THE CAMBRIDGE COM
AMERICAN TRAVEL WRITING

Travel writing has always been intimately linked with the construction of American identity. Occupying the space between fact and fiction, it exposes cultural fault lines and reveals the changing desires and anxieties of both the traveler and the reading public. These specially commissioned essays trace the journeys taken by writers from the pre-revolutionary period right up to the present. They examine a wide range of responses to the problems posed by landscapes found both at home and abroad, from the Mississippi and the Southwest to Europe and the Holy Land. Throughout, the contributors focus on the role played by travel writing in the definition and formation of national identity, and consider the diverse experiences of canonical and lesser-known writers. This Companion forms an invaluable guide for students approaching this new, important, and exciting subject for the first time.

THE CAMBRIDGE
COMPANION TO

AMERICAN TRAVEL WRITING

EDITED BY
ALFRED BENDIXEN
Texas A&M University

AND

JUDITH HAMERA
Texas A&M University

CAMBRIDGE
UNIVERSITY PRESS

CAMBRIDGE UNIVERSITY PRESS
Cambridge, New York, Melbourne, Madrid, Cape Town, Singapore, São Paulo, Delhi

Cambridge University Press
The Edinburgh Building, Cambridge CB2 8RU, UK

Published in the United States of America by Cambridge University Press, New York

www.cambridge.org
Information on this title: www.cambridge.org/9780521678315

First published 2009

Printed in the United Kingdom at the University Press, Cambridge

A catalogue record for this publication is available from the British Library

Library of Congress Cataloguing in Publication data
The Cambridge companion to American travel writing / edited by Alfred Bendixen
and Judith Hamera.
p.   cm.
Includes bibliographical references (p. 279) and index.
ISBN 978-0-521-86109-0 – ISBN 978-0-521-67831-5 (pbk.)
1. Travelers' writings, American – History and criticism.   2. American prose
literature – History and criticism.   3. National characteristics in literature.   4. Travel in
literature.   5. Americans–Foreign countries – Historiography.   6. Travel writing – History.
I. Bendixen, Alfred.   II. Hamera, Judith.   III. Title.
PS366.T73C36   2008
810.9'355 – dc22   2008033445

ISBN 978-0-521-86109-0 hardback
ISBN 978-0-521-67831-5 paperback

CONTENTS

NOTES ON CONTRIBUTORS

ALFRED BENDIXEN is Professor of English at Texas A&M University and founder of the American Literature Association, which he currently serves as Executive Director. His books include *Haunted Women* (1985), an edition of the composite novel *The Whole Family* (1986), *"The Amber Gods" and Other Stories by Harriet Prescott Spofford* (1989), and *Edith Wharton: New Critical Essays* (1992). He is also the associate editor of the *Continuum Encyclopedia of American Literature* (1999).

TERRY CAESAR has taught at Clarion University, Pennsylvania; Mukogawa University (Japan); and San Antonio College, Texas. He is the author of *Forgiving the Boundaries: Home as Abroad in American Travel Writing* (1995). He has also published academic essays on the subject, as well as personal essays of his own travel to such places as Saudi Arabia, China, and Brazil. He has co-edited with Eva Bueno a collection of essays on Latin American popular culture, *Imagination Beyond Nation* (1998). He is currently a columnist for the online journal, *Inside Higher Ed.*

WILLIAM MERRILL DECKER is Professor of English at Oklahoma State University, where he teaches American literature and serves as Director of Graduate Programs in English. He is the author of *The Literary Vocation of Henry Adams* (1990) and *Epistolary Practices: Letter Writing in America before Telecommunications* (1998), and is a co-editor of and contributor to *Henry Adams and the Need to Know* (2005).

PHILIP GOULD is Professor of English at Brown University, Rhode Island. He is the author of *Barbaric Traffic: Commerce and Antislavery in the Eighteenth-Century World* (2003) and former President of the Society of Early Americanists. He is currently working on a study of loyalist writing in Revolutionary America.

JUDITH HAMERA is Professor and Head of the Department of Performance Studies at Texas A&M University. She is the author of *Dancing Communities: Performance, Difference and Connection in the Global City* (2007), the editor of *Opening Acts: Performance in/as Communication and Cultural Studies* (2006) and co-editor of *The Handbook of Performance Studies* (2006). She is also the recipient of the National Communication Association's Lila Heston Award for Outstanding Scholarship in Interpretation and Performance Studies.

CHRISTOPHER MCBRIDE completed his PhD in English at the Claremont Graduate University, California, and is currently a member of the English faculty at Solano College, California. He is the author of *The Colonizer Abroad: American Writers on Foreign Soil, 1846–1912* (2004) as well as articles on American conjure stories, Herman Melville, William Dean Howells, and Mary Austin.

CHRISTOPHER MULVEY is Professor Emeritus of English and American Studies at the University of Winchester. He is the recipient of awards from the Arts and Humanities Council, the British Academy, Cambridge University, and the University of Virginia. His books include *Anglo-American Landscapes* (1983), *Transatlantic Manners* (1990), *New York: City as Text* (1990), *Frank Thomas Morrell: Edwardian Entrepreneur* (1994), *Black Liberation in the Americas* (2001), and *Dominic St. John Mulvey: London Irishman* (2005). He is a General Editor with Henry Louis Gates and Maria Diedrich of The African American Research Library, for which he has created an electronic scholarly edition of the first African American novel, William Wells Brown's *Clotel, or the President's Daughter* (London, 1853) published online by Virginia University Press in March 2006. He is presently working on an electronic scholarly edition of Phillis Wheatley's *Poems* (London, 1773) and a history of American transportation and culture. He has recently established the Winchester University Press and is planning a Museum of the English Language for the City of Winchester.

HILTON OBENZINGER teaches writing and American literature at Stanford University. He is the author of *American Palestine: Melville, Twain, and the Holy Land Mania*, as well as articles on American Holy Land travel, Mark Twain, Herman Melville, and American cultural interactions with the Middle East. His current project is *Melting Pots and Promised Lands: Early Zionism and the Idea of America*. A recipient of the American Book Award, he has also published books of poetry, fiction, and oral history.

DEBORAH PAES DE BARROS is Associate Professor of English at Palomar College, California. She is the author of *Fast Cars and Bad Girls: Nomadic Subjects and Women's Road Stories* (2004).

MARTIN PADGET lectures in American Studies at the University of Wales, Aberystwyth. He is the author of *Indian Country: Travels in the American Southwest, 1840–1935* (2004) and *Photographers of the Western Isles* (2008). His current research examines travel writing and the Southwest from the Spanish colonial era to the present day.

SUSAN L. ROBERSON is Chair and Associate Professor of English at Texas A&M University–Kingsville. She is the author of *Emerson in His Sermons: A Man-Made Self* (1995) and the editor of *Women, America, and Movement: Narratives of Relocation* (1998) and of *Defining Travel: Diverse Visions* (2001). She is currently at work on a book-length study of travel and mobility in the writings of antebellum American women.

THOMAS RUYS SMITH is a Lecturer in American Literature at the University of East Anglia. He is the author of *River of Dreams: Imagining the Mississippi Before Mark Twain* (2007), and is currently at work on a social and cultural history of New Orleans.

VIRGINIA WHATLEY SMITH is an Associate Professor of English at the University of Alabama, Birmingham, where she teaches African American literature. She has presented papers or been published on Richard Wright, W. E. B. Du Bois, John A. Williams, Ann Petry, Sarah Baartman, and others. She published *Richard Wright's Travel Writings*, an essay collection, in 2001. Currently, she is writing a biography on Richard Wright.

WILLIAM W. STOWE is the Benjamin Waite Professor of English at Wesleyan University, Connecticut. His work on travel writing began with *Going Abroad: European Travel in Nineteenth-Century American Culture* (1994). Recent publications include studies of landscape and leisure in Thoreau, Jewett, Fuller, Henry Ward Beecher, and Henry James, and an essay on literary aspects of the rural cemetery movement entitled "Writing Mount Auburn: Language, Landscape, and Place."

JUDITH HAMERA AND ALFRED BENDIXEN

Introduction: new worlds and old lands – the travel book and the construction of American identity

[W]hat would happen, I began to ask, if travel were untethered, seen as a complex and pervasive spectrum of human experiences? Practices of displacement might emerge as *constitutive* of cultural meanings rather than as their simple transfer or extension.[1]

James Clifford

Travel and the construction of American identity are intimately linked. This connection undergirds commonplace descriptions of America as a nation of immigrants and a restless populace on the move. It lies at the heart of the politics of Manifest Destiny, in complex relationships between the technology, commerce, and aesthetics of the car culture, and in migration narratives from those of the Hopis and Zunis to those of the Beats. American travel writing both acknowledges this connection and deploys it to perform complex ideological and cultural work. It simultaneously exposes inter- and intra-cultural contradictions and contains them. It creates American "selves" and American landscapes through affirmation, exclusion, and negation of others, and interpellates readers into these selves and landscapes through specific rhetorical and genre conventions. Thus, after Clifford in the epigraph above, American travel writing, like travel itself, is constitutive, a tool of self- and national fashioning that constructs its object even as it describes it.

The Cambridge Companion to American Travel Writing brings together thirteen new essays that explore the ways in which travel writing has defined, reflected, or constructed American identity. Although the travel book has always attracted a wide readership and the talents of major authors, it has only recently won significant attention from scholars. Too often unjustly ignored or unfairly dismissed as unimaginative hackwork, the travel book is receiving the thoughtful consideration it deserves as a literary genre with its own conventions, principles, and values. *The Cambridge Companion to Travel Writing*, edited by Peter Hulme and Tim Youngs, demonstrated the vitality and importance of this body of writing, and provided invaluable surveys that establish the richness and diversity of the genre as well as the emergence of new ways of reading travel. In some respects, this *Companion* builds on the work of its predecessor and shares some of the same goals. Like Hulme and Youngs, we recognize the need to offer "a tentative map of a vast, little explored area."[2] Readers of American literature may be surprised to discover how much travel writing has been produced by Americans and how much has been written about various places and aspects of the United States. Many of the authors presented here have a firm place in the canon and in the classroom. Travel writing has consistently attracted the talents of major authors, many of whom produced travel books either as early apprenticeship works designed to launch a literary career, or as part of their later roles as public intellectuals. The essays in this volume place the work of these major figures into an important historical and intellectual context. In addition, this *Companion* also seeks to enlarge our concept of the American literary canon by introducing readers to a large number of writers who have been unjustly forgotten and neglected.

American travel writing raises particularly complex questions of definition. Michel de Certeau notes that every story is a travel story[3] and American literary and expository writings take this literally from their earliest beginnings. In chapter 1, Philip Gould states that "eighteenth-century British American travel writing was not really an identifiable literary genre. Rather, discourses of travel permeated all sorts of genres and writings that included a wide array of audiences and intentions" (p. 13). Travel writing became a capacious framework for harmonizing multiple interests, each in and of itself central to nation-building and management: commercial, spiritual, socio-political, scientific, and, of course, literary. Yet despite this consolidating function, American travel writing also exposes cultural and genre fault lines. It exists betwixt and between the factual report and the fictional account, personal memoir and ethnography, science and romance. The genre is itself in motion and, in the process, reveals much about the changing cultural desires and anxieties both of the traveler and the American reading public. The essays in this volume focus mostly on travel writing as a non-fiction genre based, at least in theory, on the real experiences of actual travelers rooted in the specific factual details of both history and geography. Nevertheless, these essays also recognize that the boundary between travel writing and fiction can be especially murky, and that there are particular novels, and even poems, that must be taken into account. This is not just a matter of genre allegiance. Fact and fiction also intermingle in individual works as well. In this respect, travel writing is much like autobiography, another non-fiction genre that we are only now learning how to read. Sometimes a travel book may, in fact, be part of an autobiographical project, part of a larger attempt to explain oneself to the world or at least to the reading public. On the other hand, many travel books take a completely different stance, subordinating the presentation of the self to a greater focus on the external details of nature and society in a specific location. These kinds of travel works often intrude into the territory occupied by other forms of non-fiction, including history, political analysis, art criticism, journalism, sociology, and scientific observation. The essays in this volume recognize the fluidity of travel writing, but also recognize that it emerges in unique ways in response to the historical, political, and aesthetic particulars of a given context.

The complex, fluid, multiple-layered nature of travel writing generally, and American travel writing in particular, presents considerable editorial and organizational challenges. No simple survey of specific texts and/or authors is sufficient to address the rich complexity of American travel writing. Furthermore, it is not possible to examine all forms of this writing in a single volume. With these challenges in mind, we have chosen a thematic organization for this *Companion*, with essays focusing on central issues and sites as these emerge in key texts. For the purposes of this *Companion*, "American travel writing" refers both to accounts of travel by "Americans," itself a category in flux across these essays, and to travel about what is now the United States by those writing in English. Space limitations prevent us from including the vast number of important and often fascinating works written in French, Spanish, German, Russian, and other languages. The essays are grouped into three broad categories: I Confronting the American landscape; II Americans abroad; and III Social scenes and American sites. The shifts in location and time described in these essays are particularly important, because the ways Americans viewed their own physical and cultural landscapes were, and remain, intimately linked to their real and imagined engagements with other places and times, with "elsewhere." Thus, as many of the essays in the volume explain, the American "here and now" exists in dialogic tension with various "theres and thens."

An attention to diverse constructions of "Americanness," combined with examinations of the rhetorical work of specific genre conventions, binds these essays together. These two concerns are interrelated because American travel writing simultaneously constructs the traveler, the nation, and specific publics and readerships. These essays examine how crucial works of travel writing appeal to their readerships through conventions that ultimately define and redefine the genre. For instance, these texts construct race, gender, and class norms in their portrayals of travelers' personae (e.g., "the manly explorer," "the Gentleman abroad," "the adventuress"), impose standards for judging veracity (e.g., the rigors and romance of exploration and participant observation), and engage in the fundamentally political act of representing cross-cultural exchange.

It is important to note that the three sections of this volume are not autonomous, hermetically sealed units. On the contrary, just as boundaries blur and borders shift throughout the American national project, individuals, issues, texts, and sites appear and reappear in multiple essays across all three sections. Thus, the issues of landscape introduced in Part I recur in Deborah Paes de Barros' final essay on the road, tying the volume together. Race, gender, and class cross all three sections, often illuminating these distinctly American dilemmas. Landscapes are inherently social scenes, and natural wonders "over here" are read against real and imagined intersections of nature and culture "over there." Nevertheless, the three thematic parts provide a framework for understanding the genre's development and complexity.

It seems natural to begin a book on American travel writing with a section entitled, "Confronting the American landscape." James Houston writes, "The world's landscapes are but the screen on which the past, present, and anticipated cosmic vanity of mankind is written. Land is the palimpsest of human needs, desires, meaning, greed, and fears."[4] As the essays in Part I indicate, connections between landscape, writing, and this psychosocial palimpsest are especially acute in New World accounts; contacts with America's "natural wonders" generate and expose crucial dilemmas. The first such dilemma is both the simplest and the most complex: is this landscape empty or is it full? In "Property in the horizon," William Stowe observes that the fictional "'Daniel Boon' . . . sees the landscape as happily empty," a useful precondition for positing himself, and the flesh and blood settlers who come later, as "rightful inheritor[s]" (p. 27). This putative emptiness was rhetorically productive, a stimulus for others to fill it and, in literary terms, a generative blank slate for genre reinvention, as in Richard Lewis' pastoral adventure "A Journey from Palapsco to Annapolis, April 4, 1730" (Gould).

Genre considerations blur into those of nation-building in other accounts by those who found the landscape "full"; taxonomies of flora and fauna, rubes and rustics, and ethnographic accounts of Native peoples produce "Americanness" as an effect of cataloguing the former and excluding the latter. Indeed, the presence of Native Americans exposes the paradoxical view of the American landscape as both full and empty of others who were here first but are simultaneously "inevitably" disappearing: "the waste lands of the wandering tribes will be divided and sold by the acre, instead of the league. The dozing Mexican will be jostled on the elbow, and will wake from his long trance to find himself in the way" (Susan Wallace in Padget, p. 88).

Empty, full, or both, the American landscape provides multiple kinds of cultural patrimony. Fecund emptiness was a commercial invitation and an opportunity for scientific investigation. It provided a kind of providential capital that could be deployed against the presumed cultural superiority and relative geological modesty of Europe. The sublime beauty of the Grand Canyon and Niagara Falls could speak back to European works of art, even as they attested to a more muscular American geography: "Either Nature has wrought with a bolder hand in America, or the effect of long continued cultivation on scenery, as exemplified in Europe, is greater than is usually supposed" (Nathaniel Parker Willis in Mulvey, p. 51).

Personal spiritual capital could be read into the landscape as well, particularly in the exotic, mysterious Southwest, the majestic Niagara Falls, and the arterial Mississippi; as Thomas Ruys Smith notes, the navigation of the Mississippi, and specifically "the ritualistic element of river travel" (p. 74), functioned as a uniquely American psychospiritual pilgrimage. As the case of the Mississippi makes clear, the "Americanness" asserted, discovered, or constructed in response to landscape was often ambivalent. The Mississippi is "laden with the burdens of a nation" (Eddy Harris in Smith, p. 74), with overlapping and interanimating images of frontier optimism and/as "Emerson's 'antidote' for the 'passion for Europe'" (p. 67), the horrors of the slave trade, and grinding rural poverty. The Southwest is simultaneously a timeless repository of American authenticity and a series of simulacra – representations of representations of places. Perhaps, given this palimpsest of burdens and opportunities written onto and read from the landscape, it is no surprise that American self-assertion is more vigorous on foreign soil, the subject of the essays gathered in Part II, "Americans abroad."

The essays in this section deal with important books about Europe, the Holy Land, Latin America, and the Pacific, and embody a variety of approaches, but they share an underlying concern with the ways in which American identity is defined by contact with other people and other places. In *Travelers, Immigrants, Inmates: Essays in Estrangement*, Frances Bartkowski writes:

> The demands placed upon the subject in situations of unfamiliarity and dislocation produce a scene in which the struggle for identity comes more clearly into view as both necessary and also mistaken . . . The subject, no matter how decentered, cannot *not* be a subject or it lapses into aphasia. We must speak, and once we do so we enact an enabling fiction of identity that makes social life possible.[5]

American accounts of travel abroad simultaneously presume and construct the United States as an imagined community. Furthermore, an enabling fiction of "Americanness" frequently works synecdochally with the portrayal of the traveler: the traveler's persona stands in for Americanness. As Hilton Obenzinger observes, Mark Twain's *The Innocents Abroad, or The New Pilgrim's Progress* is a paradigm case. Describing Twain's mock eulogy at the Tomb of Adam in the Church of the Holy Sepulchre, Obenzinger notes that Twain not only asserts his own persona as an American, but also repackages the site itself as an American product: "[B]y bringing Twain's book – and his irreverence – he [General U.S. Grant] also participated in what had become a uniquely American tourist practice: Grant visited the Tomb of Adam because it was the place where Mark Twain had wept. Twain had given an American meaning to the place, and he inscribed his own persona upon the shrine through burlesque" (p. 154).

Other personae that produced "Americanness" through assertion or negation include the "expat"; the tourist – depending upon the period either "the overawed students of an old and sophisticated civilization" or the representatives of a superpower flushed with "heroic self-regard" (Decker, p. 136); the pious pilgrim (Obenzinger); the good-natured American gentleman (Bendixen); the sailor who goes native only to flee to literally save his skin, thus both negating and affirming "civilization" at the same time (McBride); and the adventurer (Caesar). Personae exist in dialogic tension with the others they meet and describe. Thus, Christopher McBride examines the ways in which nineteenth-century travelers to Hawaii and Cuba fashioned the islands as proxies for negotiating issues of race, and assertions of racial superiority, at home. In a similar vein, Terry Caesar notes that South America served as a surrogate frontier for travelers with implicit or explicit neo-colonial, neo-imperial agendas. Travels to Palestine, as Hilton Obenzinger demonstrates, "posed ultimate questions" even as its material conditions often disappointed or, in some cases, inspired "infidel counter texts" (p. 151). Alfred Bendixen explores the way in which pre-Civil War American travelers in Europe fashioned conventions that reflected and responded to their own cultural anxieties.

As the idea of counter-texts suggests, writings by Americans about travel abroad demonstrate that genre conventions are often functions of personae, not the other way around. Thus, when Irving adopts the role of Geoffrey Crayon, Gent., or other writers identify their books as "written by an American," the selection of the persona ultimately shapes both the choice of subjects and the nature of the response. Where one privileged Euro-American traveler might construct travel to Europe or the Middle East in terms of various "origin myths," as return visits to lands that are part of one's historical or cultural ancestry, African American travelers pointedly problematize these myths by naming complicity with slavery and white amnesic nostalgia as their core, if unacknowledged, components. Theodore Roosevelt's "zoo-geographic reconnaissance," in *Through the Brazilian Wilderness*, is shaped by his performative production of himself as "a man of action as well as observation," and not simply an "ordinary traveler" (Caesar, p. 187).

The essays in Part III, "Social scenes and American sites," reexamine and synthesize these same themes and conventions. Here, contacts with the landscape and confrontation with irreducible difference give birth to new genre conventions and reinvigorate existing ones. "Americanness" is again in flux in the texts discussed here: discovered, asserted, resisted, disavowed, but generally never simply unproblematically given. Readers are cast as co-conspirators, as empowered witnesses, as passive consumers. In the texts discussed in this section, travel itself becomes a trope, a stand-in for a range of unfinished projects, from personal and national identity to modernity itself.

In *Moving Lives: 20th-Century Women's Travel Writing*, Sidonie Smith posits, "If the mode of moving a body through space affects the traveler who moves through space as that body, then the mode of motion informs the meaning that the traveler sends back home in narration."[6] While Smith's observation resonates across all the essays in this volume, it is especially pertinent to Part III. In the three essays that comprise this section, modes of travel and their attendant means for organizing bodies signal profound differences in the impetus for travel from enslavement to tourism. Further, these modes of travel prospectively and retrospectively frame "home" in complex and contradictory ways, and shape the resulting narratives as resistance, as nostalgia, as collective response, or intrapsychic monologue. As all three essays demonstrate, "America" is produced as an effect of these sometimes exuberant, sometimes deeply fraught experiences of both mobility and home.

Mobility and corporeality are intimately linked. Perhaps it is no surprise that those relegated by white patriarchal elites to the status of wholly "body," as opposed to "mind," specifically here African Americans and women, address this interrelationship with special clarity in their travel writing. Virginia Whatley Smith notes that a palpable sense of corporeality is central to African American contributions to the form. She explores the slave narrative as a discursive vehicle for "shocked bodies and fractured psyches," one that would speak back to the holds of the slave ships, to confinement, beatings, and the multiple unrelenting physical and psychic assaults of slavery (p. 198). Gender and/as embodiment also emerges, sometimes directly, sometimes obliquely, in travel writing by women. As Susan Roberson attests, "In addition to other risks and dangers of the road, women were subject to sexual risk, to themselves being the territory that is explored and conquered by others" (p. 223). In a dramatically different key, and from a dramatically different social position, "New Journalists" Tom Wolfe and Hunter S. Thompson represent intersections of corporeality and mobility by focusing on the sensory and the intrapsychic. In their attempts to fuse narrative and experience on the road and on the page, "[s]ensation, atmosphere, emotion, and consciousness define experience, and the mundane gesture becomes as essential to history as culturally celebrated moments" (Paes de Barros, p. 233).

Mobility implies "to" and "from" somewhere and, as these essays suggest, that "somewhere" is often "home." "Home" in the context of American travel writing is rarely simple, and may sometimes even be dystopian, whether as the terminus of the slave ship's voyage and beginnings of bondage in the slave narrative or the infinitely more comfortable bourgeois domesticity that conjured prospects of psychic and aesthetic bondage for the Beats. Home was, or was not, Africa or Paris for some African American travel writers; it both was and was not the road itself for John Steinbeck and William Least Heat-Moon. "Making a home out of the wild or the foreign seems to be an occupation with women travel writers," according to Roberson (p. 219). Further, the construction or negation of these various concepts of home stood in for that of America itself, whether as intractably racist or as a psychedelic frontier.

Genre innovations are often introduced even as America is produced in the accounts discussed here, though others actively resist such formal or thematic risk-taking. For example, Roberson writes, "[t]here is a conservative quality in much of women's non-fiction travel writing despite whatever other freedoms or adventures their tales may relate" (p. 225). On the other hand, Smith notes that African Americans actively refashion the conventional leisure-class tourist account by explicitly addressing aspects of sociopolitical context, including race, that are often absent in white texts. Finally, Deborah Paes de Barros notes that contemporary travel writers, beginning with the Beats, recast the genre entirely from the social to the explicitly psychobiographical, wherein travel becomes both literal movement and a tool for examining inner as well as outer landscapes.

All the essays in this volume speak to social scenes and/as American sites by explicitly or implicitly raising questions of who gets to choose to travel and who does not, and of the American landscape as "out there," "in here," as resource, backdrop, impediment, or monument. All examine what counts as an "American" or an "un-American" site, and how frequently one definition is asserted through the negation of another. Directly or indirectly, all reckon with the possibilities and limits of travel as metaphor for the American national project itself. All take up the issue of alterity and its representations "at home" and abroad, an issue that lies at the very core of the American social imaginary. In so doing, these essays demonstrate the ideological and rhetorical, as well as the aesthetic work of travel writing, and the centrality of this work to ongoing processes of national self-fashioning in an always already global context.

Notes

1. James Clifford, *Routes: Travel and Translation in the Late Twentieth Century* (Cambridge, MA: Harvard University Press, 1997), p. 3 (emphasis in original).
2. Peter Hulme and Tim Youngs, eds., *The Cambridge Companion to Travel Writing* (Cambridge: Cambridge University Press, 2002), p. 1.
3. Michel de Certeau, *The Practice of Everyday Life*, trans. S. Rendall (Berkeley: University of California Press, 1984), p. 115.
4. Quoted in Mark Neumann, *On the Rim: Looking for the Grand Canyon* (Minneapolis: University of Minnesota Press, 1999), pp. 5–6.
5. Frances Bartkowski, *Travelers, Immigrants, Inmates: Essays in Estrangement* (Minneapolis: University of Minnesota Press, 1995), pp. xix–x.
6. Sidonie Smith, *Moving Lives: 20th-Century Women's Travel Writing* (Minneapolis: University of Minnesota Press, 2001), p. xii.

I

CONFRONTING THE AMERICAN LANDSCAPE

I

PHILIP GOULD

Beginnings: the origins of American travel writing in the pre-revolutionary period

In eighteenth-century British America travel writing was not really an identifiable literary genre. Rather, the discourses of travel permeated all sorts of genres and writings that included a wide array of audiences and intentions. While some of these early travel writings actually do resemble modern travel narratives, most took shape in the context of other kinds of concerns: scientific, political, or religious. Travel writing, for example, sometimes involved mapping America for transatlantic readers interested in settling the frontier, especially in the aftermath of the British victory over France in the Seven Years War (1756–63). Or, alternatively, it involved the religious itinerant traveling simultaneously across spiritual and actual landscapes. Colonial American travel writing thus took shape in the context of other genres like nature writing, promotional writing about settling the American frontier, spiritual autobiography, and military history. This writing included poetic forms as well. Early eighteenth-century poets in British America adapted well-established English literary traditions such as pastoral and satire because they had cultural legitimacy. Both prose and poetic accounts of travel remind us that these accounts of American places often were written and published for metropolitan readers with particular (or potential) interests in North America.

One of the earliest forms of travel literature is the promotional writing meant to attract emigrants and funding for British colonies. Probably the most notable instance of this kind of promotional writing was William Penn's "Some Account of the Province of Pennsylvania in America" (1681), which aimed to sell English migrants and capitalists on the future of his new colony. Penn's writing deals more in hopeful ideals than in historical realities. It fits Wayne Franklin's summation of early travel writing: "The simplest and most delightful variety of the New World travel book is less narrative than declaratory, less concerned with the details of an actual endured journey than with the general design of America as a scene for potential ones."[1] For an English Quaker founding a colony supposedly on the principle of religious toleration, Penn's promotional writing appears surprisingly secular in many ways. It emphasizes, for example, the "luxury and corruption of manners" of contemporary English society as a way of attracting settlers looking for a better life. What he emphasizes is the availability and fertility of the land, so that the "Pennsylvania" that emerges here is a trope for "freedom" itself. In this way, Penn forecasts what Crevecoeur would do much later on in *Letters from an American Farmer* (1782). Introducing a suggestion of what would eventually be called the American Dream, Penn declared, "A plantation seems a fit place for those ingenious spirits that being low in the world, are much clogged and oppressed about a livelihood."[2]

Much more attuned to the social realities of early British America is the colonial travel journal. The practice of journal keeping had various sources in the early eighteenth century, but none more important than the Protestant tradition of keeping an account of one's spiritual condition. In colonial New England, this tradition eventually became secularized to the point where the temporal and physical reality of travel contended with (and sometimes overtook) the religious theme of the soul's journey. This is certainly the case with Sarah Kemble Knight's *Journal* (1704–05), which was composed to be shared (and probably read aloud) among her coterie of friends and acquaintances. The *Journal* thus remained in manuscript for quite some time and was not published until 1825. As a secular, even comic, version of the Protestant spiritual journey, Knight's *Journal* recounts the trip she made from Boston to New York in 1704–05. This was a long and difficult one at the time, and it was all the more tenuous for a woman traveling alone. This in itself says much about the spirit of its female protagonist, who, sometimes seriously, but more often ironically, represents herself as a kind of vulnerable pilgrim engaged in a difficult quest. She makes mock-serious classical allusions and breaks into poetic interludes about moonlit landscapes.

The *Journal*'s great literary value stems from the cultural position Knight creates for herself – and for her immediate coterie of readers. As David Shields has shown, the manuscript form was meant to solidify social relations and reinforce cultural values among this select group.[3] The form and its intended readership complicate the boundaries between "private" and "public" spheres kinds of writing that we normally think of today. Knight's sense of herself and her writing in this social context helps to explain the *Journal*'s preoccupation with the important category of "manners." There is no better display during this relatively early era of what this term meant to an urban provincial traveling the rustic countryside. Throughout, Knight offers disparaging, and sometimes humorous, commentary on the impoverishment of colonial culture – the country bumpkins, drunkards, and ill-bred strangers who make her journey more difficult and her writing more interesting. Knight's humor relies on social contrast, irony, and "low" types, such as "Jone Tawdry" and "Bumpkin Simpers," for example, which will later populate New England humor writing. Sometimes these ironic contrasts reflect back unexpectedly on Knight and belie her own cultural provinciality. But the *Journal* also offers perceptive analysis of social and material differences, for example, between Boston and New York. It even ranges into Native American ethnography, local customs regarding divorce laws, commercial differences, leisure and entertainment, and governmental elections and court rulings.

The *Itinerarium* of Dr. Alexander Hamilton offers an even more extended and thorough account of colonial American mores. Hamilton was a Scottish physician who emigrated to Maryland in 1739. Traveling to improve his health, Hamilton's round-trip journey in 1744 from Annapolis to York, Maine covered well over 1,000 miles. Upon his return, he, along with several Annapolis friends, formed the Ancient and Honorable Tuesday Club in 1745. It was one of the more important social organizations shaped around the Shaftesburyan ideal of literary wit and masculine sociability, which ideally worked to "smooth the edges" of its members. Its *History*, composed by Hamilton as the Club's secretary, provides one of the best examples of one version of manners in eighteenth-century British America: the importance of wit and ironic humor, the value of knowledge of the world, disdain for bigotry and zealotry of all kinds, especially that associated with theological controversy.

The social context of the Tuesday Club helps to explain the prominent thematic and stylistic features of the *Itinerarium*. Throughout, Hamilton's keen eye for social observation locates myriad colonial characters inhabiting societies that barely qualify as civilized. Drunken disputants, evangelical preachers, surly innkeepers, coquettes, eccentric European visitors, Native Americans: all of these (and more) come under his scrutiny that often verges into irony and sometimes even farce. Consider, for example, his assessment of his lodging outside Baltimore:

> I found nothing particular or worth notice in my landlord's character or conversation, only as to his bodily make. He was a fat pursy man and had large bubbies like a woman. I supped upon fried chicken and bacon, and after supper the conversation turned upon politicks, news, and the dreaded French war; but it was so lumpish and heavy that it disposed me mightily to sleep. The learned company consisted of the landlord, his overseer and miller, and another greasy thump'd fellow who, as I understood, professed physick and particularly surgery. In the drawing of teeth, he practiced upon the house maid, a dirty piece of lumber, who made such screaming and squalling as made me imagine there was murder going forwards in the house.[4]

Here is the distance that the *Itinerarium* characteristically maintains between Hamilton and the rustic social worlds he encounters. In the colonial setting devoid of a hereditary aristocracy, there is the ongoing narrative project of maintaining such distance and thereby securing one's status as a "gentleman." This project tends to dehumanize the lower orders, reducing them either to grotesque bodies unable to cut a fine public figure; or, worse, it simply turns people into things ("a dirty piece of lumber"). Hamilton's social status, moreover, is tied to different forms of consumption that ideally secure one's health. Here food and conversation are metaphors for one another, to the extent that "lumpish and heavy" social interaction puts one to sleep.

The obsession with manners in Knight and Hamilton also characterizes William Byrd's travel writings. These include the lesser-known *A Progress to the Mines*, the result of a trip made in 1732 to inspect Governor Spotswood's iron mines, and *A Journey to the Land of Eden*, which recounts his 1733 trip to survey a new estate he had bought in North Carolina. But Byrd is best known for the two versions he wrote of the surveying party that was appointed in 1728 to resolve the boundary dispute between Virginia and North Carolina. Like the writings of Knight and Hamilton, moreover, Byrd's histories of this episode remained in manuscript for selective audiences, and were not published until the nineteenth century. Byrd kept a journal of the difficult trek, which he first turned into the *Secret History of the Dividing Line*, a manuscript meant for only an intimate audience of friends. The *Secret History* is a highly satirical work that spills into farce. It is filled with lewd scenes of sexual aggression, and allegorically comic names for the members of the surveying party, drawn from the Restoration comedy that Byrd had known during his youth in London. If it is not so detailed in colonial politics and geography, it nevertheless offers a more brutally realistic account of travel through the southern Appalachian frontier.

The History of the Dividing Line was the expurgated and revised version of the *Secret History* that Byrd later reconstructed in the late 1730s. The *History* is pristine by comparison, since it was intended for a wider readership that included political authorities in Britain, as well as learned naturalists like Peter Collinson and Mark Catesby on both sides of the Atlantic. Not only its classical allusions but also its ethnographic commentary on Native Americans, its scientific details of flora and fauna, and the historical context of English colonization framing the work (meant, of course, to vindicate Virginia's territorial claims), all show this very different literary intention. Byrd's ironic and contemptuous portrayal of the North Carolinian backcountry emphasizes the local inhabitants' sloth and ill-health – they are "uncultivated" in many ways, prone to disease and disfiguration, truly "savage" in their manners. His perspective is that of an aristocratic "creole" – a complex term broadly signifying Byrd's local status – who nevertheless had spent much of his life in London among elite literary and scientific milieus, frequenting places like Will's Coffee House (where the English poet John Dryden held court) and being admitted to the Royal Society. His famous library at Westover would exceed 4,000 volumes, and he considered himself an able naturalist and physician. His is a transatlantic perspective on the American frontier, at once genteel and politically conscious of the importance of the expedition to metropolitan authorities in London, yet asserting his superiority as a provincial, somewhat paradoxically, whose distance from London provides a particular kind of experiential authority.

During this era the travel journal took literary form in verse as well. Poetic accounts of travel were generally more stylized and often either more satirical or more idealistic accounts of journeys made in British America. The poetic form, in other words, was conducive to satire, pastoral, and other traditional English ways of representing human and physical landscapes. Two of the important travel poems from this era, Richard Lewis' "A Journey from Patapsco to Annapolis, April 4, 1730" (1732), and Ebenezer Cooke's "The Sot-Weed Factor; or, a Voyage to Maryland" (1708), exemplify these different poetic intentions. Both writers were notable figures in colonial American letters and politics (Lewis simply proclaimed himself poet laureate of Maryland), and their poems exemplify the complex meanings of "travel." Lewis' "Journey" obviously uses an English model of the pastoral, where classical allusion and idealized image enhance (or create) the beauty of the inviting natural landscape. Indeed its epigraph is from Virgil's *Georgics*, which the English poet John Dryden had translated into English in 1697. From the colonial periphery, then, Lewis accesses this classical source via metropolitan cultural authority. Indeed the lofty language of "Journey," its Latinate syntax, its serious use of the heroic couplet, and stock religious lessons afforded by observing God's natural creation all show Lewis trying to identify himself – and Maryland – in this larger cultural purview. The poem's material texture is thus relatively thin – the landscape is more an idealized portrait of pastoral idyll, though disturbed intermittently by wild storms and animal violence.

"The Sot-Weed Factor" makes the transatlantic context for travel all the more explicit. Written in a Hudibrastic style, whose lilting rhythms and strange rhymes tend to comically deflate affected pretenses, the poem travesties the English emigrant's encounter with colonial realities. It was first published in London and probably had these dual audiences in mind. Part burlesque, part picaresque, the speaker's social and cultural disdain for the comparatively primitive life in colonial Maryland probably resonated humorously for many different kinds of readers. But subtle clues throughout the poem also suggest that metropolitan ignorance is also an important theme. Balancing the ill-mannered (and often drunken) behavior of colonials with the pedantic pretenses and self-delusions of the Factor himself, the poem conducts a comic survey of all sorts of social and racial "types" in the New World. Perhaps less important as a "realistic" account of travel in colonial Maryland, the poem is nevertheless a serious cultural commentary on the clash between imperial and provincial manners by a writer who spent time in both places. It thematically negotiates frontier rudeness and imperial elitism as it works its way towards an understanding of civilized manners mediating between these two extremes.

The great wars for empire between the British and the French, which dominated mid-century politics and society, provided a major context for American travel writing of the 1750s and 1760s. Most military narratives remained in manuscript, since they had highly specialized intentions and audiences; some, like George Washington's, were later printed. This narrative recounted his volunteer mission from Virginia to deliver an ultimatum to the French commandant demanding French withdrawal from the Ohio Valley; it was published in 1754 in Williamsburg as *The Journal of Major George Washington*, and then reprinted in colonial newspapers and in a London pamphlet. (Washington had written an earlier journal, "A Journal of my Journey over the Mountains began Friday the 11th of March 1747/8," which was not published.) But this one had widespread political and cultural importance. The ostensible audience for the journal is Washington's superior officer, Robert Dinwiddie, but its publication suggests an awareness of the audiences on both sides of the Atlantic who were interested in frontier conditions along Appalachia, especially in the Native American tribes inhabiting the region, as well as the activities of the French army. Washington's prose, though dry and factual, contains original insights into military defense and strategy. It also includes a speech by the "Half King" (the Seneca sachem Tanacharison), supposedly given to the French, which undoubtedly was meant to vivify the narrative with Indian eloquence (much as Thomas Jefferson later used Chief Logan's speech in *Notes on the State of Virginia*). The journal dramatizes the intrigue of diplomatic acumen along a frontier setting where alliances, even identities, are unstable and in flux.

There were also numerous travel narratives published after the conclusion of the Seven Years War (1756–63), when Britain finally established itself as the dominant political power in North America. These writings were significant on many accounts: naturalistic and geographical detail, Indian ethnography, and sometimes daring adventure. Some of the most prominent ones were, for example, William Smith's *An Account of Bouquet's Expedition*

Against the Ohio Indians (1765), Major Robert Rogers' *Journals* and his *Concise Account of North America* (1765), William Stork's *An Account of East Florida* (1766), and James Adair's *History of the American Indians* (1775). Modeled on classical works by Horace and others, they combine autobiography with natural history – a broad term encompassing the fields of meteorology, geology, botany, zoology, and ethnology.[5] They were written for both colonial and British audiences keenly interested in the American frontier. Ironically, then, while the British government's imposition of the Proclamation line of 1763 forbade future settlement, at least temporarily, these military histories/travel accounts "opened up" the West imaginatively. This is apparent, for example, in William Stork's *Account*, which was republished along with a journal John Bartram wrote of a trip he made up the St. John River. Stork wrote the prefaces for both works, which were meant to promote financial and political interest in a region that, as he complains, had been unfairly characterized as "unhealthy" and "infertile." Its imperial purpose was explicit and precise: "The design of this work is not only to fix attention of the ministry upon an object of great national importance; but also to point out to individuals, especially to persons of a middling fortune, to take up grants from the crown." His preface to Bartram's journal similarly aimed to "gratify the curiosity of the speculative."[6]

These writings sometimes took the form of the journal or memoir, but their autobiographical dimensions submerged personal stories within larger political or scientific designs. In some cases the autobiographical "I" all but disappears, as in Mark Catesby's *Natural History of Carolina, Florida, and the Bahama Islands* (1731–47). In most cases, the prefaces to travel accounts are self-effacing and emphasize the future use to which the account may be put. Yet these works also exhibit the self-confidence of an autobiographical observer empowered with a particular kind of knowledge. This is a *colonial* form of knowledge that metropolitan readers desperately wanted, offering valuable information for future investment, settlement, and imperial policies.

The salient tensions permeating the colonial position of authority are apparent, for example, in the Introduction to perhaps the most popular travel narrative of the period, Jonathan Carver's *Travels through the Interior Parts of North America* (1778). First published in London with a British readership in mind, *Travels* was widely reprinted over the next few decades on both sides of the Atlantic. Carver was a former officer in the British army who was seeking the Northwest Passage in the upper Mississippi region (today's northern Midwest). His Introduction displays the tensions of the provincial writer cautiously assuring his readers that his work would "furnish an ample fund of amusement and gratify their most curious expectations." Some day, Carver claims, future settlers "will reap, exclusive of the national advantages that must ensue, Emoluments beyond their most sanguine expectations. And . . . perhaps they may bestow some commendations and blessings on the person that first pointed out to them the way."[7] Throughout these opening remarks, and the lengthy narrative that follows, are the conflicting energies of self-assertion and self-effacement, which produce the images both of heroic individual and dutiful subject to the Crown's authority. But though Carver's name appears on the title page, and later editions after his death included flattering biographical sketches of him, his self-image as a writer did not claim the kind of artistic achievement we assume today. "And here it is necessary to bespeak the candour of the learned part of my Readers in the perusal of it, as it is the production of a person unused, from opposite avocations, to literary pursuits" (p. xvi). Literary deficiency supposedly proved historical accuracy – an assertion that was all the more ironic for a work that was immensely popular yet factually inconsistent.

Later expeditions used narratives like these as guides to alien worlds. The frontier travel narrative aims to domesticate these worlds – both physical landscapes and the Native American tribes living there – and make them comprehensible. Stylistically, this produces rhetorical tensions between order and disorder. There is no better example of this than the writings of John Bartram. A Pennsylvania Quaker, and the most famous American botanist in the middle of the eighteenth century, Bartram traveled widely, collected American materials vigorously, while corresponding with British patrons and advisors. His celebrated garden in Philadelphia contained American specimens collected from his travels, and shows the period's penchant for discovery and categorization. His *Observations* (1751), published in London, were based on a trip he made in 1743 with Conrad Weiser, whom the Pennsylvania government appointed to travel north on a diplomatic mission to the Six Nations, as well as the cartographer Lewis Evans, who produced a map of the journey. (The Treaty of Lancaster eventually resulted from Weiser's two trips to the Canadian frontier.) This work was first published as *A Journey from Pennsylvania to Onondaga in 1743*, along with *Extract from the Journal of Lewis Evans* and Weiser's *Report on the Journey to Onondaga*. (The volume also includes a description of Niagara Falls by the Swedish naturalist Peter Kalm.) In this context, Bartram's naturalistic detail is not simply scientific but political as well. His journey is part of the larger project of British American frontier politics and the larger designs of the British Empire. Accounting for nature means taking possession of it, making it "knowable" to oneself and to one's British readers. To this end, Bartram's style is highly and dryly factual, though it does include interesting anecdotes that, as in the killing of a rattlesnake, have almost mythic overtones.

Bartram's prose exemplifies natural history's overall preoccupation with Native Americans. Like so many of these works, his frontier journals make meticulous observations of Native American culture and society, at once emphasizing strange and alien peoples, and subtly assimilating them into Eurocentric registers of meaning. Bartram observes them carefully though not objectively. His tone ranges from sincere curiosity to mild irony, particularly regarding Indian religion, though his writing certainly cannot be reduced to "racist" formulas. Like most eighteenth-century narratives of this sort, Bartram's speculates on the historical origin of North American Indians, and though he views them as part of the human race, he also summarily concludes that the Six Nations are "a subtle, prudent, and judicious people in their councils, indefatigable, crafty, and revengeful in their wars, the men lazy and indolent at home, the women continual slaves . . ."[8] Scenes describing Indian rituals, like the rites conducted after slaying a bear, are underwritten by Enlightenment and Protestant thinking. More often than not, however, Bartram withdraws moral judgment and lets the moment speak for itself. There are even times that reverse cultural categories and exhibit, though perhaps reluctantly, changes taking place in his own identity: "As soon as we alighted they shewed us where to lay our baggage, and then brought us a bowl of boiled squashes cold. This I then thought poor entertainment, but before I came back I had learnt not to despise good *Indian* food" (p. 35).

The frontier travel journal generally contained more benign and balanced imagery of Native Americans than did the captivity narrative. Readers of Mary Rowlandson's *The Sovereignty and Goodness of God* (1682), her account of the eleven-week captivity she endured during King Philip's War (1675–76), recognize that her demonic representation of Satan's minions gives way to a more intimate, complicated portrayal. This was true of literally dozens of captivity narratives that appeared in colonial New England, which offered readers glimpses into alien cultures as well as foreign landscapes. Yet the relation between captivity narrative and travel writing is problematic because the genre's protagonists were generally not trained naturalists or surveyors. Narrative location, moreover, was usually eclipsed by the sheer trauma of the experience and by the larger thematic designs of spiritual autobiography emphasizing the soul's chastening. So while Rowlandson's narrative does offer an account of travel, its movements are structured according to a series of "Removes," which chart her gradual loss of a cultural and psychological "center" as she proceeds further into the New England wilderness.

But other forms of spiritual autobiography produced more detailed accounts of American locales. Quaker narratives, for example, often involved itinerant preaching across the British American colonies (and sometimes even the West Indies) because of fundamental features of Quaker piety. Quakerism was originally a radical Protestant sect founded during the seventeenth-century English Civil Wars. Founded by George Fox, whose *Journal* later became a model for Quaker autobiographies on both sides of the Atlantic, Quakerism was initially the driving force behind the founding of Pennsylvania. By the middle of the eighteenth century, there were numerous Meetings (or congregations) established in the colonies, principally in the middle Atlantic. Believing in the "Inner Light" – the idea that there is the spark of divinity in every living thing – Quakers were pious, idealistic, non-violent humanitarians who emphasized inner spiritual movements and direct relations with the divine. Quaker autobiography emphasized the subject's conversion as well as his – or her – ongoing mission of communicating the spirit of God (Quaker "testimony") to others through preaching, good works, and living the exemplary moral life.

This emphasis upon spiritual movement created the need for physical movement – for travel – to spread the Truth of God's Inner Light. Perhaps the most famous Quaker autobiography was *The Journal of John Woolman*, published posthumously in 1774, which recounts Woolman's religious conversion and subsequent life of itinerant preaching. He traveled widely throughout the colonies, making two trips, for example, to the South, where he witnessed the horrors of slavery and became an early and ardent abolitionist. His writing contains some of the earliest instances of what would later become in the nineteenth century the abolitionist critique of the Southern plantation. He also traveled to the western frontier of Pennsylvania, after the Seven Years War, where he preached among the Native American tribes decimated by imperial wars. Quaker writers like Woolman, however, were not as immediately concerned with giving exact details of social life in America; these arise almost residually and within the primary concern with piety and conversion. But the Quaker process of "seeking" – of spreading the Truth – was democratic enough to embrace all regions and peoples.

This egalitarian ideal extended to Quaker women as well. One of the more important prose works by an eighteenth-century colonial woman is the Quaker spiritual autobiography, *Some Account of the Fore Part of the Life of Elizabeth Ashbridge*, which was published in England in 1774. Ashbridge's *Account* offers an autobiographical version of the transatlantic adventures of the "fallen woman" that Daniel Defoe had popularized in his novel *Moll Flanders* (1722). Beginning in England, and then moving to Ireland and British America, the *Account* shows Ashbridge's ongoing struggle with patriarchal authority. Her passage to America, however, does not idealize the immigrant experience. Rather, the *Account* is structured according to the motifs of captivity and seduction, as Ashbridge must navigate an often brutal, deceptive colonial world. This culminates with her marriage to an abusive, drunken husband, and her subsequent conversion to Quakerism, which takes on both spiritual and gendered significance. It represents her attempt at establishing her own autonomy against her abusive husband, and it legitimizes the terms of her future travel – escaping his authority to attend Quaker meeting, and later preaching the Word on her own. One way of thinking about her *Account*, then, is as a kind of picaresque experience of colonial Pennsylvania and New Jersey, with its social realities and social spaces – homes, taverns, churches, meeting houses, and the like.

Itinerant preaching changed the religious landscape of colonial America in general. Spiritual accounts of the travels of gospel preachers were perhaps more common in private correspondence and unpublished manuscripts. But the religious journals and letters that were printed in local newspapers or as pamphlets and books did constitute a form of travel writing. During the era before the American Revolution there was no more popular itinerant minister than George Whitefield, whose journey from Britain to Georgia in 1740 caused a popular sensation. As one historian has summarized it, "Pro-revival correspondence and publication began flooding across the parishes of the [British] empire, further enhancing the sense of a dynamic movement that knew no bounds. George Whitefield's *Journals* appeared at regular intervals throughout his first American tour, permitting readers to trace the Spirit's path throughout southern New England, across the Atlantic, and along the colonial coastline."[9] Evangelical religion depended upon an expanding print culture to promote its cause, and Whitefield was the best at manipulating American newspapers to wage his own publicity campaign. While his *Letters and Journals* were later published as large monographs in London (and had large British American audiences through their imported sales), they were often parsed out strategically to keep his revival movement going. Readers would learn about revivals recently held (or soon to be held) in other areas of British America. Though not primarily about these distant places, or particularly detailed about them, such accounts did promote a larger inter-colonial consciousness. It was an important medium through which highly localized cultures in colonial America could imagine themselves in the larger social and geographical context of British America.

One of the more important genres that evolved during this period of religious revivals known as the "Great Awakening" was the missionary history, which combined Protestant piety, Native American ethnography, and even more secular elements of travel. Though not ostensibly concerned with such matters, the missionary history did reveal many important realities surrounding frontier life in the eighteenth century. Probably the most famous instance of this genre was *An Account of the Life of the Late Reverend David Brainerd*, which the famous New England minister Jonathan Edwards edited and published in 1749. As Edwards' protégé, Brainerd represented an exemplary (though often melancholic) piety and sense of Christian duty that led to his years of service trying to convert Algonquian Indians. Brainerd's mission lasted during the middle 1740s in western Massachusetts, eastern New York, and New Jersey. He preached to and proselytized Native Americans, working through an interpreter, and eventually helping to translate the Psalms into Algonquian. The *Life* is as much Edwards' as his own narrative, and, though focused mostly on Brainerd's interior journey, it does stage important features of the cultural contact that took place in what the *Account* calls the "howling wilderness" between Anglo- and Native Americans. It also provides moments of social commentary, not unlike that of Byrd's Histories, which scorns the "savage" behavior of white (and unconverted) frontier settlers.

The Protestant traditions of spiritual autobiography and captivity narrative also inform the writings of eighteenth-century black subjects. Indeed, the dynamics of captivity and liberation shape probably the earliest instance of eighteenth-century black writing in which travel predominates. *The Narrative of the Uncommon Sufferings and Surprising Deliverance of Briton Hammon* (1760) is something of a generic hybrid, combining captivity narrative and transatlantic travel narrative. Hammon's *Narrative* recounts a thirteen-year odyssey of shipwreck and captivity in the Caribbean where he was held captive by the Spanish and Native Americans. The *Narrative* concludes with Hammon's fortuitous rediscovery of his "good Master" Winslow on board a ship bound from England to New England, and his symbolic reunification with him. Whether actually writing or only orally relating their lives, slave narrators like Hammon drew on multiple discourses as a way of cultivating such complex identities that lay ambiguously within and without contemporary norms. No black autobiographer during this era wrote completely outside the norms of "civilized" or "Christian" identity – one that was more often than not associated directly with "Englishness." He claims this kind of civilized identity and, presumably, the traditional rights that accompany it.

In 1771, as the American Revolution was quickly approaching, Benjamin Franklin wrote (but did not then publish) Part One of his famous *Autobiography*. Written on the eve of the American Revolution, this part charts the young Franklin's emergence from obscurity and poverty to economic success as a printer. Ironically, this most "American" of success stories has important transatlantic contexts and intentions. It was composed in England, while Franklin was there for years as an agent of the British colonies, and it was addressed to his eldest son William, who was then Governor of New Jersey and a staunch Loyalist to the British Crown. The work itself dramatizes Franklin's movements from Boston to Philadelphia; from Philadelphia to London and back again; and his rise through the ranks of Pennsylvania social and political ranks of power. In the context of the diverse modes of travel narrative discussed above, Franklin's *Autobiography* reads like a unique, even ingenious, version of the promotional design of so much early travel writing about British America. Its portrait of the opportunities to be found in cosmopolitan Philadelphia fulfills this design. Promoting himself and America simultaneously, Franklin's work was intended for elite groups of readers on both sides of the Atlantic who were meant to recognize the potential rewards of Franklinian virtues played out in an American scene. This was true of many other kinds of travel writing before the American Revolution. War narratives, exploration accounts, the naturalistic travel journal, spiritual autobiography, evangelical diaries and journals: all of these forms of early travel narrative were on some level promotional writings that most often targeted transatlantic audiences with information about the kinds of "wealth" or resources available in British America.

Notes

1. Wayne Franklin, *Discoverers, Explorers, Settlers: The Diligent Writers of Early America* (Chicago: University of Chicago Press, 1979), p. 21.
2. William Penn, "Some Account of the Province of Pennsylvania in America" (1681), n.p.
3. David Shields develops this idea in *Civil Tongues and Polite Letters in British America* (Chapel Hill: University of North Carolina Press, 1997).
4. Carl Bridenbaugh, ed., *Gentleman's Progress: The Itinerarium of Dr. Alexander Hamilton* (Pittsburgh: University of Pittsburgh Press, 1948), p. 7.
5. For further information, see Pamela Regis, *Describing Early America: Bartram, Jefferson, Crevecoeur, and the Influence of Natural History* (Philadelphia: University of Pennsylvania Press, 1992).
6. *An Account of East Florida, with a Journal Kept by John Bartram of Philadelphia, Botanist to his Majesty for the Floridas, upon a Journey from Saint Augustine up the River St. John's* (London, 1767), pp. iii–iv.
7. Jonathan Carver, *Travels through the Interior Parts of North America, in the Years 1766, 1767, and 1768*, 3rd edn (London, 1781), p. vii.
8. *A Journey from Pennsylvania to Onondaga in 1743, by John Bartram, Lewis Evans and Conrad Weiser* (Barre, MA: Massachusetts Imprint Society, 1973), p. 90.
9. Timothy Hall, *Contested Boundaries: Itinerancy and the Reshaping of the Colonial American Religious World* (Durham, NC: Duke University Press, 1994), p. 83.

2

WILLIAM W. STOWE

"Property in the horizon": landscape and American travel writing

Landscape is "a construct of the mind and of feeling," according to Yi-Fu Tuan, a human invention that "can take place only in the mind's eye."[1] "[D]escriptions of the environment are never merely empirical," writes Robert Lawson-Peebles. "They are strategies which encode the interests and concerns of the writer as well as the physical nature of the terrain, the climate, and so on."[2] "Miller owns this field, Locke that, and Manning the woodland beyond," writes Emerson, "[b]ut none of them owns the landscape. There is property in the horizon which no man has but he whose eye can integrate all the parts, that is, the poet."[3]

All three of these writers consider the apprehension of a landscape to be a creative act involving the active perception, organization, and interpretation of a set of empirical givens. Judith Adler says much the same about travel which, when it is "undertaken and executed with a primary concern for the meanings discovered, created, and communicated as persons move through geographical space," has the ability to "bestow[] meaning on the self and the social, natural, or metaphysical realities through which it moves."[4] Moving through the world, observing one's surroundings, giving shape and meaning to what one sees, these activities combine the satisfaction of study and the exhilaration of creative art with a sense of ownership, of "property in the horizon."

From their earliest encounters with the American land, European-Americans used exploration, travel, and the representation of landscape to help define themselves and their place in the world. Pioneers, survey-ors, adventurers, and scientists tried to represent the land, plants, animals, and indigenous peoples as accurately as possible. Artists, poets, and culti-vated tourists sought and described scenes of picturesque beauty and sublime grandeur. Travelers in more developed regions integrated farms and villages, cities and even factories, into their landscape descriptions.

A thorough history of the place of landscape in American travel writing would require several volumes. It would build on the work of landscape specialists like Barbara Novak (*Nature and Culture*), John Brinckerhoff Jackson (e.g., *Discovering the Vernacular Landscape*), and John Stilgoe (e.g., *Common Landscape of America, 1580–1845*; *Landscape and Images*); studies of exploration and adventure such as William Goetzmann's *Exploration and Empire*; accounts of the genteel search for the picturesque such as Beth Lueck's *American Writers and the Picturesque Tour* and John Conron's *American Picturesque*; and histories of travel and tourism like Dona Brown's *Inventing New England*, M. H. Dunlop's *Sixty Miles from Contentment*, Earl Pomeroy's *In Search of the Golden West*, John F. Sears' *Sacred Places*, and Anne Farrar Hyde's *An American Vision*. What I am attempting here is something more modest: a brief account of the ways in which American travelers have used landscape to establish personal and national identities, take scientific account of the world around them, and bear witness to the awe and wonder it can inspire. Some of the figures I discuss are conventional travel writers, but more are what I would call traveling writers or writing travelers, "poets" in the Emersonian sense, who create meaningful landscapes from the welter of facts and impressions that make up the American scene.

Landscape and personal identity

In the introduction to *Landscape and Power*, W. J. T. Mitchell invites readers "to think of landscape not so much as an object to be seen or a text to be read but as a process by which social and subjective identities are formed."[5] Perceiving, defining, and describing a landscape is a way of placing oneself in the world by claiming a particular subject position or exploring a more intimate sense of selfhood.

Some travelers pictorialize the passing scene as a way of dominating the world around them. John Filson's fictionalized "Daniel Boon" casts himself as an articulate and sensitive pioneer who sees the landscape as happily empty and claims to be its rightful inheritor. Having "gained the summit of a commanding ridge," he "surveyed the famous river Ohio that rolled in silent dignity, marking the western border of Kentucke with inconceivable grandeur . . . All things were still. I kindled a fire near a fountain of sweet water, and feasted on the loin of a buck, which a few hours before I had killed."[6] "Boon" uses what Mary Louise Pratt calls the "monarch-of-all-I-survey" moment[7] to assert his domination of the scene, validated by his accomplishment in attaining the height, his aesthetic appreciation of the vista before him, and his ritual consumption of the game he has killed. A later description confirms his claim by depicting the newly settled "Kentucke, lately an howling wilderness," as "a fruitful field" (*Colonel Daniel Boon*,

p. 49) and the site of future cities "situated on the fertile banks of the great Ohio, rising from obscurity to shine with splendor, equal to any other of the stars of the American hemisphere" (p. 50).

While "Boon" uses landscape description to claim the role of conqueror, other early travelers use it to affirm subject positions defined by gender, class, and race. William Bartram, usually a mild and unassuming naturalist, illustrates Annette Kolodny's claim in *The Lay of the Land* that landscape description can serve as a vehicle for claiming the privileges of *maleness* by imagining a scene in West Georgia as a perfect vale of Arcady, peopled by "companies of young, innocent Cherokee virgins, some busy gathering the rich, fragrant fruit, others having already filled their baskets . . . reclined under the shade of floriferous and fragrant native bowers." In this scene the land, its fruits, and its very inhabitants seem to invite the male travelers to more than Platonic contemplation. Indeed, "the sylvan scene of primitive innocence was . . . perhaps too enticing for hearty young men long to continue idle spectators," so "nature prevailing over reason, we wished at least to have a more active part in their delicious sports."[8] Caroline Kirkland, in the fictional persona of Mary Clavers, uses landscape description to claim an identity defined by *class* and good sense. In describing the wild flowers of Michigan she declares her sophistication by calling upon Shelley, Lamb, and Bulwer.[9] On a "charming drive" through "wilderness literally 'blossoming as the rose'" (*A New Home*, p. 114), she shows a more sensible, self-mocking, but still superior side, as she loses one of her "silly thin shoes" (p. 115) in the marshy ground. By asserting her familiarity with English poets and making fun of her inappropriate dress, Kirkland declares her difference from both vulgar settlers like the good-hearted Mrs. Danforth (pp. 13–16) and unfortunate souls like the fastidious Mrs. B–, who has built a fine log house, and furnished it with elegant pieces brought from the east, but who is also desperately poor, saddled with an indolent husband, and completely out of place in the Michigan woods (pp. 115–21). Clarence King affirms his *racial* superiority by peopling his Sierra landscapes with Native Americans conceived as racial others, amusing, "picturesque," fit objects for the traveler's gaze, but of no importance for their own sakes: "The charm of this forest life, in spite of its scientific interest, and the constant succession of exquisite, highly colored scenes, would string one's feelings up to a high though monotonous key, were it not for the half-droll, half-pathetic *genre* picturesqueness which the Digger Indians introduce."[10]

More recent travelers have tended to think of identity in more individualistic terms, using their encounters with landscape to meditate on their own particular relations to the natural world. Terry Tempest Williams, traveling the landscapes of her native Utah in *Refuge* (1991), seeks out landscapes that speak to her of change, loss, and the possibility of regeneration, as she contemplates the way nature wars with nature in the flooding of the Great Salt Lake and the spread of cancer cells in the bodies of her female relatives. William Least Heat-Moon, exploring a single Kansas county in *Prairy-Erth*, intersperses reflections on the economic, social, personal, and natural history that the landscape reveals with meditations on his own place in the world. "I'd come into the prairie out of some dim urge to encounter the alien," he writes, "and I had begun to encounter it as I moved among the quoins, ledgers, pickled brains, winds, creek meanders, gravestones, stone-age circles."[11] Diana Hume George uses her journeys across the length and breadth of America as occasions to combine meditations on her own feelings with philosophical, literary, and political reflections. Her visit to the Pryor Mountains Wild Horse Range on the Wyoming/Montana border prompts a vivid description of the Bighorn Canyon along with comments on the recreational killing of wild animals, the effects of dams on wild rivers, the psychological effects of heights and edges, the erotic component of the urge to jump, the connections between sex and death, Mrs. Moore's experience of the Malabar Caves in E. M. Forster's *A Passage to India*, and her own father's suicidal plunge from an eleventh-floor hotel room in Cleveland forty years earlier.[12]

All of these writers provide representations of the American land that are as "composed" as any landscape painting. Their elements are the forms and features of the natural world, but also the associations and metaphors that these material givens inspire. Like painters, these writers describe a scene, but in the process they also claim a particular perceiving identity, a persona that can be understood in both historical and psychological terms.

Landscape and national identity

Landscape description has also been important in the establishment of national identities. In *Landscape and Memory*, Simon Schama reminds us that "national identity . . . would lose much of its ferocious enchantment without the mystique of a particular landscape tradition."[13] American travelers helped establish and maintain such a tradition, first by using the magnificence of the American landscape to claim superiority to European scenery, and later by describing the relations between people and the land in distinctly American contexts.

The painter Thomas Cole asserted that "American Scenery . . . is a subject that to every American ought to be of surpassing interest" since "it is his own land; its beauty, its magnificence, its sublimity – all are his."[14] Meriwether

Lewis anticipated Cole when he described the falls of the Missouri as an American treasure, a "truly magnificent and sublimely grand object, which has from the commencement of time been concealed from the view of civilized man."[15] Francis Parkman followed Lewis in his celebration of American wildness, describing the prairie surrounding the Platte river in terms of its "stern and wild associations" not with the heroic past, as would be the case in Europe, but with the pressing demands of the present. "[F]or here each man lives by the strength of his arm and the valor of his heart. Here society is reduced to its original elements, the whole fabric of art and conventionality is struck rudely to pieces, and men find themselves suddenly brought back to the wants and resources of their original natures."[16] The arrival of the railroads brought tourists and vacationers to the scenes that Lewis and Parkman had reached with such difficulty, and the first visitors were quick to name the distinctive qualities of the landscape and to claim them as quintessentially American. "The view of the Rocky Mountains from the divide near Kiowa Creek is considered one of the finest in Colorado," writes Bayard Taylor. "I know no *external* picture of the Alps which can be placed beside it."[17] For Samuel Bowles, Colorado embodies the special relation between America and nature, both in the grandeur of the landscape and in the promise of its resources:

> Here, where the great backbone of the Continent rears and rests itself; here, where nature sets the patterns of plain and mountain, of valley and hill, for all America; here, where spring the waters that wash two-thirds of the western Continent and feed both its oceans; here, where mountains are fat with gold and silver, and prairies glory in the glad certainty of future harvests of corn and wheat – here indeed is the center and central life of America[.][18]

In 1872 William Cullen Bryant consolidated the association of landscape and nation in *Picturesque America*, a monumental collection of prose sketches and engravings of the most popular tourist destinations in the country. Bryant's introduction glows with national pride, claiming that the United States offers "some of the wildest and most beautiful scenery in the world."[19] The individual articles guide armchair travelers through classic American scenes such as Niagara Falls, the Brandywine Valley of Pennsylvania, the California coast, or the Yellowstone geyser basin, as well as such favorite tourist cities as Newport and St. Augustine.

These last examples remind us that landscape is not limited to strictly *natural* scenes, habitats, or settings. The word itself originally meant shaped or managed land, "a unit of human occupation" (Schama, *Landscape and Memory*, p. 11), "a collection of dwellings and other structures crowded together within a circle of pasture, meadow, and planting fields and surrounded by unimproved forest or marsh."[20] Travelers from Timothy Dwight to William Least Heat-Moon have shared this view of landscape, describing the American land socially or economically, and defining the nation in terms of its human inhabitants, their identities and their activities.

Dwight was well aware of the appeal of "beautiful and magnificent scenes of nature."[21] He also recognized that history formed an important part of landscape, even in a new country (*Travels*, p. 4), but his overriding purpose in his travel writing was to bear witness to the humanization of the American land, "the conversion of a wilderness into a desirable residence for man" (p. 7). For him, the ideal landscape is neither sublime nor conventionally picturesque, but cheerful, "neat," and prosperous. "A succession of New England villages, composed of neat houses, surrounding neat schoolhouses and churches, adorned with gardens, meadows, and orchards, and exhibiting the universally easy circumstances of the inhabitants, is, at least in my own opinion, one of the most delightful prospects which this world can afford" (p. 7). Not every scene lived up to Dwight's ideal,[22] but he did describe town after town in glowing terms, taking account of the layout, the soil, the trees, crops, and livestock, the condition of local industry, as well as churches, schools, historical events, and notable natives. The result is a rich sense of the dynamic, evolving landscape of the northeastern United States in the first years of the nineteenth century, and a set of mythic images that live on in magazine and calendar art to this day.

Dwight began his travels in 1796 and made his last journey in 1815. Early in this same period some very different travelers helped create a much broader sense of the American landscape by describing the homes of the native peoples of the American Northwest. Thomas Jefferson's instructions to Meriwether Lewis included a request for a detailed report on native peoples, their customs, culture, "food, clothing, and domestic accommodations" (*Journals*, p. xxv). The members of his expedition were constantly aware that the land they "explored" served as home and hunting ground for others, and that the landscape was likely at any moment to contain the figures, friendly or hostile, of native peoples. The American Indians are part of the landscape throughout the journey: "a butiful Countrey on both Sides of the river," Clark writes on October 24, 1804. "We have Seen no game on the river today – Indians hunting in the neighbourhood passed a Island on the S.S. made by the river . . . on this Isld. We Saw one of the Grand Chiefs of the Mandins, with five Lodges hunting" (p. 69). The following August, Lewis describes a classic encounter in some detail, beginning with the lone figure in the distance ("I discovered an Indian on horseback about two miles distant" [p. 222]), and continuing through an uneasy and ultimately unsuccessful attempt to make contact. The presence of the American Indian suggests that this land is part of a native economy, and so perhaps supplied with a "road" leading west through the mountains. In fact, the party discovers such a road, which leads them eventually to a sizeable "encampmen[t] on the river in a handsome level and fertile bottom" complete with a "lodge made of willow brush and an old leather lodge which had been prepared for our reception" (p. 228). Here as throughout their prodigious travels, Lewis and Clark describe a landscape alive not only with wild creatures but with American Indian peoples.

Margaret Fuller discovers a differently peopled landscape in her travels in the newly settled upper Midwest some years later. She describes a landscape in the process of being settled, tamed, domesticated; she is particularly interested in the place of women in the scene she describes, but also disturbed by the condition – and the spectacle – of the native peoples she encounters. Her landscape descriptions seem at first conventionally romantic. "Our stations were not from town to town but from grove to grove," she writes. "These groves first floated like blue islands in the distance. As we drew nearer, they seemed fair parks, and the little log houses on the edge with their curling smokes, harmonized beautifully with them."[23] Three factors disturb Fuller's idealized picture, however. First is the "slovenliness" (*Summer on the Lakes*, p. 46) of too many settlers, who, lacking the American Indians' instinct for siting and habits of preservation, are despoiling the landscape and "obliterat[ing] the natural expression of the country" (p. 47). Second is the very different experience of the two sexes in this landscape, where men find healthy labor in the fields and "recreation with the gun and fishing-rod" while women, often ill-prepared for the frontier life by their refined education (p. 62), are confined to rude dwellings with neither domestic help nor congenial society. Third is the monitory presence of the American Indians, doomed, as Fuller conventionally believed, to extinction (p. 195), but providing a constant reminder of their superior sensitivity to the natural world and their cruel mistreatment by whites (p. 183).

Fuller traveled west in the relatively brief period between the first settlements and the arrival of the railroads and, with them, the beginnings of modern tourism. When Samuel Bowles went to Colorado for "a summer vacation in the Switzerland of America" a generation later, settlement was well established and the landscape filling with people and industrious development. Along the tracks between Chicago and Omaha the travelers "wonder alike at the richness of the soil, the beauty of the rolling prairie, the abundance of the harvests, the rapid settlement and cultivation of the country" (*Parks and Mountains*, p. 41). In the mountains themselves the delightful scenery is interspersed with "little wooded parks or open fields, where grain grows or flocks feed, and somebody keeps 'a ranch'" (p. 74).

In such settings, Bowles predicts, "whole families, – mothers and babies included, – will, with covered wagon and a saddle-horse or two, make a pleasure visit to the mountains" (p. 76). As a patriotic booster of post-Civil War America – the Vice-President of the United States accompanied him for part of his travels in Colorado – Bowles takes pains to depict a prosperous and peaceful nation. For him, as for Fuller, however, the American Indians mar the picture. His solution to the problem is brutal and frank, revealing the racist assumptions beneath the idealized vision of an "American" landscape peopled entirely by white settlers. Give the American Indian food and clothing, he writes, "the means to help himself in the simplest forms possible," "add such education as he will take, such elevation as he will be awakened to, and then let him die, – as die he is doing and die he must" (p. 147).

When Bowles vacationed in the West, the nation was still expanding and the territorial conflict between whites and American Indians was still very much alive. For twentieth-century travelers the frontier was closed, the wilderness was enclosed, the peopled landscape was a given, and the American Indians confined by and large to reservations. The American Guide series, produced by the Depression-era Federal Writers' Project, sets the tone for mid-century travel and redefines the national view of landscape in its state-by-state guidebooks, which include introductory essays on history, ethnic groups, agriculture, labor, and transportation as well as detailed descriptions of roadside scenes. While the writing in *Picturesque America* aspired to the condition of landscape painting, the Guide writers depict landscapes in historical, sociological, and scientific terms. The typical tour provides accounts of natural history and geology, early settlements, local history, and current economic and social life along with amusing anecdotes and occasional brief accounts of the appearance of the scene, which together produce a thickly described, inhabited landscape. Even the most spectacular settings are treated this way. The description of the approach to Yellowstone Park from Bozeman, Montana, through the Gallatin Valley, to take an extreme example, bows briefly to the grandeur of the scenery ("the summits of the mountains form a tremendous background for the quieter landscapes near at hand"[24]) but spends most of its time on American Indian history and legend, natural history, and agriculture. There are also detailed discussions of ranching practices and the lives of ranch workers (*Montana: A State Guide*, pp. 275–76) as well as an account of the professional training and demanding duties of Forest Service rangers (p. 277). The American Indians, meanwhile, have become tourist attractions, "provid[ing] the local color relished by tourists" (p. 237), and giving guidebook writers the opportunity to criticize their treatment by earlier generations.

Guidebooks to Southern states have an even more difficult past and a more disturbing present to deal with. The solution in the Alabama volume is to describe the landscape in "objective" terms, and let the ruins of war and the signs of African American poverty speak for themselves.

> West of Tuskegee the highway is through the rich Black Belt, where cotton is still the money crop and Negro tenant cabins dot the plantations. Wide fields, mostly cotton and corn, spread far on both sides of the highway . . . Plantation big-houses, some standing deserted and dilapidated amid groves of ancient trees, are visible along the highway. Newer farm houses have supplanted some of the old dwellings and the introduction of tractors has deprived many Negro tenant farmers of their jobs.[25]

Booker T. Washington and George Washington Carver are mentioned, it is true, but "Negroes" serve mostly as landscape features and the subjects and sources of such charming bits of folklore as the fugitive slave song, "Run nigger run," which "Negroes of today still sing" (*Alabama*, p. 343).

Later twentieth-century travel writers who set off in search of America follow the Guides' lead in depicting working landscapes with stories to tell. In *Travels with Charley in Search of America*, which may be taken as the prototype of the genre, John Steinbeck combines descriptions of land, people, customs, and history to provide an updated personal portrait of the nation. Later on, Bill Bryson seeks "the lost continent" in what he sees and hears in "small-town America,"[26] while reflective travelers like William Least Heat-Moon, John McPhee, and Jonathan Tilove seek the human as well as the natural in the landscapes they describe. In *PrairyErth*, Heat-Moon provides a deep geography of the cartographic quadrangles of Chase County, Kansas. At Matfield Green, for example, he turns as his Native ancestors did to the four cardinal directions, associates each with an indigenous plant, and meditates on the people who used it. In Thrall-Northwest he surveys the possible site of a Tallgrass Prairie National Park (since established), recounts the history of the park idea, and discusses its current supporters and opponents. In *Encounters with the Archdruid*, McPhee takes a different tack, looking at landscapes through the eyes of the famous environmentalist, David Brower, and three manipulators of landscape: a geologist who sees copper where others see scenery; a real estate developer who thinks of himself as a "true conservationist";[27] and a legendary head of the Bureau of Reclamation who sees dam-building as a holy mission and takes pride in having created the landscape of Lake Powell while submerging the landscape of Glen Canyon beneath its waters. And most recently, in *Along Martin Luther King*, Tilove explores the streets that bear the martyred leader's name, relating every kind of landscape from the rural bucolic to the urban frenetic to the lives of the

African American people who inhabit them, celebrating successful lives and deploring oppressive conditions.[28]

"America" has been identified with its landscape, and travelers have sought the grand, the picturesque, and the typical in their landscape excursions. Travel writers have used the grand natural landscape to claim American uniqueness and boost American pride, but they have also shown how the passing scene can reflect American history and society in somewhat more troubling ways. Representing a landscape is often a celebratory act, but it can be analytical and critical as well, teaching readers and viewers how to see their surroundings in moral and political as well as aesthetic terms.

Scientific observations

If one reason for traveling is to claim a personal or national identity, another is to describe the outside world as accurately as possible. The men and women I call scientific travelers are not analytic scientists but acute observers, either natural historians interested in landscape as habitat, or surveyors and geologists interested in the shape, the history, even the composition of the land.

The first great American natural historian and travel writer is the same William Bartram whom we have already seen restraining his masterful virility in the face of the virgin landscape and the Cherokee maidens. Bartram is better known for his detailed accounts of Southeastern swamps and forests, equally inspired by Linneaus' classificatory intelligence and his own enthusiasm for the beauty and variety of the divine Creation. He makes his two aims apparent from the very beginning of his *Travels*, expressing his hope "that his labors will present new as well as useful information to the botanist and the zoologist" as well as his joyful view that "[t]his world, as a glorious apartment of the boundless palace of the sovereign Creator, is furnished with an infinite variety of animated scenes, inexpressibly beautiful and pleasing" (*Travels*, p. 15). His descriptions of particular scenes attempt to fulfill both purposes, testifying to his pleasure in the created world and recording his observations of its contents. Bartram's two aims can make for awkward prose, veering from conventionally overwrought rhetoric to flat-footed list-making, but his writing serves his purposes very well and no reader can doubt his aesthetic responsiveness or his dedication to precise scientific reporting.

Two mid-nineteenth-century naturalists and travel writers managed their mixed purposes with more grace. Henry Thoreau traveled widely in Concord and beyond, and published accounts of his journeys throughout his career. His landscape descriptions include detailed accounts of plants and animals as well as metaphoric leaps and philosophical musings. Susan Cooper confined her travels to her home region near Cooperstown, New York. She, too, paid close attention to the natural world, but she saw it in more conventionally moral and religious terms.[29]

In his best-known travel essay, "Ktaadn," Thoreau provides striking descriptions of Mount Katahdin's forbidding landscape and a memorable meditation on the place of "spirit" in the physical world of rocks and trees and bodies.[30] In *A Week on the Concord and Merrimack Rivers*, he pays more attention to natural history, but even here he cannot content himself with mere physical description. His account of the Muskatequid marshes describes the plant life along the river in some detail, while painting a colorful picture of the scene and even allowing himself a quick classical allusion.

> The snakehead, *Chelone glabra*, grew close to the shore, while a kind of coreopsis, turning its brazen face to the sun, full and rank, and a tall dull red flower, *Eupatorium purpureum*, or trumpet-weed, formed the rear rank of the fluvial array. The bright blue flowers of the soap-wort gentian were sprinkled here and there in the adjacent meadows, like flowers which Proserpine had dropped[.] (p. 19)

Thoreau sketches the scene with a botanist's attention to plant life and a painter's sensitivity to color and composition. A little further along, he comes upon a fisherman and his dog standing "like statues" by the stream, providing both visual interest and a chance to comment on nature's ability, "by one bait or another," to "allure[] inhabitants into all her recesses" (p. 21). The bait he alludes to seems at first to be fish, and the sentence a clever reversal of the usual sense of the scene. Thoreau goes on, however. First he remembers another Concord fisherman who was drawn into nature by a very different lure – "His fishing was not a sport, nor solely a means of subsistence, but a sort of solemn sacrament and withdrawal from the world" (p. 22). Then he returns to the fish, first to assert that "the fruit of the naturalist's observations is not in new genera or species, but in new contemplations still" (p. 22) and then to spend several pages describing the appearance and habits of the most common river fishes. Thoreau varies the focus and perspective of his landscape descriptions, moving gracefully among scientific information, verbal pictures, and "contemplations" to produce his own particular version of travel experience.

Susan Cooper's best-known work is *Rural Hours*, an account of the natural and social life of her region, based on her walks and excursions. She was a serious student of natural history but no slave to "long-winded Latin polysyllables."[31] Instead of tedious classification, she describes small and large-scale landscapes, provides plant lore and practical information, and draws moral and religious lessons from her observations. In the entry for May 16, her travels take her to a favorite landscape which she describes first in sensory terms, then religiously, and finally morally. "Strolled away from the village in quiet fields by the river, where sloping meadows and a border of wood shut one out from the world," she writes. The scene is "sweetly calm"; there is "nothing stirring but the river flowing gently past, and a few solitary birds flitting quietly to and fro like messengers of peace . . . At hours like these," she goes on, "the immeasurable goodness, the infinite wisdom of our Heavenly Father, are displayed in so great a degree of condescending tenderness to unworthy, sinful man, as must appear quite incomprehensible[.]" Despite the goodness of God, however, "[t]here is sorrow on earth amid the joys of spring as at other seasons," and it behooves true Christians both to console the sufferers as best they can, and to remind them of the "eternal comfort" offered by "the Word of God" (pp. 45–46).

Generations of naturalists followed Cooper's example – think of Celia Thaxter, John Burroughs, Mabel Osgood Wright – traveling intensively in their neighborhoods. In our time, naturalists often combine more adventurous travels with their accounts of the natural world. One of them is Ann Zwinger, who travels the mountains, rivers, and deserts of the West, describing the scene, explaining the geology, drawing the plants. In *Run, River, Run*, she describes "a naturalist's journey" down the Green River from its source in the Wind River Mountains to its confluence with the Colorado. Along the way she uses her way with verbs to animate the landscape ("snow rounds into water, seeps and trickles, splashes and pours and clatters, burnishing the shattered gray rock, and carols downslope"[32]) and her knowledge of science to show us its own dynamic life, from the life cycle of the midge (p. 11) to the dynamics of a glacial river from the point of view of a hydrologist ("Ripples form only in sand, not in loose gravels or cohesive muds" [p. 57]) and a canoeist ("If a rock broaches the surface, there is no problem, but if under the surface – a 'sleeper' – one must learn to read its depth by the bolster it makes" [p. 40]).

Another group of scientific observers is more interested in terrain and topography than local habitat. Meriwether Lewis and William Clark were self-educated naturalists as well as explorers, but their main job was to chart new territory. John Charles Frémont was a professionally trained surveyor who was commissioned to map and measure the land; Clarence King studied science at Yale, learned field geology while working on the California State Geological Survey, and later served as the first director of the United States Geological Survey. A century later, John McPhee, a professional writer and geological autodidact, has spent part of his brilliant career helping Americans understand the American land.

Thanks in large part to the guidance of Thomas Jefferson, Lewis was ideally qualified to describe the Western landscape. His travel journals combine detailed observations and measurements, comments on the political and commercial significance of the land, and aesthetic reactions. He describes the "Clifts" of the upper Missouri, measuring their height, analyzing their composition, and assessing their susceptibility to erosion (*Journals*, pp. 143–44). His description of Maria's River combines political, commercial, and aesthetic elements, commenting on its likely role in boundary disputes, its utility in providing "safe and direct communication" to fur country, and its passage through "one of the most beautifully picteresque [*sic*] countries that I ever beheld" (p. 153). His celebrated account of the Great Falls of the Missouri moves from surveyor's observations – "a cascade of about fifty feet perpendicular streching [*sic*] at rightangles [*sic*] across the river from side to side to the distance of at least a quarter of a mile" – to a comparison of two of its cataracts couched in the conventional vocabulary of the picturesque traveler – "at length I determined between these two great rivals for glory that this was *pleasingly beautiful*, while the other was *sublimely grand*" (p. 163).

Like Lewis, John Charles Frémont strove to provide an objective picture of the American West for the benefit of the nation and the edification of settlers and developers. Working forty to fifty years after Lewis, Frémont could rely on far more sophisticated scientific training, technique, and instrumentation to produce more precise maps and more reliable data. His reports are more polished than Lewis'; he seems to have exchanged the awed enthusiasm of the pioneer for the calmer authority of the scientific cartographer and the observant naturalist. Each morning and evening he reports the precise temperature, barometric pressure, and, weather permitting, the latitude and longitude as determined by celestial observation. Having established his location, he makes precise geological observations, noting, for example, that the ridge on the left bank of the upper Platte "is composed entirely of silicious pudding stone" arranged in strata which "incline to the northeast with a dip of about fifteen degrees."[33] Frémont is also an ambitious word-painter and a connoisseur of scenery who sometimes finds himself distracted from his scientific duties by the beauty of his surroundings:

Viewed in the sunshine of a pleasant morning, the scenery was of a most striking and romantic beauty, which arose from the picturesque disposition of the objects, and the vivid contrast of colors. I thought with much pleasure of our approaching descent in the canoe through such places; and . . . did not now dwell so much as might have been desirable upon the geological formations along the line of the river.   (*Narratives of Exploration*, p. 143)

Clarence King, the Yale-trained geologist, admirer of Ruskin and author of *Mountaineering in the Sierra Nevada*, combines objective description of landscape with self-consciously literary writing and high-cultural allusion. The first sentence sets the tone: "The western margin of this continent is built of a succession of mountain chains folded in broad corrugations, like waves of stone upon whose seaward base beat the mild small breakers of the Pacific" (*Mountaineering*, p. 1). The first clause appears to be a statement of fact: the west coast is indeed defined by parallel mountain ranges. In the next two phrases ("folded in broad corrugations, like waves of stone"), King provides a comparison that calls attention to his role as perceiver and writer. His goal, it seems, is not simply to state facts but to convey impressions. In the final clause he asserts his literary presence and authority even more firmly by providing a surprising characterization of the Pacific, whose "mild small breakers" contrast so effectively with the mountainous "waves of stone." Throughout his text, King uses the double authority of science and literature to establish a privileged relation with the natural world, which he understands in geological, botanical, historical, cultural, and personal terms. He displays his scientific expertise by describing the Sierra as a product of barely imaginable geological processes in unthinkably distant periods – the Paleozoic, the Triassic, the Jurassic. Then he demonstrates his high-cultural authority and poetic sensibility by comparing the history of the mountains to the "trial of fire and the desperate ordeal of water" undergone by "the characters of the *Zauberflöte* [*Magic Flute*]" (p. 4).

John McPhee is another Easterner with Ivy League credentials who combines adventurous travel with scientifically informed observation, a modest and elegant writing style, and a sensitivity to the poetry of even the most unprepossessing landscape. Not a scientist, McPhee casts himself as a well-read amateur who travels the country with naturalists and geologists, helping the reader see the landscape and its animals, plants, and geological features through their eyes. In *Rising from the Plains*, he travels Wyoming with the "autochthonous geologist" David Love, helping his readers see unlovely scenes with new eyes.[34] Just west of Rawlins, for example, is a landscape which would never "lift the stock of Eastman Kodak," "a dispassionate world of bare rock, brown grass, drab green patches of greasewood, and scattered colonies of sage," crossed by an interstate described in geological terms as originally "lithified as white concrete" but "now dark with the remains of ocean algae, cremated and sprayed on the road" (pp. 22–23). "Why stop here?" McPhee asks, and Love shows him. To the educated eye this barren landscape reveals more geologic history than the Grand Canyon, "reach[ing] back into the Archaen eon and up to the Miocene epoch" (p. 23). McPhee looks at what he sees and then imagines a time-lapse view of the scene, taking us from "a deep and uncontinented ocean sluggish with amorphous scums" (p. 23), through a barren desert, "a Jurassic landscape of particularly dramatic dinosaurs," "the great Cretaceous seaway," a Paleocene swamp, and an Eocene river "running off a mountain into lush semi-tropical plains, where puppy-sized horses were hiding for their lives" (p. 24). Unaffected by the conventions of sublime and picturesque, untroubled by the need to associate his word-pictures with European models, McPhee gives us landscapes, whether in Wyoming or Maine, Alaska or New Jersey, as they look to an observant visitor and as they can be made to live through knowledge of their history, whether natural or human or both.

Landscape and metaphysics

To many American travelers, landscape has a religious or cosmological significance: it is a site for meditation on ultimate meanings, a sign of the benevolence, indifference, or even hostility of the divine. Early promoters of American settlement conceived of the landscape as a *locus amoenus*, the gift of a benevolent God; others, including many of the settlers themselves, thought of it as the home of the devil, waiting to be conquered and redeemed.[35] Nineteenth-century American painters treated landscape as "a holy text which revealed truth."[36] Emerson wrote that nature "always speaks of Spirit" (*Nature*, p. 40), and even such a resolute materialist – an "earthiest" as he calls himself – as Edward Abbey finds himself wondering if the canyon landscape he explores is "at last the *locus Dei*."[37]

For many early American travelers nature and landscape are quite simply the residence of the Creator. The world, for Bartram, is "a glorious apartment of the boundless palace of the sovereign Creator" (*Travels*, p. 15). The poet and traveler Lydia Huntley Sigourney sees divinity in all manner of landscapes. At Niagara she senses a sublime and ineffable presence: "This is thy building, Architect Divine!"[38] At Daniel Wadsworth's country estate near Hartford, the landscape bears witness to a more benevolent, personal God, as the very plants "own the Hand that paints the flower, / That deals the sunshine and the shower, / That bears the sparrow in its fall, / Is kind, and good, and just to all" (*Scenes in My Native Land*, p. 53). Though he casts his first journey to the Maine Woods in unmistakable metaphysical terms, Thoreau is less willing than Bartram or Sigourney simply to celebrate God's presence and assume his benevolence. The scene near the summit of Mount Katahdin is a parody of pastoral, "where rocks, gray, silent rocks were the flocks and herds that pastured" (*The Maine Woods*, p. 638) and "Nature . . . seems to say sternly, why came you here before your time? This ground is not prepared for you" (p. 640). Thoreau's admirer John Muir describes his experience of God in the landscape in language that seems more spontaneous than Bartram's or Sigourney's and less skeptical than Thoreau's. "Who could ever guess," he asks, "that so rough a wilderness should yet be so fine, so full of good things . . . God himself always seems to be doing his best here, working like man in a glow of enthusiasm."[39] "Looking back through the stillness and romantic enchanting beauty and peace of the camp grove, this June seems the greatest of all the months of my life, the most truly, divinely free, boundless like eternity, immortal" (*Mountains of California*, p. 68). Muir's most famous mountaintop experience is precisely the opposite of Thoreau's: rather than being chased away from the heights he is challenging, and forced to confront his human alienation from the entirely spiritual and the merely physical, he is rescued at a crucial moment by the coming-together of the two.[40]

In the twentieth century Annie Dillard combines Muir's exuberance with Emerson's transcendental spirituality. Like Susan Cooper, she is primarily a local traveler. "I explore the neighborhood," she writes. "Like the bear who went over the mountain, I went out to see what I could see."[41] What she sees, more than anything else, is something she calls "mystery," and what she means by mystery seems to be the unmistakable but incomprehensible revelation of the numinous in the phenomenal world. Dillard's landscapes pulse with meaning and mystery. Her neighborhood creeks "are an active mystery, fresh every minute. Theirs is the mystery of the continuous creation and all that providence implies" (*Pilgrim*, pp. 2–3). The nearby mountains "are a passive mystery . . . Theirs is the one simple mystery of creation from nothing, of matter itself anything at all, the given" (p. 3). The scenes she explores are thresholds of revelation, rarely realized but always possible. Once in a very long while, sun and dew and a simple cedar combine to produce momentary illumination. Looking at that sparkling tree "was less like seeing than like being for the first time seen, knocked breathless by a powerful glance." It is a "vision" she lives for, Dillard writes, "the moment when the mountains open and a new light roars in spate through the crack, and the mountains slam" (p. 34).

Edward Abbey's view of the landscape appears to be the direct opposite of Dillard's. "I know nothing whatever about true underlying reality," he writes, "never having met any . . . I am pleased enough with surfaces – in fact they alone seem to me to be of much importance" (*Desert Solitaire*, p. xi). Despite his self-declared "earthism," the landscapes he travels challenge him to ask metaphysical questions. Floating down the Colorado River through the doomed Glen Canyon, Abbey repeatedly wonders about God, and repeatedly denies his importance if not his existence (pp. 180, 185). He admits that the "secretive little side canyons," each with its "tiny spring" and single cottonwood tree tempt him to imagine "a rainbow-colored corona of blazing light, pure spirit, pure being, pure disembodied intelligence, *about to speak my name*," but he sees these fantasies as signs of weakness. "If a man's imagination were not so weak," he writes, "he would learn to perceive in water, leaves, and silence more than sufficient of the absolute and marvelous, more than enough to console him for the loss of the ancient dreams" (p. 200).

Abbey's mid-century materialism is an exception among landscape writers, as two very different contemporary examples make clear. Neither Terry Tempest Williams nor Barry Lopez is a neo-Transcendentalist like Dillard, but both find mystery beneath the surface of the places they describe. Williams travels her native Utah, chronicling the effects of the rising level of the Great Salt Lake. Having "learned at an early age that God can be found wherever you are, especially outside," she writes reverently of the Bear River Bird Refuge, of the desert, of the lake itself. She relates the fertile wetlands, "emeralds around Great Salt Lake," life-giving but threatened by flood, to human families and nurturing communities, also life-giving but threatened by disease.[42] By the end of the book, however, she has moved from the fatalism that these parallels imply to an angry awareness that while changes in the landscape are inevitable and perhaps even divinely ordained, her family's cancers may have as much to do with bomb testing and nuclear fallout as with fate or genetics (*Refuge*, pp. 281–90).

Lopez is both a meticulous naturalist and a fabulist who often uses a magical realist mode to produce an intensity of connection with the natural world that mere description cannot provide. The landscape descriptions in *Arctic Dreams*, his account of his far Northern travels, are mesmerizing in their beauty and their approach to inherent but inexpressible meaning. In one passage he describes the colors of the aurora borealis and then tells of "turn[ing] over a weathered caribou antler once on the tundra and [finding] those same two colors staining its white surface . . . Such correspondences," he goes on, "like that between a surfacing guillemot and an Eskimo man rolling upright in his kayak, hold a landscape together."[43] Like Dillard, he also sees "such correspondences" as revealing the essence of the land itself, which is mysterious and, ultimately, sacred. "The land retains an identity of its own, still deeper and more subtle than we can know." "Our obligation toward it" includes being "alert for its openings, for that moment when something sacred reveals itself within the mundane, and you know the land knows you are there" (p. 228). His accounts of such moments help readers cultivate an alertness to landscapes as things of beauty and parts of a cosmic whole.

Travel writers and landscape observers are creative artists, Emersonian poets who use the power of imagination to organize experience and perception into coherent and meaningful wholes. They are also, to a greater or lesser degree, reporters who seek to provide a faithful representation of the world and their experience of it. Just as there is no representation without interpretation, however, so there is no journey that is not inflected by the traveler's knowledge, intelligence, and sensibility, and no landscape that is not composed from an observer's literal, psychic, social, and spiritual point of view. In their attempts to represent and interpret the American scene, travel writers have combined natural and artificial features of the observed world with their own personal, social, ethical, and philosophical concerns to create literary landscapes that contribute to an understanding of American experience.

Notes

1 Yi-Fu Tuan, "Thought and Landscape: The Eye and the Mind's Eye," in *The Interpretation of Ordinary Landscapes: Geographical Essays*, ed. D. W. Meinig (New York: Oxford University Press, 1978), pp. 89–90.
2 Robert Lawson-Peebles, *Landscape and Written Expression in Revolutionary America* (Cambridge: Cambridge University Press, 1988), p. 6.
3 Ralph Waldo Emerson, *Nature*, in *Essays and Lectures*, The Library of America (New York: Literary Classics of the United States, 1988), p. 9.
4 Judith Adler, "Travel as Performed Art," *American Journal of Sociology* 94:6 (May 1989), p. 1368.
5 W. J. T. Mitchell, *Landscape and Power* (Chicago: University of Chicago Press, 1994), p. 1.
6 John Filson, *The Adventures of Colonel Daniel Boon* (Wilmington, NC: James Adams, 1784), p. 55.
7 Mary Louise Pratt, *Imperial Eyes: Travel Writing and Transculturation* (New York: Routledge, 1992), pp. 201–05.
8 William Bartram, *Travels* (1791; rpt. New York: Penguin, 1988), p. 289.
9 Caroline Kirkland, *A New Home – Who'll Follow? or, Glimpses of Western Life* (New York: Charles S. Francis, 1841), p. 8.
10 Clarence King, *Mountaineering in the Sierra Nevada* (1872; rpt. Yosemite National Park: Yosemite Association, 1997), p. 33.
11 William Least Heat-Moon, *PrairyErth* (Boston: Houghton Mifflin, 1991), p. 105.
12 Diana Hume George, *The Lonely Other: A Woman Watching America* (Urbana: University of Illinois Press, 1996), pp. 40–45.
13 Simon Schama, *Landscape and Memory* (New York: Vintage, 1996), p. 15. See also Mitchell, *Landscape and Power*, p. 15.
14 Thomas Cole, "Essay on American Scenery," *American Monthly Magazine* (January 1836), p. 1.
15 Meriwether Lewis and William Clark, *The Journals of Lewis and Clark*, ed. Frank Bergon (New York: Penguin, 1995), p. 161.

16 Francis Parkman, Jr., *The Oregon Trail*, ed. David Levin (New York: Penguin, 1982), p. 106.

17 Bayard Taylor, *Colorado: A Summer Trip*, ed. William W. Savage, Jr. and James H. Lazalier (Niwot: University of Colorado Press, 1989), p. 35.

18 Samuel Bowles, *The Parks and Mountains of Colorado: A Summer Vacation in the Switzerland of America, 1868*, ed. James H. Pickering (Norman: University of Oklahoma Press, 1991), p. 36.

19 William Cullen Bryant, "Introduction," *Picturesque America* (New York: D. Appleton, 1872), vol. I, p. iv.

20 John Stilgoe, *The Common Landscape of America, 1580–1845* (New Haven: Yale University Press, 1982), p. 12.

21 Timothy Dwight, *Travels in New York and New England*, ed. Barbara Miller Solomon (Cambridge, MA: Harvard University Press, 1969), vol. I, pp. 3, 4.

22 On his disappointments see Jane Kamensky, "'In These Contrasted Climes, How Chang'd the Scene': Progress, Declension, and Balance in the Landscapes of Timothy Dwight," *New England Quarterly* 63:1 (March 1990), pp. 80–108.

23 Margaret Fuller, *Summer on the Lakes in 1843* (Boston: Little and Brown, 1844), p. 40.

24 Federal Writers' Project, *Montana: A State Guide Book* (New York: Viking, 1939), p. 275.

25 Writers' Program of the Works Project Administration, *Alabama: A Guide to the Deep South* (New York: Richard R. Smith, 1941), p. 281.

26 Bill Bryson, *Lost Continent: Travels in Small-Town America* (New York: Harper and Row, 1989).

27 John McPhee, *Encounters with the Archdruid* (New York: Farrar, Straus, and Giroux, 1971), p. 95.

28 Jonathan Tilove, *Along Martin Luther King: Travels on Black America's Main Street* (New York: Random House, 2003).

29 Rochelle Johnson makes the comparison in "Placing *Rural Hours*," in *Reading Under the Sign of Nature*, ed. John Tallmadge and Henry Harrington (Salt Lake City: University of Utah Press, 2000), pp. 64–84.

30 Henry Thoreau, *A Week on the Concord and Merrimack Rivers, Walden, The Maine Woods, Cape Cod* (New York: Literary Classics of the United States, 1985), p. 646.

31 Susan Fenimore Cooper, *Rural Hours*, ed. Rochelle Johnson and Daniel Patterson (Athens: University of Georgia Press, 1998), p. 83.

32 Ann Zwinger, *Run, River, Run: A Naturalist's Journey Down One of the Great Rivers of the American West* (Tucson: University of Arizona Press, 1975), p. 2.

33 John Charles Frémont, *Narratives of Exploration and Adventure*, ed. Allan Nevins (New York: Longmans, Green & Co., 1956), pp. 154–55.

34 John McPhee, *Rising from the Plains* (New York: Farrar, Straus, and Giroux, 1986), p. 4.

35 See Roderick Nash, *Wilderness and the American Mind*, 3rd edn (New Haven: Yale University Press, 1982), pp. 23–43. On the *locus amoenus* see Kenneth Myers, "On the Cultural Construction of Landscape Experience: Contact to 1830," in *American Iconology: New Approaches to Nineteenth-Century Art and Literature*, ed. David C. Miller (New Haven: Yale University Press, 1993), pp. 62–64.

36 Barbara Novak, *Nature and Culture: American Landscape and Painting, 1825–1875* (New York: Oxford University Press, 1980), p. 7.

37 Edward Abbey, *Desert Solitaire: A Season in the Wilderness* (New York: Ballantine, 1968), pp. 208, 200.

38 L. H. Sigourney, *Scenes in My Native Land* (Boston: James Munroe, 1845), p. 4.

39 John Muir, *My First Summer in the Sierra* (1911; rpt. New York: Penguin, 1987), p. 60.

40 John Muir, *The Mountains of California* (1894; rpt. San Francisco: Sierra Club, 1988), p. 52.

41 Annie Dillard, *Pilgrim at Tinker Creek* (New York: Harper and Row, 1974), p. 11.

42 Terry Tempest Williams, *Refuge: An Unnatural History of Family and Place* (New York: Vintage, 1991), pp. 14, 28, 22.

43 Barry Lopez, *Arctic Dreams* (1986; rpt. New York: Bantam, 1989), p. 229.

3

CHRISTOPHER MULVEY

New York to Niagara by way of the Hudson and the Erie

Four scenes

In the middle decades of the nineteenth century, the five-hundred-mile journey from New York City by way of the Hudson River Valley and the Erie Canal to Niagara Falls arranged itself in a ready-made sequence of perfect landscape types. The urban setting, the picturesque scene, the technological landscape, and the sublime site called for different kinds of language and for different displays of emotion. Each stage of the journey demanded its set-piece, and American and British travelers rapidly established four sub-genres that became a demanding series of writerly tests. It is true, as Alan Wallach argues, that in this period "landscape tourism in the United States tended to focus on scenes of awesome grandeur" – waterfalls, mountains, rivers.[1] It is even more true that criticism of travel literature has emphasized the naturally awesome, but the people on the ground, as it were, did not overlook the technologically impressive, and, following Wordsworth, they believed that the Earth "has not anything to show more fair" than a great city seen at the right time in the right light. The canal and the city would not supplant the river and the falls, but they could complement and offset them in the great journey.

The basic route is outlined in a remarkable document not formally published until 1849 when William W. Campbell included it in *The Life and Writings of DeWitt Clinton* under the title "His Private Canal Journal – 1810." Clinton's "Canal Journal" is not an account of a journey along the Erie Canal but an account of a journey from New York City to Niagara made to plot the path of the Erie Canal. The great decision of the New York State Assembly lay in the fact that the legislators resisted the short cut to the nearer Lake Ontario, and they determined to dig the 363 miles from the Hudson to Lake Erie. Clinton says nothing about either New York City or the Hudson Valley, but daily entries provide detailed descriptions of the route through Western New York. Clinton's "Private Canal Journal" is prosaic, but its outcome was the Erie Canal, dug between 1817 and 1825, and the canal was so much associated with him that it was called "Clinton's Ditch," first as a political insult, then as a nationwide compliment.[2]

Clinton's imagination was excited by the political, commercial, and national potential of a great passage between New York City and trans-Appalachian America. He records legend as information, and he does not approach his subject – even Niagara – with awe. His treatment of landscape shows an eighteenth-century sensibility, and that makes him a traveler very different from those who were to celebrate Niagara after reaching their goal by way of his canal. Some of the greatest writers of the United States and the United Kingdom made the journey, but it has to be said that few if any appreciated the full significance of Clinton's Ditch. Perhaps Walt Whitman alone understood: "Something for us is pouring now, more than Niagara pouring," he wrote.[3] The canal had been built to open the West, and Walt Whitman believed that Erie's streaming humanity would be much greater than Niagara's Thundering Waters.

Not every traveler started from New York City, nor completed all four sections of the demanding route, nor, if they did complete all four, did they do so in the one journey. But very many did make the journey that William Leete Stone describes in a short piece called "A Trip from New York to Niagara."[4] He begins his travelogue by saying that he and his wife started from New York at 5 p.m. on October 10, 1829 when they boarded the *New Philadelphia* to journey up the Hudson overnight to Albany. Like Clinton's "Private Canal Journal," Stone's "Trip from New York" is at the boundary of travel literature, at an instructive boundary. Exploration of these boundaries represents my return to themes I first engaged in *Anglo-American Landscapes* (1983). The return is with two important differences. First, the viewpoint of American travelers is now included; *Anglo-American Landscapes* includes only British accounts of American landscapes. Second, the present study is written with an understanding that the Erie Canal is a key to the development of modern America, not merely a mode of transport.

New York City: "a scene of opulence and industry"

Some of the best encapsulations of New York City, descriptions of the whole as the equivalent of a natural wonder, come from outsiders, and among the most expressive were the Britons; but before taking the British view, it is worth looking at an American description of New York that appears in another form of travel text that is at another boundary of travel literature – the travel guide. Through many versions and editions between 1822 and 1840, the most popular guide for the New York to Niagara trip was Gideon

Miner Davison's *Traveller's Guide through the Middle and Northern States, and the Provinces of Canada*. Davison's work started out as something closer to a travel book than a travel guide because in 1822 it was called *The Fashionable Tour; or, A Trip to the Springs, Niagara, Quebeck, and Boston, in the Summer of 1821*, and its evolution into a travel guide offers an opportunity to show the differences in the genres. The guide suppresses the book's narrative, the story of the journey, and as Barbara Korte says "a text about a journey is not normally considered an account unless the journey is narrated."[5] When, in 1833, the first edition of the *Traveller's Guide* appeared, Davison published with it a *Map of the Routes Through the Middle & Northern States and the Provinces of Canada: Designed to Accompany The Travelers Guide*, and that graphical abstraction of *The Fashionable Tour* marks an ultimate stage in the removal of narrative from the description of a journey. Thinking about (but probably not looking at) New York City, Gideon Davison starts his description by saying that "The city is situated on the point of York Island, at the confluence of the Hudson and the East rivers, in latitude 40."[6] By contrast, the Englishman William Cobbett coming upon the city from the Atlantic says: "Man's imagination can fancy nothing so beautiful as the bay and port, from which two immense rivers sweep up on the sides of the land, on which the city is." And he adds the further thought "The city is a scene of opulence and industry: riches without indolence, and labour without grudging."[7] Cobbett is fired by the scene as Davison is not. The Englishwoman Fanny Trollope was even more impressed than Cobbett: "My imagination is incapable of conceiving anything of the kind more beautiful than the harbour of New York," she writes towards the end of *Domestic Manners of the Americans*. It rose, like Venice, from the sea. "New York, indeed, appeared to us even when we saw it by a soberer light, a lovely and a noble city."[8]

Brightness was a difference between New York and Liverpool that struck Sarah Mytton Maury, a resident of the English port: "The clearness of the atmosphere, and the absence of coalsmoke" in the city of New York were particularly pleasing after "the dingy mud coloured walls of the houses in Liverpool."[9] The sky above the bay of New York reminded Lady Emmeline Stuart Wortley of Italy.[10] The fact that it is easy to find breathtaking descriptions of both city and bay in nineteenth-century British travel writing does not mean that Americans have not appreciated what the foreign eye so readily sees. But American appreciations are deeper, more embedded in the full texture of American writing, more likely, that is, to appear in the novel or the poem. No Briton writes of Manhattan as Walt Whitman, "of Manhattan the son," writes in "Mannahatta" of the "City of hurried and sparkling waters! city of spires and masts! City nested in bays! my city!" (*Leaves of*

Grass, pp. 585–86). Equally Edith Wharton's descriptions of Old New York in her collection of that title allow the reader to visit the city and enter its dining rooms, drawing rooms, and bedrooms in a way that no visiting Briton ever did. And perhaps the greatest descriptions of New York are those that Henry James provides in *The American Scene*; but Whitman, Wharton, and James are special cases from which no useful generalizations can be made except to say that they are New Yorkers who did not overlook New York. New York City is itself a special case in the journey from New York to Niagara, and the uneven treatment given it by American and British travel writers contrasts with the consistent treatment that both sets of writers give to the next stage – the Hudson River Valley.

The Hudson River Valley: "one of Nature's felicities"[11]

The American landscapes most frequently described as picturesque were those views associated with the Hudson River, views that gave rise to the first distinctly North American landscape school, which came into being exactly with the completion of the Erie Canal: "The traditional and by now almost hallowed date for the beginning of the Hudson River School," says John K. Howat, "is 1825, when Thomas Cole was discovered by three of New York's leading artists, John Trumbull, William Dunlap, and Asher Durand."[12] Gideon Miner Davison's *Traveller's Guide* suddenly and briefly becomes a travel book for the pages in which he describes the Hudson: "To the gratification derived from a prospect of the beautiful and sublime objects of nature," he says, "the effect of the most striking contrast is added, to render the scene truly picturesque and enchanting. On the one hand are seen summits, crowned with forests, apparently impenetrable to the footsteps of cultivation; and on the other, beautiful and extensive lawns, checkered with the abodes of husbandry, and glowing in all the rich verdure of summer" (p. 121). British and American writers were in agreement with Davison about the picturesque beauty of the Hudson, and any disagreement came from the writers who asserted that the scenes were more than picturesque. Davison himself claims that the range of scenes – plains and mountains, towns and villages, forests and fields – imparted "to the beholder all the charms of novelty, with the highest emotions of the sublime" (p. 121). His use of the sublime here may seem facile, but he makes no similar claim for Niagara, which he describes in a pedestrian fashion.

In 1833, the English actress Fanny Kemble presented full descriptions of the Hudson Valley, at all points from New York City to Albany – the city where the traveler's journey turned west along the Mohawk Valley. The poetic mode that Kemble employed for her descriptions was Wordsworthian;

in that, she was following a fashion of British travelers: "and rock and river, earth and sky," she writes, "shone in intense and dazzling brilliancy." As her steamboat bears her up river, Fanny Kemble allows her readers to experience with her the growing intensity of her mood, the steady heightening of sensibility. "Far away the distant summits of the Highlands rose one above another, shutting in the world, and almost appearing as though each bend of the river must find us locked in their shadowy circle, without means of onward progress." The boat, Fanny Kemble, and the reader move through what became, effectively, a series of lakes in the progress north. "At every moment the scene varied; at every moment, new beauty and grandeur was revealed to us."[13]

The view from the Catskill's Mountain House was held by many to be the greatest view between New York and Albany. Harriet Martineau wrote: "I may be singular; but I own that I was more moved by what I saw from the Mountain House than by Niagara itself."[14] Martineau originally made her claim in her *Retrospect of Western Travel* of 1838, but her passage on the Hudson's beauties was quoted by the New Yorker and preacher-poet Charles Rockwell in his 1867 anthology, *The Catskill Mountains and the Region Around*. Rockwell's appreciation of the beauty of the Catskill Mountain House and its view is not inferior to that of Harriet Martineau nor her general appreciation of the Hudson greater than that of the Americans in whose company Rockwell places her: James Fenimore Cooper, Willis Gaylord Clark, Tyrone Power, N. P. Willis, Park Benjamin, and Bayard Taylor. However, Martineau is very strong on the subject of the Mountain House: "I think," she says, "I had rather have missed the Hawk's Nest, the Prairies, the Mississippi, and even Niagara, than this" (Rockwell, *The Catskill Mountains*, p. 224).

But valuing the Mountain House scene above Niagara to the point of calling it "sublime" was either to use the word too casually, as Davison does, or to strive for a contrived reaction, as Martineau does. The special quality of the Hudson Valley was that it was a domesticated landscape. The through-flow of businessmen, tourists, and immigrants – Whitman's "more than Niagara pouring" – made the Hudson entirely safe and familiar. Danger lay 363 miles away at the end of the Erie. As John Conron says of the Mountain House view: "The painters of the Hudson River School are clearly drawn to the vista in part as a means of representing the manifold effects of the Anglo-American civilization (or domestication or refinement) of the natural landscape."[15] That is the idea expressed by Thomas Cole himself in his "Essay on American Scenery," published in *The American Magazine* in January 1836: "Without any great stretch of the imagination we may anticipate the time when the ample waters shall reflect temple, and tower, and dome, in every variety of picturesqueness and magnificence."[16]

British writers like Fanny Kemble, Harriet Martineau, Fanny Trollope and Thomas Hamilton cannot fairly be blamed for not realizing as they traveled through the Hudson Valley between Albany and New York that they were moving through landscapes that were the focus of intense American interest. However, the sites that British travelers were appreciating were those that had already been identified by American travelers. The initial popularity of the Mountain House, originally referred to as Pine Orchard, says Alan Wallach, is attributed "to a series of articles that William L. Stone, editor of the Federalist New York *Commercial Advertiser*, published in his newspaper in 1824" ("Thomas Cole," p. 31). Moreover, the Hudson landscapes were a main focus of Nathaniel Parker Willis' *American Scenery*, a book that opens with the assertion that

> Either Nature has wrought with a bolder hand in America, or the effect of long continued cultivation on scenery, as exemplified in Europe, is greater than is usually supposed. Certain it is that the rivers, the forests, the unshorn mountain-sides and unbridged chasms of that vast country, are of a character peculiar to America alone – a lavish and large-featured sublimity, (if we may so express it,) quite dissimilar to the picturesque of all other countries.[17]

A nationalism that slighted Europe's landscapes – Willis was familiar with the Lake District, the Rhine Valley, and the French Alps – did not mean that America's landscapes were not being genuinely appreciated. His defensive nationalism was only a bolder statement of Thomas Cole's more tentative defense of the landscapes of his beloved adopted country: "the Alleghanies and the Catskills are in no point higher than five thousand feet; but this is no inconsiderable height," says the man who at the age of seventeen had followed his father from England; "Snowdon in Wales, and Ben-Nevis in Scotland, are not more lofty" ("Essay on American Scenery," p. 102).

The Erie Canal: "the wondrous stream"

The truly remarkable object in the whole journey from New York to Niagara was the Erie Canal. There were other cities, other river valleys, and other waterfalls, but only in China was there another continuous canal that ran for 363 miles. At the time of its digging the longest canal in Great Britain was just over 30 miles and the longest European canal was France's Canal du Midi at 150 miles. The idea of the Erie had seemed to President Thomas Jefferson so preposterous that he thought Clinton's plan "little short of madness," and he refused to allow the Federal Government to have any part in its planning.[18] It eventually came about as the creation of New York State alone, and it began to figure in the accounts of travelers even before it was complete. In 1819, the New Hampshire lawyer Estwick Evans published his *Pedestrious Tour*, a record of 4,000 miles that he had walked (dressed in buffalo skins) the previous year. His initial stage of 744 miles was the walk from Portsmouth in New Hampshire to Detroit (in what would be Michigan), taking him through the Mohawk Gap and along the planned route of the Erie Canal. He writes, "I may here introduce some facts relative to the grand canal in the State of New York. The object of this great undertaking is to facilitate the inland commerce of the State, by uniting the waters of Lake Erie with those of the Hudson."[19] A traveler like Evans willing to go the distance on foot was already going at the pace of the horse-drawn canal boats that started to make the through journey in 1825. However, those boats had the advantage of moving twenty-four hours a day, seven days a week except for those of the "Six-Day Lines" which observed the Sabbath.[20]

The boostering language into which Evans moves when speaking of the canal and "her Clinton" was a rhetoric that came easily to Americans writing of an accomplishment which, though entirely an achievement of New York State, was at once recognized as a triumph of the American nation. In the *Traveller's Guide*, Gideon Miner Davison begins his account of the canal with a standard encomium: "This magnificent structure was commenced under the patronage of the state, on the 4th July, 1817, and was completed in 1825, uniting the waters of the Erie and the Hudson, at an expense of less than seven millions of dollars – a sum trivial in comparison with the immense advantage derived to the state from such communication" (p. 230). Davison gives descriptions of fifty-one points on the canal starting with Albany and ending with Buffalo, but he early raises the great problem with traveling on the Erie: boredom. Novelty wore off in the first hour, and for those who went all the way by canal, the traveling time was a minimum of fifty hours of complete inertia.

Nathaniel Hawthorne made this unchallenging challenge the basis of the article about the Erie that he published in the *New-England Magazine* towards the end of 1835. "I embarked," he writes, "about thirty miles below Utica, determining to voyage along the whole extent of the canal, at least twice in the course of the summer." It is an unusual instance of round-trip travel writing, and he adopts the deliberating distance of the *flâneur* as the pose suitable for negotiating the Erie experience. "I was inclined," he says, "to be poetical about the Grand Canal." He knows that he is suspended between the great poetical subjects of the Hudson Valley and the Niagara Falls, but he chooses to celebrate instead the man-made and the commercial. However, the *flâneur* is only "inclined" to be poetical; he does not say that he actually will be. What he is, is whimsical, imagining "DeWitt Clinton as an enchanter" whose "simple and mighty conception had conferred inestimable value on spots which Nature seemed to have thrown carelessly into the great body of the earth, without foreseeing that they could ever attain importance." Hawthorne's Nature is of a kind with the surprised and "sleepy Dutchmen" whose "unmarketable produce" has been turned into gold. Hawthorne's urbanism leads him to see "the wondrous stream" as flowing "between two continuous lines of buildings, through one thronged street, from Buffalo to Albany."[21] "One thronged street" to describe 363 miles of canal is a masterly image that captures an effect of the Erie that most travelers noted only where it had transformed villages into cities. By 1835, the process had peaked with Rochester and Buffalo presenting themselves as model boom towns – those points in the frontier where the American economy arrived with such force that the business of growth from settlement to city could be completed in a year. When Basil Hall reached Rochester in 1827, he found a boom well underway. Building was going on everywhere; streets were being cut through the forest, and settlers were all the time arriving; Hall relished the heady mixture of the new and the primeval.[22] Three years later, the Scotsman Thomas Hamilton reported that "Rochester is a place worth seeing. Twenty years ago there was not a house in the neighbourhood, and now there is a town containing thirteen thousand good Americans and true . . . Such a growth is more like forcing in a hot-bed, than the natural progress of human vegetation" (*Men and Manners in America*, vol. II, p. 308). Rochester, like Buffalo, was distinguished by its very activity and life; its unfinished, reckless appearance was redeemed for most of its visitors by the very promise of success. This was a landscape that spoke of the future, and as long as it did so with confidence, it had a lurid fascination for English visitors even though they were used to the more finished quality of the cities of their own country.

For a few Americans, the Erie landscape spoke of the past. For James Fenimore Cooper, the achievement of the heroic American who was DeWitt Clinton, Canal Builder, spelled the end of the heroic American who was Natty Bumppo, Pathfinder. As Edith Wharton in New York City could take her readers where travel books could not, Cooper in his homeland of Western New York shows a feeling for its landscape that goes beyond the travelers, British or American. *The Last of the Mohicans* gains a vertiginous perspective from his ability to superimpose hugely contrasting landscapes in the same frame. The gap between the Pathfinder's vision and that of the Canal Builder is less than that of a lifetime and both are looking at the same piece of the planet, but they see different worlds:

> The tourist, the valetudinarian, or the amateur of the beauties of nature, who, ... in quest of information, health, or pleasure floats steadily toward his object on those artificial waters which have sprung up under the administration of a statesman who has dared to stake his political character on the hazardous issue, is not to suppose that his ancestors traversed those hills, or struggled with the same currents, with equal facility. The transportation of a single heavy gun was often considered equal to a victory gained; if, happily, the difficulties of the passage had not so far separated it from its necessary concomitant, the ammunition, as to render it no more than a useless tube of unwieldy iron.[23]

Notwithstanding the novelist's sorrow, 200 years later, the gash that Clinton made in the primeval world has been so long healed that "those artificial waters" have become part of the natural landscape, a place of peace and escape when the rural reaches of the canal can be found.

Niagara Falls: "this most sublime of moving scenes"[24]

"By the beginning of the nineteenth century," says Elizabeth McKinsey in *Niagara Falls: Icon of the Sublime*, "the exploration of Niagara Falls was virtually complete." What remained to be done was the exploitation of the Falls, and to that end, after 1834, "the guidebook market became more specialized with the first appearance of volumes devoted entirely to Niagara (instead of the whole Northern Tour)."[25] The century's evolution of the guidebook in North America is shown in eight titles, dating from 1809 through to 1893, that have been collected as *Niagara Falls Guidebooks from the 19th Century* (Western New York Library). They trace a pattern from explorer through traveler to tourist. The first title is Thomas Cooper's *A Ride to Niagara*, and it describes a 700-mile round-trip wilderness journey in 1809 between Albany and Buffalo. Cooper is a traveler who writes; he is not a writer who travels. His is not a standard nineteenth-century commercial travel book of the kind that Harriet Martineau and Charles Dickens or Margaret Fuller and Mark Twain made popular. The final title in the Western New York collection is *The Niagara Book: A Complete Souvenir of Niagara Falls, Containing Sketches, Stories and Essays* by "W.D. Howells, Mark Twain, Prof. Nathaniel S. Shaler, and Others." It was published in 1893 as a kind of literary album – an outcome not only of the traveling ease with which they all reach Niagara but also of the fatal ease of the overwritten subject. Clichés, worn phrases, and stereotypes fill *The Niagara Book*. Published in Buffalo and with two such powerful names as its lead writers, it was guaranteed good on-site sales, although, of its ten articles, Twain's facetious "First Authentic Mention of Niagara Falls" is among the less attractive. Howells' strong piece, "Niagara, First and Last," shows that plain description of what the traveler sees and feels could still produce good Niagara-writing, and it gains from the fact that Howells layers his discussion with a lifetime of visits so that he is able to comment on the changes in both the Falls and himself. Contrasting what he sees now with what he saw then, he is not drawn into the babbling or the freezing that threatens Niagara travel writing from 1825 onwards.

What kind of voice could be found with which to talk about Niagara that would not expose the writer as gushing fool or insensitive boor? In February 1835, Nathaniel Hawthorne published, anonymously, "My Visit to Niagara" in the *New-England Magazine*, and an ambiguity in the stress of the title – is it "*My* Visit" or "My *Visit?*" – suggests the difficulty posed for the essayist. Nonetheless, Hawthorne finds a relatively successful voice that is midway between those of Washington Irving and Henry James:

> I am quite ashamed of myself here. Not that I ran, like a madman, to the falls, and plunged into the thickest of the spray – never stopping to breathe, till breathing was impossible: not that I committed this, or any other suitable extravagance. On the contrary, I alighted with perfect decency and composure, gave my cloak to the black waiter, pointed out my baggage, and inquired, not the nearest way to the cataract, but about the dinner-hour. The interval was spent in arranging my dress. Within the last fifteen minutes, my mind had grown strangely benumbed, and my spirits apathetic, with a slight depression, not decided enough to be termed sadness. My enthusiasm was in a deathlike slumber. Without aspiring to immortality, as he did, I could have imitated that English traveler, who turned back from the point where he first heard the thunder of Niagara, after crossing the ocean to behold it.[26]

Henry James himself included a Niagara piece in *Portraits of Places*, and though the book was published in 1884, the essay "Niagara" was first published in 1871. He avoids the limpness of Hawthorne, though there are touches of the *flâneur* in his description of his approach, as near as he dare, to watch the waters rush over the Horseshoe: "You are able at last to stand on the very verge of the shelf from which the leap is taken, bathing your boot-toes, if you like, in the side-ooze of the glassy curve."[27] But he gives his essay strength and direction by structuring it as the "drama of Niagara," taking that to be a work of Nature in a series of acts starting at the mouth of Niagara River. "From this point," he says, "I think, you really enter into relations with Niagara," and from there he travels to Livingston to take the train to the Falls. At Livingston, he looks down from the great cliffs to the river below: "This is the first act of the drama of Niagara; for it is, I believe, one of the commonplaces of description that you instinctively convert into a series of 'situations'" (p. 365). The Falls themselves become the middle act of the drama, and there James counterpoints the standard response with his own: "The common feeling just here, I believe, is one of disappointment at its want of height; the whole thing appears to many people somewhat smaller than its fame. My own sense, I confess, was absolutely gratified from the first; and, indeed, I was not struck with anything being tall or short, but with everything being perfect" (p. 368). James' not being afraid to say that the Falls satisfied him countermoves the clamorous majority, but he does follow suit with the mob in comparing the Falls to the work of the great artists, first cleverly comparing the "sordid" foreground of the tourist and souvenir scene with Turner's use of the same kind of foreground as a foil to a grand subject (p. 367) and then later telling his readers that "in the matter of line [the Horseshoe] beats Michael Angelo" (p. 370). Remarkably for James, if not uniquely, he even follows popular pattern and begins talking about God, something that every Victorian felt obligated to do at Niagara, telling his reader that the genius who invented the Horseshoe was "certainly the first author of the idea that order, proportion and symmetry are the conditions of perfect beauty" (p. 372). James succeeds in writing well about Niagara by refusing to be panicked by the subject, by refusing to be disappointed by it, and by refusing to feel obliged to be original about it. He succeeds by massed effects of fine writing.

After reading James, it is instructive to return to Gideon Miner Davison and to see how cautiously the guide writer treats the subject: "The view from the table rock, has been generally considered preferable; but this point must be decided by the different tastes of visitants," says Davison, and he goes on to say that "visitants desirous of passing in the rear of the great sheet of water, are supplied by the keeper of the stairs with dresses for that purpose, and with a guide" (*The Traveller's Guide*, pp. 268–69). Davison is sober and constrained. He refers to his readers as "visitants" rather than "tourists," and that word betrays his unease about what he should say and how he should say it. But Davison's respectful treatment of his readers has a straightforwardness about it that exposes James' domination of his readers. Davison is conceding that he is not up to the subject but will give it the nine pages that it deserves; James will concede nothing, and, with all its porcelain success, "Niagara" remains a cold piece of writing.

Like Henry James, the minor British poet Alfred Domett came to the Falls by way of Canada. He had left Cambridge without a degree but did not appear to think himself much disadvantaged by that. He was, however, wary of failing in a degree of good taste and he knew that Niagara posed traps: "It is said," he wrote in his diary, "to be bad taste to attempt a minute description of the falls of Niagara, and perhaps correctly so. Nevertheless a few words may serve to give some idea of the relative situation of at least the prominent parts." It was not a promising start. "It is," he said of Niagara, "as when you look at a foxhunt or an army in full march." The Falls grew on most people, but Domett soon became bored; that he admits with a hint of self-congratulation: "It was something to learn that it was possible to look with a listless eye even at this cataract of cataracts, to yawn in the face of Niagara."[28] Domett was frightened of the danger of the subject – the plunge into bathos that would leave the writer looking ridiculous. The nature of this fall was well illustrated by a temptation put before Harriet Martineau; it was one that she resisted with her customary good sense: "A lady asked me many questions about my emotions at Niagara, to which I gave only one answer of which she could make anything. 'Did you not,' was her last inquiry, 'long to throw yourself down, and mingle with your mother earth?' – 'No.'"[29]

Conclusion: "from New York City to Niagara Falls"

From New York City to Niagara Falls is the subtitle of a modern-day *Frommers* guidebook to New York State, and its title suggests that the way in which the state began to see itself in 1825 remains the state image to the present day. However, there have been several stages in the travel history of this journey, and they have been dictated by technology. The classic form of New York travel was the result of DeWitt Clinton's having pushed the limits of canal technology. At the beginning of the digging of the Erie, there were a number of problems waiting to be solved; and they were solved as the men went along, notably the construction of tree-grubbing machines and the discovery of a wet-setting cement known as meager limestone.[30] By the time that the Erie Canal was opened, everything necessary for the building in North America of canals of unlimited length was fully understood. However, within three years, the railroad appeared. By 1836, work was begun on an Erie Railroad, and the Erie Canal began to disappear from travel literature in the 1850s. After the Civil War, the Hudson was bridged at Albany and the Hudson River Valley began to disappear from travel literature in the 1860s. In the 1870s, the Falls themselves began to diminish when John Wesley Powell's explorations of the Colorado River led the people of the United States to believe that God's grandeur and America's glory were better demonstrated by Colorado's Canyon than by Niagara's Falls.[31] In 1876, Colorado was admitted as the thirty-eighth state of the Union, and its vast new landscape redefined the sublime. Niagara Falls did not cease to attract visitors, but they were no longer the place where even Henry James could feel the presence of "the first author."

It was the habit of British travelers to complain that Americans did not appreciate their own scenery. "The utter insensibility of the generality of Americans to the beauty and sublimity of nature is," says Fanny Kemble, "nothing short of amazing" (*Journal*, vol. II, p. 256). However, she was echoed by Nathaniel Hawthorne, who said the same thing about the English and the English landscape. "It is," he says, "only an American who can feel it."[32] As they praised landscapes but criticized people, travelers were usually on some kind of release from everyday life; they were not necessarily on holiday, but they were usually cut off from the business of home and could mistake detachment for superiority. The gaze of the traveler took possession of what Emerson called the poet's property: "Miller owns this field, Locke that, and Manning the woodland beyond. But none of them owns the landscape. There is a property in the horizon which no man has but he whose eye can integrate all the parts, that is, the poet,"[33] but the poet and the traveler's title deeds to their landscapes cut them off from the world at which they were gazing.

The fact that Hawthorne and James wrote essays about Niagara is not insignificant. British travelers did not write that kind of essay. Early nineteenth-century Britons who wrote about Niagara were necessarily in the middle of a very great journey. They had already had to cross the 3,000 miles of the Atlantic and they had yet to recross it. That represented 6,000 most dangerous miles, occupying at least eight weeks before the 1840s and the steamship. Once in North America, Basil Hall, Thomas Hamilton, Fanny Trollope, Fanny Martineau, and fifty more planned several thousand miles of land travel. They were not inclined, by and large, to playfulness, and their mind-set and finances led them to think in terms of the travel book not the travel essay. The situations of the New Englander and the New Yorker were different; they were investing much less in the act of travel. Working closer to home led Hawthorne to plan a journey that involved a summer month's round-trip on the Erie Canal as its only object. With the mind-set induced by this plan, an attitude very different from that of the Britons became available. Hawthorne set out to write an essay not a book, and the tone he adopted was that of the metropolitan who looked at both scene and people in the hope of some mild amusement. What resulted was the *flâneur*'s view, but a danger of the *flâneur*'s style is that it can become infected by facetiousness as it does in Mark Twain's "First Authentic Mention of Niagara Falls."

Mark Twain was more the humorist than the *flâneur*, and his flippant manner was just as pronounced in his travel books such as *Europe and Elsewhere*. To collect the material for these, he had to travel as far and as hard as the Britons coming to America, and Twain was not the only nineteenth-century American writer to write comic travel books about

England. David R. Locke's *Nasby in Exile; or Six Months of Travel*, published under the pseudonym of Petroleum V. Nasby, also worked in the humorist style, exactly the kind of thing (though not quite so well done) as Charles Dickens does in *The Uncommercial Traveller* but not the kind of thing that Dickens does in *American Notes*. There are moments of genuine comic writing in the *Notes*, but it does not consist of a steady stream of flippancies and wisecracks of the kind that Petroleum V. Nasby pours out. Britons did not start doing comical tours of the United States until the twentieth century, and their books about nineteenth-century America maintain a fairly serious tone. Anger is an emotion often expressed, and that is an emotion not available to the *flâneur*. Neither Hawthorne nor James admits the anger that often overwhelms the Briton when the hucksters' booths spoil the sublime landscape. Americans distanced themselves from the immediate scene through the pose of the *flâneur*, but Americans were also fully adapted to their republican world and preferred to laugh rather than rage at democratic excesses. While the foreign traveler often saw more, the home-based traveler often understood more.

Notes

1. Alan Wallach, "Thomas Cole: Landscape and the Course of American Empire," in *Thomas Cole and Landscape into History*, ed. William H. Truettner and Allan Wallach (New Haven: Yale University Press, 1994), p. 31.
2. The canal diary appears in William W. Campbell, *The Life and Writings of DeWitt Clinton* (New York: Baker and Scribner, 1849). For a recent account of the building of the canal, see Peter L. Bernstein, *Wedding of the Waters: The Erie Canal and the Making of a Great Nation* (New York: Norton, 2005).
3. The line is from "Rise, O Days" from the "Drum Taps" section of *Leaves of Grass*, in Walt Whitman, *Complete Poetry and Collected Prose*, ed. Justin Kaplan (New York: Library of America, 1982), p. 427.
4. William Leete Stone, "A Trip from New York to Niagara in 1829," *Magazine of American History* 20 (October–December 1888), pp. 321–24; 395–99; 489–94.
5. Barbara Korte, *English Travel Writing from Pilgrimage to Postcolonial Explorations*, trans. Catherine Matthias (Basingstoke: Macmillan, 2000), p. 9.
6. Gideon Miner Davison, *The Traveller's Guide through the Middle and Northern States, and the Provinces of Canada* (New York: G. & C. & H. Carvill, 1834), p. 97.
7. William Cobbett, *A Year's Residence in the United States of America*, ed. J. Morpurgo (Fontwell, Sussex: Centaur, 1964), pp. 230–31.
8. Frances Trollope, *Domestic Manners of the Americans* (London: Whittaker, Treacher, 1832), pp. 268–70.
9. Sarah Mytton Maury, *An Englishwoman in America* (London: T. Richardson and Son, 1848), p. 163.
10. Emmeline Stuart Wortley, *Travels in the United States, etc. During 1849 and 1850*, 3 vols. (London: Bentley, 1851), vol. 1, p. 1.

11. Thomas Hamilton, *Men and Manners in America*, 3 vols. (Edinburgh: Blackwood, 1833), vol. II, p. 287.

12. John K. Howat, *The Hudson River and its Painters* (1972; New York: Penguin, 1978), p. 29.

13. Frances Anne Butler Kemble, *Journal*, 2 vols. (London: Murray, 1835), vol. I, pp. 260–63.

14. Quoted in Charles Rockwell, *The Catskill Mountains and the Region Around: Their scenery, legends, and history; with sketches in prose and verse, by Cooper, Irving, Bryant, Cole, and others* (New York: Taintor Brothers, 1867), p. 224. The selection from Harriet Martineau's *Retrospect of Western Travel* (1838) appears on pp. 224–29.

15. John Conron, ed., *The American Landscape: A Critical Anthology of Prose and Poetry* (New York: Oxford University Press, 1973), p. 118.

16. Thomas Cole, "Essay on American Scenery" (1836); rpt. in *American Art: Sources and Documents, 1700–1960*, ed. John W. McCoubrey (Englewood Cliffs, NJ: Prentice-Hall, 1965), p. 106.

17. Nathaniel Parker Willis, *American Scenery; Or, Land, Lake, And River Illustrations Of Transatlantic Nature* (London: George Virtue, 1840), p. iii.

18. Evan Cornog, *The Birth of Empire: DeWitt Clinton and the American Experience, 1769–1828* (New York: Oxford University Press, 1998), p. 113.

19. Estwick Evans, *A Pedestrious Tour, of four thousand miles, through the western states and territories, during the winter and spring of 1818. Interspersed with brief reflections upon a great variety of topics* (Concord, MA: Joseph C. Spear, 1819), p. 120.

20. Ronald E. Shaw, *Erie Water West: A History of the Erie Canal, 1792–1854* (Lexington: Kentucky University Press, 1966), p. 227.

21. Nathaniel Hawthorne, "The Canal Boat," *New-England Magazine* 9 (December 1835), p. 398.

22. Basil Hall, *Travels in North America, in the Years 1827 and 1828*, 3 vols. (Edinburgh: Cadell, 1830), vol. I, p. 150.

23. James Fenimore Cooper, *The Last of the Mohicans: A Narrative of 1757* (London: George Routledge, [n.d.]), p. 170.

24. Richard Cobden, *The American Diaries of Richard Cobden*, ed. with an introduction and notes by Elizabeth Moon Cawley (Princeton: Princeton University Press, 1952), p. 149.

25. Elizabeth McKinsey, *Niagara Falls: Icon of the Sublime* (Cambridge: Cambridge University Press, 1985), pp. 37, 134.

26. Nathaniel Hawthorne, "My Visit to Niagara," *New-England Magazine* 8 (February 1835), p. 91.

27. Henry James, *Portraits of Places* (Boston: James R. Osgood, 1884), p. 369.

28. Alfred Domett, *The Canadian Journal of Alfred Domett*, ed. E. A. Horsman and Lillian Rea Benson (London, Ontario: Western Ontario University Press, 1955), pp. 27–30.

29. Harriet Martineau, *Society in America*, 3 vols. (London: Saunders and Otley, 1837), vol. III, p. 81.

30. In addition to the works by Bernstein and Shaw cited above, useful information on the canal may be found in Carol Sheriff, *The Artificial River: The Erie Canal and the Paradox of Progress, 1817–1862* (New York: Hill and Wang, 1997).

31. John Rennie Short, *Representing the Republic: Mapping the United States 1600–1900* (London: Reaktion, 2001), pp. 194–95.

32. Nathaniel Hawthorne, *Our Old Home: A Series of English Sketches* (Edinburgh: Patterson, 1884), p. 47.

33. Ralph Waldo Emerson, *Nature*, in *The Collected Works of Ralph Waldo Emerson*, vol. 1 (1836; rpt. Cambridge, MA: Belknap Press, 1971), p. 12.

4

THOMAS RUYS SMITH

The Mississippi River as site and symbol

So the story goes: not long before his death in 1986, Jorge Luis Borges made a pilgrimage to Hannibal, Missouri. Though eighty-three years old and nearly blind, the Argentinian author insisted on visiting one site as soon as he arrived in the town that had been the childhood home of Mark Twain. He was escorted to the river. Then – accounts differ – Borges completed his pilgrimage by dipping his hand or, more dramatically, by wading bodily into the current of the Mississippi. Either way, his moment of contact with the river led him to the same conclusion: "Now I understand the essence of America."[1]

Apocryphal though Borges' moment of enlightenment may have been, it tells in miniature a story that has been rewritten for centuries. Since the moment Hernando De Soto and his party of conquistadors first arrived at the banks of the Mississippi in 1541, travelers of every variety have flocked to and along this representative river to better comprehend the country through which it flows. Both as a conduit for trade and travel, and a destination in its own right, the river's role in national life has changed dramatically over the centuries. It no longer commands the social and economic power of its antebellum zenith. Nevertheless, it continues to occupy a unique place in American travel writing – and the American consciousness.

In the early nineteenth century, Reverend Timothy Flint felt that his first sighting of the river "left on my mind a most deep and durable impression, marking a period, from which commenced a new era in my existence."[2] For T. S. Eliot, a child of St. Louis, the river was innate: "a strong brown God – sullen, untamed and intractable . . . within us."[3] Even William Least Heat-Moon, a child of the Missouri who has attempted in his own travels "to testify to the capital allure of rivers other than the Mississippi," has conceded its "encompassing mystique" that "still holds us in a grand cultural thrall."[4] The Mississippi remains a vital location in the symbolic geography of America.

Mark Twain understood the river's symbolic nature. He was taught the lesson while learning to pilot a steamboat on the Mississippi; what he learned remains fundamental for successfully piloting a course through the river's manifold representations. He came to understand that there were two rivers: the physical Mississippi, running from Lake Itasca to the Gulf of Mexico; and the Mississippi of the imagination, meandering through the mind. For a steamboat pilot, the imagined Mississippi took precedence. Horace Bixby, Twain's piloting mentor, instructed him: "you can always steer by the shape that's *in your head*, and never mind the one that's before your eyes."[5]

So too for its travelers, the river has often been as much a symbol as a site. Twain also made the discovery that this most written-about river was in itself a book – a book that, in time, revealed itself more fully than any travel account could render: "There never was so wonderful a book written by man; never one whose interest was so absorbing, so unflagging, so sparklingly renewed with every re-perusal" (*Mississippi*, p. 118).

The story of Mississippi travel writing can, in one sense, quickly be told in an apparently circular list of its changing modes of transport: the canoes of its explorers; the flatboats of early settlement; the steamboats of the Golden Age; the shantyboats of the early twentieth century; and the canoes of those attempting to navigate the river's course today. If each era's travel writing has been defined by a mode of transport, its concomitant relationship with the river has been profoundly different. A series of metamorphoses is contained within the succession from dugout to plastic canoe. In turn, the river has been an enigma, and an emblem of imperialism; the essential highway of a young nation moving west; the realm of profit, increasing urbanization, slavery, and war; a limbo of lost splendor and increasing dismissal; the scene of imaginative resurrection; an escape route to a forgotten America; and, today, an arena in which to test personal limits. The most significant accounts of the Mississippi have been able to assess the river with a profound awareness of its history, and yet still see it with acute, contemporary eyes – the site, as well as the symbol. Connective tissue links the most disparate accounts of its waters. Mark Twain knew this, too: "A glance at these tourist-books," he wrote, speaking for all ages, "shows us that in certain of its aspects the Mississippi has undergone no change since these strangers visited it, but remains to-day about as it was then" (*Mississippi*, p. 292).

The Mississippi emerged onto the world stage cloaked in mystery. Its tantalizing possibilities as a conduit of empire were slow to be fully apprehended, and the key to much of its early appeal lay in the superimposition of an established myth. The Mississippi was imagined as a solution to the vexed question of the Northwest Passage – the Passage to India, a navigable water route between Europe and Asia. Nation by nation, Old World powers dispatched explorers to the river and laid claim to its course. As well as slowly clarifying information about the physical Mississippi, the early travel accounts that resulted served a double role: they fueled imperial desire, and they established certain paradigmatic relationships between travelers and the river. Broken dreams and ruined fortunes soon littered its banks. On occasion, they also introduced a trend for exaggeration. Knowledge of the river grew, but so too did the inventions of some of its travelers.

The Spanish were first. Even before De Soto, Spanish expeditions to the Gulf Coast had reported telling hints of a great river that emptied there. Of course, De Soto and his troops did not embark upon a perilous journey into the unknown to find a river. They went looking for gold. Landing in Florida in 1539, the Spanish troops slowly fought and marched westward in fruitless pursuit of riches. Their discovery of an immense river on May 8, 1541 – immediately dubbed the "Rio Grande" – was, after two years in the field, the discovery of another obstacle to surmount. "He went to look at the river," wrote the anonymous "Gentleman from Elvas" in 1557, describing his commander's resolutely militaristic first sighting of the Mississippi, "and saw that near it there was much timber of which piraguas might be made, and a good situation in which the camp might be placed."[6] A year later they reached the river again in disappointed retreat. Struck by fever, De Soto died and was buried in the Mississippi. His remaining troops effected an extraordinary escape, floating downriver and along the coast to Mexico in makeshift boats.

It took over 130 years for an imperial European power to officially reach the Mississippi again. France took up the baton. Stimulated by rumors of a large waterway – already a "renowned river" – that ran through the interior of North America, Father Jacques Marquette and Louis Joliet reached the Mississippi from Canada in 1673. Marquette experienced "a joy that I can not express." The Native tribes they encountered were eager to warn them about its perils: "They told me," Marquette recorded, "that the Great River is very dangerous, unless the difficult parts are known; that it was full of frightful monsters who swallowed up men and canoes together; that there is even a demon there who can be heard from afar, who stops the passage and engulfs all who dare approach."[7] It was a useful warning.

Marquette and Joliet opened the way for the efforts of a man who fully understood the Mississippi's potential. The singular, prescient vision of René-Robert Cavelier, Sieur de la Salle, focused on one central idea: control of the Mississippi meant control of the continent. His plan, continually frustrated in its execution, was to establish a firm French presence in the interior of North America by the construction of a chain of forts stretching from the St. Lawrence to the Mississippi's outlet. La Salle achieved much. His eventual 1681–82 expedition to the Mississippi was the first to follow, and furnish proof of, the river's course to the Gulf of Mexico. There, La Salle formally took possession "of this country of Louisiana" for France: "from the mouth of the great river . . . and the rivers which discharge themselves therein," to its still obscure source far in the North.[8] But soon, La Salle was dead – shot in 1687 by disgruntled members of his disastrous expedition to establish a colony near the Mississippi's mouth. His plan for the colonization of the river survived him.

La Salle's expeditions contained another lesson for the river's future: the importance of timely publication. In 1679, on an early expedition to the west, La Salle had dispatched a small party of men to explore the Upper Mississippi. One of their number was Louis Hennepin, a Franciscan friar. Departing in February, the party journeyed as far north as the series of falls near the Minnesota River – which Hennepin "called St. Anthony of Padua's." Then, in April, they were taken prisoner by a Sioux war party. Before their rescue in July, the captive Frenchmen were forced to travel widely in the region. Such were Hennepin's pioneering experiences on and around the river – at least, in reality. On paper, he engaged in a process of embellishment and exaggeration, producing three extremely popular volumes about America. His first account was a largely authentic record of his experiences. By 1698, however, Hennepin's audacity had increased. He claimed to have beaten Marquette and Joliet to the Mississippi, and even La Salle himself to the Gulf.

Popular interest in the exotic New World, particularly the great river which bisected it, was enormous. Hennepin's travel accounts therefore answered a demand and went through numerous editions. His Mississippi retained a romantic mystique designed to appeal to his readers. Its fecundity was extraordinary: "We regarded the river . . . with great pleasure . . . We wanted neither buffalo nor deer, nor beaver, nor fish, nor bear meat, for we killed these animals as they swam across the river" (Shea, *Discovery and Exploration*, pp. 116–18). The Missouri, in his account, flowed from a mountain, from the top of which a traveler could see the sea. Other writers, many with even less experience of America than Hennepin, capitalized on the fashion and brought their own visions of the Western River system before the public. The infamous Baron de Lahontan claimed to have ascended the Mississippi in 1701, and to have discovered a great tributary leading to the west. This "Rivière Longue," as he named it, led him to magical lands inhabited by great civilizations. Such accounts ensured that the imagined Mississippi still shadowed its physical counterpart.

This duality was true of an equally influential British travel account. Elements in Britain had long been aware of the Mississippi's imperial significance. In 1699, for example, Daniel Coxe attempted to found a colony near the river's mouth – only to be turned away by the French. Not until the French–Indian War did Britain gain significant footholds on the Mississippi, and a chance for exploration. Captain Jonathan Carver was a native of New England who had served in the recent war. He had a passion for exploring, and a passion for the Mississippi, particularly its potential as a western artery of British America. The "great river," he predicted, would allow its inhabitants "to establish an intercourse with foreign climes" and, therefore, "an extensive and profitable commerce."[9] In 1766, without official sanction, Carver set out to discover the source of the Mississippi. His journey was continually hampered – by conflict between the Sioux and the Chippewa, a lack of supplies, even suspicions of treachery. Because of significant personal problems, including bigamy, his *Travels Through the Interior Parts of North America* was not published until 1778. Then, at last, it appeared at a propitious time and quickly went through over forty editions. Again, this fame was a product of controversy. Poverty-stricken in London, Carver sold his manuscript to a publisher. With or without his knowledge, his original account – which included much valuable information about the Upper Mississippi – was embellished with a series of fantastical stories (including some taken from Hennepin and Lahontan). Carver died destitute in 1780.

Thomas Jefferson owned first editions of all three of Hennepin's books, copies of Lahontan's and Carver's accounts, even Daniel Coxe's promotional pamphlet *Carolana* – indeed, almost all printed matter pertaining to travel along the river and through the trans-Mississippi West. Under Jefferson's aegis, as a result of his fascination with this material, the early promise of the river and its tributaries would be brought to fruition. In 1803, the Louisiana Purchase ensured the Mississippi's Americanization. It fully opened the river to travel, brought about a pressing demand for further exploration, and allowed Jefferson to oversee the execution of plans that he had been formulating for decades. In 1804, Meriwether Lewis and William Clark, using the Mississippi as a stepping-stone for their route along the Missouri, made their way to the Pacific coast – finally laying to rest the dream of a Northwest Passage. As a contemporary commentator remarked, the party was not "amused by such tales as were told to Hennepin" and "did not expect to meet with the Spirits and Pigmies"; there remained a great deal "to excite imagination in the wide region before them."[10] At the same time, Zebulon Pike was sent to find the source of the Mississippi. Securing the prize of the river's head had a symbolic significance for its new owners. The journey was hard and laborious, and, in truth, stopped eighty miles short. Still, Pike himself was pleased with the accomplishment: "I will not attempt to describe my feelings on the accomplishment of my voyage, for this is the main source of the Mississippi."[11] His journal, when it was published in 1810, resonated with a public eager for information about their river. The Mississippi, culturally as well as geographically, entered fully into the American sphere.

By the time that Henry Rowe Schoolcraft laid claim to the discovery of its true source at Lake Itasca in 1832 – "What had been long sought, at last appeared suddenly" – the nature of river travel had changed profoundly.[12] Even at the time of the voyages of discovery, change was on the horizon. In August 1807, Robert Fulton undertook the inaugural trial of his steamboat on American waters. He steamed one mile up the East River. Flushed with the success of his pioneering voyage, one thought was uppermost in Fulton's mind: "Everything is completely proved for the Mississippi," he wrote to Robert Livingston, his business partner and the man who had negotiated the Louisiana Purchase, "and the project is immense."[13]

In 1841, Ralph Waldo Emerson wrote to Margaret Fuller about his yearning to embark upon a journey that had become symbolically linked to important aspects of the national character:

> If I had a pocketful of money, I think I should go down the Ohio & up & down the Mississippi by way of antidote to what small remains of the Orientalism – (so endemic in these parts) – there may still be in me, to cast out, I mean, the passion for Europe by the passion for America.[14]

In the antebellum years, steamboat travel on the Mississippi was a definitive American journey. The river became a vivid symbolic representative of the nation through which it ran as an increasingly vital artery. The cabin of a Mississippi steamboat became an authoritative vantage point from which to judge young America and to assess the spirit of the times. The Golden Age of steamboating was, therefore, the Golden Age of Mississippi travel writing. The seeds were sown in 1811 when Nicholas Roosevelt, a partner in the Mississippi Steamboat Navigation Company with Fulton and Livingston, piloted the *New Orleans* downriver. The arrival of this first steamboat on the Mississippi was a landmark event, long looked for on the river frontier. As well as opening up the river's economic potential, it inaugurated a passenger trade that revolutionized life on the Mississippi. River travel became feasible for all. Steamboats proliferated: 200 arrived at New Orleans in 1820; 1,000 in 1830; 2,000 in 1841; 3,000 in 1847. As Giacomo Beltrami declared in 1828, "what used to be a journey is a *promenade*."[15] Exploration gave way to tourism.

Of the innumerable accounts of the river that appeared in this period, most significant were those written by the eminent Victorians who arrived from the Old World to judge the New. America bristled at their criticisms – both real and perceived. It devoured their accounts all the same. As such, their portraits of the river became definitive. For the most part, these descriptions were unflattering. In sharp contrast to the pioneering joy of its early explorers, the Mississippi was continually traduced and bemoaned. For Frances Trollope, in her highly influential *Domestic Manners of the Americans* (1832), the river was a "murky stream . . . utterly desolate." Worse still were the Americans she encountered on the river: "I would infinitely prefer sharing the apartment of a party of well conditioned pigs." As for those attempting to colonize the river's "unwholesome banks," she had never "witnessed human nature reduced so low."[16] Many agreed. Frederick Marryat "could only regret that life was so short, and the Mississippi so long." He was driven to "disgust at the idea of perishing in such a vile sewer, to be buried in mud, and perhaps to be rooted out again by some pig-nosed alligator."[17] For William Makepeace Thackeray, the Mississippi was "dreary & funereal," and gave him "pain." It could only exude a "great fierce strong impetuous ugliness."[18]

These reactions were partly a result of the Mississippi's failure to meet the criteria of established aesthetics: it was neither picturesque like the Ohio, nor sublime like Niagara. Yet extreme European repulsion was more than a matter of the view. Antebellum Old World travelers often hated the river for the same reasons that Americans came to regard it as a positive symbol of democratic national spirit: the social equality of the steamboat cabin; the promise of national growth and expansion; its role as the mythical birthplace of popular Jacksonian cultural heroes like Mike Fink – in short, Emerson's "antidote" for "the passion for Europe." Other travelers had a more specific reason for their distaste. The Mississippi was unavoidably the jugular of slavery. Travel on its waters necessitated a confrontation with its realities. The river would have been "far pleasanter," reflected the well-traveled Ida Pfeiffer, if "one did not remember that the greater part of its population . . . are in bondage."[19]

When he traveled in America in 1841, Charles Dickens experienced a conflation of both reactions. Dickens spent only a brief time on the Mississippi, at the end of a journey from Cincinnati to St. Louis. The journey was long enough, however, for him to develop a profound loathing for the "foul stream." He had already suffered many ideological disappointments in the New World. The Mississippi became the focus and the prime example of his frustrations with both democracy and slavery. His fellow passengers repulsed him. A "magnetism of dulness" reigned. The river itself compounded horror upon horror: "liquid mud . . . monstrous bodies . . . giant leeches . . . mud and slime on everything." And in his final dismissal of the "intolerable river," the specter of slavery made its presence felt. Dickens left the Mississippi "dragging its slimy length and ugly freight abruptly off towards New Orleans."[20] It was a rare traveler who could view the river differently. Harriet Martineau, in sharp contrast to her conservative compatriots, was one. She upbraided America for its lack of true democracy, and, though a passionate abolitionist, was able to see more in the Mississippi than the repudiation of promise. Though the river "may reveal no beauty to the painter," she argued, "to the eye of one who loves to watch the process of world-making, it is full of delight." In Martineau's view, the Mississippi was representative of the newest and most fertile aspects of the New World – still in flux, and therefore still cause for optimism.[21]

Of course, for all the egalitarian trappings that so many Old World passengers chafed against, cabin passage in a Mississippi steamboat, however rudimentary, was a luxury beyond the means of many. River travel in the antebellum era had another aspect. The poor, often emigrating to America, were obliged to take deck passage and travel in the open air, crowded together, close to the waters of the Mississippi. Unsanitary surroundings, exposure, disease, and danger characterized their voyage. Few accounts of this world exist. John O'Connor, an itinerant gambler who traveled widely on the Mississippi, attested to its hardships: "Deck passengers were stowed like hogs . . . they were made to feel all the degradation of poverty in the brutal and disgraceful treatment they received from the petty officers belonging to the boat."[22]

One way for the poor to avoid such depravations, at least imaginatively, emerged in 1846. The level of public interest in river travel, stimulated by the diverse multitude of its travel accounts, led to the emergence of an art form: the moving panorama of the Mississippi. The moving panorama was an enormous painted canvas fastened between two rollers, wound at a steady pace from one roller to the other in front of a paying audience. The Mississippi panoramas presented the viewer with a succession of river views from the point of view of a traveler in a steamboat cabin – the expurgated highlights of its long course condensed into a ninety-minute spectacle. They were enormously popular, and carried the Mississippi around the world. During its residency in London at the close of 1848, over half a million viewers traveled along the river in front of John Banvard's panorama. Charles Dickens was one. Finding the virtual Mississippi far more enjoyable than the real thing, he recommended it as "an easy means of travelling, night and day, without any inconvenience from climate, steamboat company, or fatigue."[23] For the millions whose impression of the Mississippi came from travel by moving panorama, its effect could still be impressive. Henry David Thoreau visited one in Concord. Its effect on him was complete and profound: "As I worked my way up the river in the light of to-day, and saw the steamboats wooding up, counted the rising cities, gazed on the fresh ruins of Nauvoo, beheld the Indians moving west across the stream . . . I felt that *this was the heroic age itself.*"[24] In the antebellum years, the river's symbolic power could transform canvas and paint into muddy water, and muddy water into the lifeblood of America.

Very soon, this "heroic age" was at an end. The river, already under severe pressure from the railroads in the 1850s, was forced to close its waters at the advent of the Civil War. Travel writing was displaced by military dispatch. When the river was again opened for freight and passenger traffic, it flowed through a very different landscape. Slavery was gone, the railroads were dominant, and the steamboat trade was suffering from mortal wounds.

The river's cultural life was about to begin anew – all because the Civil War forced a young steamboat pilot named Samuel Clemens from his chosen occupation. Born in 1835, Clemens was a child of the river in its frontier days. From 1857 until 1861 he was a steamboat pilot in the trade's last flush years. Then he headed west, and became Mark Twain. As large as Twain's shadow looms across the Mississippi, it is impossible to overestimate his importance. Throughout his writing – though particularly in *Life on the Mississippi* (1883), and *Adventures of Huckleberry Finn* (1884) – Twain guaranteed the river a continued place in world literature. Steeped in the river, he was uniquely well placed to tell its story. As he expressed his imaginative copyright: "By a series of events – accidents – I was the only one who wrote about old times on the Mississippi . . . the Mississippi was a virgin field . . . Here then was my chance, and I used it."[25] He remains a catalytic presence. Twentieth-century accounts of the river, at least in some regard, float on Mark Twain's Mississippi.

Though Twain left the river in 1861, he never left it imaginatively. It appeared as a backdrop, and as an agent of transformation and license, in *The Gilded Age* (1873) and *The Adventures of Tom Sawyer* (1876). Twain drew heavily on the river for "Old Times on the Mississippi," serialized in the *Atlantic Monthly* in 1875, a work that recalled his experiences as a young pilot. More vitally, and by his own reckoning, his Mississippi years indelibly informed his consciousness – whether comparing the pyramids to river bluffs in *Innocents Abroad* (1869), or assessing "all the different types of human nature": "When I find a well-drawn character in fiction or biography, I generally take a warm personal interest in him, for the reason that I have known him before – met him on the river" (*Mississippi*, p. 217). In April 1882, accompanied by his publisher and a stenographer, Twain finally returned to the Mississippi with the express purpose of writing a book about his experiences. From St. Louis he steamed downriver to New

Orleans. Then he steamed back to the Upper Mississippi, spending three days in his boyhood home. Then came composition of the definitive Mississippi travel narrative. Meandering like the river, or like gossip in the pilothouse, *Life on the Mississippi* took in the whole panorama of the Mississippi. The first three chapters dealt with geography and the river's history; the next eighteen reprinted and expanded Twain's memories of "the flush times of steamboating"; and the final two-thirds of the book were devoted, with significant detours, to his return to the river (*Mississippi*, p. 61).

To its critical detriment, this miscellaneous structure has been placed alongside Twain's own intemperate remarks about its apparently agonizing birth. In October 1882, he wrote to William Dean Howells about the intolerable "burden of the contract," complaining, "I have nothing more to borrow or steal."[26] Soon, it had become "this wretched God-damned book."[27] Such explosions have overshadowed Twain's later fondness for the book, as well as his initial conception of what the purpose of this travel account should be. As early as 1871 he wrote to new wife Olivia about his plans for the future: "when I come to write the Mississippi book, *then* look out! I will spend 2 months on the river & take notes, & I bet you I will make a standard work."[28] Viewing *Life on the Mississippi* as the attempted consummation of a long-held desire to produce a "standard work" is revealing, not least in bringing a greater sense of coherence to the text. And as Horst Kruse has proved, Twain's most significant incorporation of other writings on the river dated from an early stage of the book's composition. His organizing approach was, therefore, intentionally threefold: reminisce, revisit, and research. Inevitably, therefore, *Life on the Mississippi* is a work of contrasts.

Descriptions of antebellum life, when "the great Mississippi, the majestic, the magnificent Mississippi" was the animating spirit of the towns along its banks, illuminate the opening chapters. As such, the most immediate contrast is the downturn in the river's fortunes in the late nineteenth century. "Mississippi steamboating was born about 1812," Twain eulogizes, "at the end of thirty years, it had grown to mighty proportions; and in less than thirty more, it was dead! A strangely short life for so majestic a creature." Yet throughout the book, the past refuses to offer an easy resting place. This is true of Twain's return to Hannibal. Though he is "a great deal moved," sentiment soon gives way to memories of unexpiated guilt (*Mississippi*, pp. 64, 256, 524). It is also true of his treatment of the river's Victorian commentators. The inclusion of extracts from writers like Trollope, Dickens, and Marryat provides a counterpoint and contrast to his luminous memories of steamboating's glory days. Continually caught between past and present, the Mississippi provides Twain with the only true constant, and with the book's true organizing principle. "It had suffered no change," he lovingly wrote of the river view from Holiday's Hill in Hannibal, "it was as young and fresh and comely and gracious as ever." Whatever man's mutability, the "lawless stream" rolled on (*Mississippi*, pp. 525, 302).

For twentieth-century travelers, Twain's journey to the Mississippi in 1882 had another vital outcome. Returning to the well-spring of his creativity allowed him to finish a book that he alluded to in *Life on the Mississippi*: "which I have been working at, by fits and starts, during the past five or six years" (*Mississippi*, p. 42). Huck and Jim's resulting journey downstream remains the archetypal Mississippi voyage. "Other places do seem so cramped up and smothery," Huck described, "but a raft don't. You feel mighty free and easy and comfortable on a raft . . . Sometimes we'd have that whole river all to ourselves for the longest time."[29] If not quite by raft, then the fertile new phase of river travel that followed in Twain's wake was characterized by two forms of transport that expressed their passengers' connate desire for some form of escape. The house or shantyboat provided shelter for travelers fleeing society; the canoe allowed them to attempt a route back to their essential selves. In either instance, aspects of river travel have become familiar tropes. For William Least Heat-Moon, "taking a craft of whatever configuration down the Mississippi . . . has become so repeated it's on the way to developing into a ritual for a nation shy on communal rituals" (Introduction, Jonk, *Journey*, p. x).

To some degree, the river's ongoing appeal as a subject for "touristbooks," and its status as the definitive American river, has been a curse as well as a blessing. Eddy Harris, canoeing down its course in the late twentieth century, was continually disheartened on his journey by strangers who told him of others making an identical pilgrimage, and in more unorthodox ways – people like "the couple last year who floated down the Mississippi in some sort of raft made of all kinds of junk they collected along the way. People are doing this sort of thing all the time."[30] There is another sad irony for modern travelers attempting to commune with the river wild. In the early twentieth century, the process of improving and restricting the river's unpredictable course accelerated. By the 1950s, the upper river between Minneapolis and St. Louis was more canal than river. Levees and wing dams controlled the Lower Mississippi. Such is the landscape that characterizes modern Mississippi travel writing.

The shanty- and houseboat phenomenon of the early twentieth century gave birth to a distinct breed of travelers enchanted, like Kent and Margaret Lighty, by "the simple miracle of being able to carry our household bodily over the waters."[31] For houseboaters, the boundaries of travel and life dissolved, and a river journey became an open-ended, potentially lifelong, experience. Escaping the demands of conventional society, they proudly drifted into an alternative America briefly flourishing on the banks of the Mississippi. Ben Lucien Burman estimated that in his years steamboating on the river in the 1920s and 1930s as many as 30,000 houseboats were scattered along the Mississippi and its tributaries. According to the Lightys, this proliferation was a result of the way that the river had "slipped out of the public consciousness into a fertile kind of obscurity." The Mississippi had "become a frontier once more": "the last frontier of those who will not live by laws other than their own, and for those who have broken laws elsewhere" (*Shantyboat*, p. vi). This assessment was characteristic. The houseboater was, if nothing else, a philosophical outlaw. As Richard Pike Bissell, river novelist and long-term houseboater, described his own conversion: "I went crazy for houseboats . . . and the nutty, independent, don't-care-now-and-I-won't-care-later people that lived in them."[32]

Behind this flippant, antisocial pose lay more serious concerns, and the imprint of another guiding inspiration: when Clarence Jonk reached Red Wing in his houseboat in 1933, he symbolically resolved "to pay homage to Thoreau by climbing Barn's Bluff." Travelers like Jonk imaginatively transformed the Mississippi into Walden Pond. For Jonk himself, the river provided a vital outlet from the Depression – economically as well as emotionally. Financially poor himself, and "sympathetic with the poverty stricken peoples of the earth," Jonk embraced the river's "inexpensive way of life." This meant a life away from the conventions of a society governed by market forces. Tellingly, Jonk's houseboat only left its moorings because of the continued disapproval, and numerous petitions, of his landlocked neighbors. It also allowed Jonk an immersion in the natural world of the river that he recorded with Thoreauvian attention to detail. "A cage is not really a cage," he asserted, "if it is capable of motion and direction" (*Journey*, pp. 128, 16, 220, 34).

Thoreau's influence on Mississippi houseboaters found its fullest expression in the life and writing of Harlan Hubbard and his family. Setting off down the Ohio in a self-built houseboat in 1944, the Hubbards took six years to reach New Orleans. *Shantyboat* (1953) is a record of this intermittent journey through a "strange new world" – "beyond the law, beyond taxes and the ownership of property." On the one hand, their river experiences were a testament to the delights of the slow process of becoming "better acquainted with that restless companion to which we had attached ourselves." On the other, they were an attempt to live "a more unhampered life." Hubbard's river journey, therefore, developed into as much manifesto as travel account: "I merely wanted to try living by my own hands . . . I wanted to grow my own food, catch it in the river, or forage after it. In short,

I wanted to do as much as I could for myself." Though such sentiments prefaced growing concerns within the wider world, alternative America would not flourish for long on the river. "It is to be regretted," Hubbard accurately lamented, "that the race of shantyboaters is dying out."[33]

The canoeists who took their place on the river were a different breed. As early as 1875, Nathaniel Bishop had undertaken a seminal voyage downriver in a sneak-box, a twelve-foot craft. It was Albert Tousley, when he canoed the length of the Mississippi in 1928, who set the template for those who followed. His ambition was "not the dream of a rabid idealist." Though he wanted to "associate with the spirits of Indians and explorers," the significance of his journey was largely internal: "Mine was to be the battle with the elements, mine the achievement or failure! The challenge of the stream was there!" So too was the final lesson that the river imparted: "within oneself there is freedom from practically everything."[34] The ritualistic element of river travel, highlighted by Moon, is most apparent in its modern canoe narratives. A wide variety of travelers have recorded their experiences by means of a litany that soon becomes familiar: incompetence gives way to growing expertise; the river's mysteries are slowly revealed; initial enthusiasm wanes; disaster – the threat of drowning or violence – steels the will; finally, the destination is reached. The Mississippi is respectfully conquered. Emphasis is placed upon individual effort and self-improvement.

The most compelling of these modern canoe narratives is Eddy Harris' *Mississippi Solo* (1988). It is, simultaneously, archetypal in its description of the canoeist's endeavors, and unique because of one simple fact: Harris is black. Despite, or perhaps because of, the river's role in the history of slavery, Harris was the first black writer to produce a travel narrative of the Mississippi since its antebellum appearances in fugitive slave narratives. From the book's opening line, Harris travels on a Mississippi "laden with the burdens of a nation." As an old friend cautions him, his journey spans an America "from where there ain't no black folks to where they still don't like us much." Yet Harris himself rhetorically negates the issue: "I would not make race an issue out here." Though racism, both casual and vicious, is often apparent – like Huck and Jim, Harris discovers that leaving the river means entering into a world of "anger and rage" – it is not the dominant theme of his account. Rather than Twain or Thoreau, Harris declares himself to be "haunted by the ghost of Ernest Hemingway," and rugged individualism is paramount. He is even involved in a shoot-out. His experiences are wholly mediated through their effect on his own consciousness: "The river god had been testing me . . . I had to fight through. I did it, and the river smiled approval." By his own reckoning, but speaking for the ranks of twentieth-century canoeists as a whole, Harris leaves the river "a better man" (pp. 1, 7, 67, 221, 29, 176, 243).

Perhaps fittingly, the twentieth century's most significant account of the Mississippi was connected to the journeys of houseboaters and canoeists, but distinct from both. Jonathan Raban had an outboard motor when he traveled from Minneapolis to the Gulf in a sixteen-foot boat – not large enough to inhabit, but sufficient to accommodate a comprehensive traveling library. "It is called the Mississippi," he explains early in *Old Glory* (1981), "but it is more an imaginary river than a real one." Closer to the cultural heritage of the Mississippi than any traveler since Twain, Raban weighs anchor at the confluence of powerful currents. In large part, his journey downriver is an attempted retreat to a sanctuary, "the great good place of my childhood," conjured up by Twain, George Caleb Bingham's paintings, and the incantation of river towns found on the map. But Raban is also aware of the conventions of "odd foreigners" traveling to the river, particularly the Victorian critics who stand as his inevitable forebears. Neither imaginative model is sufficient, as Raban discovers at his own first sighting of the Mississippi: "It wasn't the amazing blue of the cover of my old copy of *Huckleberry Finn*. Nor was it the terrible chocolate flood of Charles Dickens and Frances Trollope." It is, in fact, "just a river." Just a river – but a river that leads Raban on a definitive journey through modern America. Along its course, he finds communities divided along lines of race, and characterized by poverty and flight; powerfully Christ-haunted, and in search of salvation; neglectful of the great river which was once their *raison d'être*, and yet indelibly tied to its waters. It does not lead to easy conclusions. Raban's eventual arrival at the Gulf is an arrival at a primordial "*nothing*" – without glory, but rich with the potential of rebirth.[35]

In 1993, Raban returned to the river to witness that summer's record-breaking floods, stretching from Minneapolis to the Mississippi's junction with the Ohio at Cairo, Illinois. Despite the best efforts of the Corps of Engineers, the Mississippi is still able to climb out of its banks at will. Its elemental power, its essential wildness, remains untamable. For Raban, this "wild beast in the heart of the heartland" was not unfamiliar in its inundation. Rather, feeling a "surge of vicarious pride," he knew that this terrible vision of the Mississippi in eruption was a vital aspect of its representative power: "People do see its muddy turmoil as a bodying-forth of their own turbulent inner selves . . . there's a note in their voices that says, *I have it in me to do that . . . I know how it feels.*"[36]

Eliot's strong brown God is alive and well, and it continues to draw a steady stream of pilgrims onto its long course. On occasion, the river still demands a tribute. Two men attempting to canoe the Mississippi drowned in 1997. Undaunted – and undoubtedly spurred on by the danger that remains inherent – travelers eagerly take to its waters. In August 2005, for example, Michael Porath and Vaughan O'Brien set out to canoe from Lake Itasca to the Gulf. That is, by now, a familiar story. What is not yet familiar is the means of its transmission: whilst the men progressed downriver, Porath filed regular reports to his local newspaper which were posted on the Internet; his readers were invited to contact him, anywhere along the river's course, by e-mail. As Ben Lucien Burman was told by a young deckhand when he returned to the river late in life, "It ain't the same Mississippi you knew noways." But as his captain knew, and as those who have traveled and written about the Mississippi know intimately, "She's still the same old river."[37] And so the procession persists, of those hoping to find the essence of America in the muddy waters of the Mississippi River.

Notes

1. As quoted in Stephen E. Ambrose and Douglas G. Brinkley, *The Mississippi and the Making of a Nation* (Washington: National Geographic Society, 2002), p. 204.
2. Timothy Flint, *Recollections of the Last Ten Years in the Valley of the Mississippi* (Carbondale: Southern Illinois University Press, 1968), pp. 64–66. Originally published in 1826.
3. T. S. Eliot, "The Dry Salvages," in *Four Quartets* (London: Faber, 1994), p. 23.
4. From William Least Heat-Moon's introduction to Clarence Jonk's *River Journey* (St. Paul, Minnesota: Borealis Books, 2003), p. xi. First published in 1964.
5. Mark Twain, *Life on the Mississippi* (Boston: James R. Osgood and Company, 1883), p. 104.
6. Edward Gaylord Bourne, ed., *Narratives of the Career of Hernando De Soto*, 2 vols. (London: David Nutt, 1905), vol. I, p. 112.
7. John Gilmary Shea, ed., *Discovery and Exploration of the Mississippi Valley* (Albany: Joseph McDonough: 1903), pp. 10–18. First published in 1852.
8. Francis Parkman, *The Discovery of the Great West* (Boston: Little, Brown and Company, 1869), p. 282.
9. Jonathan Carver, *Travels Through the Interior Parts of North America* (London: The Author, 1778), pp. 527–28.
10. *Quarterly Review* 12 (1815), pp. 317–68, 319.
11. Elliott Coues, ed., *The Expeditions of Zebulon Montgomery Pike*, 3 vols. (New York: Francis P. Harper, 1895), vol. I, p. 254.
12. Henry Rowe Schoolcraft, *Narrative of an Expedition Through the Upper Mississippi to Itasca Lake* (New York: Harper & Brothers, 1834), p. 56.
13. Alice Crary Sutcliffe, *Robert Fulton and the Clermont* (New York: The Century Co., 1909), p. 201.
14. Emerson to Margaret Fuller, in *Letters of Ralph Waldo Emerson*, ed. Ralph L. Rusk, 6 vols. (New York: Columbia University Press, 1939), vol. II, pp. 394–95.

15. Giacomo Beltrami, *A Pilgrimage in Europe and America*, 2 vols. (London: Hunt and Clarke, 1828), vol. II, p. 33.

16. Frances Trollope, *Domestic Manners of the Americans*, 2 vols. (London: Richard Bentley, 1832), vol. I, pp. 3–5, 19.

17. Captain Frederick Marryat, *A Diary in America with Remarks on its Institutions*, 3 vols. (London: Longman & Co., 1839), vol. II, pp. 125, 142–43.

18. *The Letters and Private Papers of William Makepeace Thackeray*, ed. Gordon N. Ray, 4 vols. (London: Oxford University Press, 1946), vol. III, p. 589.

19. Ida Pfeiffer, *A Lady's Second Journey Round the World*, 2 vols. (London: Longman, Brown, Green and Longman, 1855), vol. II, p. 241.

20. Charles Dickens, *American Notes for General Circulation*, 2 vols. (London: Chapman and Hall, 1842), vol. II, pp. 110–12, 146–48.

21. Harriet Martineau, *Society in America*, 3 vols. (London: Saunders and Otley, 1837), vol. I, pp. 208–12.

22. John Morris [John O'Connor], *Wanderings of a Vagabond* (New York: The Author, 1872), pp. 432–33.

23. Charles Dickens, "American Panorama" (1848), in *Dickens' Journalism*, ed. Michael Slater, 4 vols. (London: Dent, 1997), vol. II, pp. 135–37, 136.

24. Henry David Thoreau, "Walking," in *Civil Disobedience and Other Essays* (New York: Dover Publications, 1993), p. 60. Originally published in 1862.

25. Horst Kruse, *Mark Twain and "Life on the Mississippi"* (Amherst: University of Massachusetts Press, 1981), p. 127.

26. *Mark Twain's Letters*, ed. Albert Bigelow Paine, 2 vols. (New York: Harper & Brothers, 1917), vol. I, p. 424.

27. Samuel Charles Webster, ed., *Mark Twain, Business Man* (Boston: Little, Brown and Company, 1946), p. 207.

28. *Mark Twain's Letters, Volume 4: 1870–1*, ed. Victor Fischer and Michael B. Frank (Berkeley: University of California Press, 1995), p. 499.

29. Mark Twain, *The Adventures of Huckleberry Finn* (London: Chatto & Windus, 1884), pp. 177–79.

30. Eddy L. Harris, *Mississippi Solo* (New York: Henry Holt and Company, 1998), p. 98. First published 1988.

31. Kent and Margaret Lighty, *Shantyboat* (New York: The Century Co., 1930), p. 3.

32. Richard Pike Bissell, "For Houseboaters the Livin' is Easy," *Sports Illustrated*, 15:8 (August 21, 1961), pp. 38–39. With thanks to the University of Iowa Library.

33. Harlan Hubbard, *Shantyboat* (Lexington: University Press of Kentucky, 1977), pp. 28, 3, 28, 38, 3. First published 1953.

34. Albert S. Tousley, *Where Goes the River?* (Iowa City: Tepee Press, 1928), pp. xi–xii, 4, 295.

35. Jonathan Raban, *Old Glory* (London: Collins, 1981), pp. 11, 17, 41, 38, 527.

36. Jonathan Raban, "Mississippi Water," *Granta* 45 (Autumn 1993), pp. 127–59, 129–30.

37. Ben Lucien Burman, *Look Down that Winding River* (New York: Taplinger Publishing Company, 1973), pp. 177, 192.

5

MARTIN PADGET

The Southwest and travel writing

In August 1830 James Ohio Pattie traveled back to the United States after a five-year odyssey through the mountains, canyonlands, and arid plains of the region between Santa Fe, New Mexico and San Diego, California. He had set out to make a fortune in the fur trade, but returned with neither money nor possessions. The only asset he possessed was the remarkable story of his extensive travels. He collaborated with Timothy Flint, whose frontier histories include a biography of Daniel Boone and a novel set in New Mexico, to produce *The Personal Narrative of James O. Pattie* (1831), one of the earliest American-authored works in which the Southwest is described. The book records a relentless slaughter of beaver, bears, and buffalo, and details frequent interactions with Native Americans that vary from mutual accommodation to outright violence. While the factual value of the account is in parts suspect, Pattie's frontier narrative nevertheless provides fascinating insights into a region that was little known to Americans until the 1820s and 1830s.[1]

The boundaries of the Southwest were only vaguely drawn when Pattie entered the small town of San Fernando de Taos in northern New Mexico on October 26, 1825.[2] Recollecting the event five years later, Pattie states:

> The alcaide asked us for the invoice of our goods, which we showed him, and paid the customary duties on them. This was a man of a swarthy complexion having the appearance of pride and haughtiness. The door-way of the room, we were in, was crowded with men, women and children, who stared at us, as though they had never seen white men before, there being in fact, much to my surprize [*sic*] and disappointment, not one white person among them. I had expected to find no difference between these people and our own, but their language. I was never so mistaken. The men and women were not clothed in our fashion, the former having short pantaloons fastened below the waist with a red belt and buck skin leggings put on three or four times double. A Spanish knife is stuck in by the side of the leg, and a small sword worn by the side. A long jacket or blanket is thrown over, and worn upon the

Glasgow University Checkout / Receipt

Customer name: Devolder, Elsie

Title: Politics, identity, and mobility in travel
writing / edited by Miguel A. Cabaas, Jeanne
Dubino, Vero
ID: 30114016184205
Due: 05-01-18

Title: The global politics of contemporary travel
writing / Debbie Lisle.
ID: 30114013773182
Due: 05-01-18

Total items: 2
08/12/2017 10:26
Overdue: 0

Please Retain your Receipt for your Record

shoulders. They have few fire arms, generally using upon occasions which require them, a bow and a spear, and never wear a hat, except when they ride. When on horseback, they face towards the right side of the animal. The saddle, which they use, looks as ours would, with something like an arm chair fastened upon it.[3]

These sentences create a striking impression of a region that only recently had become accessible to American trappers and traders. The linguistic and cultural differences noted in this initial encounter suggest that, before he arrived in Taos, Pattie had envisaged a certain equality existing between Americans and the Hispano population. However, on arrival, Pattie's Yankee dislike of social hierarchy and officialdom combined with a deeply ingrained disregard for the mestizo identity of most New Mexicans to convey a clear sense of superiority over the local population. Pattie lingered only briefly in Taos before proceeding to Santa Fe, the capital of New Mexico, where his party gained official permission to trap beaver along the Gila River.[4]

Pattie was in the vanguard of the American movement into the southern half of the Rocky Mountain region. He had traveled up the Missouri and Platte rivers from St. Louis before heading southwest with a traders' caravan across the plains to the Arkansas River, where the party bartered with Ute Indians for deerskins and beaver pelts and then headed across the plains to New Mexico. He had traversed country north of the Mexican border into which the American explorers Zebulon Pike and Stephen Long had ventured in their reconnaissance of the far West in 1806–07 and 1819–20 respectively. In the early 1820s, the centers of Mexican governance in San Antonio, Texas; Santa Fe, New Mexico; and Monterey, California were relatively small settlements set upon a vast terrain over much of which Mexico had only a nominal hold. Opportunistic American merchants opened the Santa Fe Trail to New Mexico in 1822, the year after Mexico gained its independence from Spain, in order to exploit what soon became a lucrative trade between Missouri and northern Mexico. As a consequence of the Texas War of Independence in 1835–36, the annexation of Texas in 1845, and the subsequent US–Mexico War of 1846–48, about half of Mexico's northern territory was incorporated into the United States. So too were myriad American Indian tribes drawn into the Union – among them Comanches, Utes, Southern Paiutes, Hopis, Havasupais, Navajos, Pueblos, Akimel O'odham (Pimas), Mojaves, and Apaches – as a consequence of the American conquest of northern Mexico.[5]

The image of the Southwest conveyed by travel writers would change dramatically over the course of the nineteenth and twentieth centuries as

Americans sought to master the region's geography. One of the most striking aspects of Pattie's narrative is the degree to which it provides details
about certain locations and noteworthy events, particularly those involving points of crisis, but without an overt attempt being made to provide
such information in a larger unfolding narrative structure. This is in contrast to succeeding travelers, such as John Russell Bartlett, who relied on his
extensive fieldwork as the American Commissioner of the United States and
Mexican Boundary Commission in 1850–53 to construct a personal narrative that is rich in precise detail about flora, fauna, topography, mineral
wealth, ethnological data, and the chronology of his travels.[6] The attempts of
government-appointed officials and, in particular, the Army Corps of Topographical Engineers to provide an effective reconnaissance of the Southwest
in the fifteen years after the signing of the Treaty of Guadalupe in 1848, were
strengthened in the aftermath of the Civil War. Survey teams led by Ferdi-
nand V. Hayden, Clarence King, George Wheeler, and Major John Wesley
Powell sought to map the terrain and physical resources of the western territories as a whole, authoring reports in which accounts of travel through
inspirational monumental landscapes such as Yellowstone and the Grand
Canyon were a conspicuous feature.[7]

By the 1880s, when both the Southern Pacific and Santa Fe transcontinental railroads had been completed, a more benign image of the Southwest had
come to the fore than is found in the accounts of Pattie and other travelers of
the antebellum period. But there is a sense in which neither the region's arid
and often forbidding landscapes nor its ethnically diverse populations of
Native Americans and Hispanos could be neatly contained by the exercise
of an Anglo traveler's sentimental imagination. One gains the sense from
reading descriptive books such as George A. Dorsey's *Indians of the Southwest* (1903) and John F. Huckel's *American Indians: First Families of the
Southwest* (1913), published by the advertising departments of the Santa Fe
Railway and its companion organization the Fred Harvey Company, that
the image they promote of native cultures of the Southwest is overly ordered
and circumscribed.[8] The superficially affirmative tone of such publications,
in which Taos Indians are praised for their biculturalism ("enjoying two
widely different religions, two sets of implements as far apart as the Stone
Age and the locomotive" [Huckel, *American Indians*, n.p.]), is undermined
by the racial hierarchies they construct among Southwestern tribes. Thus
Pueblo Indians are regarded as more highly civilized than Navajos, who
are, in turn, "far in advance of the Plains Indians of the country north."
Meanwhile, Apaches, viewed as a lower type of Indian than each of these
tribal cultures, are reductively assessed as being "adept in the gentle art of
murder" (Huckel, *American Indians*, n.p.). Arguably, it is this specter of

American Indian enmity and of the power of the Southwestern environment to undermine efforts to rationalize and control its more destructive capacity that continues to haunt the imaginations of travelers through the region, as shall be seen in the cases of Edward Abbey and Charles Bowden later in the discussion.

The Santa Fe and Taos Trails

Through the publication of Pattie's narrative and a host of reports of military reconnaissance and exploration, travelogues and captivity narratives, a more accurate and detailed yet ideologically loaded image of the Southwest's physical and cultural geography emerged at the height of American territorial expansion in the 1830s and 1840s. The trader Josiah Gregg published *Commerce of the Prairies* (1844) after making the journey between Independence and Santa Fe on eight occasions, beginning in 1831. Gregg casts himself as an adventurer and health-seeker, noting Washington Irving's travelogue *A Tour on the Prairies* (1835) as his inspiration. The lack of constraint which Gregg celebrates is also emphasized in Lewis Garrard's *Wah-to-Yah and the Taos Trail* (1850). In an early example of tourism along the Santa Fe Trail that echoes Francis Parkman's adventures on the Oregon Trail in the same year, Garrard traveled from his home in Cincinnati at the tender age of seventeen to St. Louis; from there he explored the Southwest. His reading of John L. Stephens' *Incidents of Travel in Central America, Chiapas, and Yucatan* (1841), William H. Prescott's *History of the Conquest of Mexico* (1843), and John C. Fremont's *Report of the Exploring Expedition to the Rocky Mountains in the Year 1842, and to Oregon and North California in the Years 1843–44* (1845) had fired his imagination at the prospect of traveling beyond the confines of established American society: "Anyone, in the Far West, is romantically inclined."[9] Garrard traveled with a large caravan to Bent's Fort, located on the Arkansas River in southeastern Colorado, which between 1832 and 1849 lay at the heart of the Southwestern fur trade. There he freely interacted with traders, trappers, and Cheyenne Indians, providing a valuable record of backwoods humor articulated in a rich vernacular voice.

After news arrived of an uprising in the Taos locale in which Governor Charles Bent had been assassinated, Garrard joined a party of twenty-three men to "kill and scalp every Mexican to be found" (*Wah-to-Yah*, p. 123). But his emotive patriotism was checked by the injustice he witnessed in Taos as the men implicated in the insurrection were condemned to hang after cursory trials: "It certainly did appear to be a great assumption on the part of the Americans to conquer a territory and then arraign the revolting inhabitants for treason" (p. 172). Garrard traveled, then, in the context of war and was politically and socially aligned with the American conquest, yet his book calls into question the moral grounds on which American authority was exercised in New Mexico. The lingering attention that he gives to the deaths of the six men implicated in the revolt, in the only eyewitness account that exists, suggests his repulsion at the execution: "The bodies swayed back and forth, and, coming in contact with each other, convulsive shudders shook their frames; the muscles, contracting, would relax, and again contract, and the bodies writhed most horribly" (p. 198).

When eighteen-year-old Susan Shelby Magoffin set out from Independence, Missouri with her trader husband Samuel in June 1846, she was the first white American woman to travel the Santa Fe Trail. Similar to many women travelers on the overland trails in the 1840s, she kept a diary of a journey that took in El Paso del Norte and Chihuahua as well as Santa Fe. Although not written for publication, the journal was probably composed with the thought that family members would read her account. The initial part of the journey, from Independence to Bent's Fort, allowed her to escape the confines of the domestic sphere. Similar to Gregg, whose book she carried and often cited, Magoffin celebrates the liberation she felt during her journey, commenting: "There is such independence, so much free uncontaminated air, which impregnates the mind, the feelings, nay every thought, with purity. I breathe free without that oppression and uneasiness felt in the gossiping groups of a settled home."[10]

Her sense of self was called into question by two events at Bent's Fort. As she lay confined in bed by the sickness that soon resulted in the loss of her unborn child, she contrasted her situation with that of an Indian woman who had just given birth at the fort. Magoffin, who was amazed to hear that this mother had bathed herself in the river only half an hour after giving birth, reflects: "It is truly astonishing to see what customs will do. No doubt many ladies in civilized life are ruined by too careful treatments during child-birth, for this custom of the hethen [sic] is not known to be disadvantageous, but it is a 'hethenish [sic] custom'" (Down the Santa Fe Trail, p. 68). Travel beyond American settlements and into the Mexican borderlands provided an opportunity, then, to reconsider accepted practices within the United States concerning childbirth, and to question just what constituted civilized and primitive behavior. Magoffin also questioned the logic of warfare with Mexico. Her journey from Independence had started in June 1846 at a point when President Polk had already declared war on Mexico, and Bent's Fort was the launching point for the march on New Mexico by General Stephen Watts Kearny's Army of the West during her twelve-day stay there. Of her convalescence, she writes:

Though forbidden to rise from bed, I was free to meditate on the follies and wickedness of man! Of a creature formed for nobler and higher purposes, sinking himself to the level of beasts, waging warfare with his fellow man, even as the dumb brute. And by his example teaching nothing good, striving for wealth, honour and fame to the ruining of his soul, and loosing a brighter crown in higher realms. (p. 69)[11]

The Grand Canyon

In the course of his travels through the Southwest, Pattie may have encountered the Grand Canyon. He recounts reaching a point of the Colorado River "where the mountains shut in so close upon its shores, that we were compelled to climb a mountain, and travel along the acclivity, the river still in sight, and at an immense depth beneath us" (*Personal Narrative*, p. 89). For Pattie, the canyon, whether seen in actuality or conjured from stories he had heard from fellow mountain men, was primarily an obstacle to his free movement through the Southwest. Certainly he did not possess the capacity to understand the processes by which the canyon had been formed, as would become the case when government-sponsored survey teams mapped Western resources after the Civil War. Pattie's lack of intellectual curiosity about the canyon echoes that of the Spaniard Captain García López de Cárdenas, who visited the South Rim in 1540. Cárdenas was a member of the large Spanish expeditionary force, led by the conquistador Francisco Vasquez de Coronado, which had traveled through the interior of New Spain to search for the fabled Seven Cities of Cibola. Cárdenas set out from a winter camp near Zuni Pueblo in New Mexico with American Indian guides to establish the existence of a great river lying to the west that might offer a means of access from the interior to the sea. Upon reaching the South Rim at modern-day Desert View, his party searched for a means of accessing the Colorado River. The chronicler Pedro de Castañada later recorded:

They spent three days on this bank looking for a passage down to the river, which looked from above as if the water were six feet across, although the Indians said it was a half league wide . . . Those who stayed above had estimated that some huge rocks on the sides of the cliffs seemed to be about as tall as a man, but those who went down swore that when they reached these rocks they were bigger than the great tower of Seville.[12]

In spite of its imperial might, Spain did not possess the intellectual capacity to make sense of this discovery.[13]

When Major John Wesley Powell set out from Green River, Wyoming heading a team of ten volunteers in May 1869 to travel the length of the

Green, Grand, and Colorado rivers, the time had arrived when the American cultural imagination could grasp the meaning of the Grand Canyon. The high Colorado Plateau country through which he journeyed was the last part of the contiguous United States to be explored, and Powell's fellow Americans celebrated an accomplishment that helped bind together a nation deeply divided by the Civil War. Powell's lyrical narrative of his river journey is one of the classic accounts of travel through the American West. The author's use of the historical present lends a sense of immediacy to the day-to-day reckoning. On August 13, the party began its journey into the Grand Canyon. While Powell's journal entry for the day is brief, his subsequently written narrative provides an appropriate sense of occasion:

> We are now ready to start on our way down the Great Unknown . . . We are three quarters of a mile in the depths of the earth, and the great river shrinks into insignificance as it dashes its angry waves against the walls and cliffs that rise to the world above; the waves are but puny ripples, and we but pigmies, running up and down the sands or lost among the boulders. We have an unknown distance yet to run, an unknown river to explore. What falls there are, we know not; what rocks beset the channel, we know not; what walls rise over the river, we know not. Ah, well! we may conjecture such things. The men talk as cheerfully as ever; jests are bandied about freely this morning; but to me the cheer is somber and the jests are ghastly.[14]

Powell conveys the epic scale of the canyon by contrasting its solid physical presence with the insignificant and temporary passage of his party. It was not simply the spatial qualities of the canyon that captured Powell's imagination but also the geological processes working through deep time that had created it. The sublimity of the Grand Canyon as a grand spectacle of nature was inextricably linked, in the age of Charles Lyell and Charles Darwin, to new ways of comprehending the age of the earth and the evolution of life. Powell's coming to age had occurred when geology, evolution, and Darwinism battled with religious fundamentalism for supremacy in the American mind, and he had firmly aligned with rationalism and secularism.[15]

As Powell's men progressed through the Grand Canyon, fearful of starvation and the great distance they might yet have to travel, morale dropped. The tone of the narrative reflects the fluctuating temperament of the team, hence the canyon becomes a "granite prison" (*Exploration*, p. 89) while the men can still thrill to a "wild exhilarating ride" (p. 91). But for all the grandeur of the canyon, the men wished their trial to conclude. Powell, who had lost an arm at the Battle of Shiloh during the Civil War, likened his great sense of relief at completing the passage to that of the soldier

who has been chained by wounds to a hospital cot until his canvas tent seems·
like a dungeon cell, until the groans of those who lie about tortured with probe
and knife are piled up, a weight of horror on his ears that he cannot throw off,
cannot forget, and until the stench of festering wounds and anesthetic drugs
has filled the air with its loathsome burthen, – when he at last goes into the
open field, what a world he sees! (pp. 102–03)

Running boats through the canyon had not only tested the party physically
but also burdened the men psychologically. The view from the river was too
often confining, and only the deep sleep that comes from profound physical
tiredness provided respite from the unceasing roar of the water.

In contrast to Powell's predominant view from the river in his expedition of 1869, the men he later commissioned to survey the Grand Canyon
locale for the US Geological Survey could look down on the Colorado from
panoramic vistas. Between the completion of Powell's journey and the publication of Clarence Dutton's *Tertiary History of the Grand Cañon District*
in 1882, the region was subjected to a great multidisciplinary onslaught in
which geological science, cartography, topographic art, photography, and
painting were combined in an overarching effort to forge a unified understanding of canyon country. Dutton stresses the immense scale and age of the
canyon and pays particular attention to its visual qualities, detailing form,
shadow, and light. He yokes together the languages of science and aesthetics
in articulating the view from Point Sublime: "In all the vast space beneath
and around us there is very little upon which the mind can linger restfully.
It is completely filled with objects of gigantic size and amazing form, and as
the mind wonders over them it is hopelessly bewildered and lost."[16]

For Dutton, the great challenge in studying the geology of the canyon
and the surrounding Colorado Plateau lay in putting together a totalizing
vision of the region's ever evolving natural history. The Grand Canyon
represented to Dutton and Powell a vast intellectual puzzle which revealed
just how the forces of nature – upheaval, faulting, flooding, and above all
erosion – were responsible for creating some of the most spectacular scenery
known. Accordingly Dutton insists that in order to comprehend the Grand
Canyon, there has to be enough time in which to orient oneself sufficiently to
appreciate its unique qualities. He warns readers that the "lover of nature,
whose perceptions have been trained in the Alps, in Italy, Germany, or
New England, in the Appalachians or Cordilleras, in Scotland, or Colorado,
would enter this strange region with a shock, and dwell there for a time
with a sense of oppression, and perhaps with horror" (*Tertiary History*,
p. 141). And yet within two decades of Dutton's remark the Grand Canyon
had become a spectacle to which American tourists traveled in ever greater

numbers after the Santa Fe Railway completed a spur line to the South Rim in 1903. As George Wharton James puts it in his guidebook *Arizona the Wonderland* (1917): "One may take his seat – aye, the most delicate of transcontinental travelers may take her Pullman drawing-room, in Chicago, and ride direct to El Tovar, the perfect Fred Harvey hotel on the rim of the Canyon – and without a moment's weariness, ennui or deprivation of any accustomed luxury, gaze upon this wonderland of form, color and mystery."[17]

The ethnological Southwest

By the early 1900s many ethnologists and archeologists had traveled from the East to study the native cultures of the Southwest. The Bureau of Ethnology, together with the Smithsonian Institution, sponsored the fieldwork of professional ethnologists, while also publishing the work of talented amateurs in its annual reports and frequent bulletins. The Army officers John Gregory Bourke and Washington Matthews studied the native people they encountered in the course of their postings to Southwestern locations. Bourke, who also wrote a popular account of General Crook's campaign to contain Apaches during the mid-1880s, published *The Snake-Dance of the Moquis of Arizona* with Scribner's Press in 1884, while Matthews translated Navajo myths, including a monograph entitled *The Night Chant: A Navaho Ceremony* (1902). Soon the Field Museum of Natural History in Chicago, which opened during the 1893 World's Fair, also sent ethnologists to the Southwest and beyond to conduct research and collect tribal artifacts. During the 1920s and 1930s, anthropologists trained under the guidance of Franz Boas created intricate studies of Southwestern American Indian cultures that include Ruth Bunzel's *The Pueblo Potter* (1929) and Ruth Benedict's *Patterns of Culture* (1934).

Frank Hamilton Cushing became the best-known ethnologist to visit the Southwest in the late nineteenth century. He traveled to Zuni Pueblo in 1879 as part of an expedition co-organized by the Bureau of Ethnology and the Smithsonian Institution and commanded by James Stevenson. Cushing, only twenty-two years old, had been instructed by his mentor, Spencer Baird of the Smithsonian, to "find out all you can about some typical tribe of Pueblo Indians."[18] He remained at Zuni for over four years, living in the tribal governor's household and immersing himself in the day-to-day life of the Pueblo. He also gained admission to the association of warriors known as the Society of the Bow, which in turn facilitated his access to the ceremonial organization and political governance of Zuni society. In the course of his long stay, Cushing became one of the first participant observer ethnographers and a prototypical figure in pursuing a relativistic stance towards the study of American Indian cultures. Anticipating the work of the anthropologist Franz Boas, whose pedagogical influence would be felt at universities throughout the United States from the 1920s on, Cushing did not believe that all humankind developed a uniform path of social evolution. Instead cultures developed in ways that were particular to their own history and location. Comprehending Zuni society required not only collecting artifacts and folklore, as was common practice among his contemporaries, but employing an empirical, intuitive, and speculative approach to the reconstruction of tribal culture.[19]

Cushing provided a popular account of his stay in a series of articles published as "My Adventures in Zuñi" in *Century* magazine between 1882 and 1883. A particularly interesting episode records the response of Zunis to his practice of sketching and note-taking during ceremonial dances. Similar to ethnologists and travelers in general during the late 1800s, Cushing assumed a right of access to native ceremonies and the esoteric knowledge associated with them. Thus he ignored Zuni leaders who told him to relinquish books and pencils when viewing ceremonies. Ventriloquizing the voice of Zunis collectively, Cushing writes: "If you put the shadows of the great dance on the leaves of your book to-day, we shall cut them to pieces."[20] Cushing was determined to persist in his effort, brandishing a knife in defiance at the Zuni leaders and resuming sketching later that day. Some weeks later Cushing again represented a ceremony from a rooftop. According to Cushing's account, the Dance of the Great Knife, which traditionally required a sacrificial victim, had been organized to intimidate him into giving up his offensive activities. Cushing persisted in sketching this ceremony despite performers making violent gestures toward him: "Soon they began to point wildly at me with their clubs. Unable as I was to understand all they had been saying, I at first regarded it all as a joke, like those of the *Keó-yi-mo-shi* [koyemshi: ritual clowns], until one shouted out to the other, "'Kill him! kill him!'" ("My Adventures," p. 72). Cushing claims to have quickly neutralized the situation by waving his hunting knife threateningly and then laying it on the open pages of his sketchbook, signifying his intention to continue recording ceremonies. He also claims that for this action, which appears to have earned him the respect of his challengers, he received the "wildly shouted applause" (p. 73) of Zuni onlookers.

Cushing's sojourn at Zuni was undertaken with a serious scientific purpose but his popular narrative, in which he placed himself at the center of a human drama and relegated all other whites to the margins, creates an evocative image of adventure and cultural discovery. The account, insofar as it articulates a deep-seated appreciation of the complexity and spirituality of Zuni life, also reveals a search for a sense of authenticity and presence that increasingly seemed to Cushing and so many others of his generation to be missing from late-nineteenth-century American society. By the early 1900s it had become increasingly common for not only ethnologists but also writers and artists to sojourn with Southwestern tribes. The ethnological impulse thus became intermingled with the tourist's urge to consume the spectacle of native cultures.

Forging the land of enchantment

After viewing the ongoing construction of the Atlantic and Pacific Railroad (later to become part of the Atchison, Topeka, and Santa Fe Railway) through New Mexico in 1879, the author Susan Wallace wrote:

> If you would dream dreams and see visions, now is the time to come. If you would taste the wild charm, hasten to catch it before the wear of every-day travel tramples out the primitive customs. It is still to a good degree a country apart from the rest of the United States; mountain-locked and little known, severed, as it has been, from the great highways of commerce. Its history is a romance and a tragedy, and, as in every country imperfectly explored, it holds more or less of the mysterious. Here are extensive ruins; unparalleled natural phenomena; mountains, "flaunting their crowns of snow everlastingly in the face of the sun," that bear in their bosom undeveloped mines, dazzling the imagination; cañons with perpendicular sides a mile in height; savages merciless and bloodthirsty, who in undying hate still dispute the progress of foreign civilization. But the civilizer is coming; is here. The waste lands of the wandering tribes will be divided and sold by the acre, instead of the league. The dozing Mexican will be jostled on the elbow, and will wake from his long trance to find himself in the way.[21]

Wallace had traveled to Santa Fe from her home in Crawfordsville, Indiana, with her husband Lew Wallace, the governor of New Mexico between 1879 and 1881 – a period in which he completed the best-selling novel *Ben-Hur* (1880). Unlike the industrializing and urbanizing East and Midwest, the Southwest appeared to be a region where small-scale subsistence farming, artisanal arts and crafts, intimate communal life, and "superstitious" religious practices continued at the heart of everyday life. Wallace points out the region's arid and mountainous landscapes and its ethnically diverse population of American Indians and Hispanos, inviting readers to discover an exotic location that lies on the margins of the United States. Americans will find much of interest there, including the long-deserted dwellings of ancient Puebloans (the "Anasazi"), monumental nature, and the romance of old Spain. However, Wallace continues, all this is about to change with the arrival of the railroad:

> the epic of history cannot abide the screech of the locomotive nor its penetrating headlight. It requires broken, disconnected threads, doubtful testimony, dim lights – above all, the mist lines of distance. The locomotive brings the ends of the earth together, and dashes into nothingness delicate tissues woven in darkness, like certain laces, whose threads break in the weaving by day.
>
> (*The Land of the Pueblos*, p. 96)

The Land of the Pueblos stands at the outset of a fifty-year period in which the commercial Southwest took full shape in the consciousnesses of Americans. When Wallace left New Mexico, her husband having been appointed the US Minister in Turkey, a unified sense of what constituted the Southwest had yet to emerge. But the impact of the railroad and the speculators, tourists, and settlers that it carried was profound. Although the Santa Fe Railway did not immediately promote the attractions of the American Indian Southwest in its advertising literature, by the 1890s the company, in tandem with the Fred Harvey Company, had created a distinctive regional iconography that drew on the work of an extended network of artists that included well-known figures such as Thomas Moran, E. Irving Couse, and Maynard Dixon. The invention of the half-plate for the reproduction of photographs in books, and chromolithography for the distribution of books, calendars, and postcards with color illustrations, facilitated the creation of advertising imagery that appeared to take readers into the heart of American Indian country. The rapidity of this process needs emphasizing for although the motif of discovery remained commonplace in popular representations of the Southwest in the late 1800s and early 1900s, it soon took on a manufactured quality in the pages of tourist guides. Passengers on board Santa Fe trains had long possessed the opportunity to interact with American Indians selling arts and crafts at stations and hotels along the line, but by the mid-1920s they were being offered the chance to take an American Indian Detour that would allow them to "feel the lure of the real Southwest beyond the pinched horizons of your train window."[22]

Some four years after Wallace left New Mexico, a twenty-five-year-old man named Charles Fletcher Lummis first encountered the Hispano settlements of southern Colorado and northern New Mexico during a 3,507-mile walk from Chillicothe, Ohio to Los Angeles. Lummis' "tramp across the continent," as he called it, was a typical endeavor for this athletic and promotionally minded soul, who boasted that he could walk up to seventy-five miles in a twenty-four-hour period. From his trek he sent two sets of letters, eastward to the *Chillicothe Leader* and forward to the *Los*

Angeles Times. The letters sent back to Ohio show how Lummis' sensibilities towards both Mexican Americans and American Indians changed in the course of his travel. From Alamosa in southern Colorado, Lummis remarks that Mexicans "are a snide-looking set, twice as dark as an Indian, with heavy lips and noses, long, straight, black hair, sleepy eyes, and a general expression of ineffable laziness."[23] Walking southwards through New Mexico, Lummis changed his mind as he tried out his newly acquired, but strictly limited, Spanish vocabulary and received the hospitality of humble rural people.

For all that Lummis associated with ordinary folk in New Mexico, he most admired those with position and power. Thus the most memorable aspect of Lummis' time in New Mexico was his stay with the socially elite family of Don Manuel Chaves in San Mateo. There Lummis shaved and shook off his "dude" identity in an effort to make himself more presentable to the "upper crust" family, especially a young woman who possessed the seductive beauty of the "true Spanish type": "Blue eyes are sweet and alluring, but for solid magnetism it takes two orbs of jet, framed in lashes and brows still darker, and showing the sparks of a fire that is apt to blaze up at any minute" (*Letters from the Southwest*, p. 207). That Lummis, who was married, would give such frank expression of libidinal desire in a newspaper article is itself interesting, but this sentence also points to the limitations of his cultural relativism. In future years he would continue to celebrate the beauty of the "Spanish-American face," heaping praise on visages in which the European was deemed to be most dominant.[24] He would also seek to emulate the lifestyle of the Chaves family, calling himself Don Carlos and singing folk songs in Spanish in hospitable gatherings at his home, El Alisal, in Los Angeles. Making such observations about female beauty and mimicking the patriarchal role of an elite Hispano effectively demonstrates how Lummis truly admired only limited aspects of Mexican American culture.

Lummis continued to Los Angeles, where he took up the position of city editor at the *Los Angeles Times* and soon became immersed in the social and political culture of southern California. After three years of overwork that resulted in a debilitating stroke, Lummis returned to the heartland of the Southwest for his rehabilitation. In New Mexico he first stayed for almost a year with the Chaves family before moving to Isleta Pueblo, where he dwelled for a further three years until his return to Los Angeles. This immersion in New Mexican culture led to a new career as an author and promoter of the Southwest. From New Mexico he sent numerous articles and short pieces to newspapers and magazines located outside the region; he also produced thousands of photographs, on which engravings could be based, to illustrate his writings. Building on his magazine publications, Lummis then wrote a number of books for Eastern publishers during the 1890s, including explorations of Hispano and Pueblo Indian folklore (*A New Mexico David and Other Stories and Sketches of the Southwest*, 1891) and the travelogues *Some Strange Corners of Our Country* (1892) and *The Land of Poco Tiempo* (1893). Back in California, Lummis took up the editorship of *Land of Sunshine* (later *Out West*), a journal which initially served as a promotional tool for southern California investors. The publication soon took on the imprint of his idiosyncratic and forceful personality as he proselytized on the topic of all things Southwestern and championed the historical legacy of Spanish colonialism in the New World.

The expatriate Southwest

By the turn of the century the Southwest had become, in the eyes of many Anglos, a region where the forces of industrialization and urbanization that were transforming other parts of the United States appeared not to have reached. Pueblo Indians in New Mexico appeared to Lummis and other Anglo commentators of his generation to be a repository of stable values in a modernizing society marked by economic and social instability. To Anglo writers and artists, from the late nineteenth century on, sojourning in Arizona and New Mexico offered a refuge from commercialism. Their affection for the region constituted among the citizens of a modernizing culture a nostalgic longing for aspects of their imagined past, such as a closer and more communal way of life. However, the Southwest was not only a region of refuge but also a place of new beginnings where new configurations of American cultural identity could be imagined, and where women such as Mabel Dodge Luhan, Mary Austin, and Georgia O'Keeffe could realize a high degree of personal freedom that could not be found elsewhere in the United States.

Mabel Dodge, a wealthy heiress, had held a well-known salon in Manhattan that attracted leading literary, artistic, and political figures between 1912 and 1917. Having dispatched her third husband, the painter Maurice Sterne, to New Mexico, she experienced a vision one night at home in New York in which Sterne's face transformed into that of an American Indian. Shortly thereafter she received a letter from Sterne in which he wrote: "Do you want an object in life? Save the Indians, their art-culture – reveal it to the world!"[25] Dodge took the Santa Fe Railway to New Mexico, where her life was transformed after meeting Tony Lujan, a local Taos Indian. Comparing and contrasting Sterne, from whom she had grown estranged, and Lujan, to whom she felt increasingly attracted, Dodge writes:

I had a strange sensation of dislocation, as though I were swinging like a pendulum over the gulf of mankind, between Maurice and Tony; and Maurice seemed old and spent and tragic, while Tony was whole and young in the cells of his body, with his power unbroken and hard like the carved granite rock, yet older than the Germanic Russian whom the modern world had destroyed.[26]

Mary Austin, a prolific author of novels, plays, poetry, and polemical articles on the subjects of women's rights and American Indian rights issues, had attended Dodge's salons while living in New York. In her first and most enduring book, *The Land of Little Rain* (1903), which is dedicated to Lummis' second wife Eve, she characterizes the landscape, flora, fauna, and human population of the Mojave Desert east of the Sierra Nevada in northern California. The book contains the observations of a keen-eyed naturalist and an almost gnomic mysticism where Northern Paiute and Shoshone Indians are represented. Indeed, Austin throughout her adult life demonstrated an affinity for Native American cultures by writing stories and plays in which they featured, freely translating traditional oral literature in *The American Rhythm* (1923), and declaring that in a period "so harried and hate-ridden as in this civilized age of ours" Americans in general had much to learn from native people.[27] Having unshackled herself as wife and mother in California, Austin moved to New York City in 1915, but over the following decade she became increasingly drawn towards the Southwest, until she moved to Santa Fe permanently in 1924. Austin shared with her fellow Anglo expatriates Dodge and Alice Corbin Henderson a conviction that there was a redemptive value to Native American spirituality and creative expression. Collectively, these women were attracted to what they regarded as the rooted and holistic way of life of Pueblo Indians and Navajos (Diné). Through learning from the example of native people and Hispanos, Americans might rediscover the joys of unalienated labor and forms of spirituality integrated into everyday life, and also find a refuge from the stresses of urban existence.[28]

Austin published her travelogue *Land of Journey's Ending* (1924) in the aftermath of a 2,500-mile journey through that part of the Southwest bounded by the Rio Grande in the east and the Colorado River in the west. Austin echoes the interests of Wallace and Lummis in the history of Spanish colonialism, the fate of ancient Puebloans who deserted cliff dwellings in the thirteenth century, and the livelihoods of contemporary American Indians. But Austin writes far more sympathetically about both native people and Hispanos than Wallace, while her feminist interest in the maternal and nurturing aspects of the landscape contrasts markedly with the frequently masculinist aspects of Lummis' writing about the region. There is a notable contrast between Austin "cuddling safety against the mother rock" (p. 78) in an account of visiting an ancient Puebloan cliff dwelling, and Lummis recording his energetic excavation – ("After the first four feet of digging, the relics came thick and fast" [*Letters from the Southwest*, p. 211]) – of a similarly dated ruined pueblo on the Chaves estate during his walk to Los Angeles.

The idealistic aspects of the new beginnings that both Austin and Dodge considered possible in the Southwest were radically called into question by D.H. Lawrence, who traveled to Taos at the invitation of Dodge in 1922. Lawrence, weakened by ill health and in the midst of his restless exile from Britain, appears initially to have been drawn to Dodge's mission to meld modern Anglo-dominated America with the perceived spiritual wisdom and holistic livelihood of native peoples. But in the light of actual experience in New Mexico and Arizona, he became convinced that there was a fundamental irreconcilability between white Americans and native people. In *Mornings in Mexico* (1927), the book that resulted from sojourns in New Mexico and Oaxaca, Mexico, Lawrence wrote three essays that deal specifically with native ceremonies in Arizona and New Mexico. In "The Dance of the Sprouting Corn" Lawrence details a spring Corn Dance at Santo Domingo Pueblo in New Mexico in which "the mystery of germination, not procreation, but *putting forth*, resurrection, life springing within the seed, is accomplished."[29] His essay "Indians and Entertainment," which includes a vibrant description of a Christmas Day Deer Dance at Taos Pueblo, insists on white consciousness being "different from and fatal to the Indian" (p. 55). Meanwhile the almost reverent qualities of Lawrence's account of the Santo Domingo ritual contrast dramatically with his essay on the Hopi Snake Dance that he witnessed at Hotevilla, in northern Arizona, in 1924.[30]

For over forty years Anglo observers had been drawn to ceremonies held at various Hopi villages on a biennial basis in which snakes were handled on the final afternoon of a nine-day ritual. Significantly, the ethnological and colonialist aspects of Bourke's *The Snake-Dance of the Moquis of Arizona* (1884) quickly gave way to accounts, such as Walter Hough's *The Moki Snake Dance* (published by the Santa Fe Railway in 1900), that were overtly marketed towards Southwestern tourists. In the first of two essays that he wrote on the Snake Dance, Lawrence refers to "the hopping Indian with his queer muttering gibberish and his dangling snake," and mimics the voices of Anglo onlookers: "why, he sure is cute!"[31] In producing an account which stresses the ways in which intrusive Anglo curiosity had turned the Snake Dance into "a circus," Lawrence produced a discomforting representation of the incompatible characters of whites and Native Americans. Under pressure from Mabel Dodge, who was offended by this essay, Lawrence produced a revised account which appears in *Mornings in Mexico*. The later essay lacks

the sardonic tone of the earlier account, but still Lawrence insists on fundamental cultural differences. Viewing the departure of Navajo visitors from
Hotevilla, he writes: "We say they look wild. But they have the remoteness
of their religion, their animistic religion, in their eyes, they can't see as we
see. And they cannot accept us. They stare at us as the coyotes stare at us:
the gulf of mutual negation between us" (p. 90).[32]

The post-World War II Southwest

The history of the Southwest has proved that Susan Wallace was correct
to stress the change that would come with the arrival of the railroad, the
chief symbol of the forces of incorporation that would transform the region
economically, socially, politically, and culturally. But in spite of the subsequent construction of interstate highways and air travel, Sun Belt urban
development, the annexation of vast areas of land for military bases, and the
exploitation of the region's timber, oil, gas, and uranium resources, much
of the iconography used to promote the appeal of the Southwest today continues to echo the romantic sentiments of Wallace's writing. So too have
literary writers again and again considered the Southwest as constituting a
place apart from the rest of the United States. For instance, the Australian
author Thomas Kenneally, in his travelogue *The Place Where Souls Are Born*
(1992), views the abundance of internationally branded fast food outlets,
gas stations, and ATMs in Tuba City, on the Navajo reservation in northern
Arizona, and comments: "There's a sense in which Citicard and all the rest
of it are a challenge to the writer and a sense in which they are a stimulation.
For in the Southwest, the strangenesses persist in the face of the tendency to
make the known world one great mall."[33]

But not all writers would agree with this proposition. For the British
author Melanie McGrath, in her travelogue *Motel Nirvana* (1995), the
growth of what Edward Abbey labeled industrial tourism prevents her from
viewing the Grand Canyon on her visit to the South Rim. Her postmodern
sense of uncertainty contrasts greatly with the Modernist investment in the
sanctity and aura of landscape and native cultures when she contends that
the canyon is "no longer a place, but the representation of a place."[34] She
also demonstrates great skepticism towards Anglo New Agers, concentrated
in locations such as Santa Fe and Sedona, who participate in vision quests,
sweat lodges, and drumming and dancing ceremonies to develop a sense of
deep spirituality that is supposed to be what native people possess: "The
search for transcendence goes on in our culture, but no amount of birthing
drums or suburban medicine wheel ceremonies can ever hope to capture
Indian mysticism, being empty of Indian context" (p. 214). McGrath thus

draws on the spirit of D.H. Lawrence to explore therapeutic and narcissistic aspects of American culture in the Southwest that arguably have their roots in the anti-modern turn of Mabel Dodge and her associates in the early twentieth century.

Besides the two ways of seeing the travelers' Southwest suggested by Kenneally and McGrath, there is an alternative. Since the early nineteenth century the paths of travel writing and nature writing have crossed repeatedly in American literary history. The naturalist's eye has been attracted to Southwestern landscapes in myriad texts, including John C. Van Dyke's *The Grand Canyon of the Colorado* (1920), Edward Abbey's *Desert Solitaire* (1968), and Terry Tempest Williams' *Pieces of White Shell: A Journey to Navajoland* (1984). Much of the most stirring and nuanced writing on the Southwest derives from such sources. Abbey's voice, alternately polemical, rambunctious, and lyrical, continues to rumble across the deserts and canyonlands of the region, cajoling and ushering Americans into thinking through the consequences of actions that denude the very landscapes they claim to love. Williams, quieter voiced but just as ethically committed, works through centuries of mutual hostility and wariness to find in traditional Navajo storytelling a means for all Southwestern Americans to live with humility and learn to dwell within the limits of the land.

In an age of looming environmental crisis it will become increasingly difficult for writers to express lyrical visions of transcendental nature without referring also to the dangers associated with climate change and the Southwestern population's over-reliance on finite and ever-dwindling water resources. It is more likely that writers will follow the example of Abbey by issuing jeremiads warning of the environmental and social degradation to come. Charles Bowden's *Desierto: Memories of the Future* (1991) is a case in point, a book that is difficult to categorize because of the way in which it combines aspects of investigative travel and nature writing with elements of imaginative play that blur the lines between fact and fiction. But there can be no mistaking Bowden's insistent moral vision as he plots the encroachments of modern urban society on the Sonoran Desert in southern Arizona or visits a Mexican drug trafficker to provide a dystopian vision of a borderlands region in which the excesses of consumer capitalism and a market-driven black economy are all too apparent. To what extent does such writing, compounded by Bowden's succeeding books *Juarez: The Laboratory of Our Future* (1998) and *Down by the River: Drugs, Money, Murder, and Family* (2002), change the modern reader's way of seeing the Southwest? Certainly these books take us a long way from most of the writers that I have mentioned in the course of this discussion. However, there is a sense in which Bowden's profound unease at the way in which the occupation of the Southwest by the United States over the past two centuries has resulted in urban blight, an unsustainable mode of living, and severe strain on the region's natural resources echoes earlier accounts in which the nature of American conduct towards the region's landscapes and indigenous and Hispanic population was called into question. We have only to think of Lewis Garrard's disgust at the swaying bodies of executed Hispanos and Pueblo Indians in 1847, of D.H. Lawrence's antipathy towards the rubber-necking tourists at the Hopi Snake Dance, and of Edward Abbey's aversion to the excesses of industrial tourism in the Southwest to gain an appropriate sense of the ways in which travelers have long articulated visions that cut against the grain of the nationalist and promotional rhetoric associated with the region. Contemporary accounts of travel, then, are poised delicately and sometimes awkwardly between a sense of affirmation, through which the capacity of Southwestern landscapes to compel a sense of awe and even reverence in the observer is confirmed, and anger verging on resignation at the prospect that the region's burgeoning population will inevitably pay a heavy price should residents collectively fail to forge a sustainable way of living in a largely arid environment.

Notes

1. For a detailed investigation of Pattie's travels, see Richard Batman, *James Pattie's West: The Dream and the Reality* (Norman: University of Oklahoma Press, 1986).
2. There has been considerable debate among commentators as to the geographical boundaries of the Southwest. The geographer D.W. Meinig writes: "The Southwest is a distinctive place to the American mind but a somewhat blurred place on American maps," whilst the literary historian Leah Dilworth claims that the Southwest is "a region of the imagination . . . on which Americans have long focused their fantasies of renewal and authenticity." It should be noted that the present discussion, which focuses on the representation of Arizona, New Mexico, and parts of Colorado, does not attempt to provide a holistic interpretation of literary travel in what the historical geographer Richard Francaviglia refers to as the Greater Southwest of Arizona, New Mexico, parts of Colorado, Utah, Texas, and the northern states of Mexico. See D.W. Meinig, *Southwest: Three Peoples in Geographical Change, 1600–1970* (New York: Oxford University Press, 1971), p. 3; Leah Dilworth, *Imagining Indians in the Southwest: Persistent Visions of a Primitivist Past* (New Haven: Yale University Press, 1996), p. 2; and Richard V. Francaviglia, "Elusive Land: Changing Geographic Images of the Southwest," in *Essays on the Changing Images of the Southwest* (Walter Prescott Web Lectures, no. 28), ed. David Narrett, Richard V. Francaviglia, and Bruce S. Narramore (College Station: Texas A & M Press, 1993), p. 13.
3. James O. Pattie, *The Personal Narrative of James O. Pattie* (Lincoln: University of Nebraska Press, 1984), p. 38.

4. The often hostile attitudes of nineteenth-century Anglo travelers towards His-
panos are discussed in David J. Weber, "'Scarce More than Apes': Historical
Roots of Anglo-American Stereotypes of Mexicans in the Border Region," in
Myth and the History of the Hispanic Southwest (Albuquerque: University of
New Mexico Press, 1988), pp. 153–67; and Raymund Paredes, "The Mexi-
can Image in American Travel Literature, 1831–1869," *New Mexico Historical
Review* 52:1 (1977), pp. 5–29.

5. For discussions of Southwestern travel in the antebellum period, see William
H. Goetzmann, *Army Exploration in the American West, 1803–1863* (New
Haven: Yale University Press, 1959); Mabel Major and T.M. Pearce, *Southwest
Heritage: A Literary History with Bibliographies*, 3rd edn (Albuquerque: Uni-
versity of New Mexico Press, 1972); and Eric Sundquist, "The Literature of
Expansion and Race," in *The Cambridge History of American Literature*, vol.
2, *1820–1865*, ed. Sacvan Bercovitch (Cambridge: Cambridge University Press,
1995), pp. 125–328.

6. See John Russell Bartlett, *Personal Narrative of Explorations and Incidents in
Texas, New Mexico, California, Sonora, and Chihuahua, Connected with the
United States and Mexican Boundary Commission, During the Years 1850, '51,
'52, and '53* (New York: D. Appleton and Company; San Francisco: Le Count
and Strong, 1854).

7. For historical studies of the reconnaissance and survey of the West as a whole,
see William H. Goetzmann, *Army Exploration in the American West*, and
*Exploration and Empire: The Explorer and the Scientist in the Winning of
the American West* (New York: Knopf, 1966).

8. See George A. Dorsey, *Indians of the Southwest* ([Chicago]: Passenger Depart-
ment, Atchison, Topeka and Santa Fe Railway System, 1903), and John F.
Huckel, *American Indians: First Families of the Southwest* (Albuquerque: Fred
Harvey Indian Department, 1913).

9. Lewis H. Garrard, *Wah-to-Yah and the Taos Trail, or Prairie Travel and Scalp
Dances, with a Look at Los Rancheros from Muleback and the Rocky Mountain
Campfire* (Norman: University of Oklahoma Press, 1955), p. 41.

10. Susan Shelby Magoffin, *Down the Santa Fe Trail and into Mexico: The Diary
of Susan Shelby Magoffin, 1846–1847*, ed. Stella M. Drumm (New Haven: Yale
University Press, 1962), p. 10.

11. For a discussion of how Magoffin's diary displays ambivalence towards patriotism and gender identity, see Brigitte Georgi-Findlay, *The Frontiers of Women's
Writing: Women's Narratives and the Rhetoric of Westward Expansion* (Tucson: University of Arizona Press, 1996), pp. 92–103.

12. Quoted in Herbert E. Bolton, *The Spanish Borderlands: A Chronicle of Old
Florida and the Southwest* (Albuquerque: University of New Mexico Press,
1996), p. 93.

13. For an interpretation of the various ways in which the Grand Canyon was
viewed during the Spanish colonial and American eras, see Stephen J. Pyne,
How the Grand Canyon Became Grand: A Short History (New York: Penguin,
1999).

14. J.W. Powell, *Exploration of the Colorado River of the West and Its Tributaries*
(Washington, DC: Government Printing Office, 1875), p. 80.

15. For details of Powell's intellectual development and career as head of the Geographical and Geological Survey of the Rocky Mountain Region (1870–79) and director of both the Bureau of Ethnology (1879–1902) and US Geological Survey (1881–94), see Donald Worster, *A River Running West: The Life of John Wesley Powell* (New York: Oxford University Press, 2001).

16. Clarence E. Dutton, *The Tertiary History of the Grand Cañon District, with Atlas* (Washington, DC: Government Printing Office, 1882), p. 150.

17. George Wharton James, *Arizona the Wonderland* (Boston: The Page Company, 1917), p. 98.

18. Quoted in Eliza McFeely, *Zuni and the American Imagination* (New York: Hill and Wang, 2001), p. 85.

19. This discussion draws on Curtis M. Hinsley, *The Smithsonian Institution and the American Indian: Making a Moral Anthropology in Victorian America* (Washington, DC: Smithsonian Institution Press, 1994), chapter 7; and McFeely, *Zuni and the American Imagination*, pp. 75–110.

20. Frank Hamilton Cushing, "My Adventures in Zuñi," in *Zuñi: Selected Writings of Frank Hamilton Cushing*, ed. Jesse Green (Lincoln: University of Nebraska Press, 1979), p. 70.

21. Susan Wallace, *The Land of the Pueblos* (New York: John B. Alden, 1888), p. 94.

22. *Indian Detour* (New York and Chicago: Rand McNally and Company, 1926), p. 6. An extensive literature discusses the growth in popularity of the Southwest in the late nineteenth and early twentieth centuries. See, for instance, Dilworth, *Imagining Indians in the Southwest*; Audrey Goodman, *Translating Southwestern Landscapes: The Making of an Anglo Literary Region* (Tucson: University of Arizona Press, 2002); and Martin Padget, *Indian Country: Travels in the American Southwest, 1840–1935* (Albuquerque: University of New Mexico Press, 2004).

23. Charles Fletcher Lummis, *Letters from the Southwest*, ed. James W. Byrkit (Tucson: University of Arizona Press, 1989), p. 97.

24. See Charles Fletcher Lummis, "The Spanish-American Face," *Land of Sunshine* 2:2 (January 1895), pp. 20–21.

25. Quoted in Mabel Dodge Luhan, *Movers and Shakers* (Albuquerque: University of New Mexico Press, 1985), p. 534.

26. Mabel Dodge Luhan, *Edge of Taos Desert: An Escape to Reality* (Albuquerque: University of New Mexico Press, 1987), p. 193. Also see Lois Rudnick, *Mabel Dodge Luhan: New Woman, New Worlds* (Albuquerque: University of New Mexico Press, 1984).

27. Mary Austin, *The Land of Journey's Ending* (Tucson: University of Arizona Press, 1983), p. 187.

28. For discussion of Dodge and Austin as expatriates, see Lois Rudnick, "Re-Naming the Land: Anglo Expatriate Women in the Southwest," in *The Desert Is No Lady: Southwestern Landscapes in Women's Writing and Art*, ed. Vera Norwood and Janice Monk (Tucson: University of Arizona Press, 1997), pp. 10–26. Also see Augusta Fink, *I-Mary: A Biography of Mary Austin* (Tucson: University of Arizona Press, 1983).

29. D.H. Lawrence, *Mornings in Mexico* and *Etruscan Places* (Harmondsworth: Penguin, 1960), p. 70.

30. For a discussion that focuses on Lawrence's period in New Mexico, see Tamara M. Teale, "Beyond Purity and Pollution: D.H. Lawrence on the Edge of Taos," *Studies in Travel Writing* 4 (2000), pp. 54–77. Also see Paul Fussell, *Abroad: British Literary Traveling between the Wars* (New York: Oxford University Press, 1980), pp. 141–64.

31. D.H. Lawrence, "Just Back from the Snake-Dance – Tired Out," in *Spud Johnson and Laughing Horse*, ed. Sharyn Udall (Albuquerque: University of New Mexico Press, 1994), p. 359.

32. For discussions of representations of the Hopi Snake Dance, see Dilworth, *Imagining Indians in the Southwest*, pp. 21–75; and Padget, *Indian Country*, pp. 174–93.

33. Thomas Kenneally, *The Place Where Souls Are Born: A Journey into the American Southwest* (London: Hodder and Stoughton, 1992), p. xix.

34. Melanie McGrath, *Motel Nirvana: Dreaming of the New Age in the American Desert* (London: HarperCollins, 1995), p. 85.

II

AMERICANS ABROAD

6

ALFRED BENDIXEN

American travel books about Europe before the Civil War

During the early years of the nation and throughout much of the nineteenth century, patriotic Americans often deplored the idea of foreign travel. Even Washington Irving, who spent much of his adult life abroad and did more than any other author to establish the conventions of American travel writing about Europe, proclaimed in his *A Tour on the Prairies* (1835): "We send our youth abroad to grow luxurious and effeminate in Europe; it appears to me, that a previous tour on the prairies would be more likely to produce that manliness, simplicity, and self-dependence, most in unison with our political institutions."[1] Yet, Americans were eager to learn about the lands from which they were now separated by a revolution as well as an ocean. As citizens of the new world they were fascinated with what the old one had to offer: the chance to view the monuments to history, to gaze at great works of art, to visit sights associated with great writers, to wander through the graveyards and ruins of the past, and to ponder the meanings inherent in the symbols of other cultures. European travel was thus both attractive and dangerous for Americans throughout the early national period and the years leading up to the Civil War.

The contradictory impulses underlying American travel in Europe during this time can be summed up by noting that almost every major American author made a statement condemning, ridiculing, or at least questioning the idea of foreign travel, and almost every one of them produced at least one travel book. The most famous example is probably Emerson, who labeled traveling "a fool's paradise" in his famous remark in "Self-Reliance," and then spent years writing *English Traits* (1856). The travel books Americans produced about Europe in this period reflect, and sometimes attempt to reconcile, contradictory impulses: a nationalistic aversion to praising anything foreign, undemocratic, and un-American; and an aesthetic desire to affirm and celebrate the achievements of art and culture embodied in European scenes.

The dominant note of most American travel writing about Europe before 1865 is a strong sense of nationalism, which sometimes emerges in savage criticism of European scenes, individuals, and values, but most often assumes gentler and more humorous forms. Today we often assume that the traveler goes abroad to learn something and to be transformed by the experience of travel, but the antebellum American was often suspicious of any transformative experience arising out of travel abroad or foreign influences. The goal of travel and of travel writing thus became a greater appreciation of one's own home and country. The antebellum American travel writer is generally more likely to lecture than to learn, more likely to preach the gospel of nationalism than to become a convert to foreign enthusiasms of any kind. These underlying biases shape what their travel books cover and what they exclude. For instance, we know that many travelers went abroad for their health, and that it was common for well-to-do New England ministers to travel abroad to recover from overwork and attain some kind of physical and psychic renewal. Nevertheless, the travel writings they produce never turn to the obvious underlying metaphors of their experiences, never suggest that Europe could be a healthier place than America, or that foreign travel has offered some redemptive experience not available at home. The nationalism of antebellum American writing closes off certain aspects of travel from honest consideration.

In some cases, the travel writer clearly knows what he is going to say about a particular foreign scene before he leaves home. Indeed, two of our most important writers of the early national period, Royall Tyler and James Kirke Paulding, actually wrote travel books about England without ever going abroad. Tyler's *The Yankey in London* (1809) and Paulding's *A Sketch of Old England, by a New England Man* (1822) lack the descriptive detail one expects from the genre, but in their basic assumptions and arguments they are remarkably like many of the genuine books of travel by Americans that appeared throughout the early nineteenth century. For both authors, the central target is the British travel writer who has dared to criticize American scenes and democratic values. In the first half of the nineteenth century, Americans frequently satirize the British traveler for being dull-witted, narrow-minded, and incapable of traveling wisely. Much of this apparent animosity stems from the offense Americans took at the writings by British travelers who remained sharply critical of the United States until the 1850s.[2] Thus, Tyler emphasizes the eagerness of the British to criticize other nations while remaining blind to their own faults. He even tells of an English traveler who could not tolerate America's sunny weather and had to seek relief in a blacksmith's shop, where he found the smoky air that reminded him of a London fog. However, he assures us that his attacks on the British are not serious, for if they were, he ironically remarks, "I should abhor myself, and feel degraded from the rank of intelligent beings, and reduced to a level with *English travellers*."³ Americans make fun of British travelers in their books on Italy and France as well as in their works on England.

Tyler assumes the role of the good-natured and somewhat innocent American traveler whose travels lead him to a comic assessment of the British. Thus he goes to the House of Commons with high expectations of discovering "the talents, the learning, the wisdom of a wise nation collected in one brilliant focus" (*The Yankey in London*, p. 18) but discovers vulgar men talking about horse races. He is so shocked that he proclaims: "I felt the dignity of my nature violated. I felt more – I remembered I was of English descent, and I blushed for the land of my ancestors" (pp. 27–28). In the House of Lords, he finds "a subject abstruse in itself . . . rendered more so by eloquence of the learned counsel" (p. 204). The sights of British government present a perversion of rational principles so great that the Yankee's appreciation of his own government grows. Tyler prefigures later American travel books in both his nationalistic stance and his adoption of another role characteristic of the form: the traveling moralist whose experience of foreign scenes leads him to muse on human vanity and folly. He goes on to mock foreign fashions in dress and has many sharp remarks to make about contemporary British language and writing. He also has an intriguing chapter defending literary hoaxes, arguing that the merit of the work is more important than its origin. While Tyler's book is itself a literary hoax, it is also an important and often lively book which anticipates later non-fiction accounts in its merging of moral judgment and satiric comedy into a nationalistic assessment of foreign lands.

In Paulding's longer and less successful two-volume *A Sketch of Old England*, comedy soon gives way to a dull and vituperative tract on the political and literary decay of England. Nevertheless, his sometimes vicious criticisms reflect many of the conventions of nationalistic travel writing. He begins by assuring the reader that he will correct the overly generous judgments of other American writers, a statement that reflects a clear assault on the writings of Washington Irving with whom Paulding once collaborated on the *Salmagundi Papers* (1807–08), but is also part of the antebellum convention in which American travel books reject other works of travel as dishonest. This honest traveler thus affirms his own integrity while also emphasizing the need for Americans to free themselves from the corrupting influences of Europe. Paulding's strategy typifies the nationalistic approach: he asserts that everything good in England is part of the past which Americans can claim as their heritage. He contrasts the glorious heroic past – "the time, or perhaps just before, our ancestors came to Plymouth" – with a shabby present marked by "profligate kings, a dissipated nobility, a lazy and luxurious clergy, a paper system, and unexampled taxes" to conclude: "Every day, and every country I visit, add to my affection for my home, and my attachment to a republican form of government."[4]

Like most American travelers, Paulding emphasizes the superiority of his own land's natural beauty, ironically remarking: "Far be it from me to flout these people for not having larger rivers, higher mountains, finer waterfalls, and broader lakes. They cannot help it" (*A Sketch of Old England*, vol. I, p. 60). He discovers nothing picturesque in the landscape except the presence of beggars and assails those who admire the great aristocratic homes whose "walls were reared upon the miseries of thousands" (vol. I, p. 22). He finds the British people to be cold, greedy, selfish, and dishonest, and he even wonders whether it is the rotten weather or their habit of drinking beer that gives them "that peculiar cast of bluff and gruff stupidity" (vol. I, p. 25). He provides lengthy praise for British literature from the time of Shakespeare to that of the Augustans, which affirmed both liberty and simplicity, but has only harsh words for contemporary British writing, which has foolishly glorified feudal customs, aristocracy, and other absurdities, instead of defending morality and freedom. This is an argument that will reappear in later travel books by many other Americans, including Longfellow and Emerson.

These fictional works suggest the limitations of the nationalistic writer who is so closed to foreign influences that he can produce a travel book without traveling. However, these works also remind us that the boundaries between fact and fiction may be very fluid, and that the literary skill of the writer and the mastery of specific conventions may be more important in travel writing than the actual experience of the traveler. After the success of *Innocents Abroad* (1869), Mark Twain actually hired someone to do the traveling for him for a series, "Around the World," that he published in the *Buffalo Express*; the traveler, D.R. Ford, sent back factual details that Twain would then work into a more literary form. Twain hoped to continue this procedure for a book about a journey to the African diamond mines, but the person he sent to gather the material died on route.[5] Marietta Holley also produced a successful series of fictional works about the adventures of Samantha Allen and her family, including such best-sellers as *Samantha at Saratoga* (1887) and *Samantha in Europe* (1895), many of which involved travel to sites that Holley herself never saw.

Not all of the antebellum travel books Americans produced reflected an awareness of literary form. Some were little more than collections of rough notes, or diary sketches, or unpolished letters sent home. For instance, the five volumes of James Fenimore Cooper's *Gleanings in Europe* (1836–38) lack any real sense of coherence, consisting largely of unrevised letters that occasionally express a shrewd insight but more often give way to bad temper. Cooper was one of the few travel writers who managed to insult both Americans and Europeans. Thus, his volume on England states that British women "speak with great precision and beauty, though they often appear cold and repulsive," and that "the American press is highly creditable to the American nation, corrupt, ignorant, and vulgar as so much of it notoriously is."[6] His *Gleanings* sold badly and largely deserved the bad reviews they received.

Those writers who recognized the importance of working the material of travel into a coherent form with a polished style usually relied on the conventions established by Washington Irving in *The Sketch Book of Geoffrey Crayon, Gent.* (1819–20), one of the first great American best-sellers. He published *The Sketch Book* in parts, each of which offered a mixture of sentiment and comedy, tales and essays. The result was a loosely organized collection of pieces held together primarily through the genial personality of Irving's persona, Geoffrey Crayon. The descriptions of English scenes and the meditations that those scenes inspire make up over three-fourths of *The Sketch Book* and established the basic literary strategies for many of the travel writers that followed him. Although many antebellum American travel books about Europe are more nationalistic and thus more critical of Europe than Irving, they often share his tendency to glorify peaceful rural scenes and to lapse into sentimentality, as well as his fascination with aesthetic issues and scenes associated with famous authors. The pseudonym of "Geoffrey Crayon, Gent." must be regarded as an assertion of American capabilities, as a rejection of foreign critiques of American vulgarity and crudeness, and an insistence that citizens of the new democracy possessed the refinement needed to appreciate and judge the achievements of European culture. Although Irving's graceful style provided the foundation for the sentimental, superficial, and genteel writing that dominates much of later nineteenth-century American literature, *The Sketch Book* is actually much more complex than most scholars have recognized. The character of Geoffrey Crayon is built around a series of contradictions: he is the bachelor who affirms the value of wife, home, and family; the traveler who longs for a settled life; the antiquarian who mocks a pedantic interest in the past; the lover of dreams and escapes who knows that dreams are not real and that escapes are impossible.[7] Whatever Crayon is, he is not simple.

And his views of England are also not simple. Many of the comments in his introductory sketch, "The Author's Account of Himself," are consistent with the values found in more overtly nationalistic travel writing. Thus, Irving offers a paragraph of florid prose to show that "never need an

American look beyond his own country for the sublime and beautiful of natural scenery."[8] When he goes on to describe the attractions of foreign scenes, he incorporates the nationalistic assertion of America's "youthful promise" and the implication that the English qualities he treasures – "the charms of storied and poetical association" – belong to the past and not to the present (*The Sketch Book*, p. 9).

Furthermore, Irving's meditations on "quaint peculiarities," "mouldering stones," "ruined castles," and "falling towers" lead inevitably to his great theme of mutability, which involves a deflation of all human pretension. Some of that is directed at the traveler, at Geoffrey Crayon himself, but much of it is also aimed at European pretensions. It is hard to mistake the mocking tone when he declares that: "I will visit this land of wonders and see the gigantic race from which I am degenerated" (p. 9). It is easier to miss the process of ironic deflation in essays which, on the surface, seem filled with genuine admiration. For instance, "Westminster Abbey" ultimately concludes that monuments to cultural achievements are really just "a treasury of humiliation; a huge pile of reiterated homilies on the emptiness of renown, and the certainty of oblivion!" (p. 141). Irving and other American travelers found the theme of mutability appealing because it enabled them to engage in a process of meditation that both establishes the refined sensibility of the traveler and makes the monuments to foreign accomplishments less intimidating to citizens of a new country that could boast of few monuments and few accomplishments.

Although Irving is more ambivalent and less of an Anglophile than most scholars have suggested, he clearly prizes one aspect of English life: the sense of stability, home, and family that he affirms throughout the book, particularly in scenes dealing with rural life. Later travel writers would follow Irving in contrasting the European appreciation of leisure that takes life more patiently, slowly, and fully with the haste of American commercial life. They would also join Irving in admiring the strong European sense of home and family that was supported by generations of the same family living in the same place. Even very nationalistic voices acknowledged that the great mobility of American life hampered the development of family tradition and often admired the greater devotion to home and family that they found in much of Europe.

For American authors, the travel book provided a special means of affirming the importance of artistic creation for a nation devoted to commerce and more practical matters. Thus, Crayon is pleased to note that visitors to Westminster Abbey show more reverence for the memorials to poets than to warriors or rulers. Irving's affirmation of the literary artist also underlies his comments on "the charms of storied and poetical association," an allusion to the common belief that the value of any particular site depends largely on specific historical or literary associations. In other words, writers give meaning to landscapes that would otherwise be uninteresting. Irving's literary essays often confront his own anxieties about the place of the artist in commerce-loving America. In "Roscoe," he speaks of the Liverpool banker who authored a famous history, explicitly noting the relevance for "the citizens of our young and busy country, where literature and the elegant arts must grow up side by side with the coarse plants of daily necessity" (p. 17). "A Royal Poet" turns King James I of Scotland into something of a democrat who was also the first to cultivate the literary genius of his people and win them to an appreciation of "the gay, the elegant, and the gentle arts" (p. 77). His famous essay, "Stratford-on-Avon," emphasizes the way that Shakespeare left his home town in disgrace but returned in triumph as the result of his literary achievements – as Irving himself clearly hoped to do. It also suggests that the young Shakespeare drew crucial inspiration from his apparently aimless wandering in rural scenes and shared many of the same values that mark *The Sketch Book*. Thus, his various portrayals of writers are really veiled self-portraits that address Irving's own specific fears and ambitions.

Scholars have not yet paid sufficient attention to the way that travel books enable authors to articulate a set of literary values and aspirations. Irving not only put Stratford-on-Avon on the map of sites that must be seen by American tourists, but also made the literary pilgrimage into an important part of travel books. In the process of visiting a scene associated with a famous writer, the traveler demonstrates that he possesses sufficient poetic sensibility to understand the sources of inspiration that lead to great art and to interpret the qualities that define the true artist. In his meditations, the traveler partakes imaginatively in the act of artistic creation, defines the qualities that make art great, and thus affirms a set of aesthetic values. The literary pilgrimage thus often becomes a peculiar combination of literary manifesto and veiled autobiography that reveals more about the travel writer than the purported subject.

Irving established the basic conventions of the literary travel book about Europe: a series of familiar essays with a good-natured narrator who balances an appreciation of the European past with a nationalistic affirmation of the American future and offers both moments of genial humor and serious moralizing. Most of Irving's later works offered more fiction than travel material. *Bracebridge Hall* (1822) unsuccessfully attempts to stretch out some of the material from *The Sketch Book* into an excuse for the telling of tales. In *Tales of a Traveller* (1824), the travel material is reduced to a handful of pages. *The Alhambra* (1832) offers a great deal of graceful description, but the heart of that book consists of the Spanish legends that Irving skillfully retells. Irving eventually wrote a travel book about America, *A Tour on the Prairies* (1835), but his main influence on American travel writing rests almost entirely on *The Sketch Book*.

Irving's influence is clearest in Henry Wadsworth Longfellow's *Outre-Mer: A Pilgrimage Beyond the Sea* (1835), Donald G. Mitchell's *Fresh Gleanings* (1847), and Henry T. Tuckerman's *The Italian Sketch Book* (1835; revised and expanded 1837 and 1848), all of which contain fiction as well as travel writing. While Longfellow's decision to establish his literary career with a work modeled on Irving is understandable, it was also unfortunate. In preparation for his position as Professor of Modern Languages at Bowdoin College, he spent much of 1826–29 in Europe, mostly France, Spain, and Italy. The letters he wrote home were lively and graceful, and should have provided the foundation for a good travel book.[9] Instead of relying on them, however, he spent years producing a book that was ultimately too self-consciously literary and artificial, too much a clumsy imitation of Irving. Although he ultimately abandoned the persona of "The Schoolmaster" that he used for the first magazine publications of his travel writing, there is, as Newton Arvin has noted, "something curiously unyouthful" about this work.[10] One might extend this remark and note that there is something curiously unyouthful about most of the American travel writing about Europe during the entire antebellum period. The writer usually does not present himself as a young man whose travels lead to some kind of initiation, but as an older man, a sage who lectures and moralizes. The best travel works of the period are often by older individuals, established writers who feel more comfortable with the role of the sage. Although marred by clumsy moralizing and sentimentality, *Outre-Mer* refuses to subject European sights to a nationalistic, and frequently provincial, critique. For Longfellow, "the old World was a kind of Holy Land" (vol. I, p. 9), and his travel was both a pilgrimage and the start of a lifelong endeavor to make Americans appreciate the achievements of European literature.

Donald G. Mitchell's *Fresh Gleanings; or, a New Sheaf from the Old Fields of Continental Europe* was also designed to launch a literary career. Mitchell, who wrote under the pseudonym, Ik. Marvel, was a superb stylist whose later *Reveries of a Bachelor* (1850) and *Dream Life* (1851) established him as one of the most popular authors of his time. His narrator is a weak man in poor health, easily intimidated, and too good-natured to complain, even when being cheated by guides, innkeepers, and merchants. Instead of the nationalistic prejudices that mark much antebellum American travel writing about Europe, we have Ik. Marvel's genial admiration of the scenes he visits, especially rural scenes that evoke a sentimental affirmation of home and pleasant memories of his own Connecticut farm. Nowhere in American travel writing about Europe is there a stronger pastoral impulse than that manifested in his continuous glorification of peaceful and quiet rural life as a rebuke to the commercial haste that seemed to mark life in the United States. The book is also distinguished by its focus on such rarely visited sites as the Island of Jersey, the towns of the French countryside, Hungary, and Austria and Holland, but the longest and most vivid of its five sections explores "The World of Paris." Mitchell asserts that the good traveler will shun guidebooks and explore out of the way scenes with the hope of understanding and appreciating different modes of life. There are a few moments of analysis when Ik. Marvel comments on national characteristics, but the strength of the book comes from vivid descriptions and character sketches that illustrate various features of common life abroad and capture some of the humorous moments inherent in travel.

Henry T. Tuckerman has been largely and unjustly forgotten. His most important work is *America and Her Commentators: With a Critical Sketch of Travel in the United States* (1864), a long study of the most important foreign writings on antebellum America, but he also produced important books about Italy, England, and France. He began his literary career in 1835 with the first edition of *The Italian Sketch Book*, a slim volume that he enlarged and revised until it grew into the substantial work of over 400 pages in the third edition of 1848. His love for Italy was so great that it also shaped his poetry and *Isabel; or Sicily* (1839), a prose work blending travel material with the romance. The first edition of *The Italian Sketch Book* contained an introduction that explicitly defined the ideal traveler as a genial optimist whose travels both reaffirm his faith in humanity and enlarge his appreciation of art and antiquity. Tuckerman's traveler will not allow the appearance of poverty and injustice to prevent him from valuing scenes rich in poetic sentiment and will not see ruins as signs of decay but as evidence of the capacity of the human spirit to achieve greatness. The third and final edition of *The Italian Sketch Book* incorporated the more nationalistic and more critical essays on Italian scenes that Tuckerman originally published in *Rambles and Reveries* (1841) but largely maintains this commitment to an optimistic and generous assessment. While other Americans assailed political despotism in Italy and severely criticized the Catholic Church, he emphasizes the natural beauty of the landscape, the rich heritage of artistic achievement, and the honest vitality of its people. His final and most important chapter of the book, "Modern Italy," is an ambitious attempt to redefine the proper American outlook, which, he asserts, should discover cause for political hope in this land's rich artistic heritage: "The energy, the tact, the sentiment that once made her great, whose symbols are yet in her bosom, fascinating the stranger's gaze, now in the grandeur of a temple, and anon in the smile of a Virgin, here in the grim Tuscan's verse, and there in Angelo's marble outline – still exist in the very blood of her sons."[11]

For Tuckerman, travel provided an opportunity to escape from the prosaic nineteenth century into a more poetic world and travel writing was a means to praise the enduring power of art and literature, themes that are crucial to his *A Month in England* (1853), a collection of nine essays focusing on literary and historical associations. In many respects, Tuckerman is quite representative of characteristic American attitudes, particularly in his affection for the British writers of the past "who are our intellectual ancestry"[12] and his fascination with exploring the conditions that produce great literature. Tuckerman notes that each land has a distinctive appeal for the traveler: "In Greece, it was especially architecture and statuary; in Italy, it is painting; in Germany, music; in France, military glory; in America, scenery; and in London, literature" (p. 98). When he attempts to explain the flourishing of British literature, however, he ends up concluding that the presence of social injustice and inequality provides the novelist with abundant material while the unpleasant climate makes outdoor life impossible and encourages the solitary labor of literary production. The achievement of British literature thus rests on some unpleasant facts.

The ambiguity behind Tuckerman's view of England – his love for scenes associated with a literary past and his contrasting criticism of the social and political realities of the present – is quite characteristic of antebellum American travel writing. In his chapter "The Drudge and the Duke" Tuckerman asserts that "the English laborer lacks both the Italian's ability to enjoy the charms of his climate and the American's ability to hope that toil will eventually lead to prosperity" and concludes that even a poetic temperament will feel a reformer's impulse when he sees "a beautiful girl's finger worn to the bone by the process of making steel pens, or a weaver's eyes fevered with rebellious speculations as he bends such hollow and pallid cheeks over the never-resting loom" (pp. 77–78). Tuckerman suggests that the American will be troubled by British arrogance and the way a concern with money and power pushes aside other, more poetic values, but also feel an ongoing affection for the land that produced Shakespeare and other wonderful writers. This kind of ambiguity runs throughout many of the most thoughtful American antebellum travel books about England, especially those by Hawthorne and Emerson.

Tuckerman's *Maga Papers About Paris* (1867) relies less on personal experience and more on biting social and political commentary. His central metaphor portrays France as a theater: he views French life as an entertaining spectacle filled with beauty and grace but devoid of natural and honest feeling:

> The social economy of Paris is based on a combination of narrow means with bright conceptions; we see it in the graceful but frail upholstery; the exquisite fit of a plain muslin robe, the bewitching trim of a cheap bonnet, the variety of a two-franc dinner, the *bon-mot* which atones for the inability to read, the absorption over a game of dominos, the philosophic air with which a cigarette is smoked, and the elitist ruffle of a chemisette; the prolific fun educed from an anecdote, and the light impression made by a revolution; the incurious notice of what is comprehensive, and the intense desire to make capital of the frivolous.[13]

Once again, Tuckerman's views are typical. There is a strong anti-French attitude in much of the American travel writing of this period that seems to stem partly from a feeling that France had failed to uphold the American revolutionary tradition, had failed to prove that democratic republics were superior forms of government. The violence and instability of French political life seemed to challenge the validity of American political theories. Travel writers generally agreed with Tuckerman that the real problem was not democratic principles but the French, who were too frivolous to make democracy work.

The nationalistic bias that marks Tuckerman's text assumes a fiercer shape when anti-Catholic bigotry is added to the mix. American travel writing about Europe probably played a significant role in the development of the anti-Catholic prejudices and condemnation of foreign influences that led to the formation of the Know Nothing Party of the 1850s. Joel Tyler Headley and Daniel Clarke Eddy were clergymen who wrote best-selling travel books about Europe and also served as state representatives for the Know Nothing Party. Eddy's *Europa: Scenes and Society in England, France, Italy, and Switzerland* (1852), which went through fifty editions by 1860, is actually more of a guidebook than the usual collection of essays. He provides the traveler with much factual information, including the expenses that can be expected, but also details the appropriate patriotic response to European scenes, thus continually assuring the reader of American superiority. Headley produced *Letters from Italy* (1845); *The Alps and the Rhine* (1847), one of the most complete descriptions of Swiss and German scenery in the American travel writing of this period; and *Sketches and Rambles* (1850), a collection of essays on France, England, and Italy. The popularity of Headley's work probably lies in his capacity for extravagant rhetoric and melodrama. For example, his meditations on the French Revolution assume a crudely dramatic form in which God first punishes the French nobles for their oppression by bringing about the violent revolution and then punishes the revolutionaries for their atheism. Headley's God is quite willing to use violence, and he assures us that England, France, and Italy can all expect to be purged. Both Eddy and Headley emphasize a religious focus in their treatment of art, nature, and society. Art is always judged according to whether or not it is consistent with Protestant practices. They both show interest in Switzerland and mountain scenery, which is presented as an opportunity to view the glory of God as represented by natural wonders. Their Swiss travels lead to reflections on how Protestant countries love liberty and to praise of Calvin. Both portray England, France, and Italy as lands of poverty and misery, lands suffering from political injustice, the absurdities of aristocracy, and a lack of moral values. Both condemn the Catholic Church, which is presented as a defender of tyranny, an oppressor of the people, and a violator of all true religious principles.

The same kind of bigotry mars *Notes of Travel and Study in Italy* (1860) by Charles Eliot Norton, one of the most distinguished American scholars of the nineteenth century. Norton attacks Catholic ceremonies as tasteless and vulgar spectacles, compares the glorification of saints and relics to the selling of quack medicine, and denounces Church censorship and the preference of commentary over biblical text. He condemns the selling of indulgences but despairs of change "because, so far as Italy is concerned, there is no freedom of discussion, and men's minds are not stirred with the suggestion of other and more rational forms of beliefs and modes of worship."[14] Norton, who shared Ruskin's belief that art and architecture recorded the spirit of an age and nation, offers Americans a democratic mode of interpreting European art. Thus he discovers both a true fervor of religious faith" and "the prevalence of the democratic element" in the Gothic cathedral (pp. 104–05). He asserts that:

> The spirit of the earlier artists was incongruous with the worldly pomp and selfish display of the capital of the Popes; but Michael Angelo's genius gave just expression to the character of the Papacy in its period of greatest splendor, and Bernini is the fit representative of its weakness and decline . . . Instead of being the minister of truth, the purifier of affections, the revealer of the beauty of God, Art was degraded to the service of ambition and caprice, of luxury and pomp, until it becomes utterly corrupt and false.   (pp. 62–63)

In *Notes of Travel*, both the creation and the interpretation of art become moral and political acts.

For a view of the nationalistic perspective at its most entertaining, one should turn to the books on France and Italy produced by James Jackson

Jarves, who was probably the finest American travel writer of the mid-nineteenth century. As a young man, Jarves left his native New England to seek his fortune in the Hawaiian Islands, but soon demonstrated more talent for writing than business. He edited one of Hawaii's first newspapers and wrote a travel book and a history of Hawaii. His mastery of the skills of journalism and historical research are evident in *Parisian Sights and French Principles, Seen Through American Spectacles* (1852) and its "Second Series" (1855). As a good American traveler, Jarves admires the sights and deplores the principles. But he brings more to his work than national prejudice; he offers portraits of foreign lands unsurpassed for their wealth of detail. More than any other travel writer of his time, Jarves cites statistics, presents facts, and quotes passages from books, documents, and periodicals. Yet his work is also filled with direct observation and detailed analysis. When he offers such conventional fare as the chapter recording everything seen during a stroll, the reader leaves feeling that Jarves has seen more than anyone else would, and that he has usually seen more deeply.

The France that Jarves describes has been torn apart by violence. Having witnessed the bloodshed in Paris during Louis Napoleon's seizure of power, he attempts to explain why: "Though there has been blood enough spilt in France to regenerate a world, it has enriched no soil but that of despotism."[15] Again and again, his amused rationalism gives way to impassioned anger at the bloody crimes committed in France in the name of revolution. His overriding concern with explaining the failure of democratic and republican principles in France provides a thematic unity to his work that is rarely found in the rambling familiar essays that make up many travel books. *Parisian Sights and French Principles* also contains a vivid chapter describing Louis Napoleon's *coup d'état* and another one that details the failure of the National Assembly. Finding that the French are incapable of a democratic republic, Jarves prefers the order imposed by a despot like Louis Napoleon to the violence of the radicals, whose secret societies, conspiratorial aims, and initiation rites he describes in sensationalistic fashion. Like many other Americans, he blames the failure of democratic revolution partly on the Roman Catholic Church, which, he complains, stifles individual judgment and rational thought by emphasizing obedience and implicit faith. He objects to Catholic ritual, because: "Where there is so much machinery and ceremony, there can not fail to be a proportion of tinsel and heartlessness" (p. 72). Insisting that "the religious education of the Americans is at the bottom of their republicanism" (p. 89), Jarves asserts that the moral influence of plain New England churches is more precious than the magnificent appearance of Parisian churches. Nevertheless, Jarves also demonstrates an ability to enjoy Paris as he describes everything from the process of finding an apartment there to the French marriage agencies where "one can order a wife or husband, and have either served up in less time than a new coat" (p. 30). No one is better at delineating the sexual lasciviousness that Paris represented for Americans of this period.

With its blend of precise and thorough description, political analysis, entertaining anecdotes, and mild sensationalism, *Parisian Sights and French Principles* became popular enough to warrant a "Second Series" in 1855 with many illustrations presenting the changes that Paris underwent as Baron Haussman demolished its narrow winding streets and installed wide boulevards. The essays, and those that comprised his next book on Italy, also appeared in *Harper's Monthly*, where they attracted a wide readership. The "Second Series" relies less on statistics and analysis and more on historical material, abstract statement, and narrative.

Jarves' finest travel writing appears in *Italian Sights and Papal Principles, Seen Through American Spectacles* (1856). Jarves is still the precise observer and meticulous reporter, the social analyst and the moral critic, the gatherer of the amusing and the scandalous. His American spectacles remain firmly in place as he condemns the Papal Government and criticizes the Roman Catholic Church, but Italy inspired his genuine devotion and his best prose. He is still the reliable advisor who alerts us to the inconveniences of renting a palace in Florence, the treacherousness of the climate, the social necessity of a carriage and box at the opera, but he now tends to convey the experience of travel through dramatic situations in which he is participant as well as observer. No other American travel writer has done a better job of dramatizing the frustrations and inconveniences of travel, of portraying the abuses and overcharges of custom officials and the ignorance and interference of guides. With these people, the traveler must engage in a battle of wits that has elements of the confidence game and perhaps a hint of the mock heroic, but Jarves extends the satire to those who debase travel into the "frigid duty" of "Sight-seeing," those who "neither study, examine, nor look" and simply wish to be able to say: "They have been there."[16] The party of "sight-seers" become the cast of a comedy:

> It consisted of a young lady, who preferred youthful beaus to old ruins; a fashionable matron, who would like to see what fashionable people want to see – but in as ladylike a manner as possible, and who much preferred the use of her own tongue to that of another; a young gentleman, to whom every thing but cards and suppers, and talking were unmitigated bores; and your humble servant, who went because it would have been so stupid to have staid behind. (p. 139)

Jarves also mocks the "guide, who pointing to the lake, gravely informed us that it was a lake" (p. 140) and undercuts much of the romantic pretensions associated with Italian travel.

Comedy is not the only literary mode Jarves has mastered. There is a tragic tone underlying much of the best descriptive writing in this book. His finest piece of writing is the long essay describing his visit to Pompeii, which moves from the conventional act of solitary meditation on the significance of the ruins to a powerful imaginative re-creation of the volcanic eruption and the acts of courage and despair of the city's doomed inhabitants. "Rome that Was and Is" vividly describes the physical wasteland surrounding the city as an emblem of its moral and economic decay: "Real Rome is dirty, comfortless, and torpid; the home of beggars, indolence, and superstition" (p. 351). "A Dream of Venice" offers one of the best Ruskinesque analyses of architecture and history produced by an American. His comments on art and architecture throughout the volume represent a rare achievement in the travel writing of this period – criticism that is both thoughtful and entertaining. Much of the book discusses the past, including vivid chapters on the origins of the charitable society, the *Misericordia*, and on Savonarola, the fervent priest whose violent quest for political freedom led to his execution. Over a quarter of the book focuses on Holy Week in Rome, with the description of the ceremony serving as a vehicle for the usual American and Protestant attacks on lavish spectacle. He argues that the Catholic Church opposes the development of democratic ideals: "Their intent is not to make citizens, but to make subjects – to train disciples, and not masters" (pp. 310–11). Nevertheless, he expresses great admiration for the Italian people, who possess "lively imaginations, quick perceptions, and great elasticity of spirit, with a natural taste for the beautiful" (p. 53). Jarves loved Italy so much that he spent the rest of his life there and eventually removed his American spectacles. In 1883, he produced another travel book, *Italian Rambles*, in which he almost completely reverses his position, emphasizing how much Americans could and should learn from Italy. The change in political perspective says something about Jarves but it also reflects the greater cosmopolitanism that marked American life after the Civil War.

Although the dominant force behind American travel writing about Europe in the antebellum period is a defensive nationalism, other kinds of books also attracted popularity and merit some attention. The chatty and gossipy essays that Nathaniel Parker Willis produced under the title, *Pencillings by the Way* (1835; expanded edition 1844), and reprinted under a variety of titles, boasted of being "eminently superficial" and of not relying on "*inquiry, study*, and *reflection*."[17] What he offered his readers were the first impressions of a skillful observer who gains access to the fashionable and famous, and records their conversations and actions. His mastery of the art of name-dropping and his indiscretion are clearly represented in the following passage:

> Bulwer was very badly dressed, as usual, and wore a flashy waistcoat of the same description as D'Israeli's. Count D'Orsay was very splendid, but very undefinable. He seemed showily dressed till you looked to particulars, and then it seemed only a simple thing, well fitted to a very magnificent person. Lord Albert Cunyngham was a dandy of common materials; and my Lord Durham, though he looked a young man, if he passed for a lord at all in America, would pass for a very ill-dressed one.[18]

The book also contains some description of scenery and famous sights and occasionally rises above the superficial (most notably in his accounts of the cholera epidemic in Paris and of the influx of refugees from Poland), but the portraits of famous contemporaries gave the book its popularity in the nineteenth century and whatever historical value it still possesses.

Among those inspired by Willis was Bayard Taylor, who grew up with two goals: he wanted to be a poet and he wanted to travel. In 1844, at the age of nineteen, he published his first volume of poetry and sailed for Europe with only $140 and some commissions for travel letters from several newspapers. After two years of traveling around Europe, usually by foot and always cheaply, he returned to the United States and published *Views-a-Foot* (1846), which went through six editions during the first year and twenty editions by 1855, when Taylor revised the book for a uniform edition of his *Travels*. By then, he had already established himself as America's best-known professional travel writer, with journeys to Africa, Asia Minor, and the Far East as well as to the gold mines of California, which led to his most important book, *El Dorado* (1850). His writings about Europe appear in *Views-a-Foot, By-Ways of Europe* (1869) and in some of the essays collected in the two series of *At Home and Abroad* (1859 and 1862). Unfortunately, these are not very good books: one of his contemporaries aptly noted that: "Bayard Taylor has travelled more and seen less than any man living."[19] His writings capture some of the thrill of visiting foreign lands but offer little more than superficial description along with the conventional patriotic and anti-Catholic assessments. What was not conventional was the bold idea of the walking tour and of seeing Europe inexpensively. The chapter of practical advice added to the eighth edition contains a list of expenses, showing that it was possible to spend two years in Europe for less than 500 dollars; it suggests that one could travel from Milan to Genoa for only sixty cents and spend five weeks in Paris for only fifteen dollars.

Views-a-Foot was proof that youthful enthusiasm, determination, and the American spirit of self-reliance could overcome all obstacles including a lack of money.

One of the most remarkable books is Cyrus Augustus Bartol's *Pictures of Europe Framed in Ideas* (1855). A Unitarian minister and minor figure in the Transcendentalist movement, Bartol offers a series of sermons that attempt to develop a theory of travel. He was not an original thinker, and he was not afraid to contradict himself, but his book aptly sums up many of the ideas underlying American travel writing. Thus, the first essay, "Abroad and at Home," explains how travel is only valuable when it brings the pilgrim to a greater appreciation of home and country. American clergymen tended to have a greater interest in describing natural scenery than other travelers to Europe and they tended to read nature, as Bartol puts it, as "a book of prayer, a service of praise."[20] He devotes an entire chapter to "The Beauty of the World" and another hundred pages, about a quarter of the book, to specific chapters delineating the metaphorical and theological implications of mountains, rivers, lakes, and the sea. Much of his book, however, affirms his faith in progress, which he calls the true "theology of travel" (pp. 160–61). His essentially Hegelian view of history allows him to read the history of violence written on the battlefields of Europe as evidence of a world moving inevitably towards peace. A number of chapters deal with the role of religion, sometimes affirming the value of a universal religious reverence inherent in human nature and expressed in religious art and architecture, and, at other times, extolling the superiority of the plain puritan heritage and deploring the failures of the Catholic Church. *Pictures of Europe* has been largely ignored but it deserves attention as a neglected document of Transcendentalism and as a valuable guide to American intellectual history.

In addition to having a greater interest in natural scenery, especially mountain scenery that seemed imbued with the grandeur of God, American clergymen also tended to be more interested in Germany, apparently because it was the land of Luther and the Reformation. While the works of Headley and Eddy demonstrate an enormous capacity for intolerance, the travel books by members of the liberal clergy seem to be among the most appreciative and least prejudicial of American travel writers. Bartol provides the clearest guide to their attitudes and beliefs, but they are also exemplified in James Freeman Clarke's *Eleven Weeks in Europe* (1852), which is both typical and undistinguished, and Harriet Beecher Stowe's *Sunny Memories of Foreign Lands* (1854), which includes extracts from the diary of her brother, the Rev. Charles Beecher, and which shows a fine mind confronting important political, religious, and aesthetic issues.

For most nationalistic travelers, European condemnations of American slavery simply represented national prejudice and reflected the hypocritical delight foreigners took in attacking an American institution while ignoring their own more serious social problems. Stowe's triumphal tour of England raised similar criticisms in the American press, forcing her to go to great lengths throughout her travel book to defend the warmth, integrity, and sincerity of both the British anti-slavery movement and of the British people. *Sunny Memories* thus provides one of the most positive pictures of Great Britain in American travel books of this time. Her British are kind and generous people, and their anti-slavery commitment simply reflects the love of freedom that unites both England and the United States. Stowe's desire to read the world in religious terms appears most clearly in her meditations on ruins and in her descriptions of the Alps, but her work also features a number of comic moments devoted to the irritations of travel and to the absurdity of relics. Although she has some problems in finding nice things to say about the French, Stowe is among the most tolerant and generous of American writers. Her work also frequently deals with aesthetic issues, especially when she describes works of art or visits scenes associated with great writers. In fact, it would be easy to extract a literary manifesto from her travel writing. She consistently prefers works that express religious ideas forcefully and passionately to more polished but less moving works, qualities she discovers in Shakespeare, whose family life she reconstructs "as a sort of Elizabethan counterpart" to her own upbringing.[21] Her quest for a painting that will move her to some higher awareness of life is finally resolved when she views a work by Rubens, whose power, she asserts, "forces you to accept and forgive a thousand excesses."[22] For Stowe, the travel book was a vehicle for defining and affirming the aesthetic, religious, and political values that mattered most to her.

The attack on slavery also plays a role in books produced by two African Americans during the antebellum period. William Wells Brown's *The American Fugitive in Europe; Sketches of Places and People Abroad* (1855), a revised and expanded version of *Three Years in Europe* (1852), contains numerous anti-slavery comments, but the main goal seems to be to prove that a freed slave is capable of traveling wisely and writing gracefully. It views both the English and French positively, emphasizing their abhorrence of slavery and their willingness to treat him as a human being and not as a piece of property. There are some vivid moments assailing slavery, perhaps most notably when a customs inspector is shocked to find slave shackles in his luggage, and some passages devoted explicitly to racial issues, such as the depiction of the remarkable Joseph Jenkins, a black man who thrives in Europe by assuming a variety of jobs and roles. Nevertheless, Brown's account of visits to famous people and famous sights is surprisingly conventional in its choice of subjects and its comments. Completely unconventional is David F. Dorr's *A Colored Man Round the World* (1858), which merges attacks on racial injustice and a remarkable fascination with the exotic and the erotic. Dorr offers the most sexually charged and sexually explicit account of travel in France and the Middle East in American travel writing. His behavior is often surprising and sometimes outrageous, including the moment in the chapter "The Dogs Provoke me, and the Women are Veiled" where he discovers he cannot buy a certain woman in Constantinople for twenty-five dollars because he is not a Mohammedan. Dorr was technically a slave during his travels but he adopts the perspective of a free New Orleans gentleman who views life abroad as an excuse for hedonistic pleasures. His book is an amazing and entertaining aberration in both the worlds of American travel writing and abolitionist literature.

For many thoughtful American writers of the period, the problem of the travel book was the need to reconcile conflicting values – the nationalistic impulse that led to criticism of Europe, and an aesthetic appreciation of great cultural achievements. The struggle to reconcile these conflicting feelings shapes the travel books of James Russell Lowell, Ralph Waldo Emerson, and Nathaniel Hawthorne. In the four essays describing his travels in Italy in the second half of *Fireside Travels* (1864), Lowell proclaims various patriotic sentiments but has some difficulty reconciling them with a romantic longing for a simpler, slower, more poetic way of life. He continually objects to the haste of American commercial life and laments the absence of imagination in an increasingly rational and scientific age. While he deplores Catholicism, he insists that "one must take his Protestant shoes off his feet" when entering St. Peter's, "the only Church that has been loyal to the heart and soul of man, that has clung to her faith in the imagination, and that would not give over her symbols and images and sacred vessels to the perilous keeping of the iconoclast Understanding."[23] Much of what Lowell sees in Italy appeals to his romantic sensibility, which wants to retreat into imaginative musings on a glorious past, but this is always balanced by a strong comic sense which undercuts any drift into sentimentality and transforms the inconveniences and absurdities of travel into a source for good natured humor. At various points, he pokes fun at guides, British travelers, and "guide-book poetry, enthusiasm manufactured by the yard" for those who lack real imagination (p. 188). Although *Fireside Travels* is often charming and amusing, it is finally an uneasy blend of humor, sentiment, and nationalism. Lowell is never fully able to reconcile his comic apprehension of reality, his desire for a more poetic and imaginative age, and his nationalistic affirmation of democratic values.

Similar problems affect Emerson's *English Traits* (1856) which has puzzled critics who continue to debate whether the author ends up admiring or attacking the British. Emerson opens his summary chapter with the sentence "England is the best of actual nations"; and then fills up a long paragraph with a harsh summation of British faults.[24] In some respects, *English Traits* seems very unconventional. The core of the book consists of what Howard Mumford Jones has called "the great generalizing chapters" (Introduction, *English Traits*, p. xvi). Only the opening and closing sections, much of which focus on Emerson's experiences with famous British writers, deal with personal experience, and remarkably little of his analysis of British life is rooted in the details of specific observation. Noting that the book seems to move "from a predominantly positive to a predominantly negative view of the English," Philip L. Nicoloff argues that Emerson's organizing ideas suggest a nation facing inevitable decline: "America was young, Europe was old, and historical necessity would take care of the rest."[25] The theory of history that Nicoloff emphasizes helps to explain some of the apparent inconsistencies in the book, but it also clearly places it in the tradition of American travel writing which tends to confront the European past by pointing to the future glories of the United States. In fact, *English Traits* actually reflects many of the conventions that have been described throughout this chapter, including the attempt to balance a set of moral meditations with a genial sense of comedy. There is a comic impulse underlying many of the essays that is more characteristic of American travel books than of Emerson's other works. Many of his satiric remarks on the limitations of the British are surprisingly like the comic critique of the narrow-minded British traveler that runs through the genre. Thus Emerson tells us that: "An English lady on the Rhine hearing a German speaking of her party as foreigners, exclaimed, 'No, we are not foreigners; we are English; it is you that are foreigners'" (p. 96). In describing their national prejudices, he notes that "They hate the French, as frivolous; they hate the Irish, as aimless; they hate the Germans, as professors" (p. 79). His chapter, "Literature," has puzzled scholars disturbed by his sweeping rejection of most of the literary giants of nineteenth-century Britain, but that is consistent with the literary nationalism expressed in his earlier essays and in most antebellum American travel books, which tended, as Emerson does, to emphasize the achievement of Renaissance authors and disparage contemporary works. *English Traits* is clearly the work of a Transcendentalist who will not allow a foolish consistency to prevent him from perceiving the complexity of his subject, but it is also quite characteristic of the American travel writer who is torn between admiring foreign achievements and defending American values.

Hawthorne's *Our Old Home* merits attention for its polished prose and its careful balancing of affectionate praise for an ancestral homeland with satirical commentary. After finally abandoning his plans to write a romance set in England, Hawthorne decided to write a collection of essays with an organizing theme: the American's special relationship to England. The form of the travel sketch – the graceful, rambling familiar essay – allowed a freedom that Hawthorne could not find in the novel. Moreover, the well-established conventions of American travel writing about England led him to admire and affirm the same qualities in English life that other Americans had lovingly described in their travel books: the sense of venerable antiquity, rural peace, and a settled way of life that is in sharp contrast with the haste and turmoil of modern commercial America. These conventions also enabled him to respond to those aspects of the British character that annoyed him with good-natured humor and wit. Like many other Americans, he valued England more than the English and even jokingly suggests a plan to annex the island,

> transferring their thirty millions of inhabitants to some convenient wilderness in the great West, and putting half or a quarter as many of ourselves into their places. The change would be beneficial to both parties. We, in our dry atmosphere, are getting too nervous, haggard, dyspeptic, extenuated, unsubstantial, theoretic, and need to be made grosser. John Bull, on the other hand, has grown bulbous, long-bodied, short-legged, heavy-witted, material, and, in a word, too intensely English.[26]

Unsurprisingly, some of his remarks offended British readers.

At the heart of *Our Old Home* is the nationalistic affirmation of home and country that is basic to American travel writing. Hawthorne thus joins a long tradition that assumes that travel can be psychologically and morally destructive unless the traveler maintains a strong allegiance to his American values. The possible dangers of an American's attachment to England form the core of the opening essay, "Consular Experiences," and thus introduce the theme that is developed throughout the text: England is the American's old home, but it is not, should not, and cannot be his present home. *Our Old Home* also takes one of the great conventions of American travel writing about Europe, the literary pilgrimage, and adapts it into a fictional form that is rich in moral and psychological inquiry in two brilliant essays, "Recollections of a Gifted Woman," which focuses on Delia Bacon's obsession with the idea that Francis Bacon had actually written the works of Shakespeare, and "Lichfield and Uttoxeter," which explores an act of penance committed by Dr. Johnson. The best of the essays in *Our Old Home* stand as among the finest achievements of American travel writing in this period.

Mark Twain's *The Innocents Abroad* (1869) appeared after the Civil War but in many ways it is the capstone to a literary genre whose conventions were first established in the early national period and developed throughout the first half of the nineteenth century. Twain's comic portrayal of the difficulties and absurdities of travel and his deflation of European pretensions are rooted in the tradition of travel writing described in this chapter. In the post-Civil War period, American travel books about Europe often reflected a greater cosmopolitanism, a greater openness to the possibility of foreign influence. In this respect, Twain's masterpiece is more closely connected to the nationalistic works that preceded it than to the travel books that followed it. Understanding the tradition of travel writing about Europe established by American authors during the formative years of our literary traditions enables us to place many of our most important writers into a more accurate and meaningful historical context and enables us to appreciate the ways in which a set of conventions develops to meet the special demands of specific times and places.

Notes

1. Washington Irving, *A Tour on the Prairies*, ed. John Frances McDermott (Norman: University of Oklahoma Press, 1944), p. 55.
2. The most famous British criticisms of America are the travel books of Frances Trollope, Basil Hall, Captain Frederick Marryat, Harriet Martineau, and Charles Dickens, which appeared during the third, fourth, and fifth decades of the nineteenth century, but anti-American travel writings appeared much earlier. For a more thorough account of British attacks on America, see Henry T. Tuckerman, *America and Her Commentators* (New York: Charles Scribner, 1864) and Allan Nevins, ed., *America Through British Eyes* (New York: Henry Holt and Co., 1926). Martin Crawford notes that harsh criticism of America stopped appearing in British travel books by the 1850s in his article, "British Travellers and the Anglo-American Relationship in the 1850s," *The Journal of American Studies* 12 (August 1978), pp. 203–19. The most useful recent books on American travel writing are Terry Caesar *Forgiving the Boundaries: Home as Abroad in American Travel Writing* (Athens: University of Georgia Press, 1995); Christopher Mulvey, *Anglo-American Landscapes: A Study of Nineteenth-Century Anglo-America Travel Literature* (Cambridge: Cambridge University Press, 1983) and *Transatlantic Manners: Social Patterns in Nineteenth-Century Anglo-American Travel Literature* (Cambridge: Cambridge University Press, 1990); and William W. Stowe, *Going Abroad: European Travel in Nineteenth-Century American Culture* (Princeton: Princeton University Press: 1994).
3. Royall Tyler, *The Yankey in London* (New York: Isaac Riley, 1809), p. 165. Thomas Tanselle's *Royall Tyler* (Cambridge, MA: Harvard University Press, 1967) contains an appreciative discussion of this work on pp. 189–205.

4. James Kirke Paulding, *A Sketch of Old England, by a New England Man* (New York: Wiley, 1822), vol. 1, pp. 279–80.

5. Jay Martin, *Harvests of Change* (Englewood Cliffs, NJ: Prentice-Hall, 1967), pp. 170–71. Martin's chapters on Twain have much to say about the importance of travel and travel writing to the shape of his career.

6. James Fenimore Cooper, *Gleanings in Europe: England*, ed. Robert E. Spiller (New York: Oxford University Press, 1930), pp. 277, 254.

7. The most useful discussion of Irving's *Sketch Book* remains William Hedges, *Washington Irving: An American Study 1802–1831* (Baltimore: Johns Hopkins Press, 1965), pp. 128–63.

8. Washington Irving, *The Sketch Book of Geoffrey Crayon, Gent.*, ed. Haskell Springer (Boston: Twayne, 1978), pp. 8–9.

9. Andrew Hillen, ed. *The Letters of Henry Wadsworth Longfellow*, vol. 1 (Cambridge, MA: Harvard University Press, 1966). For an instance of how these letters are superior to the travel book, compare the description of scenery near Bayonne in vol. 1, p. 220 with the same scene on pp. 189–90 in vol. 1 of Henry Wadsworth Longfellow, *Outre-Mer: A Pilgrimage Beyond the Sea*, 2 vols. (New York: Harper and Brothers, 1835).

10. Newton Arvin, *Longfellow: His Life and Work* (Boston: Little, Brown and Company, 1963), p. 42. For a discussion of the ways the travel book helped Longfellow to understand his future career, see Thomas H. Pauly, "*Outre-Mer* and Longfellow's Quest for a Career," *The New England Quarterly* 50 (March 1977), pp. 30–52.

11. Henry T. Tuckerman, *The Italian Sketch Book*, 3rd edn (New York: J.C. Ricker, 1848), p. 408.

12. Henry T. Tuckerman, *A Month in England* (New York: Redfield, 1853), p. 54.

13. Henry T. Tuckerman, *Maga Papers About Paris* (New York: Putnam, 1867), pp. 26–27.

14. Charles Eliot Norton, *Notes of Travel and Study in Italy* (Boston: Houghton Mifflin, 1887), p. 217.

15. James Jackson Jarves, *Parisian Sights and French Principles, Seen Through American Spectacles* (New York: Harper, 1852), p. 216.

16. James Jackson Jarves, *Italian Sights and Papal Principles, Seen Through American Spectacles* (New York: Harper, 1856), pp. 136–37.

17. Nathaniel Parker Willis, *Pencillings by the Way* (London: Macrone, 1836), p. v. These comments occur in the preface to the second British edition; the textual history is quite complex. The most complete edition is the 1844 American edition, but Willis later reprinted many sections of *Pencillings* in volumes with various titles.

18. Nathaniel Parker Willis, *Pencillings by the Way* (New York: Morris & Willis, 1844), p. 31.

19. The comment was made by Park Benjamin and is quoted in Paul C. Wermuth, *Bayard Taylor* (New York: Twayne, 1973), p. 29. For a more generous assessment of Bayard Taylor, see the chapters devoted to him in Larzer Ziff, *Return Passages: Great American Travel Writing, 1780–1920* (New Haven: Yale University Press, 2001); Ziff regards him as one of five great American travel writers of the nineteenth century.

20. Cyrus Augustus Bartol, *Pictures of Europe Framed in Ideas* (Boston: Crosby, Nichols, 1855), p. 51.
21. Forrest Wilson, *Crusader in Crinoline: The Life of Harriet Beecher Stowe* (Philadelphia: J.B. Lippincott Co., 1941), p. 362.
22. Harriet Beecher Stowe, *Sunny Memories of Foreign Lands*, 2 vols. (Boston: Philips, Sampson, 1854), vol. II, p. 163.
23. James Russell Lowell, *Fireside Travels* (Boston: Ticknor & Fields, 1864), pp. 288, 290–91.
24. Ralph Waldo Emerson, *English Traits* (Cambridge, MA: Harvard University Press, 1966), p. 194.
25. Philip L. Nicoloff, *Emerson on Race and History: An Examination of "English Traits"* (New York: Columbia University Press, 1961), pp. 36, 236.
26. Nathaniel Hawthorne, *Our Old Home* (Columbus: Ohio State University Press, 1970), p. 64.

7

WILLIAM MERRILL DECKER

Americans in Europe from Henry James to the present

From the decade following the Civil War to the early years of the twenty-first century, American accounts of European travel reflect every conceivable variable of touring style and literary representation. Neither class nor color has effectively offered a bar to this journey; women as well as men, old as well as young, have penetrated every corner of Europe and recorded their experience in a multitude of contexts and narrative forms. Most of this work appears as non-fiction prose but the era also abounds in travel poetry and fiction popularly read as travelogue.[1] In the course of this period the relation of Old to New World continuously evolves: as Europe becomes a field of carnage as well as the site of a museum past, the USA assumes a dominant role on the world stage. In the decades following World War II, Americans circulate as the inadvertent emissaries of a hegemonic power and typically travel en masse. Detaching themselves as they can from the group, writers of the European sojourn tour the cynosures of established pilgrimage but seldom halt there: absenting themselves from the grand boulevard and floodlighted cathedral, they seek a quaint, rural, pre-modern Europe or, alternatively, a contested, ravaged, reinvented Europe beyond the Cold War's breached partition. If here they find flowers, recipes, old peasant customs, everywhere they may also look misery straight in the eye. For a literature of leisure that traditionally affects to abandon high seriousness in pursuit of holiday pleasure, travel writing in this time frame excels in limning a world of twisted and tragic line.

Before the Great War

With the exception of Jack London, the major travel authors of the prewar era are conspicuously and even poignantly privileged. Henry Adams, Henry James, and Edith Wharton exemplify modes of European travel whose days at the turn of the century are numbered. All came of age at a time when the Grand Tour was thought to complete an elite education; all crossed the ocean

127

in flight from a homeland they regarded as culturally thin. Eurocentric in unexamined ways, each approaches the Old World as "a passionate pilgrim" (in James' phrase) to the wellsprings of Western Civilization. To be in Europe is to behold antiquity, the Middle Ages, and the Renaissance, even as the present compels attention in the form of awkward democratizations ("cockneyfication" is James' favored term) and the shadow of wars to come. Almost all have read John Ruskin and follow the cathedral trail, yet each adopts secular means of celebrating the monuments of a European Christian past. Each aspires to the company of aristocrats, artists, and intelligentsia; all ponder their American identities through genealogical connections with some parts of Europe and not others. They also write in anticipation of a Great War that would provide the implicit point of departure for the succeeding generation.

James' travel writings, first collected in *Portraits of Places* (1883), build vigorously on Washington Irving's proposition that to travel is to compile impressions from ephemeral contact with venerated foreign sites. His earliest portraits began as sketches in letters home that family members urged him to revise for publication in the *Nation*.[2] "Sketchable" occurs in his writing as a term of approbation as does "compose" in the painterly sense of heterogeneous objects harmonizing under the spell of the painter's management. The Thames and environs formed "a masterly composition." A chance view of the Warwickshire countryside "made a perfect picture" and he writes in praise generally of what English details "can accomplish for the eye."[3] Walking about on arrival in Venice, the sundry impressions "began, as the painters say, 'to compose.' " Whether viewing Chartres Cathedral or Tintoret's Crucifixion or commoners of the street – Venice for instance is full of "good-looking rascals" – the rapture of travel is visual; moreover it is a solitary pleasure achieved apart from "one's detested fellow-pilgrim."[4] Although "the sentimental tourist" as James designates his travel persona may interact with the local populace, he remains in a predominantly spectatorial relationship with the place visited: if the object in view is not a sketch, a watercolor, or a painting, it is a dramatic scene observed from the shelter of a box seat. Beneath the spectatorial motif there is never any question that the literary traveler imposes his fancy on the place visited almost as though he were imagining the whole thing.

As readers of his fiction would expect, James the travel author principally writes about England, France, and Italy; and as is generally true in Anglo-American writing the path south conveys the traveler from the seeming familiarity of the British Isles to an exotic and morally ambiguous olive-skinned otherness. Travel writing of this era is notable for its casual and unapologetic ethnography, its ready differentiation of the world's people into putative racial groupings. Italy and Spain provide the great contrast; John Hay's *Castilian Days* (1871) is an early example of the literary colonization of Iberia. Hay, James, Wharton, and Adams all write of the distinct peoples of Europe as though racial character were immutable and Anglo-Saxon superiority an established fact. Given his Anglo-Irish genealogy and his desire as a cultivated late-nineteenth-century American to emulate the ways of the upper-class English, James, like Irving and Emerson before him, finds in England a homelike foreignness; observing the ugliness of London house walls "corroded with soot and fog" he concedes: "If I were a foreigner it would make me rabid; being an Anglo Saxon I find in it what Thackeray found in Baker Street – a delightful proof of English domestic virtue, of the sanctity of the British home." Yet in the Anglo-Saxon homeland profound distinctions attach to differences of class, and since one of the most pervasive themes in American travel writing concerns the impoverished face the world presents to the American traveler, James' recurrent notation of the poor as picturesque is conspicuous. He writes in fascination of "the London rabble, the metropolitan mob"; his sketchbook contains "studies of low life . . . stage villains of realistic melodrama" (*English Hours*, pp. 114, 119–20, 137). In Paris, James greets proletarian threat with a patronizing attitude, available to an elite American whose native culture officially deprecates such rigid class structure as provokes insurrection in the Old World: "The Paris *ouvrier*, with his democratic blouse, his expressive, demonstrative, agreeable eye, his meager limbs . . . is a figure that I always encounter again with pleasure" (*The Continent*, p. 728).

Sympathetic as he may be with such a personage, James prefers a status quo that preserves the Old World as old, the common preference of the American tourist. His self-description as "sentimental tourist" or "cosmopolite" consciously brackets political and social life as not primarily relevant to what he and his American reader consider the pleasures of travel. But James cannot ignore the ethics of his position. He recognizes that the charm of Europe depends on the sufferings of those oppressed by ancient disparities of wealth and privilege. The glory of Venice, he understands, is deeply rooted in human suffering: its misery "stands there for all the world to see; it is part of the spectacle – a thorough-going devotee of local colour might consistently say it is part of the pleasure." If "the Venetian people have little to call their own," even so "they lie in the sunshine; they dabble in the sea; they wear bright rags; they fall into attitudes and harmonies; they assist at an eternal *conversazione*. It is not easy to say that one would have them other than they are, and it certainly would make an immense difference should they be better fed." Nevertheless, James concludes, "the rich Venetian temperament may bloom upon a dog's allowance" (*The Continent*, pp. 288–89).

In England one sees the same paradox: "There are ancient charities in these places . . . so quaint and venerable that they almost make the existence of respectful dependence a delectable and satisfying thought" (*English Hours*, p. 173).[5]

An antidote to this way of seeing would be offered by Jack London in *People of the Abyss* (1903), a mock travelogue and literary sociology of London's East End that portrays the district as a distant land unknown to average Londoners to say nothing of American tourists. In James' writing, Europe's glory redeems its poverty and the poor are assigned venerable roles in the ongoing pageant. In *People of the Abyss*, squalor, unemployment, domestic violence, alcoholism exist as sheer wretchedness and the underclass appear as the objects of willful neglect. This is a Europe that authors like Zola and Marx urged readers to see, and that well-heeled Americans avoided by way of preserving images garnered from readings of Thackeray and Scott. In recollecting his first landing in Liverpool and subsequent passage through the "Black District" of Birmingham, Henry Adams would recall shrinking from the abyss as he rushed toward a London that leaped from the pages of the *Spectator* and *Vanity Fair*.[6]

Yet far more than it did for James, Europe would exist for Adams in its complicated sociopolitical dimensions and the conflict between Anglo-American and English cousin is more pronounced. Family tradition (four generations in the foreign service) disposes Adams to geopolitical analysis and his early travels on a polarized continent, documented in *The Letters of Henry Adams*, provide matter for study. In Berlin fresh from Harvard, a would-be scholar of the civil law, he is obliged to enroll in a secondary school to ground himself in German, and this offers him an inside view of the educational system of the emerging Prussian state. A first tour of Austria and Italy permit observation of imperial rule and regional resistance, even a brief interview with Giuseppi Garibaldi in battle-scarred Palermo. Following a short return to the United States, he begins a seven-year residence in London as the private secretary to his father, Lincoln's ambassador to Great Britain, and in these years Adams comes to know Europe as an evolving world of visibly destabilized institutions. By vocation a historian and theorist of social change, Adams takes professional interest in how the European site – Rome's Ara Coeli, say, or Chartres Cathedral – articulates the society that produced it. Such material embodiments of old ideals exist for Adams as reference points by which to ascertain the bearings of a contemporary world.

Adams' insistence on seeing the deep European past in contrast with a global present driven by American forces (democracy, industrialism) achieves major statement in the companion volumes of his late phase, *Mont*

Saint Michel and Chartres (1904) and *The Education of Henry Adams* (1907). Of the two, the first is more obviously an example of travel literature inasmuch as this learned study of twelfth-century France proceeds as a narrative of a summer tour undertaken by an uncle and his niece with the aim of visiting medieval sites and retracing scenes of a Norman ancestry. Adams reads a detailed social history in the monumental architecture that for him exists in human time and provides only momentary refuge from a world of escalating conflict. Still, he is as susceptible as James to the art's enduring power: sitting in Chartres Cathedral on a Sunday afternoon,

> your mind held in the grasp of the strong lines and shadows of the architecture; your eyes flooded with the autumn tones of the glass; your ears drowned with the purity of the voices . . . you or any other lost soul, could, if you cared to look and listen, feel a sense beyond the human ready to reveal a sense divine that would make that world once more intelligible . . .

Yet, as he observes of the cathedral in his closing meditation on the "heavy tower," "vagrant buttress," and "irregularities of the mental mirror," "danger lurks in every stone" (*Democracy*, pp. 505, 695). The failure of Christian civilization to contain humanity in a gothic utopia leads to the multiplicity of the twentieth century, epitomized for Adams in the polarization of militarized state and anarchist bomb. The passionate pilgrim to gothic shrines and continental hinterlands is ever recalled to a violent present: in Troyes he learns of the assassination of the Russian interior minister, in Hammerfest, Norway, that of an American president. The result is familiar to twenty-first century travelers unable to slip beyond the broadcast range of CNN: "Martyrs, murderers, Caesars, saints and assassins, – half in glass and half in telegram; chaos of time, place, morals, forces and motive – gave him vertigo" (*Democracy*, pp. 1150–51).

Like James, Edith Wharton approaches the European scene as an exercise in aesthetic appreciation. Like Adams she is erudite in the history of a locale. In the familiar manner of the elite traveler she delights in "the absence of tourists and Baedekers" and rejects "the stock phrase of the stock tourist." Profoundly influenced by *The Stones of Venice*, she predictably rejects Ruskin's censure of Renaissance art. Her eye is painterly and she sounds a Jamesian note in speaking of "those Turneresque visions which, in Italy, are perpetually intruding between the most conscientious traveller and his actual surroundings." She has a learned appreciation of Italian garden design. France and especially Italy represent an agreeably erotic foreignness. Anticipating Paul Bowles, Wharton's attraction to the Mediterranean eventuates in her passage to an even more exotic

North Africa. As with James and Adams, the visual consumption of beauty represents the culmination of European travel: in Milan, for instance, "the eye is led by insensible gradations of tint to Foppa's frescoes in the spandrils – iridescent saints and angels in a setting of pale classical architecture – and thence to another frieze of tera-cota seraphs with rosy-red wings against a background of turquoise-green." As with James, the experience is private if not solipsistic: there is no way to determine "how much the eye receives and how much it contributes; and if ever the boundaries between fact and fancy waver, it may well be under the spell of the Italian mid-summer madness."[7]

If the travelogue that fills the pages of "Italian Backgrounds" and "A Motor-Flight through France" (a journey undertaken in the company of James) is conventional albeit highly accomplished, the observations of her wartime essay, "Fighting France: From Dunkerque to Belfort," represent a signal departure. A partisan and active volunteer long before the USA entered the war, Wharton toured the battle lines northeast of Paris in 1916, months after the initial German invasions but a year before the massive operations that drenched the region in blood. The war forced Wharton to replace her view of Europe as a more or less catalogued museum storehouse with recognition that the provincial landscape is the site of trench warfare. Her depiction of mobilized troops retains the painterly aesthetic:

> once the eye has adapted itself to the ugly lines and the neutral tints of the new warfare, the scene in that crowded clattering square becomes positively brilliant. It is a vision of one of the central functions of a great war, in all its concentrated energy, without the saddening suggestions of what, on the distant periphery, that energy is daily and hourly resulting in.

Yet the appearance of the "éclopés" or walking wounded drives home the sense of results, as does the physical wreckage of the French rural scene as the car rolls into "Laimont, a large village wiped out as if a cyclone had beheaded it." As a member of a generation accustomed to being in implicit command of where they were and what they saw in touring Europe, Wharton's visit to the front articulates moments of profound disorientation when it comes to location and personal identity. It is Europe radically defamiliarized: "I stood there in the pitch-black night, suddenly unable to believe that I was I, or Châlons Châlons, or that a young man who in Paris drops in to dine with me and talk over new books and plays, had been whispering a password in my ear to carry me unchallenged to a house a few streets away!" Such a passage serves well as a prelude to the Europe of succeeding generations (*Edith Wharton Abroad*, pp. 135, 147, 150).

Interwar and postwar

Those generations often voice an implicit skepticism of travel writing as such. War correspondence becomes a dominant model as writers as different as Ernest Hemingway, Louise Bryant, Jack Reed, and John Dos Passos adapt journalist convention to the scrutiny of traumatized sites. Travel experience increasingly provides the basis of memoir, as in *The Autobiography of Alice B. Toklas* (1933) and *A Moveable Feast* (1958), and study of specific cultural practices, as in *Death in the Afternoon* (1932), Hemingway's paean to bullfighting. It provides the basis for novels, such as *The Sun Also Rises* (1926), that redefine what it means to write about travel and summon generations of youth to a season of European adventure.[8]

Older than the "lost generation" on whom she bestowed the phrase, Gertrude Stein is the great transitional figure, settling in Paris towards the close of the *belle époque* and residing there through two world wars. She too produced her portraits of places, such as "In the Grass (on Spain)" and "Accents in Alsace" from *Geography and Plays* (1922) or the book-length *Paris France* (1940). In "Geography" she takes up the issue of travel and representative language: "I stands for Iowa and Italy. M stands for Mexico and Monte Carlo."[9] As narrative, however, her travels and those of her partner are recorded most fully in *The Autobiography of Alice B. Toklas*. Perhaps it is more accurate to describe the *Autobiography* as a book about a special kind of residence, life in a place of cultural experiment that accommodated same-sex partnerships and that contrasted generally with their native middle-class America. If travel writing assumes at some level a point of origin and return, Paris exists for Stein and Toklas as the spiritual home to which they are recalled from American exile; it is the metropolis they annually quit for Florence, Madrid, and Majorca; it is the threatened city they must temporarily flee, seeking refuge in England. Like Wharton, Stein and Toklas joined the war relief effort and the *Autobiography* depicts roadtrips through the devastated French countryside ("Accents in Alsace" derives from these travels) with Stein at the wheel of her Ford. Naturalized as Stein becomes to Paris and environs, however, she preserves a sense of English as her birth tongue: "there is for me only one language and that is english."[10] In this way her adopted residence retains the status of a foreign place.

For Hemingway, Paris was never to be the settled home, but it figures as the hub of his early European travels, site of much urban sauntering or *flânerie*, and the elective seat of memory. In *A Moveable Feast* (1958), his retrospect of life in interwar Paris, he portrays the young author as engaged in writing his early Michigan stories at a series of Left Bank cafés, becoming part of an expatriate community, and keeping house on straitened economies with his first wife. Paris exists as the incarnation of worldliness that never-theless harbors a season of comparative innocence, the young and vulnerable marriage protected by the author's obscurity and the couple's poverty. Writing from the perspective of achieved celebrity, he represents a life in which the penurious couple and infant son find ways to possess the good of the earth, residing in France and wintering in Austria, their happiness stalked by overnight fame and the moneyed corruption fame attracts. Living hand to mouth in deliberate contact with a European populace, Hemingway's expatriates contrast with the genteel Americans depicted in the novels of James and Wharton who do not frequent the café or racetrack, much less head to the mountains to fish. His account of American residence in Europe contrasts likewise with that of Stein, whose preoccupations with art and literature are far removed from Hemingway's concern with the affirmation of male identity.

Perhaps no American author has been more influential when it comes to projecting an image of male bourgeois-bohemian Americans ceasing to be mere tourists and naturalizing themselves, within distinct limits, to a life of expatriation. It is for this reason that one of the great examples of American travel writing is *The Sun Also Rises*, for although technically a work of fiction the book has been read as a guide and encouragement to travel (prior to its publication Pamplona's Fiesta de San Fermin was a regional event). As with Wharton, James, and Adams, conventional middle-class tourism is subject to mockery: en route to Spain, Jake Barnes and Bill Gordon find themselves on a train monopolized by Catholic pilgrims from Dayton, Ohio, and share a compartment with an American family from Montana traveling in Europe for the first time having decided to "See America first!" Yet worldly as Jake Barnes has become, serious questions arise as to the legitimacy of his position and in a memorable passage Hemingway proves that he is as much the critic as he is the exemplar of expatriate life. "You're an expatriate," Bill scolds Jake in a moment of serious drunken facetiousness. "You've lost touch with the soil. You get precious. Fake European standards have ruined you. You drink yourself to death. You become obsessed by sex. You spend all your time talking, not working. You are an expatriate, see? You hang around cafés."[11] Bill's tirade echoes what Hemingway, in *A Moveable Feast*, attributes to Stein when she pronounced his generation "lost": "All of you young people who served in the war . . . You have no respect for anything. You drink yourself to death."[12] In neither the novel nor the memoir are we offered images of battle per se, but the war's traumatic marking of this generation is understood and its effect is seen in the fragility of relationships. The limits to Jake's assimilation to Europe become especially evident during his stay in Pamplona with his English and

American friends (the old propinquity of England and America resurfaces as the Anglo-American company visits the ethnically distinct Spain). Acting as accomplice to Lady Bret Ashley's predatory design on the nineteen-year-old bullfighter, Pedro Romero, Jake alienates Montoya, the hotel proprietor and fellow *aficion* whose friendship represents a touchstone connection with the Old World.

In a more cynical if insistently ecstatic mode, Henry Miller in *Tropic of Cancer* (1934) exalts the expatriate life, but with a class consciousness that explodes in antibourgeois polemic and that seeks to affront middle-class piety in a phallocentric narrative that nevertheless affirms Victorian patri- archal values and Paris as the outlet for repressed sexuality. As a travel writer Miller is more interesting in *The Colossus of Maroussi* (1942). As he narrates his wanderings in Greece on the eve of World War II, his pen- chant for egoistic affirmation is tempered by an absorption in an unfamiliar country, his active conjuration of a pre-Christian and pre-capitalist past, and his consciousness of the disaster about to befall Europe. Miller's quest for a chthonic Old World is by the thirties a modernist commonplace, Hem- ingway's attraction to the bullfight being the prime example. Pagan Europe beckons all manner of middle-class literati. In *A Voyage to Pagany* (1928), William Carlos Williams draws upon his 1924 European trip to construct a fantasy travelogue: a New Jersey physician goes abroad to attend a med- ical seminar in Vienna but also – in a variation on a theme that runs from Hawthorne and James through Miller – to cultivate his erotic and poetic sensibility. Although *Pagany* includes conventional American-in-Paris-and- Rome scenarios, it provides retrospectively chilling views of a depressed post-Versailles Austria, views replicated by Paul Bowles' impressions of proto-Nazi Berlin. Bowles chronicles life abroad towards the close of the interwar years and reinforces the myth that US provinciality compelled an American avant-garde to reside and travel in Europe. As well, Bowles assists in building a thesis advanced before him by Hemingway: American perme- ation of Europe erodes Europe's necessary otherness. In *Without Stopping* (1972), Bowles recounts his youthful arrival in Paris, his forays into Ger- many, Italy, and Spain, and his gravitation towards a Mediterranean that would lead to a sustained North African sojourn and the novels and travel essays for which he is best known. Bowles delineates a borderland between the familiar if alien European world and the great non-European unknown; in this he follows Clemens, Wharton, Hemingway, and Dos Passos, parallels Langston Hughes and Edmund Wilson, and anticipates Paul Theroux and Robert D. Kaplan.

Then there is Russia. Henry Adams had been among the first to recog- nize that the Czar's empire, with its geographic reach and demographic ferment, presented something of a mirror image to the USA, an observation that gained force with the 1917 revolution that Louise Bryant breathlessly chronicles in *Six Red Months in Russia* (1918) and Jack Reed logs in *Ten Days That Shook the World* (1919). For American travelers, the USSR represented one vast mystery, a marginally European nation extending deep into Asia, undertaking a political experiment on a grand American scale. Poverty, racism, and ultimately the Great Depression motivated numerous writers to approach the USSR as potentially instructive and black writers were among the first to investigate the Soviet model. Between 1926 and 1959, W.E.B. Du Bois made four trips to the USSR and from first to last regarded it as "the only European country where people are not more or less taught and encouraged to despise and look down upon some class, group, or race."[13] In 1931, at the invitation of the Soviet film institute, Langston Hughes and twenty-one other young African Americans were invited to Moscow to make a film depicting race relations in the American South. The project, as Hughes narrates the adventure in *I Wonder as I Wander* (1956), is a fiasco, beginning with the improbabilities of the Soviet-produced script and extending to the inability of the college-educated northern blacks to act, sing, or otherwise entertain, but Hughes is impressed by the progress of the Soviet social experiment. In 1928, at the full blush of his leftist phase, Dos Passos made the journey, but in the "Russian Visa" chapters of *In All Countries* (1934) registers a premonitory frisson at evidence of government massacre. In *Soviet Russia* (1936), Edmund Wilson recounts a 1935 trip to the USSR and in his detailed observation of city and countryside and, memorably, his six-week confinement in the scarlet fever ward of an Odessa hospital, compiles the profile of an empire in which progressive ideals contend with premodern folkways and where "an extraordinary heroism" persists beneath constraints of "official terror."[14] The USSR would thus increasingly chasten its enthusiasts.

Those who crossed the Atlantic between the wars did so with an attitude altogether different from that of previous generations. Formerly even the best-prepared Americans had traveled as the overawed students of an old and sophisticated civilization, but the notion that US entry into World War I had "saved" Europe diminished the American's sense of cultural inferiority. World War II reinforced the conviction that Europe, with its blood feuds and totalitarian regimes, required the USA periodically to rescue it. A heroic self-regard encouraged Americans to look upon the world, like the blighted couple in Hemingway's "Hills Like White Elephants," as theirs to possess, yet intervention would prove practically and morally perilous. If World War I lent a troubled dimension to American comprehension of Europe, World War II, prelude and aftermath, set Europe beyond the bounds of tragic understanding.

Although Miller dismisses the idea "that America is the hope of the world,"[15] writers wary of US geopolitical aims preserved nonetheless a sense of mission rooted in democratic ideals. They rightly perceived the Spanish Civil War as a dress rehearsal in the fascist campaign to extend empire, and whereas Dos Passos in *Journeys between Wars* (1938) justly assesses an ideological complexity against the naïveté of partisan observers, the commitment of everyday Americans to aid the republican effort spoke of a popular idealism that existed apart from a corporate and imperial USA. Later, with Europe in ruins and the USA and USSR polarizing the continent in an East and West, it is just such idealism that F.O. Matthiessen brings to his Salzburg and Prague seminars in American literature from July to December 1947, an experience documented in *From the Heart of Europe* (1948). In teaching Emerson, Whitman, and Melville to a group of students from devastated rival nations, Matthiessen promotes a vision of democracy that offers a socialist middle way between the Soviet and American systems and does so at the center of a Europe already exhibiting irreconcilable cleavage. There could be no bolder temperamental contrast than that between the bohemian Miller and academic Matthiessen, yet in both cases a vision of democratic brotherhood associated with Walt Whitman (and, for Matthiessen, the late Franklin Delano Roosevelt) informs their sense of what America brings to the world at large and the degree to which the nation betrays fundamental ideals as it works to extend its spheres of influence. Edmund Wilson's *Europe Without Baedeker* (1947), John Steinbeck's *Russian Journal* (1948) and several essays from James Baldwin's *Notes of a Native Son* (1955) likewise survey the aftermath of Europe's worst human catastrophe. Wilson, writing with the American's traditional resentment of British insolence and an impatience with what he had earlier described as "a pack of little quarrelsome states," views the war ruins of England, Italy, and Greece with dispassion and a notable lack of empathy (*Soviet Russia*, p. 373). Steinbeck's portrait of utopian collective farms and his conspicuous incuriosity – during his visit to Kiev – as to the absence of Jews is strangely blind to the *holdomar* and holocaust perpetuated in his midst. Baldwin's discernment of postwar Paris, by contrast, retains its power to instruct.

African Americans in Europe

Black American experience of Europe does much to elucidate American experience generally and thus warrants special attention. In *The Sun Also Rises*, Bill Gordon speaks of a "noble-looking nigger" who squares off against the local talent in a Vienna boxing match. The black American, trouncing the Austrian instead of taking the fall as instructed, is mobbed by the crowd and has to be rescued by Gordon, who feels a national solidarity with him (p. 70). The anecdote is consistent with complications noted by black Americans traveling in Europe through the early decades of the twentieth century and reflects the presumption that African Americans cross the ocean to entertain. In the 1890s, it was possible for W.E.B. Du Bois to study and travel in Central Europe, pleasantly surprised at his near acceptance, but the post-World War I arrival of Jazz Age culture brought with it stereotypes associated with American racial semiotics. Black Americans in Europe were expected to be boxers, jazz musicians, or dancers. To white Americans they may be "noble-looking" and entitled to succor, but they remain distinctly second-class citizens. A white American in Europe may be wealthy in the manner of an Edith Wharton or Henry Adams or poor as Ernest and Hadley Hemingway, and in either case comfortably leisured, but a black American is expected to earn a living on stage.

Langston Hughes negotiates this stereotype even as he lives out the myth of being poor, American, and happy in Paris. In *The Big Sea* (1940), he writes of his 1923 arrival in France with seven dollars in his pocket, a merchant sailor on elective furlough. Having taken his first Parisian stroll, the pressing business as night descends is "to look for a colored person" and by luck a black American doorman directs him to the African American colony in Montmartre. There, inquiries about work are met with the question, "what instrument do you play?" Hughes tells the story of assimilating to the black expatriate community, working kitchen in clubs that represented a transplantation of Harlem culture. In France, the USSR, and Spain, Hughes is ever the student of the color line, studious as to whether the segregationist conventions of the USA are duplicated anywhere that a white European or Asian community coexists with a people of color. As a student of color lines he is attentive as well to those of class. In Venice he noses about areas "not stressed in the guide books" for a look at the slums and poor people unsuspected by conventional "English tourists."[16] As travel writer Hughes' perspective (like that of Du Bois, Wilson, Matthiessen, and Steinbeck) is decidedly leftist. In 1938, as a left journalist, Hughes covers the war in Spain, traveling in loyalist strongholds and studying the racial dynamics of the International Brigade. Since previous to the Spanish Civil War, African Americans in Europe were commonly entertainers, Hughes is surprised to find black countrymen from many walks of life serving as soldiers in defense of the republic. For Richard Wright, postwar Spain represents spiritual death in a part of Europe that he regards as an African borderland, no longer the scene of a lost noble cause or of a beautiful ritual violence, as it was for Hemingway. In *Pagan Spain* (1957), the "primitive" exalted by Wright's Modernist precursors lends itself to state terror, misogyny, and the curiously sexual sadism of the bullfight as Wright reads Franco's police state with eyes that have witnessed the violence of the Jim Crow South.

James Baldwin likewise presents a harsh, unromantic Europe, and in writing of a post-World War II Paris works to demythologize the Left Bank of interwar legend. "Equal in Paris" narrates a sojourn through the criminal justice system with which Baldwin becomes acquainted having borrowed a bed sheet that a countryman had stolen from a cheap hotel. Like Hughes and Wright, Baldwin writes in affirmation of Du Bois' statement that "the problem of the Twentieth century is the problem of the color-line"[17] and picks up where Hughes leaves off in his depiction of a black American Paris – although the musicians by this time have been joined by an African American intelligentsia. But whereas Hughes exemplifies the person of color seeking other such persons, Baldwin observes an ambivalence more likely to isolate the African American abroad from Americans generally as well as from the postwar African community. In a place where familiar color barriers do not exist, the black American according to Baldwin is not eager to meet with the reminders of such barriers in the form of fellow Americans, black or white. Skeptical of the pan-African bond assumed by Du Bois, Hughes, and Wright, Baldwin's "Encounter on the Seine: Black Meets Brown" examines both the gulf between African colonial and African American and the loss of the African historical root that three hundred years in America has effected. For Baldwin, black Americans may find in Europe liberation from the oppression of American color codes but with that liberation comes an introspective and aggravated solitude.

That isolation is most evident in "Stranger in the Village," a meditation on his residence in a tiny Alpine community where he is the only black person the locals have ever seen and so must endure their benign attention to his physical difference. From a testament to what it is like to be the exotic presence, an embodiment of binary difference, the essay proceeds to contemplate the degree to which Europe has intervened in his destiny as an American black and how much the European association with Africa, criminal as it may have been in origin, has shaped not only African Americans but also Europeans who left villages like this to settle in North America: "No road whatever will lead Americans back to the simplicity of this European village where white men still have the luxury of looking on me as a stranger."[18] In this and other essays from *Notes of a Native Son* and *Nobody Knows My Name* (1961), Baldwin does as much as anyone to expose assumptions white Americans make in traveling to a Europe that exists for them as genealogical and cultural origin. Even a progressive writer like F.O. Matthiessen – writing like Baldwin after World War II but following the example of James and Adams – approaches Europe as the "heart of *our* civilization."[19] If, for

Baldwin, Europe represents a portion of the African American parentage it more forcefully exists as the staging area of the enslavement and transportation of African people. Coming to Europe mindful at once of a violent history and white obliviousness to this history, he speaks volumes in observing with reference to Europeans and their pureblood American progeny that "the cathedral at Chartres says something to them which it cannot say to me" ("Stranger in the Village," p. 121).

In *All God's Children Need Traveling Shoes* (1987), Maya Angelou writes principally of her 1965 residence in Ghana, but an excursion to Europe towards the end of the narrative is illustrative of a Europe that speaks in particular ways to black Americans. Like *Mont Saint Michel and Chartres*, the book seeks genealogical sites that predate a New World diaspora, but Angelou's pilgrimage is inherently traumatic as it focuses on scenes of European and African crime against the ancestors. A trip to Berlin (conforming to the pattern of much African American travel in Europe, Angelou tours as a member of an acting troupe) takes on allegorical qualities as a journey to the heart of genocidally racist Europe, culminating in a breakfast with the family of an ex-Nazi businessman who collects African art and who, in an analogy of the slave trade, courts Angelou as a potential agent of future acquisitions.

Contemporary European travels

With the postwar power of the US dollar and proliferation of transatlantic flights, hordes of Americans would make the journey and do so in accordance with travel styles calibrated to age and income. Volumes of American writing about Europe appear in guidebooks that speak variously to the budget and interests of target audiences. Occasionally, a novel like Dan Brown's *The Da Vinci Code* (2003) – in its Special Illustrated Edition – serves double duty as airplane reading and guidebook on arrival, or a memoir like Frances Mayes' *Bella Tuscany* (1999) interweaves personal narrative and culinary appreciation. Although the guidebook as an institution is far from new, the broad demographics the genre has come to reflect suggest the magnitude of the tourist industry. Much travel writing is ancillary to this industry: although the short pieces that appear in *Condé Nast Traveler*, *Islands*, or in the airlines' monthly seat-pocket glossies aspire to the condition of literature, they do not often disturb the illusion that travel is a utopian pastime. They do not as a rule fixate on the poverty of a local population or the grossness of a town's hotels or the ruins that testify to murderous regional conflicts, much less the pornography available at the newsstand and what it has to say about a national character.

Such are, however, the emphases of Paul Theroux, prolific and best-selling author of *The Great Railway Bazaar* (1975), *The Kingdom by the Sea* (1983), and *The Pillars of Hercules* (1995), to cite those titles in which Europe significantly appears. Theroux reflects the restless and mechanized travel style of postwar American tourists and his narratives consist of quick takes generated by a predetermined itinerary structured by public transportation links. Compared to expatriate accounts of place such as one reads in Stein, Hemingway, Dos Passos, or Baldwin, Theroux's portraits evince a resistance and irony that threaten to reduce a locale's complex life to a grotesque, comic, performative phrase. The power of the affluent literary American to read and render the exotic scene is seldom questioned and the capacity of travel style and literary style to dominate vast stretches of geography is articulated in the titles of his books. As the titles also suggest, Theroux's travels typically cling to travel corridors, along which tourists interface with a culture actively soliciting tourist cash, which is why the sex trade figures prominently in his work. What distinguishes Theroux's writing, however, is that even as it mimics the typical American's restless and overreaching itinerary, it marks off paths that extend beyond American expectations of comfort and security. It records arrivals in dark villages where no hotel reservation has been made. It pursues an unfamiliar Europe that borders on an African, Middle Eastern, and Central Asiatic world. It samples foods guaranteed to subvert the American digestive tract. It beholds a world of sex and squalor that American tourists prefer to see through the eyes of someone else.

Much of Theroux's writing is darkly comic, with the American tourist and the local character (usually a hustler) the recurrent butt of his humor. Like other contemporaries, such as Bill Bryson's *Neither Here Nor There* (1995), and P.J. O'Rourke's *Holidays in Hell* (1998), Theroux writes in a vein indebted to *The Innocents Abroad*. In *The Kingdom by the Sea*, an account of his circumnavigation of the UK which includes a tramp through devastated Northern Ireland, and especially in *The Pillars of Hercules*, a narrative of his tour of the Mediterranean coast that takes him through the devastated Balkans, Theroux inscribes an experience of place in which humor and irony inadequately insulate the American observer who must somehow represent the enormity of human violence, suffering, and desperation. "Nothing was right in Durrës," he writes of his arrival in Albania. "In a filthy and deranged way it all fit together – the toasted trees, the cracked buildings, the nasty earth . . . When the people saw me it was as though they had seen The Man Who Fell to Earth and they ran towards me and screamed for me to give them something – money, food, clothes, my pen, anything."[20] Given the fleeting nature of his timetable-driven visits, Theroux – in contrast to

Robert D. Kaplan or the Susan Sontag of "Why Are We in Kosovo?"[21] – is more effective as an imagist than an analyst of human misery, although his writings feature astute if largely impressionistic social commentary.

No event has had a more profound effect on the American experience of Europe than the 1989 collapse of the Soviet bloc. Adventurous travelers had always found ways to sojourn behind the Iron Curtain but the opening of borders and promotion of tourism resulted in a rediscovery of Central Europe reemerging where for nearly half a century there had been a rigidly polarized East and West. In the 1990s, young expatriate communities established themselves in Prague and Budapest, where, for a while, the cost of living was nearly as low as in Paris during the interwar years, and the literary record of this experience materializes in such works as Arthur Phillips' *Prague* (2001), a narrative actually set in Budapest. Many accounts of travel in the former East are the work of Jewish writers, often children or grandchildren of Holocaust survivors, uncovering the history of Jewish Europe from World War II through the Cold War. Such titles often combine narrative of recovered history with travel to former Soviet Bloc sites. Stephen J. Dubner's *Turbulent Souls: A Catholic Son's Return to His Jewish Family* (1998) recounts travels to Poland (including Auschwitz). In *A Hole in the Heart of the World* (1997), Jonathan Kaufman tells the story of Jewish families that survived the war years based on interviews he conducted in Berlin, Prague, Budapest, and Warsaw. Eva Hoffman, a naturalized Canadian and US citizen, followed *Lost in Translation* (1990), her memoir of emigrating from Krakow as a teenager, with *Escape into the World* (1993), an account of travels in Poland, the Czech Republic, Hungary, Romania, and Bulgaria. One of the most perceptive travel narratives of the post-1989 decade, *Escape* is distinguished for its detail as well as for its unusual bi-national perspective, that of a former Eastern European who has become fully American in expectation and reflex. Overlapping with portions of Hoffman's itinerary, Robert D. Kaplan's *Balkan Ghosts* (1993) likewise explores an unfamiliar Europe whose ethnic and national conflicts exist as a synecdoche of matters that constitute the vast unfinished business of the twentieth century.

Travel has always contained elements of danger and throughout the 1970s, 1980s, and 1990s, the placid expectation of American tourists was occasionally challenged by IRA, Basque Separatist, and Red Brigade bombings. But following the September 11, 2001 attacks on New York and Washington, travelers perceived terrorist threat as no longer incidental but rather systemic, as it became known that a plot imagined in Afghanistan and staged in Hamburg hit home in the United States. The March 11, 2004 Madrid commuter train bombings and the July 7, 2005 attacks in London reinforce the idea of a Western Europe vulnerable to al-Qaeda machination. If such commonly held anxieties draw Europe and America together, differences between an Anglo-American and continental European response underscore ideological difference. As a component of European travel, terrorist anxiety is an emerging *topos* but as part of a more complex, evolving adjustment of US expectation to European realities.[22] Between America and Europe there has always been a gulf. Although Americans in Europe will continue to perpetuate a nostalgia for the nineteenth-century Grand Tour and the fabled bohemia of the Paris expatriates, the real Europe offers something quite different: consolidating economies, resurgent and militant ethnicities, a burgeoning Islamic community, a neo-fascist fringe, and strange appropriations of American pop culture. It is this many-sided, post-postmodern, defamiliarized Europe that the new travel writing will have to address.

Notes

1. Travel poetry has been written by nearly every significant twentieth-century American poet. Notable practitioners include John Dos Passos, Randall Jarrell, May Swarton, Elizabeth Bishop, Allen Ginsberg, W.S. Merwin, James Merrill, Audre Lorde.

2. Like his contemporary Henry Adams, James was first and ever a travel writer in his letters, a genre practiced by professional authors and everyday people alike. For centuries great quantities of travel writing have been inscribed in the contexts of private and business correspondence, published and unpublished, extant and lost.

3. Henry James, *Collected Travel Writing: English Hours, The American Scene, Other Travels* (New York: Library of America, 1993), pp. 141, 164, 181.

4. Henry James, *Collected Travel Writing: The Continent* (New York: Library of America, 1993), pp. 298, 395, 312–13, 400.

5. "Respectful dependence" replaces the first edition "poverty."

6. Henry Adams, *Democracy, Esther, Mont Saint Michel and Chartres, The Education of Henry Adams, Poems* (New York: Library of America, 1983), pp. 786–87. See also *The Letters of Henry Adams*, ed. J.C. Levenson *et al.*, 6 vols. (Cambridge, MA: Harvard University Press, 1982–88).

7. Edith Wharton, *Edith Wharton Abroad: Selected Travel Writings, 1888–1920* (New York: St. Martin's Press, 1995), pp. 89, 101, 97, 107, 98. For a characterization of Wharton as a pioneer motorist, see Sidonie Smith, *Moving Lives: 20th-Century Women's Travel Writing* (Minneapolis: University of Minnesota Press, 2001), p. 199.

8. Where travel writing leaves off and other genres begin becomes difficult to ascertain in this period. With reference to British and American work of the interwar years, Paul Fussell writes of the general "penetration by the 'travel' spirit." *Abroad: British Literary Traveling between the Wars* (New York: Oxford University Press, 1980), p. 53. Helen Carr observes that "a remarkable number of novelists and poets were *travelling* writers, whether or not they were in addition actually *travel* writers, as indeed a number were." "Modernism and Travel

(1880–1940)," in *The Cambridge Companion to Travel Writing*, ed. Peter Hulme and Tim Youngs (Cambridge: Cambridge University Press, 2002), p. 73.

9. Gertrude Stein, "Geography," in *Writings: 1903–1932* (New York: Library of America, 1998), p. 510.

10. Gertrude Stein, *The Autobiography of Alice B. Toklas*, in *Writings: 1903–1932*, p. 729.

11. Ernest Hemingway, *The Sun Also Rises* (New York: Scribner, 1926), pp. 83, 109.

12. Ernest Hemingway, *A Moveable Feast* (New York: Scribner, 1964), p. 34.

13. W.E.B. Du Bois, *The Autobiography of W. E. B. Du Bois* (New York: International Publishers, 1968), p. 39.

14. Edmund Wilson, *Soviet Russia*, in *Red, Black, Blond and Olive* (New York: Oxford University Press, 1956), pp. 374, 375.

15. Henry Miller, *The Colossus of Maroussi* (New York: New Directions, 1958), p. 137.

16. Langston Hughes, *The Big Sea* (New York: Hill and Wang, 1940), pp. 145, 189.

17. W.E.B. Du Bois, *The Souls of Black Folk* (New York: Norton, 1999), p. 5.

18. James Baldwin, "Stranger in the Village," in *Collected Essays* (New York: Library of America, 1998), p. 129.

19. F.O. Matthiessen, *From the Heart of Europe* (New York: Oxford University Press, 1948), p. 194; emphasis mine.

20. Paul Theroux, *The Pillars of Hercules* (East Rutherford, NJ: Putnam Adult, 1995), p. 260. Here as elsewhere, Theroux skirts the edge of thanatourism, the more or less programmed visitation of sites associated with horrific memory: slave dungeons, death camps, erstwhile urban war zones.

21. Susan Sontag, "Why Are We in Kosovo?," *New York Times Magazine*, May 2, 1999.

22. Terrorist anxiety appears presciently in Shay Youngblood's *Black Girl in Paris* (New York: Riverhead, 2000), a fictional sojourn set in 1986 that nostalgically invokes the Paris of Hughes, Wright, and Baldwin. Travel writing in the years ahead may find new models in narratives such as William Gibson's *Pattern Recognition* (New York: Putnam, 2003), a novel set in contemporary UK, Japan, France, and Russia, in which a jet-lagged American business traveler navigates a post 9/11 world and voyages as much in cyberspace as in a world of geographical realities.

8

HILTON OBENZINGER

Americans in the Holy Land, Israel, and Palestine

In the nineteenth century, travel books about the Holy Land, then ruled by the Ottoman Empire, were enormously popular. Travelers were thrilled to enter the holy city of Jerusalem, as well as to experience the exotic East. After World War I, travelers also came to investigate the Zionist experiment, or they at least had to address the Jewish presence in their field of vision in British Mandate Palestine. After the state of Israel was founded in 1948, a great many travel accounts appeared celebrating the *kibbutzim* and other social innovations of the new state. The Israeli–Palestinian conflict deepened after Israel occupied the West Bank and Gaza in 1967 and Israel became a central player in United States foreign policy. While the religious aspect of Holy Land travel remained and, if anything, grew even more complex, travel accounts became increasingly political, including histories, interviews with leaders, and visits to Palestinian refugee camps, Jewish settlements, and other scenes of conflict.

In this essay, I examine literary books by Americans who travel to all of these places – Holy Land, exotic East, Land of Israel, conflict zone – focusing on common characteristics. There are dramatic differences between nineteenth and twentieth-century travel accounts, because of the stark change in political circumstances from one century to the next. But they share certain modes of response to the complex religious and psychological encounter with the idea of a sacred landscape. Travel to other parts – Italy or Greece, for example – provided important meanings about culture to Americans in the nineteenth century; but travel to the Holy Land posed ultimate questions. These writers probe fundamental cultural constructions of American faith and identity in a country that demands the highest accountability because of its association with the Bible. A journey to the Holy Land was a mighty theme, as Melville would put it, and these books share a number of stylistic conventions and attitudes, as they attempt a mighty response. Mark Twain, Herman Melville, Hannah Arendt, and Saul Bellow have produced some of the best American literary works based on the journey to Jerusalem. But these exceptional authors stand out among the great output of Holy Land travel books by American authors. This large and growing library joins other texts and cultural products – paintings, religious tracts, guidebooks, panoramas, photographs, propaganda, and more – within a major fascination with the Holy Land that persists throughout both centuries.[1]

Holy Land

As General Ulysses S. Grant approached Jerusalem during his 1877–79 tour around the world, he carried three books to serve as his guides: the Bible, the standard tour guide, and Mark Twain's *The Innocents Abroad, or The New Pilgrim's Progress* (1869), the quintessentially American burlesque of Holy-Land travel books and irreverent send-up of smug sanctimoniousness.[2] Mark Twain's travel book was very popular – it remains perhaps the most popular travel book in American literature – and even though only a small portion of Twain's recorded journey covers the Middle East, *The Innocents Abroad* continues to play a crucial role in presenting Ottoman Palestine to the American imagination. Already a celebrated journalist from California and Nevada, Mark Twain made the journey as part of the 1867 tour on board *The Quaker City*. "The Wild Humorist of the Pacific Slope" was hired by a San Francisco newspaper to write travel letters as part of the very first large-scale tourist excursion cruise in American history. "I basked in the happiness of being for once in my life drifting with the tide of a great popular movement" (p. 27), he writes of the explosion of post-Civil War travel to Europe. While touring Europe – and appropriating Europe's cultural legacy – comprised most of the journey, "the grand goal of the expedition" was the Holy Land.

Much of the book satirizes the pretensions of the Northern elite who traveled with the crude Southerner reconstructed as a Westerner: "The pleasure trip was a funeral excursion without a corpse," he writes. "There is nothing exhilarating about a funeral excursion without a corpse" (p. 644). At the same time, Twain lambastes overbearing seekers of high culture, articulating the newly developing, market-place sensibilities of "the business of sight-seeing" through parody. He identifies how established opinions predetermine the traveler's response:

> I can almost tell, in set phrase, what [travelers] will say when they see Tabor, Nazareth, Jericho and Jerusalem – *because I have the books they will "smouch" their ideas from* . . . The Pilgrims will tell of Palestine, when they

get home, not as it appeared to *them*, but as it appeared to Thompson and Robinson and Grimes – with the tints varied to suit each pilgrim's creed.

(pp. 511–12)

The vast library of American and European Holy Land books created a thick textual lens. As a result, engagement with the actual place was mediated through an elaborate set of repeated travel and literary conventions. These accounts were so plentiful and so overwrought that Twain could have easily written a Holy Land travel book without even having to set foot in Jerusalem.

Holy Land geography was already deeply a part of the new republic's settler culture through intensive reading of the Bible. "As in the case of most of my countrymen, especially in New England, the scenes of the Bible had made a deep impression upon my mind from the earliest childhood," explains Edward Robinson, the founder of biblical archeology. "Indeed in no country of the world, perhaps, is such a feeling more widely diffused than in New England; in no country are Scriptures better known, or more highly prized." As a New Englander grows up, "the names of Sinai, Jerusalem, Bethlehem, the Promised Land, become associated with his earliest recollections and holiest feelings."[3]

Pliny Fisk and Levi Parsons left Boston to investigate prospects in Jerusalem as Protestant missionaries in 1819, producing the first American travel accounts of Palestine. Their reports in the *Missionary Herald* inaugurated another pattern of set characteristics: contact with actual Ottoman Palestine often clashed with readers' "earliest recollections and holiest feelings"; contact with real people and conditions conflicted with what they had visualized when they had read the Bible back home. The way the real Jaffa or Bethlehem veered from their imagined Holy Land was often very troubling – or humorous. While these accounts search out the exoticism of the East, as would travel narratives to Anatolia or Morocco, Holy Land travel books had the additional task of encountering the sacred along with the mundane.

Many of these travel writers consistently searched for evidences of biblical certainty and prophetic fulfillment in the landscape, a practice of reading sacred landscape according to whichever Christian framework they espoused. In *The Land and the Book*, William M. Thomson describes the hermeneutical character of the Holy Land. For him, Palestine's

testimony is essential to the chain of evidences, her aid invaluable in exposition . . . In a word, Palestine is one vast table whereupon God's messages to men have been drawn, and graven deep in living characters by the Great Publisher of glad tidings, to be seen and read of all to the end of time. The Land and the Book – with reverence be it said – constitute the ENTIRE and ALL-PERFECT TEXT, and should be studied together.[4]

These practices of reading sacred landscape-text in Palestine alongside scripture were developed parallel to long-standing practices established by both Puritan and other settlers to seek divine meanings in both the history and landscape of the New World colonizing project. This typological exercise – searching for fulfillment in the New World for what was first embodied in the biblical events of the Holy Land – was especially associated with the various doctrines that saw a special role for America concerning the return of Christ.

Discovering "evidences" of biblical truth invoked the believer's special relationship to the land of Palestine. As Rev. De Witt Talmage put it, "God with His left hand built Palestine, and with His right wrote the Scriptures, the two hands of the same Being. And in proportion as Palestine is brought under close inspection, the Bible will be found more glorious and more true."[5] Episcopal Bishop Henry White Warren in *Sights and Insights* (1874) formulated this relationship in a similar fashion: "God is careful to attest his word. He hath left all Palestine as one great comment on the Bible."[6] The land, in these rhetorical devices, is an exegetical sounding board. Rev. Stephen Olin extends the trope even further than the notion of an ambidextrous God or the Divine Author offering commentary on his own work: "Pilgrimage is little less than to be naturalized in the Holy Land. Only then does the Bible become *real*."[7] As the Bible becomes real, as confirmed by personal contact with the land, travelers become "naturalized" into their identities as Christians and Americans. This term echoes ideas of the "naturalization" of immigrants and of how social and political values become ordinary or "natural," and its use underscores how "evidences" of biblical truth adapt themselves to a nationalist and colonizing outlook. If Palestine is, as Bishop Warren asserts, "the first country where I have felt at home" because of its familiar, sacred geography (*Sights and Insights*, p. 246), then the traveler has already come to possess the land, even as a birthright, at least in the traveler's imagination.

For many nineteenth-century Holy Land travel books, the parallel study Thomson affirms of the Land and the Book would also link the land-text of Palestine to the land-text of North America, as yet another home and setting for divine scenarios. Most of these travelers were filled with anticipation of the millennium: tumultuous events of the nineteenth century were "signs of the times." The evidences they sought would indicate that prophecy would soon be fulfilled, or they at least wrestled with this popular religious current. As a result of these interpretations of certain passages from the Books of Daniel, Revelations, and other biblical texts, the New Israel in North America and its settlers had a special role in God's plan to prepare for the millennium.

Part of the millennial narrative was the necessity for the conversion and return of Jews to the Holy Land as a precondition for the return of Jesus. The belief in Jewish restoration was so widespread among eighteenth- and nineteenth-century ministers and thinkers, ranging from radical deists to conservative biblical literalists, that one scholar deems the doctrine "endemic to American culture."[8] The belief in Jewish restoration paralleled or reinforced the notion that the settlers of the New Israel in North America would also be restored, so to speak, or their colonial presence would be made "natural" by divine approbation: if the old Jews could be "restored" to their nation, then certainly the new, typological ones settling the North American continent could be "restored" as well. In this way, religious significance can be linked to the nationalism of America's settler society. Perhaps the most dramatic enactment of such a parallel could be seen in the account of Mormon Elder Orson Hyde's journey to Jerusalem in 1841. In one of the earliest official acts of the Latter-Day Saints, he arrived in the Holy City to hold a ceremony announcing the imminent, simultaneous restoration of the Jews to the old Holy Land and the Latter-Day Saints to the new one.[9]

Herman Melville was quite aware of this millennialist fascination. In his journal of his 1857 visit to Palestine, he describes his meetings with various American Protestant visionaries who had settled there in order "to facilitate prophecy." In particular, this meant preparing the ground for Jewish return through missionary activity, such as that described by Clorinda Minor,[10] and colonies, such as the encounters with the disastrous Adams colony in Jaffa related by Twain and others. Melville considered all their efforts futile and absurd, and he derided "this preposterous Jew mania." He thought it was impractical, a "Quixotism," that would occur "only by a miracle."[11] Yet he was also attracted to such a quixotic doctrine as a kind of insistent spiritual quest; the mania was "half melancholy, half farcical – like all the rest of the world" (*Journals*, p. 94).

In *Clarel: A Poem and Pilgrimage in the Holy Land* (1876), the pivotal character, Nathan, journeys through a series of American sects to end up converting to Judaism and setting up a precursor to a Zionist settlement in Jerusalem: "Here was an object: Up and do! / With seed and tillage help renew – / Help reinstate the Holy Land" (1.17.262–64).[12] Melville identifies the deep connection to American settlement, describing how "the Puritan – / Mixed latent in his blood – a strain / How evident, of Hebrew source . . ." (1.17.227–29). Nathan represents the exchange between Puritan and Hebrew used to sanctify the North American covenantal colonizing projects, and now "returns" to Holy Land settlement. Nathan's career was based on that of Warder Cresson, the first US consul to Jerusalem, who became so obsessed with the idea of Jewish restoration that he decided to convert to Judaism in order to facilitate prophecy by founding a proto-Zionist settlement outside of Jerusalem in 1851.[13]

As Holy Land books proliferated through the century, they displayed different aspects of these religious and nationalist constructs, as they also engaged in a wide range of common literary characteristics. When John Lloyd Stephens produced *Incidents of Travel in Egypt, Arabia Petraea, and the Holy Land* (1837) as the record of a secular American traveler, he sparked a controversy because it appeared that he had traveled through the cursed Land of Edom and survived, seeming to disprove prophecy. Edgar Allen Poe argued, with great exegetical flourish, that Stephens, although he traveled through the desert from Aqaba to Hebron, did not actually pass through biblical Edom, therefore maintaining the infallibility of prophecy.[14]

When Lt. William Lynch wrote his account of his 1847 voyage down the Jordan and around the Dead Sea, he gave the official US Navy exploration an explicitly nationalist cast. Commissioned at the time of the American victory in the war with Mexico, the adventure was more than the scientific expedition it claimed to be. Indeed, while Lynch did produce precise geographic descriptions of the Jordan River and the Dead Sea, including the discovery of where the Jordan "mingles" with the Dead Sea, his popular exploration narrative also gave readers the opportunity to enjoy the sight of American boats sailing down the mythic river and inland sea, waving the flag patriotically over sacred waters as Lynch contemplated how easy it would be to seize the land from the Sultan for "the Franks" (Westerners).[15]

Other secular writers came out with ironic, mildly irreverent accounts, including *Yusef* (1855) by J. Ross Browne and *The Lands of the Saracen* (1855) by Bayard Taylor, one of the most celebrated travel writers of the day. At the same time, sentimental religious tourists produced numerous travelogues, notably *Tent Life in the Holy Land* (1857) by William C. Prime (lampooned by Twain as "Grimes"), along with numerous books by missionaries and ministers. William Thomson's *The Land and the Book* (1859), based on his twenty-five years in the East as a missionary, proved to be one of the most popular books written by a missionary in the nineteenth century and remained a staple of Sunday school classes throughout the rest of the century.[16]

The most notable books inspired by travel to Ottoman Palestine remain Mark Twain's satirical send-up of the first American tourist cruise *The Innocents Abroad* and Herman Melville's monumental proto-modernist narrative poem *Clarel*, based in part on his remarkable 1857 journal. Both Twain and Melville reproduce the prevailing characteristics of the Holy Land book at the same time as they produce radical critiques, creating what I call infidel counter-texts ("infidel" in the nineteenth-century sense of unbridled heterodoxy). Melville's brilliant, philosophical poem was virtually unread (and his journal unpublished) then, and both journal and poem are only beginning to gain serious attention today, while Twain's travel satire was enormously popular from the moment it was published, although, as in so many of his books, Twain's comic effects allowed readers to avoid the implications of his satire. Twain's travel book is extroverted, public, and iconoclastic, while Melville's poem-pilgrimage is introverted, private, and meditative. Both offer unusual insights into American cultural preoccupations during the nineteenth century as they practice different types of literary mastery.

Writing about the Holy Land in an original fashion was not easy. As Holy Land travelers would "read" the Holy Land, their comprehension would often confirm all of their deepest, established beliefs, including their particular vision of the millennium. As Twain observes in *The Innocents Abroad*, Americans visiting Palestine "came seeking evidence in support of their particular creed; they found a Presbyterian Palestine, and they had already made up their minds to find no other, though possibly they did not know it, being blinded by their zeal." The same held true for Baptists, Catholics, Methodists, Episcopalians, all of whom came "seeking evidence indorsing their several creeds . . . Honest as these men's intentions may have been, they were full of partialities and prejudices, they entered the country with their verdicts already prepared, and they could no more write dispassionately and impartially about it than they could about their own wives and children" (p. 511).

Along with this solipsistic bias, travelers also developed a sense of sacred theatricality, allowing them to cultivate epiphanies or to stage biblical re-enactments. The first view of Jerusalem would invariably produce tears and prayers and Arab shepherds would be seen as biblical figures. As Prime would write, when his *dragoman* or guide came to his aid after he fell from his horse, his wife exclaimed that the scene reminded her of the Good Samaritan in the Bible, particularly as represented in the picture hanging on their wall back home.

Travelers were not just disconcerted by the discrepancy between the material Palestine of the Ottoman Empire and the imagined Holy Land of their preconceptions; they were often deeply, bitterly disappointed. "No country will more quickly dissipate romantic expectation than Palestine – particularly Jerusalem," Melville writes in his journal (*Journals*, p. 91). Travelers were constantly confronted by beggars calling for "baksheesh," and Arabs were often described as dirty, violent, and ignorant, although the myth of the Bedouin as noble Indians of the desert also persisted; Muslims were generally regarded with disgust, while Jews were generally depicted as uncouth and pathetic. Most Americans shared these orientalist stereotypes or chauvinist attitudes, typical of Western culture.

For Twain, Palestine is a discrepancy between the positive, biblical associations of the land, the "large impressions in boyhood," and its disappointing reality, such as its actual small size: "I could not conceive of a small country having so large a history." In order "to profit by this tour," Twain decides he must "unlearn a great many things I have somehow absorbed concerning Palestine," and he devises what he calls "a system of reduction" (*Innocents Abroad*, p. 486), bringing Palestine within an American scale of vision: "The State of Missouri could be split into three Palestines, and there would then be enough material left for part of another – possibly a whole one" (p. 479). The Galilee is a "solemn, sailless, tintless lake . . . looking just as expressionless and unpoetical (when we leave its sublime history out of the question,) as any metropolitan reservoir in Christendom." The material Galilee borders on fraud; and it certainly cannot compare to a New World wonder: The Galilee can "no more be compared to [Lake] Tahoe than a meridian of longitude is to a rainbow" (p. 508).

Catholic and Eastern Orthodox control of the shrines made Protestant travelers feel extremely uneasy, and they regularly rejected any claims to their authenticity. The Church of the Holy Sepulcher in particular was regarded as one such "pious fraud." At the same time, the gaudy-seeming ritual and persistent sectarian squabbling of the "nominal" Christians these travelers encountered deeply offended their ascetic, Protestant sensibilities. After George William Curtis visits the Church of the Holy Sepulcher, he complains of his revulsion from the different Christian sects:

> I make no other complaint than that of disgust. If Jerusalem were nearer Europe or America, it would be different, at least it would be more decent, from the higher character of the population. But going up to Jerusalem as to the holiest city of the purest faith, you are disappointed by what you see of that faith there, as you would be upon approaching a banquet of wit and beauty, to find it a festival of idiots and the insane.[17]

One consequence of this revulsion was to privilege the landscapes of Palestine over the shrines, promoting "tent-life" for travelers in the Holy Land along with new, outdoor shrines, such as the Garden Tomb, as a replacement for the Church of the Holy Sepulcher. Another consequence was the ability, under the guise of criticism of so-called "nominal" Christians, to mock the shrines, particularly since the poverty and perceptions of tawdriness interfered with their sense of true reverence. "When one stands where the Saviour was crucified," Twain writes of the Church of Holy Sepulcher, he finds it all he can do to keep it strictly before his mind that Christ was not crucified in a Catholic Church. He must remind himself every now and then that the great event transpired in the open air, and not in a gloomy, candle-lighted cell in a little corner of a vast church, up-stairs – a small cell all bejeweled and bespangled with flashy ornamentation, in execrable taste.

(*Innocents Abroad*, p. 572)

Finally, there would be meditations upon the "desolation" of the country, a perception common to most travelers. The desolation of Jerusalem, in particular, would stand as evidence of prophecy, but their impressions of ruin also confirmed their disappointment. More than a century later, Saul Bellow in *To Jerusalem and Back* (1976) would quote Twain's lament that "Palestine sits in sack-cloth and ashes . . . Palestine is desolate and unlovely. And why should it be otherwise? Can the curse of the Deity beautify a land? Palestine is no more of this work-day world. It is sacred to poetry and tradition – it is dream-land" (*Innocents Abroad*, pp. 607–08). Melville would ask, "Is the desolation of the land the result of the fatal embrace of the Deity? Hapless are the favorites of heaven . . . In the emptiness of the lifeless antiquity of Jerusalem the emigrant Jews are like flies that have taken up their abode in a skull" (*Journals*, p. 91). As witnesses to the backwards, impoverished condition of the country, travelers easily confirmed one Bible truth: the curse upon the Jews – and consequently upon the land itself – for rejecting Christ.

Palestine did seem barren when compared to the verdure of the New World and elsewhere – Melville observed that Jesus should have been born in Tahiti – although there were a few travelers who saw otherwise. For example, Bayard Taylor compared lush, blooming valleys in Palestine to the California gold country he had just visited; he referred to the new American possession as "our new Syria on the Pacific" (*The Lands of the Saracen*, p. 100). Most American travelers offered passages on God's curse like Twain's and Melville's, even though they were invariably quite ignorant of the actual causes of such desolation. At the same time, most American Holy Land travelers expressed some kind of sympathy for the constant efforts of Westerners to undermine Ottoman control through the "Peaceful Crusade" of mass pilgrimage, missionary work, and European tutelage of the various Christian and Jewish communities; these writers, like Lt. Lynch sailing down the Jordan, would regularly contemplate filibustering adventures to wrest the land from the Turks.

The fact that General Grant took Twain's book with him on his tour indicates just how Twain's burlesque of all the typical conventions of the Holy Land book captured the popular imagination – and appropriated the sacred and colonial associations into an American, capitalist framework. One example is Twain's mock lament at the Tomb of Adam in the Church of the Holy Sepulcher. To Protestant readers, the Church was the height of "pious frauds" concocted by Catholic and Eastern Christians, so Twain had some license to approach the bounds of sacrilegious irreverence. "The tomb of Adam!" Twain exclaims when he comes across the traditional spot for Adam's resting place (appropriately close to the site of the Second Adam's crucifixion) in the exaggerated, bombastic style of nineteenth-century oratory:

> How touching it was, here in a land of strangers, far away from home, and friends, and all who cared for me, thus to discover the grave of a blood relation. True, a distant one, but still a relation. The unerring instinct of nature thrilled its recognition. The fountain of my filial affection was stirred to its profoundest depths, and I gave way to tumultuous emotion...(*Innocents Abroad*, p. 567)

Twain relishes the mockery of American sentimentality, as well as the seemingly gaudy pretensions of non-Protestants and the self-important, chauvinist attitudes of Protestants. His lament for his "blood relation" goes on, reaching what one critic a few years later hailed as the height of "serio-comic weeping and wailing" and as an example of the "humorous sublime" – and the eulogy over Adam's grave became one of the most celebrated passages in the book.[18]

So popular was the Tomb of Adam passage that, years later, in 1902, a St. Louis newspaper could jokingly query, "Who is Mark Twain?" And the journalist could answer that the author was

> the man who visited Adam's tomb, the man who wept over the remains of his first parent. That beautiful act of filial devotion is known in every part of the globe, read by every traveler, translated into every language. Even the dusky savages of the most barbaric corners of the earth have heard of Mark Twain shedding tears at the tomb of Adam. By this time the ancient monument is fairly mildewed with the grief of Mark Twain's imitators.[19]

General Grant visited the Church of the Holy Sepulcher as many American travelers did before him, with Twain's book in hand. But by bringing Twain's book – and his irreverence – he also participated in what had become a uniquely American tourist practice: Grant visited the Tomb of Adam because it was the place where Mark Twain had wept. Twain had given an American meaning to the place, and he inscribed his own persona upon the shrine through burlesque. He had transformed the sacred site into a modern tourist sight, stamping it with the semiotic imprint of a commodity. In effect, Twain brought the money-changers back into the temple, and in this way anticipated the more profane, materialist, political attitudes of twentieth-century Holy Land books.

Israel and Palestine

In the twentieth century, Americans were still motivated by the desire to find evidences of the Bible, and most books employed the familiar characteristics of reading sacred landscape practiced in the previous century. Protestant fascination continued to grow, and it took new, popular forms later in the century with Billy Graham's film *His Land*, and other exegetical tours of the land, while modern Israel and Israelis would become central players in all apocalyptic scenarios, such as in *The Late Great Planet Earth* (1970) by Hal Lindsey and the *Left Behind* series (1996–2005) by Tim LaHay and Jerry Jenkins. With increasing numbers of books by Catholics, Mormons, and Jews, ecumenical and secular, rationalist sensibilities would also play more of a role in the twentieth century.

For one example, Bruce Feiler published a best-seller – *Walking the Bible: A Journey by Land through the Five Books of Moses* (2001) – as a Jewish, albeit somewhat open-minded, empiricist literary explorer.[20] Feiler assigns himself the mission to visit all the sites of the Five Books of Moses, including Mt. Ararat in eastern Turkey, the Red Sea, Sinai and the Pyramids in Egypt, Petra in Jordan, and the Negev desert in Israel. He describes his book as "a topographical midrash, a geographical exegesis of the Bible" (p. 40), and he proceeds to do his own reading of land-text. To accomplish his goal, he visits Jerusalem to meet with experts and crosses various boundaries of the Middle East conflict to reach important shrines or ruins to feel the specific mystique of each biblical place.

Bit by bit, Feiler's quest turns into a conversion story with tropes that William C. Prime would easily recognize. Again and again, a spiritual feeling for the land is awakened in him by being in a biblical place; he is increasingly drawn to the eerie landscape, particularly the desert, as he seeks out the meanings of the sacred stories. With his Israeli guide, archeologist Avner Goren, Feiler considers the attraction of the land and its intoxicating narratives as a "cultural DNA" (p. 325), open to all peoples, even Americans. The stories of the Bible in combination with the actual spirit of the land can draw him and his reader closer to a sense of God that is not bound by creeds or theologies. Although he can still read the sacred land-text in ways similar to the Protestant travelers who came before him, he also has contemporary archeology and the modern State of Israel added to his exegetical equipment.

After the British conquered Palestine and issued the Balfour Declaration in 1917, travelers were increasingly drawn to the modernist, Zionist experiment, broadening the scope of Holy Land literature in dramatically new ways. What Melville calls the "preposterous Jew mania" took an unexpected turn away from its Protestant definitions to become a secular, colonizing national movement. For many, millennialist theology changed in the late nineteenth century to encourage Jewish return – but without the necessity of Jews having first to convert – allowing broader Christian support for the secular Zionist movement. Many American travelers would delight to visit the new experiment of Jewish colonies in the Holy Land, supporting the effort out of humanitarian sentiments, reading the landscape as a story of secular, national redemption for a persecuted people with the founding of the State of Israel as its climax. Saul Bellow, in *To Jerusalem and Back* (1976), contrasts Twain's "unlovely dreamland," along with Melville's nightmarish descriptions of Jerusalem, to the orchards, sowed fields, and "thriving society" built by Zionists in the twentieth century.[21] Bellow sums up the accomplishments and anxieties of modern Israel and Israelis:

> In less than thirty years the Israelis have produced a modern country – doorknobs and hinges, plumbing fixtures, electrical supplies, chamber music, airplanes, teacups. It is both a garrison state and a cultivated society, both Spartan and Athenian. It tries to do everything, to understand everything, to make provision for everything. All resources, all faculties are strained. Unremitting thought about the world situation parallels the defense effort. These people are actively, individually involved in universal history. I don't see how they can bear it. (p. 46)

The advent of the modern is so startling that Bellow and others must devise new techniques to read the landscape. While Twain goes through a process of "reduction" to adjust his overblown notions of biblical geography, Bellow expands his sense of place and history in order to comprehend the new, world-historical State of Israel: "Because people think so hard here, and so much, and because of the length and depth of their history, this sliver of a country sometimes seems quite large. Some dimension of mind seems to extend into space" (p. 56).

Early visitors to the Zionist experiment noted the utopian aspirations of the "pioneers." In *Frontiers of Hope* (1929), Horace Kallen, pragmatist philosopher and Jewish advocate of cultural pluralism in America, visits Jewish communities in Palestine, Poland, and the Soviet Union in a kind of grand tour of Jewish fears and expectations.[22] In this book, Kallen displays many of the new conventions of reading the Holy Land as political experiment. Like other travelers, he is taken with the utopian quest of Palestine's ideologically intoxicated settlers; it is a country of "ancient history and recent heroism" (p. 80), and it is the "recent heroism" that intrigues him. Yet he is also struck by the obstacles these pioneers have to overcome, including their penchant for ideological wrangling. He observes a general strike of Jewish workers demanding exclusive Jewish labor for the new settlements:

> Jews, was the claim, should employ none but Jewish labor. But the leaders of Jewish labor demanded to apply, to a primitive agricultural economy in an impoverished land, the whole European theory of the class conflict and the trade-union notion of hours and wages and conditions of labor brought in from rich industrial countries. And there were, for each job to be done, three Arabs bidding against every Jew . . . (p. 77)

Kallen is a witness to a complex, paradoxical historical process which includes the creation of an exclusively Jewish, capitalist economy with the ideals of socialist egalitarianism.

In 1939, Adam Clayton Powell, Sr., renowned African American minister, published *Palestine and Saints in Caesar's Household*, a collection of Holy Land travel accounts and sermons.[23] As a typical Protestant traveler seeking evidences of biblical truth, he is surprised when he meets modern Jewish settlers to discover that they are not at all motivated by religion. Rev. Powell is disturbed by many of the people he meets, of whatever religion, and he relates his disappointment in a register familiar to many Holy Land travelers before him:

> Before going to Palestine, [the author] thought it was a divine place and totally different from any other spot on earth. He expected to find all men and all things holy. This expectation was exploded almost immediately. Before he had spent a week in the Holy Land, he had met people characterized by all the bad qualities possessed by the worst in New York and in the mountains of Kentucky. That little strip of land between the Jordan and the Mediterranean produced more holy characters and holy literature than any one of the five continents, but the men and their literature have had more influence for good upon the citizens of Chicago than upon the natives. It is still true that prophets are not without honor save in their own homes. (p. vii)

As other African American travelers, such as New Orleans dandy David Dorr (*A Colored Man 'Round the World* [1858]) and pan-Africanist Edward Wilmot Blyden (*From West Africa to Palestine* [1873]), Powell's responses involve a complex interweaving of a sense of Western and American superiority with identification with the East and the oppressed.

Writing on the eve of World War II, Powell is also keenly aware of "the world's rising tide of fierce, ungodly anti-Semitism." The fulminations of Mussolini and Hitler intrude upon his meditations: "The colored people should be the last, even by their silence, to give consent to the brutal persecution of the Jews. For if this campaign of inhuman cruelty against the Jews should succeed, who knows but what the same evil forces would next attempt to put the colored people on the rack" (*Palestine and Saints*, p. viii). With European anti-Semitism reaching its climax in Hitler's mass murder, a whole new set of associations attached themselves to the land.

After the war, humanitarian sympathies for Jewish survivors energized journalists' reports. In 1946, I. F. Stone would write *Underground to Palestine*, a brilliant account of a sympathetic journalist joining Jewish refugees from Displaced Persons camps in Europe as they are clandestinely smuggled on board a ship manned almost entirely by American Jews and spirited through the British blockade.[24] Stone records the anguish, passion, and ingenuity of those simply trying to reach the land, placing the ordeal within a sense of immediate politics and grand narratives: "The exodus of Jews from Europe, of which I was an eye witness, is the greatest in the history of the Jewish people, greater than the migrations of the past out of Egypt and Spain. To tell its story properly one would need to be not a newspaper reporter, but an ancient Hebrew prophet" (pp. 221–22). In a reissue three decades after this exodus, Stone writes two reflections, revising his conclusions. As a Jewish dissident, he objects to the occupation of the West Bank and Gaza, and as a supporter of Israel he reasserts his earlier dream of a single bi-national state. Disillusionment with the Zionist dream is yet another form of disappointment that pervades this literature.

Not a prophet but a philosopher, Hannah Arendt, in *Eichman in Jerusalem: A Report on the Banality of Evil* (1963), attaches the entire narrative of Hitler's "Final Solution" to the idea of being in Jerusalem.[25] She interrogates the kidnapping of Adolf Eichman from Argentina, "the fearsome, word-and-thought-defying *banality of evil*" (p. 252) embodied by the Nazi official, the machinations and manipulations of the Final Solution, and the "irregularities and abnormalities of the trial in Jerusalem" (p. 253). But there is no travel in this book, except for the bland Nazi functionary and the wounds of the Holocaust both brought to haunt a land where none of the horrors had taken place. The Holocaust became a new, overarching narrative brought to the land and added to the story of an abused people's awakening. When *Exodus* (1958) by Leon Uris and the 1960 Otto Preminger film made from the novel appeared, the American public identified as never before with the story of Jewish destruction and rebirth in the Holy Land as an American story of "pioneers" seeking justice and redemption in a new (albeit "old") land.

When Saul Bellow makes his way to Jerusalem in 1976, he is able to write a political investigation, a record of a fact-finding trip to Israel. He frames the journey within the tensions of modernity and antiquity by describing his encounter on the plane ride with a pious Hassid so cut off from the secular world that he has no idea who Einstein is. Bellow continues the contrast between the modern, rationalist side of Western thought and its opposite of medieval, non-rational attachments and dreams. In this he also draws out the same comparative link with American settlement that Melville and other Holy Land writers have employed.

> In me [the Hassid] sees what deformities the modern age can produce in the seed of Abraham. In him I see a piece of history, an antiquity. It is rather as if Puritans in seventeenth-century dress and observing seventeenth-century customs were to be found still living in Boston or Plymouth. Israel, which receives us impartially, is accustomed to strange arrivals. But then Israel is something else again. (*To Jerusalem and Back*, p. 5)

Bellow engages in his political tour, his experience of the surprising "something else" that can unite two widely different Jews, meeting with writers and historians, with the Mayor of Jerusalem Teddy Kollek and other Israeli politicians, all in the shadow of the 1973 war, the Arab oil embargo, Henry Kissinger's recent arrangement for Israel and Egypt to disengage in the Sinai, and the broader machinations of the Cold War. In the wake of the Vietnam War, the West is questioning itself, something Israel cannot afford to do, since it must face "the nightmare of annihilation. This is what Israel lives with. Although people will not often speak of it, it is always there" (p. 38). After a series of encounters and ruminations, after weighing paradoxical outlooks and world history, Bellow reaches one, basic conclusion: "The root of the problem is simply this – that the Arabs will not agree to the existence of Israel" (p. 179). Writers sympathetic to Israel would regularly reflect upon the fear of the state's destruction and the sense of being surrounded by intractable, irrational enemies.

After the 1967 war and the Israeli occupation of the West Bank and Gaza, one of those enemies, the Palestinians, increasingly entered the vision of American travelers much more distinctly than before and with yet other fears of destruction. By 1979, Edward Said would write *The Question of Palestine* (1979), advocating for those he terms "the victims of Zionism," disputing the dominant, pro-Israel perspective delineated by Bellow. Writing such books as *Out of Place* (1999) and *Reflections on Exile* (2000), he added yet another vision as a Palestinian American, that of displacement and exile, of someone whose travel to Palestine would occur mostly in memory or as a political project outside of the country.[26] His memoirs and accounts of return in the 1990s added to this sense of loss and new anguish, something very new in this travel literature.

Politics would increasingly inject itself, no matter what the religious goal. Grace Halswell initially planned to write a book about three families representing three faiths in Israel and Palestine. "And I thought to leave aside politics," she explains. "I quickly learned, however, that that would be like going to Antarctica and not mentioning the ice. 'Leave out politics!' exclaimed one resident. 'We *eat* politics morning, noon, and night.'" In *Journey to Jerusalem* (1981), she explains that "The politics is all about land."[27]

With the first Intifada, starting in 1988, a series of books visited the conflict with more sympathy to the Palestinian perspective. In *A Season of Stones: Living in a Palestinian Village* (1991), Helen Winternitz learns Arabic and stays in one West Bank village as a journalist ethnographer, wanting to learn more about Palestinian life and resistance.[28] She observes the day-to-day battles and organizing of the Intifada, as the village tries to stop a new Jewish settlement from encroaching on its land. By the time she leaves, the first Gulf War is over, and "the Palestinians and the Israelis continued with their own battles, each side angrier than before" (p. 300).

Gloria Emerson, who won the National Book Award for her reporting on Vietnam, writes *Gaza: A Personal Account of an Occupied Land* (1991), a record of a year of the uprising in the Gaza Strip.[29] Based in the Marna Hotel, a safe place respected by both sides, she meets with the popular committees of the nationalist uprising, courageous professionals, such as the human rights lawyer Raji Sourani, and ordinary people. She even has the chance "to meet a Hamas dignitary" (p. 168), and writes a witty account of the conversation between the robed Islamist and the female, secular agnostic. Emerson paints a vivid portrait of misery in the refugee camps and of youth in exuberant rebellion despite grim conditions.

In *Consider and Hear Me: Voices from Israel and the Occupied Territories* (1993), Saul Slapikoff reports on the popular organizations on the West Bank and Israeli peace groups as part of a solidarity delegation.[30] Slapikoff is a biologist, but he is also self-consciously a Jewish leftist and an American; he considers Jewish culpability and American complicity, as he documents the uprising through extensive interviews. *An American Feminist in Palestine: The Intifada Years* (1994), by Sherna Berger Gluck, is also based on traveling with solidarity delegations along with extended visits on her own to the Occupied Territories between 1988 and 1991.[31]

Thomas Friedman's National Book Award winning *From Beirut to Jerusalem* (1989) ends with the first Intifada, and it is perhaps the most widely read account of the conflict in the last two decades.[32] The complexity of the struggle becomes increasingly evident, along with the direct role of the United States and growing sympathies for the Palestinians. No longer witnesses of European colonial ambitions, Americans can now view their country as a major, imperial participant in the conflict; "mainstream" travelers must try to balance conflicting realities: US strategic support for Israel, geopolitical interests in the region overall, and American ideals of democracy. Friedman, as an American Jew, tries to cover all sides of the Middle East conflict, starting with the Lebanese civil war and the 1982 Israeli invasion of Lebanon; he seeks to be an objective journalist, capable of criticizing Israel for allowing the Sabra and Shatila massacre, which he witnessed, and Palestinians for terrorism, or at least he makes an attempt. But it is difficult. "[W]hen it comes to discussing the Middle East, people go temporarily insane," he observes. "[A] Jew who wants to make a career working in or studying about the Middle East will always be a lonely man: he will never be fully accepted or trusted by the Arabs, and he will never be fully accepted or trusted by the Jews" (p. 6).

Friedman also counters Twain's "reduction" with an enlargement of Israel because of cultural compatibility. He offers the view that "What the West expected from the Jews of the past, it expects from Israel today" (p. 432):

> News from modern Israel is more appealing and digestible for people in the West than from elsewhere, because the characters, the geography, and the themes involved are so familiar, so much a part of our cultural lenses . . . What matters is the size that country or people occupies in the super story, and when looked at that way, Israel becomes one of the largest of countries in the eyes of the West, while big countries such as China or Sudan become very small.
>
> (p. 428)

Friedman moves from Beirut under siege to the massacre of Sabra and Shatila to the life of settlers in the West Bank, and while he maintains his sympathies for Israel, the journalism he practices attempts to bridge the divide. By 1989, the American experience of the conflict has broadened, and he could observe that "Israel's victory in 1967 injected a new spirit of grandiosity, of manifest destiny, into the Jewish state" (p. 459).

Like Twain, his observations form a mosaic of scenes and anecdotes from which he draws decisive conclusions. Twain, however, seeks effects, hoping to extract truth through laughter, always mindful of the need to entertain. Friedman is a political correspondent, and his anecdotes are deployed to convey analysis, to be illustrations pointing to deeper proofs. His stories are meant to reveal truth, as he gives examples of the irrational yet deeply felt political compulsions on all sides – Lebanese Christian, Israeli Jew, Palestinian refugee – although historians and political scientists would find his anecdotes insufficient.

Friedman is keenly aware of the "super stories," the religious myths and national narratives that activate the different sides of the conflict, and he advocates the need to somehow diminish the force of these narratives in order to achieve peace. As part of this, he tries to delineate the psychology of both sides. For example, he concludes that, for the Palestinians, the first Intifada "was an expression of basic, elemental rage – rage at the Israelis who never allowed [Palestinians] to feel at home, rage at the Arabs who were ready to sell them out, and rage at a world that wanted to forget them" (p. 373). On the other hand, the Israelis were enraged "to have these 'niggers' . . . suddenly getting uppity and saying that they would not accept their second-class status any longer. More than a few Israelis wanted these 'thankless' Palestinian maids and waiters to be put back in their proper places." But then he reaches further to understand the deeper psychic phenomenon at the source of Israeli rage, which he sums up as the fact that "the Palestinians were depriving the Israelis of their sense of being at home" (p. 391). To Friedman, both Israelis and Palestinians need to feel at home, and to accomplish this comforting domesticity they both need their own states. American travelers from the nineteenth century would readily recognize the conflation of home and nation.

No matter how the conflict will be resolved, more American writers will no doubt embark on spiritual quests to the Holy Land; and more political investigations and accounts will be written about Israel and Palestine, particularly as America's imperial role increasingly affects the entire region. Many of these books will display the characteristics and themes of the nineteenth and twentieth centuries touched upon here, including the writers' reflections upon their own sense of spiritual and political home.

Notes

1. For more on the nineteenth and early twentieth-century fascination with the Holy Land, see John Davis, *Landscape of Belief: Encountering the Holy Land in Nineteenth-Century American Art and Culture* (Princeton: Princeton University Press, 1996); Hilton Obenzinger, *American Palestine: Melville, Twain, and the Holy Land Mania* (Princeton: Princeton University Press, 1999); Lester Vogel, *To See a Promised Land: Americans and the Holy Land in the Nineteenth Century* (University Park: Pennsylvania State University Press, 1993).

2. Mark Twain (Samuel L. Clemens), *The Innocents Abroad, or The New Pilgrim's Progress* (Hartford, CT: American Publishing Co., 1869).

3. Edward Robinson, *Biblical Researches in Palestine, Mount Sinai, and Arabia Petraea*, 3 vols. (1841; facsimile, New York: Arno Press, 1977), vol. I, p. 46.

4. William M. Thomson, *The Land and the Book; or, Biblical Illustrations Drawn from the Manners and Customs, the Scenes and Scenery of the Holy Land*, 2 vols. (New York: Harper and Bros., 1859), vol. II, p. xv.

5. Thomas De Witt Talmage, *Talmage on Palestine: A Series of Sermons* (1890; facsimile, New York: Arno Press, 1977), p. 140.

6. Bishop Henry White Warren, *Sights and Insights; or, Knowledge by Travel* (New York: Nelson and Phillips, 1874), p. 250.

7. Rev. Stephen Olin, quoted in Moshe Davis, "The Holy Land Idea in American Spiritual History," in *With Eyes toward Zion: Scholars Colloquium on America–Holy Land Studies*, ed. Moshe Davis (New York: Arno Press, 1977), p. 13.

8. Carl Frederick Ehle, Jr., "Prolegomena to Christian Zionism in America: The Views of Increase Mather and William E. Blackstone Concerning the Doctrine of the Restoration of Israel" (PhD diss., New York University, New York, 1977), p. 331.

9. See Elder Orson Hyde, *A Voice from Jerusalem, or a Sketch of the Travels and Ministry of Elder Orson Hyde* (Boston: Albert Morgan, 1842).

10. See [Clorinda Minor], *Meshullam! Or, Tidings from Jerusalem* (1851; facsimile, New York: Arno Press, 1977).

11. Herman Melville, *Journals*, ed. Howard C. Horsford with Lynn Horth (Evanston and Chicago: Northwestern University Press and the Newberry Library, 1989), p. 94.

12. Herman Melville, *Clarel: A Poem and Pilgrimage in the Holy Land*, ed. Harrison Hayford, Alma A. MacDougall, Hershell Parker, and G. Thomas Tanselle, with Walter Bezanson (1876; rpt. Evanston and Chicago: Northwestern University Press and the Newberry Library, 1991). Parenthetical references to this edition of Clarel will be in roman numerals according to part, canto, and line.

13. See Warder Cresson, *The Key of David* (1852; facsimile, New York: Arno Press, 1977).

14. See John Lloyd Stephens, *Incidents of Travel in Egypt, Arabia Petraea, and the Holy Land*, ed. Victor Wolfgang von Hagan (1837; rpt. Norman: University of Oklahoma Press, 1970) and Edgar Allan Poe, "Review of Stephens' Arabia Petraea," *New York Review* (October 1837).

15. See William F. Lynch, *Narrative of the United States' Expedition to the River Jordan and the Dead Sea* (1849; rpt. Philadelphia: Lea and Blanchard, 1850).

16. J. Ross Browne, *Yusef; or, The Journey of the Frangi, A Crusade in the East* (New York: Harper and Bros., 1855); William C. Prime, *Tent Life in the Holy Land* (New York: Harper and Bros., 1857); Bayard Taylor, *The Lands of the Saracen; or, Pictures of Palestine, Asia Minor, Sicily, and Spain* (New York: G. P. Putnam, 1855).

17. George William Curtis, *The Howadji in Syria* (New York: Harper and Bros., 1852), p. 190.

18. Samuel S. Cox, *Why We Laugh* (New York: Harper and Bros., 1880), pp. 58–59.

19. *St. Louis Republic*, 1 June 1902, quoted in Louis J. Budd, *Our Mark Twain: The Making of His Public Personality* (Philadelphia: University of Pennsylvania Press, 1983), p. 37.

20. Bruce Feiler, *Walking the Bible: A Journey by Land through the Five Books of Moses* (New York: William Morrow, 2001).

21. Saul Bellow, *To Jerusalem and Back: A Personal Account* (New York: Viking, 1976).

22. Horace Kallen, *Frontiers of Hope* (1929; rpt. New York: Arno Press, 1977).

23. Adam Clayton Powell, *Palestine and Saints in Caesar's Household* (New York: R. R. Smith, 1939).

24. I. F. Stone, *Underground to Palestine*, with new introduction and epilogue (1946; rpt. New York: Pantheon Books, 1978).

25. Hannah Arendt, *Eichman in Jerusalem: A Report on the Banality of Evil* (1963; revised 1964; rpt. New York: Penguin, 1994).

26. Edward Said, *The Question of Palestine* (New York: Times Books, 1979); *Out of Place: A Memoir* (New York: Knopf, 1999); *Reflections on Exile: And Other Essays* (Cambridge, MA: Harvard University Press, 2000).

27. Grace Halswell, *Journey to Jerusalem* (New York: Macmillan, 1981), p. 2.

28. Helen Winternitz, *A Season of Stones: Living in a Palestinian Village* (New York: Atlantic Monthly Press, 1991).

29. Gloria Emerson, *Gaza: A Personal Account of an Occupied Land* (New York: Atlantic Monthly Press, 1991).

30. Saul Slapikoff, *Consider and Hear Me: Voices from Israel and the Occupied Territories* (Philadelphia: Temple University Press, 1993).

31. Sherna Berger Gluck, *An American Feminist in Palestine: The Intifada Years* (Philadelphia: Temple University Press, 1994).

32. Thomas Friedman, *From Beirut to Jerusalem* (1989; rpt. with new chapter, New York: Anchor Books, Doubleday, 1995).

9

CHRISTOPHER MCBRIDE

Americans in the larger world: beyond the Pacific coast

This chapter examines travel writing by Americans during the nineteenth and early twentieth centuries that focuses on extra-continental journeys to islands. Although America was initially "discovered" by sea, the settlement of the United States by immigrants focused largely on filling the empty spaces on the continental map. However, by the mid-nineteenth century, the Western frontier was rapidly vanishing as the transcontinental railroad, telegraph service, and steamships emerged. Needing more land, the nation looked abroad, turning its attention towards the islands of the South Pacific, Cuba, and Hawaii. As the land frontier closed, the sea voyage became important for both imperial and literary exploration. The travel writing that results enables us to understand the relationship between American colonial and literary activity abroad.

To begin the study of American travel to the South Pacific, we must acknowledge the place the Marquesas Islands hold in the history of American imperialism. In 1815, American naval captain David Porter proposed to President James Madison that he be allowed to lead an American exploration voyage to the Pacific in order to explore potential commercial development and pursue military colonization.[1] After his arrival at Nukuheva, Porter notified President Madison and Secretary of State James Monroe that he had annexed the Marquesas in the name of the United States. Though neither acknowledged Porter's letters, Porter's claim established these islands in the American imagination as a possible site for overseas expansion and trade. As a result, subsequent writers adopted this model of conquest in their attitudes towards foreign cultures.

Herman Melville's first widely read publication, *Typee* (1846), continues the American interest in the Marquesas Islands. Based on Melville's whaling voyage to the South Pacific and his arrival at Nukuheva in 1842, *Typee* simultaneously reflects dominant attitudes and raises difficult questions about America's future imperial direction. Relaying his adventure, Tommo the narrator commonly portrays the islanders through stereotypes, which Homi K. Bhabha calls the "major discursive strategy" of colonial discourse.[2] But these essentially demeaning stereotypes often give way to praise for the natives, displaying Tommo's own ambivalence and uncertainty towards both the Typees and his own colonizing Western culture. Like many sailors, his first attraction is to the uninhibited young Marquesan females. While still aboard the ship, Tommo sees the "swimming nymphs . . . [with] their jet-black tresses streaming over their shoulders, and half enveloping their otherwise naked forms" and wonders: "How avoid so dire a temptation?"[3] Besides passive integration into this foreign community through interaction with these women, Tommo himself participates in his assimilation into Typee culture by embracing much of their culture. Upon his initial arrival in the Typee valley, Tommo claims no knowledge of the Typee language whatsoever, asserting that: "from our ignorance of the language it was impossible for us to enlighten [the Typees]" (p. 75). However, as his stay in the valley progresses, this ignorance gives way to an apparent understanding of the native language. Tommo is able to translate " 'Ki-ki muee muee, ah! moee moee mortarkee' " into "eat plenty, ah! sleep very good" (p. 88). But it is clear that Tommo never fully understands their culture when he expresses fear for his life and the belief that these cannibalistic natives intend to devour him. His fear of the natives seems unfounded.[4] Cannibalism is never a real threat to the narrator; it seems to function largely as a deterrent to potential colonizing outsiders. Hence, if Tommo leaves the valley with stories of Typee hospitality, the natives will lose the protection their reputation affords them. Tommo never acknowledges or even realizes this protective function, and instead, *Typee* concludes quickly with Tommo fleeing the island.

Typee seems to rely upon the predictable stereotype of cannibalism to avoid engaging the more serious racial issues raised in the text. Cannibalism would have been regarded by any of Melville's Western readers as deplorable,[5] thereby justifying Tommo's actions during his escape and allowing Western readers to categorize the Marquesans as "savages" – avoiding any thought of their condition as "racially" Other or as victims of imperialism. Such classification also defers any discussion of these islanders as racially equal to "white" Westerners, shunning the consideration of "race" in this racially volatile period for a tale of exotic foreigners and escape.[6] Nonetheless, the text has raised many questions about the nature of stereotyping, both racial and colonial, none of which are fully confronted in Tommo's narrative. If Tommo cannot function within this "racially" Other society, what are the possibilities for "black"/"white" relations in mid-nineteenth-century America when racial tension loomed before the Civil War? As a result of Melville's writing, the Marquesas and other South Seas

Islands take up a place in the American colonial imagination as "savage" locations requiring Western civilizing influence. Moreover, racial integration is portrayed as unacceptable, and Tommo returns to his own highly segregated American society. These attitudes, we will see, grow stronger in American travel literature as the nineteenth century progresses and the range of American travel writing expands.

But what did Melville, and nineteenth-century America, hope to find in the South Seas? For the young nation, Melville's adventure presented a means through which it could explore contact with the Other outside the confines of American soil. Moreover, Melville's literary excursion was part of the cultural, military, and artistic process through which America developed a sense of its identity as potential imperial power capable of asserting Anglo-Saxon "superiority." For Melville, this encounter with the Other was equally complex and influential. Clearly enamored with Typee society during his stay, Tommo nonetheless finds the need to flee and return home when the threat of cultural assimilation arises. By articulating these contradictions about race and imperialism in antebellum America, Melville is writing as much about the difficulties of racial coexistence in the United States as about cultural contact in the Marquesas. For Melville and America, a foreign culture allowed exploration of the "dark" underside of the country's ostensible commitment to freedom, liberty, and equality. Addressing this formative travel and literary treatment of race, I believe, is also essential for understanding Melville's "big" books. As both a cultural marker and metaphorical device, race plays a prominent role in many of Melville's later novels of the sea, including *Moby-Dick* (1851) and "Benito Cereno" (1855).

Herman Melville was not the only writer of the period who used his experiences at sea as a source for his travel writing. With the publication of his seafaring narrative *Two Years Before the Mast* (1840), Richard Henry Dana, Jr. introduced Americans to the California coast by relating his experiences as an ordinary sailor traveling from Boston to California and back. Dana's descriptions of California's burgeoning trade, natural wonders, and developing cities – such as San Diego and San Francisco – were an important precursor to later treatment of seafaring by American writers such as Herman Melville and Jack London. Because of this influence, *Two Years Before the Mast* has been the subject of numerous literary studies.[7] Dana's travel narrative, *To Cuba and Back: A Vacation Voyage* (1859), has received less critical attention. As a colonial text, *To Cuba and Back* may also help us to understand *Two Years Before the Mast*, including its power as a promotional tract for additional colonization of California. Such a supplementary cultural function becomes more fully visible with a critical study of *To Cuba and Back*.

While Dana relates the details of his maritime journey and subsequent overland tour of Cuba, the narrative is laced with significant subtexts. For example, a predilection towards stereotyping appears immediately upon his arrival in Havana, as a wide array of foreign scenes crosses Dana's sight. Gazing into a crowd at the harbor, he sees "here and there the familiar lips and teeth, and vacant, easily-pleased face of the Negro."[8] Such condescending portrayal of "black" characters recalls Dana's background as a white male from antebellum America, where a racial hierarchy thrived even in the non-plantation north. Moreover, Dana's stereotypes are not reserved for the black residents of the island. Checking into his Havana hotel, he derides a "swarthy Spanish lad" for "looking very much as if he never washed" and providing poor service as a bellhop (*To Cuba and Back*, p. 12). In these scenes and in the majority of his cultural interactions, Dana retreats to the more comfortable position of critical observer of Cuba which allows him to maintain a position of superiority for the remainder of his tour.[9]

Particularly significant within *To Cuba and Back* are Dana's plantation visits, which place his stereotypical notions of race literally and imaginatively deeper into Cuba, and highlight the economic underpinnings of slavery. As Dana visits the sugar plantations lining Cuba's interior, his narrative further exposes attitudes towards non-white characters – particularly slaves on sugar plantations, who were the majority of Cuban residents at the time.[10] In many ways, visiting these plantations was the ultimate goal of Dana's visit, and his guarded enthusiasm is clear in a number of his descriptive passages. He notices "Negroes, men and women and children, some cutting the cane, some loading the carts, and some tending the mill and furnace" (p. 48). Observing this labor, Dana generally ignores the difficulties these enslaved workers face, and offers only cursory mention of the harsh labor conditions. Instead, black plantation workers are treated with the same observant eye as the natural scenery. As he turns his focus back to his own privileged status as genteel traveler, Dana fails to offer social commentary, instead maintaining the role of observer even when confronted with glaring racial inequality worthy of his attention. His time on this plantation, and the accompanying first-hand knowledge of the slave system he gathers, has not led Dana to pointed evaluation of slavery in Cuba and America.

Of course, we might view Dana's narrative descriptions with little surprise since he is an American writing in 1859, and the product of a country that countenanced slavery in half its territory. However, he was also a member of the Free Soil Party, which argued against the expansion of slavery as a central part of its political platform. Seeing the evils of slavery for the first time, Dana is faced with an opportunity to apply his political ideals to an active critique that would be read by a number of Americans, particularly in the north. Instead, he capitulates to the overriding culture of his day – a culture rooted in the burgeoning American imperialism of the nineteenth century. An essential trading partner, able to supply sugar and serve as a market for American exports, Cuba held an important place for prominent American business interests. As a member of the American elite, Dana simply reinforces this dominant American policy through his representation of the island in this book. In a telling illustration of this cultural–literary connection, he concludes *To Cuba and Back* with a focus on Cuba's abundant material resources. The usually detached observations of this "vacation voyage" are finally transformed into agents of an imperial promotional tract. Dana closes his discussion of Cuban resources by further highlighting the island's commerce, suggesting strongly that America pursue the commercial opportunities available on the island. Though his narrative provides a detailed introduction to Cuba for many of his readers, he also portrays the island as inferior to America, thereby maintaining a sense of American cultural hegemony. Any concerns for the victims of colonialism are generally omitted in Dana's exploration of Cuba, as the mixed racial component and his own connection to America's developing overseas commerce blind him to the injustice on the island.

By the second half of the nineteenth century, the Hawaiian Islands began to receive significant attention from the United States. Mark Twain's *Letters from Hawaii*, written for the *Sacramento Union* in 1866, illustrate both Twain's development as a literary persona, and the ways in which postbellum American concerns are addressed through literary exploration abroad. Arguing for American population of the islands, Twain offers the country a way to work through its concerns about the effectiveness of Reconstruction.

On January 13, 1866, the steamer *Ajax* initiated a service between San Francisco and Honolulu, Sandwich Islands – a route that dramatically reduced travel time from twenty-one to ten days each way and raised American awareness of these Pacific islands. The *Sacramento Union* agreed to pay him for a series of travel letters describing life on the Sandwich Islands and cover his travel expenses, so on March 7, 1866, Samuel Clemens sailed aboard the steamship *Ajax* for Honolulu. The twenty-five letters Clemens sent back to California under his pen name Mark Twain played a significant role in the continuing exploration of America's domestic and foreign identity.[11] Twain begins his first letter with humor: "There are a good many mosquitoes around tonight and they are rather troublesome; but it is a source of unalloyed satisfaction to me to know that the two millions I sat down on a minute ago will never sing again."[12] One of the nuisances of life in the tropics is the presence of insects, and since he was always straightforward in his "journalistic" letters, Twain refuses to hide the realities of island life. But in choosing to write sarcastically about the "two million" mosquitoes, he is also able to lighten the subject for his readers. Twain's comedic tactics continue as he looks backward to describe his steamship journey from California to Hawaii. Throughout this letter, Twain expresses the typical impressions of a man for whom the ocean was a new, unfamiliar, and unsettling expanse. Reflecting on the "turbulent sea," he writes: "I found twenty-two passengers, leaning over the bulwarks vomiting" (*Letters*, p. 6). Of course, stormy waters and seasickness were frequent consequences of sea travel, but Twain elects to diminish these inconveniences by presenting the underlying humor of this situation and focusing instead on his promotional intent in composing the letters. Aside from simply telling his tale of sea travel and advertising steamer service to Hawaii, Twain has a deeper motive for making the journey seem acceptable to his readers – a motive strongly tied to American aims in the Pacific. He becomes less jocular when he presents a case for the sating of American imperial desires: "The main argument in favor of a line of fast steamers is [that] . . . [t]hey would soon populate the islands with Americans, and loosen that French and English grip which is gradually closing around them" (p. 12). The yearning to "populate the islands with Americans" is a direct result of the multiple Western forces influencing Hawaii, and only an increased American presence would counteract French and English power. In advocating commercial proliferation, Twain is not a unique seafarer; his literary approach echoes many of the techniques employed earlier by Dana.

Twain's complex relationship to America's developing interest in the Hawaiian Islands is most vividly expressed in his discussion of Hawaiian sugar plantations. In Letter 23, a description of all aspects of the sugar industry on the islands, he even goes as far as to predict: "When all the cane lands in the Islands are under full cultivation, they will produce over 250,000,000 pounds of sugar annually" (p. 260). For visionary capitalists in America, such economic promise would have been an enormous catalyst to explore investment in the islands.[13] Though Twain's descriptions of the Hawaiian sugar plantations and their potential for significant profit were strong drives for his writing, his letters also exhibit deeper motivations which illuminate the culture of nineteenth-century America. For example, Twain deploys racial stereotypes that seem to reflect the deeper social conflict surrounding Reconstruction. Two particular images stand out in a series of letters in which only passing mention of the just-ended Civil War is made. Traveling from Oahu to the island of Hawaii aboard the schooner *Boomerang*, Twain uses racially toned language to describe the ship's cramped deck: "When the captain and Brown and myself and four other gentlemen and the wheelsman were all assembled on the little after portion of the deck which is sacred to the cabin passengers, it was full – there was not room for any more *quality* folks" (p. 195; emphasis added). The space allocated for such "quality" gentlemen – as opposed to the "low quality" natives – is here deemed comically inadequate by the travelers who move about the islands for leisure. Shortly thereafter, Twain describes the accommodations for Kanakas (Hawaiian natives): "Another section of the deck . . . was full of natives . . . As soon as we set sail the natives all laid down on the deck as thick as Negroes in a slave pen, and smoked and conversed and captured vermin and ate them, spit on each other and were truly sociable" (p. 196). Twain's purpose here is twofold. On one hand, by consciously highlighting the racial and social differences between the diverse passengers, he is able to maintain his own superior status, thereby asserting American supremacy. But his choice of analogy – "as thick as Negroes in a slave pen" – is also par-ticularly effective for his Southern readers. The colonial message is simple: these dark-skinned people are inferior – no better than the slaves recently emancipated – so America may comfortably exploit them and their land for profit.

Twain's time in Hawaii was more than just an opportunity for testing and refining his authorial power. Since his letters were written primarily for business leaders in California, they served the related purpose of highlight-ing Hawaii's enormous economic potential. By presenting the Hawaiian as racially different and willing to relinquish control of valuable land, Twain was able to put off consideration of the damage caused by imperial incur-sions, and instead explore race outside the confines of America. These early considerations of race in his Hawaiian writings were eventually transformed into his more probing confrontation of the issue in his later masterpieces, *Adventures of Huckleberry Finn* (1884) and *Pudd'nhead Wilson* (1894); the islands were a crucial literary starting point for him. As a result of his letters, Twain not only announced himself to the literary world, but also opened Hawaii as an imperial, capitalistic, and imaginative space for the developing nation.

Not long after Twain published his Hawaii letters, Charles Warren Stod-dard fictionally recounts eight months spent roaming the South Seas in *South-Sea Idylls* (1873). Through his unique presentation of the islands, Stoddard offers Americans an alternative vision of colonial capitalism tied directly to the bodies of those to be colonized. Initially praised in literary and popular circles, but later ignored by both critics and the public, the book provides a window into Stoddard's late nineteenth-century literary and cultural world. Full of stories depicting South-Sea Islanders and clev-erly veiled homosexuality, *South-Sea Idylls* draws attention to previously unseen homoerotic aspects of American colonialism. In foregrounding such concealed behavior, the text raises crucial issues surrounding American perceptions of sexuality, leprosy, and colonized foreigners – themes inherited from Melville's *Typee* and Twain's *Letters from Hawaii*.

In the South Seas, Stoddard's unusual personal and colonial mission strongly influences all aspects of his cultural interaction. For example, the story "Pearl-Hunting in the Pomotous" expresses many of the peculiar imperial undercurrents present in Stoddard's South Sea adventures. Wishing to explore islands in the vicinity of Tahiti, the narrator embarks on a schooner to visit what he calls the "Dangerous Archipelago, or . . . the Pomotou Islands."[14] After three days of heavy swells and unsuccessful searching for land, the ship comes upon a small harbor and is met by numerous natives in canoes. The American ship becomes "for the time being the center of their local commerce" (*South-Sea Idylls*, p. 136). In the Pomotous, Stoddard's narrator reinforces this commercial use of natives once he learns that the ship will be in port for a few days. Stoddard's narrator meets a native named Hua Manu, whom he employs for his own financial gain. Pearls were a valuable resource, and the narrator hopes that he can procure a sizeable number of these treasures for later sale. However, because of the difficulty of diving for pearls, the narrator is unable to do the searching himself. Instead, the arduous work of recovering oysters will fall to the amenable Hua Manu, who dives while the narrator observes. Shortly hereafter, the pearl hunting is interrupted as the two are carried out to sea. Exposed to the vicious elements and deprived of food or water, the two wait desperately for days, hoping that the schooner might sight them on its return to Tahiti. Unable to maintain his physical and mental faculties beyond a few days in this harsh and foreign environment, the narrator deteriorates rapidly. He finds himself in "oblivious intervals" of "suspended animation" while "consumed with thirst [and] speechless with hunger" (p. 150). In a turn on the typical colonial scheme of the Westerner in power, Stoddard's narrator plays the passive role, succumbing to this hostile climate. Hua Manu, on the other hand, remains physically capable and vigilantly "on the lookout" (p. 150). In the throes of his anguish, the narrator hallucinates, explaining: "[I felt] someone gathering me in his arms . . . like an infant I lay in the embrace of my deliverer, who moistened my parched lips and burning throat with delicious and copious draughts" (p. 150). The narrator awakens some time later – hours, or, perhaps, days – to find himself being nursed to health aboard the schooner. These rescuing sailors recount how the ship found the narrator and Hua Manu on their atoll, while the narrator learns of his companion's sacrifice and consequent death. In this case, it is the Other who saves the colonizer from death, calling into question American supremacy over foreigners.

In the best-known story in *South-Sea Idylls*, "Chumming With a Savage," the narrator replicates this pattern of a homoerotic affair with a young native that results in the boy's death.[15] Part 1 of this three part story is set in Hawaii. The narrator is left to explore a valley by his companion who "thought otherwise of [his] intentions" (p. 19). After this companion leaves him for a few days, the narrator meets the next of his native love objects, Kána-aná. Finding the boy attractive, the narrator quickly initiates intimate contact and writes excitedly: "he placed his two hands on my knees, and declared, 'I was his best friend, and he was mine; I must come at once to his house, and there live always with him'" (p. 21). Their acquaintance promptly becomes affectionate, and the narrator revels in his newfound companion, intimating: "I was taken in, fed, and petted in every possible way, and finally put to bed, where Kána-aná monopolized me, growling in true savage fashion if anyone came near me. I didn't sleep much, after all. I must have been excited" (p. 25). This evasive language – "put to bed," "didn't sleep much," "must have been excited" – clearly indicates the homoerotic nature of the narrator's relationship with Kána-aná. Because he enjoys Kána-aná's company so much, the narrator has the boy brought back to the United States. However, Kána-aná becomes seriously ill and longs to return home. The narrator delineates what eventually transpired: "One day, when his condition had become no longer endurable, he stole off to sea in his canoe, thinking, perhaps, that he could reach this continent" (p. 62). Kána-aná could not paddle thousands of miles, and his body washes back to shore in the canoe days later. The story of the pair and the tragic ending that befalls Kána-aná is a case study in imperial behavior – the colonial power exploits the native until he is no longer needed. Moreover, the death of an islander would hardly have riled undiscerning American readers. His dark skin and "uncivilized" ways seem to render him as another acceptable sacrifice to American colonialism, and neither the narrator, nor the reading public, mourns the loss of this island youth.

While these stories clearly connect colonialism and homoeroticism, Stoddard and his narrator are hardly conquerors in the traditional sense; nevertheless, native islanders are subjugated through sexual exploitation and abandonment. Through his transformation of homosexuality into an element of colonialism, Stoddard's *South-Sea Idylls* significantly expands the scope of travel writing in the American imagination. But the text cannot escape the power of its time period, for American concerns over miscegenation, and tacit preoccupation with homosexuality, are ultimately punished severely. All of the homosexual, Polynesian males with whom the narrator carries on affairs die in the text, providing the narrator, and America, with convenient disposal of the results of their colonial activities abroad.

For Stoddard, however, this was his first and last "major" work – a fact that reveals how America's views of homosexuality, regardless of colonial message, could severely limit the career of an author.

As the twentieth century dawned and America saw additional settlement along the west coast, the Hawaiian Islands began to play a larger role in American expansion plans. Jack London's short story collection, *The House of Pride* (1912), is a series of six stories set on the Hawaiian Islands in the early twentieth century. Here, we can find both the triumphs and contradictions of colonization, and the troubling place of such conquests in American history. Attuned both to the horrors of leprosy and its confinement to native islanders, London's stories articulate the way that leprosy is used metaphorically to suggest race, and the means by which the destruction of Hawaiian culture through colonization can be used to further America's economic aims. The genesis of these stories was London's visit to Hawaii aboard his homemade sailboat, the *Snark*, in 1907. Particularly significant is London's depiction of the Hawaiian natives and the foreign visitors on the Islands, and the vibrant racial representations that result. With the publication of *The House of Pride*,[16] London becomes an indirect, but influential participant in the ongoing American colonization of the Hawaiian Islands, as the collection continues a pattern of "literary colonization" in American literature.

The collection begins with the title story, "The House of Pride," which explores the "tainted blood" of Percival Ford's half-brother Joe Garland. Percival Ford is a major landowner on Hawaii and "one of the big men of the Islands."[17] The son of Isaac Ford, a nineteenth-century New England missionary, Percival is, as his physician remarks, of "pure New England stock," and Percival looks at his Yankee past with reverence (p. 6). He is proud of his father's colonizing activities and his own self-perceived "righteousness." Percival believes that, as a white landlord on Hawaii, he is merely continuing his father's "spiritual" and philanthropic work by providing patriarchal and economic guidance for the natives. Never does Percival consider the social and economic domination forced on Hawaii by land-hungry Americans. A significant blow is dealt to Percival's self-constructed "house of pride" when he discovers that half-caste Joe Garland is his half-brother, the product of his father's affair with a Hawaiian woman. However, this knowledge does not compel Percival to embrace his brother as a link to his father. Rather, Percival asks his brother to go away from the islands to save him from the embarrassing knowledge of his father's history. For Percival Ford and American readers, Joe Garland is a reminder of the guilty past of American missionaries and colonizers, so he is ostracized because of his "tainted" blood.

As a piece of historical and cultural literature, *The House of Pride* is also noteworthy for its fictional treatment of leprosy on the Hawaiian Islands. Brought to the Islands by foreigners – primarily Chinese laborers – during the nineteenth century, leprosy caused a massive decline in the Islands' population so that, by 1875, the population was at its lowest point in history.[18] While leprosy's effect on Typee society was a near-destruction of their race, such widespread epidemics had been addressed on the Hawaiian Islands through establishment of the Molokai settlement.[19] Little was known of the colony by foreigners, and London's visit to Molokai provided a highly anticipated peek into this community. In many ways, London's descriptions in *The Cruise of the Snark* (1907) supply a vivid picture of the situation at Molokai, and he is careful to emphasize what he deems the pleasant and misrepresented aspects of colony life. He writes: "the segregation of the lepers on Molokai is not the horrible nightmare that has been so often exploited."[20] Because he observed these residents first-hand, London's stories in *The House of Pride* reveal sympathy and an acquired understanding of the lepers' condition and difficulties that no outside observer could provide. But these stories also raise important issues of "race" and imperialism that expose a great deal about London and the troubling influence of his historical period.

London addresses leprosy directly in the collection's best-known story, "Koolau the Leper." Here, the title character becomes the leader of a group of lepers on Kauai who, he insists, must resist their impending deportation to Molokai. In Koolau's passionate outbursts, London gives voice to the dislocated and exploited Hawaiians sent from their homes to Molokai. Because of foreign colonizers' actions in the interest of commerce, and, ostensibly, religion, the native population, like that on Nukuheva, is decimated by disease. Through Koolau, the grievances of a silent group are aired for an American audience unaware of the damage caused to the Island population. "Koolau the Leper" continues its indictment of foreign control over Hawaii in its graphic description of disfigured lepers. The narrator describes Koolau's "subjects": "They were creatures who once had been men and women. But they were men and women no longer. They were monsters – in face and form grotesque caricatures of everything human" (*The House of Pride*, pp. 49–50). While London subtly foregrounds the imperialism that underscored their infection, his broader focus is on the lepers as vibrant individuals. Even ravaged by disease, these lepers cling proudly to their adopted home and maintain Koolau's fierce criticism of foreigners on the Islands. Kapalei, whose face is featureless, "save for gaping orifices," reiterates Koolau's beliefs as he argues: "Let us live here, or die here, but do not let us go to the prison of Molokai" (p. 56). Though deportation to Molokai is allegedly carried out to prevent further spread of the disease, Kapalei stresses the lack of justice in these actions. In many cases, lepers lost not only their families, but all of their possessions. In his fierce determination while fighting against overwhelming external forces – a deadly disease and better-armed soldiers – Koolau is in many ways a typical naturalistic hero.

"Good-By, Jack," and its counterpart, "The Sheriff of Kona," are both notable within *The House of Pride* for their narrative point of view and their discussion of leprosy's impact on *haole* (the Hawaiian term for a Caucasian person) characters. Only in these two stories does London craft a first-person narrative. In "Good-By, Jack," the choice of Jack Kernsdale's first name is an obvious link to the author. Moreover, both Kernsdale and London have a strong interest in the study of leprosy. In the story, Kernsdale finds that his Hawaiian mistress, Lucy, has been infected with leprosy and will be deported. However, Kernsdale shows little concern for Lucy, nor does he bemoan the departure of this woman with whom he apparently enjoyed some intimacy. His anxiety is purely egocentric and has racial undertones important for the story's conclusion. Kernsdale immediately fears that he may now be infected. Through leprosy, white colonizers on Hawaii were able to treat the Hawaiian as Other since, in addition to a darker skin color, the disease primarily disfigured only those of Polynesian descent. Such binary segregation is undercut, however, when the possibility of a white character becoming infected is raised. Here, banishment to Molokai would force Kernsdale to face imprisonment as an Other. Moreover, if infected, he will have to bear the cultural "punishment" for miscegenation – a punishment he is obviously unprepared to accept.

Despite London's fair treatment of the natives, Hawaii possessed a larger space in the American imagination than his literary empathy could fully address. In 1890, the Census Bureau made its famous declaration that the Western frontier was closed – a limitation far more permanent than that faced during the publication of Twain's *Letters from Hawaii* or Stoddard's *South-Sea Idylls*. With opportunities for expansion therefore limited, Hawaii became an attractive commodity – a fact made salient in London's fiction. London indirectly reinforces a perceived American superiority – an attitude that fed American colonialism. Moreover, in these literary expressions, London mirrors the racial beliefs of his time, which prohibit anything more than tourism-based cultural interaction. With his popularity and attention to the details of Hawaii's riches, London's collection had an even deeper colonial impact on the Islands than he could have anticipated. His island depictions led to an increase in tourism, foreshadowing deeper American influence and Hawaiian dependence. London did not consciously strive for such a impact on the Islands, but his text functioned within a complex cultural environment of limited land and increased capitalist demands that has led, in turn, to Hawaii's current dependent status.

American traveler Charles Nordhoff wrote in 1874: "It is one of the embarrassing incidents of travel on these Islands that there are no hotels or inns outside of Honolulu and Hilo" (*Northern California*, p. 66). Of course, the Islands have changed significantly since Nordhoff's visit, to become beacons of tourism today. For London, the trip to the South Seas was an opportunity to explore the islands he had read about in *Typee*, while also testing his own mettle as skipper of the *Snark*. His collection, however, goes far deeper than adventure narrative to expose important issues in American imperialism.

As the ocean journeys of Richard Henry Dana, Herman Melville, Mark Twain, Charles Warren Stoddard, and Jack London illustrate, travel by sea was an unpredictable and often harrowing experience that tested the traveler and his writing skills. Twain, for example, would curse the rolling seas that sent many passengers leaning over the bulwarks, Stoddard would play victim to the "boisterous waves for five long weeks" (*South-Sea Idylls*, pp. 1–2), and London would lament "rolling in the trough of the sea" (*The Cruise of the Snark*, p. 15). In these nautical journeys, then, adventurous American authors became chroniclers, and the ocean became a path to artistic inspiration. When the ocean traveler arrives on foreign land, however, the creative situation changes dramatically. Here, contacts with various cultures, particularly those classified as Other, shape the writer's responses to the sea, land, and people. As America sought new frontiers upon which to test and assert its developing identity, the Marquesas, Cuba, and Hawaii served as dreamlike, extraterritorial spaces through which authors would witness and assess cultural contact. In this sense, the colonial project shaped and defined not only the writers I have studied, but the entire nation as well. Through writing, authors explore their own personal and national identities as they encounter physical frontiers abroad; at the same time, nations find their concerns, fears, and stereotypes reflected back to them through the language of their literature. Imperialism has also allowed the nation to articulate some of its greatest fears – miscegenation, cannibalism, leprosy, to name a few – on foreign soil, away from the attendant cultural difficulties that would arise in works set at home. In addition, these texts allowed America's authors to establish themselves by creation of a literary Other via travel – freeing them to write from a position of literary and cultural power. As a result, America could cast off its status as inferior, developing nation and pass this denigrating status to foreign societies. Taken collectively, these texts present a brief chronological overview of the power travel literature has to reflect and influence American culture.

Notes

1. Captain David Porter, *Journal of a Cruise Made to the Pacific Ocean* (New York: Wiley and Halsted, 1822; rpt. Annapolis, MD: United States Naval Institute, 1986). For a full discussion of Porter's trip, see John Carlos Rowe, "Melville's *Typee*: US Imperialism at Home and Abroad," in *Nationalist Identities and Post-Americanist Narratives*, ed. Donald Pease (Durham, NC, and London: Duke University Press, 1994).

2. Homi K. Bhabha, "The Other Question: Stereotype, Discrimination, and the Discourse of Colonialism," in *The Location of Culture* (New York: Routledge, 1994).

3. Herman Melville, *Typee: A Peep at Polynesian Life* (New York: Penguin, 1996), pp. 14–15.

4. See John Samson, *White Lies: Melville's Narratives of Facts* (Ithaca, NY: Cornell University Press, 1989). Samson argues that Tommo does not need to fear cannibalism, but the possibility of cultural assimilation.

5. See Caleb Crain, "Lovers of Human Flesh: Homosexuality and Cannibalism in Melville's Novels," *American Literature* 66 (March 1994), pp. 25–53, for a discussion of cannibalism in a nineteenth-century cultural context. See also Gorman Beauchamp, "Montaigne, Melville, and the Cannibals," *Arizona Quarterly* 37 (Winter 1981), pp. 289–309.

6. See Carolyn Karcher, *Shadow Over the Promised Land: Slavery, Race, and Violence in Melville's America* (Baton Rouge: Louisiana State University Press, 1980) for a discussion of Melville's position on nineteenth-century ideas about race. Karcher argues that Melville wishes to introduce readers to victims of racial oppression in his fiction.

7. See, for example, Bryce Conrad, "Richard Henry Dana, Jr. and *Two Years Before the Mast*: Strategies for Objectifying the Subjective Self," *Criticism* 29:3 (1987), pp. 291–311; Douglas B. Hill, Jr., "Richard Henry Dana, Jr. and *Two Years Before the Mast*," *Criticism* 9 (1967), pp. 312–25; Robert L. Gale, *Richard Henry Dana* (New York: Twayne, 1969).

8. Richard Henry Dana, *To Cuba and Back: A Vacation Voyage*, ed. with an Introduction by C. Harvey Gardiner (Carbondale and Edwardsville: Southern Illinois University Press, 1966), p. 8.

9. *To Cuba and Back* presents few Spanish words or explanations of Spanish terms. Only when necessary – such as identifying an *ingenio* as a sugar plantation – does he present and translate foreign words. For a discussion of the colonizer's maintenance of subject status, see Gayatri Chakravorty Spivak, *The Postcolonial Critic: Interviews, Strategies, Dialogues*, ed. Sarah Harasym (New York and London: Routledge, 1990), pp. 73–76. Spivak argues that denigration of the colonial victim allows assertion of colonial power.

10. See Louis A. Pérez, Jr., *Cuba and the United States: Ties of Singular Intimacy* (Athens: University of Georgia Press, 1990). Pérez explains that slavery was on the rise in Cuba during the nineteenth century. In 1792, there were 85,000 slaves in Cuba. By 1841, this number had swelled to 436,000. By the time of Dana's visit in 1859, the number of slaves may have been as high as 700,000.

11. For a thorough overview of Twain's time in Hawaii, see Walter Francis Frear, *Mark Twain and Hawaii* (Chicago: The Lakeside Press, 1947). As governor of

Hawaii from 1907 to 1913, Frear had intimate knowledge of Twain's influence and legacy on the islands.

12. Mark Twain, *Mark Twain's Letters from the Sandwich Islands*, ed. with an Introduction by A. Grove Day (Honolulu: The University Press of Hawaii, 1976).

13. For a discussion of American economic endeavors in Hawaii, see Noel J. Kent, *Hawaii: Islands Under the Influence* (New York: Monthly Review Press, 1983).

14. Charles Warren Stoddard, *South-Sea Idylls* (New York: Charles Scribners & Sons, 1904), p. 132.

15. The story "My South-Sea Show," for example, features the narrator bringing three natives to America for a traveling show, only to watch one die from drinking perfume.

16. The six stories in the collection originally appeared in magazines ranging from *Woman's Magazine* to *Pacific Monthly* between December 1908 and December 1910.

17. Jack London, *The House of Pride and Other Tales of Hawaii* (New York: Macmillan, 1912), p. 3.

18. Ralph S. Kuykendall and A. Grove Day, *Hawaii: A History from Polynesian Kingdom to American Commonwealth* (New York: Prentice Hall, 1949), p. 156.

19. Writing during an 1874 visit to the Islands, Charles Nordhoff notes: "Leprosy, when it is beyond its very earliest stage, is held to be incurable. He who is sent to Molokai is therefore adjudged civilly dead." *Northern California, Oregon, and the Sandwich Islands* (1874; rpt. Berkeley: Ten Speed Press, 1995), p. 101.

20. Jack London, *The Cruise of the Snark* (New York: Macmillan, 1911), p. 97.

IO

TERRY CAESAR

South of the border: American travel writing in Latin America

Writings about American travel to South America are neither as numerous nor as distinguished as the writings about American travel to Europe. Henry James never luxuriated in Buenos Aires; Mark Twain was never led astray in Rio de Janeiro. One consideration that immediately arises is the question of canon. There are some great travel books by Americans, ranging from William Herndon's *Exploration of the Valley of the Amazon, 1851–2* (1854) to Moritz Thomsen's *The Saddest Pleasure* (1992). But Herndon and Thomsen remain virtually unknown figures, and it is impossible not to speculate that this is simply because South America has not been as culturally significant to Americans as Europe.

There is another problem. Although by the end of the nineteenth century Americans had traveled to the remotest regions of the South American continent, much of the important travel writing during the century was British rather than American.[1] Whether commercial or political in motive, American travel writing about South America followed in the wake of the British, just as both took place against a broader background of European response to South America beginning at the outset of the century, as recorded in the diaries of the Spanish doctor and botanist, José Celestino Mutis (1732–1808), or as narrated in various books by the German geographer, Alexander von Humboldt (1769–1859).

Why try to isolate American travel writing about Latin America as an identifiable textual practice in the first place? There are two primary reasons. First, Latin Americans themselves recognize a specific national difference, even between Americans and British travelers. In Erna Fergusson's *Venezuela* (1939), for example, the author listens to an explanation of the local coinage by a man who calls himself Seventeen. Once the explanation is over, he asks: "Are you English, senorita?" "No, North American." " 'Oh,' he said with a sigh of comprehension, 'so that's why you don't know anything.' "[2] As indicated in the ensuing discussion, American travelers in South America proceed under the auspices of a certain distinctive ignorance about the continent, resented by the natives, if only because they experience this ignorance as a product of entitlement on the part of a strong nation over against weaker ones.

Second, American travel writing about South America plays a distinct role in the way the United States comprehends itself. As Ricardo Salvadore explains: "The American frontier myth . . . was redeployed in the Latin American context to reproduce images of empty spaces, institutional rigidities, and childish peoples inept for economic development, democratic government, and national spiritual renovation" ("North American Travel Narratives," pp. 89–90). From the very beginning of the American text, South America – the whole continent as well as individual countries – was all-too-fatefully subject to the political and cultural imperatives of North America. It is impossible to study the travel writing apart from these imperatives.[3]

Nevertheless, the writing can be divided into phases. The imperatives changed across time, and were the products of different historical periods. Mary Louise Pratt terms the "descent" upon South America by European travelers in the early decades of the nineteenth century – during the time of various South American revolutions and the rivalry between England and France as well as among both with Spain – the age of the Capitalist Vanguard, beginning in the 1820s.[4] Salvatore gives the nominal initial range as 1810–60. However, in a later article, he proposes more exact specifications for what he terms "the development of the representational machinery of the US informal empire": first "a moment of mercantile engagement (1820–1860)," and then "a moment of neo-imperial engagement (1890–1930)."[5] In the following discussion, I will adopt these two broad characterizations, and then add a third, less overtly politicized one: tourism.

Tourism does not alter the political coordinates of the American text of South American travel. To this day, typical American responses to the continent continue to take place against a vast ignorance about its histories, languages, indigenous populations, political systems, and even the geographical locations of its various countries. But tourism does alter the content of the travel text – about South America as about everywhere else. Salvatore speaks of "the master narrative of South America's incorporation within the orbit of North American knowledge" ("Enterprise of Knowledge," p. 90). It cannot remain the same narrative once incorporated, in turn, by the narrative of global tourism.

The great commercial round

Angela Pérez-Mejía defines the scientific project of the Enlightenment as "this moment of privileging of reason, of faith in the power of scientific experiment, and of vehement support for classificatory observation." What is the place of the travel writer within this project? "The enlightened traveler," she continues, "became an irreplaceable element in the acquisition of knowledge about the universe awaiting discovery."[6] A specific, identifiable American presence beginning in the 1820s comes relatively late in this Enlightenment "moment." Insofar as it concerns South America, American travel has more to do with commercial development than discovery; it is more concerned with business opportunities than exploration.

It is with good reason that Mary Louise Pratt has characterized the travelers of the 1820s and the decades immediately following as part of the Capitalist Vanguard. According to Pratt, in this travel writing, "the contemplative, estheticizing rhetoric of discovery is often replaced by a goal-oriented rhetoric of conquest and achievement . . . What are conquered are destinations, not kingdoms; what are overcome are not military challenges, but logistical ones" (*Imperial Eyes*, p. 148). American travel writing becomes an extreme example of these distinctions. Consider one of the most celebrated accounts of American travel to South America, *Exploration of the Valley of the Amazon, 1851–52* (1854), by William Herndon, a naval lieutenant appointed by the Secretary of the Navy to explore the Amazon valley. The result is celebrated because Herndon gave his book a narrative shape, within which details about crops grown or minerals extracted exist alongside descriptions of vampire bats, poisonous blowdarts, and spider webs as large as tents. Herndon is enthralled by the land he finds; the zest or wonder of exploring it is not overcome by the logistical or commercial necessity to do so. Hence, after extolling the awesome power of the Amazon, it can seem jarring when Herndon exclaims: "Its capacities for trade and commerce are inconceivably great."[7] Soon he is assessing the value of the commerce of the Missions or estimating the cost of running a small steamer between two points of Peru and Brazil, respectively, before stating thus: "[t]he trade of this region must pass by our doors, and mingle and exchange with the products of our Mississippi Valley" (p. 197).

In his editorial introduction to a modernized edition of *Exploration*, Gary Kinder finds "disturbing" the following "sentiment": "Herndon's obvious reverence for the territory and his unabashed, contradictory recommendation that it be developed quickly and fully" (p. xviii). The easiest way to reply is that what, to a later age, seems contradictory is simply not to Herndon. Because he revered the territory, he desired its development. Not only would mere reverence be too "estheticizing," in Pratt's terms; it would be ungrounded, inert – and un-American. "The Valley of the Amazon and the Valley of the Mississippi are commercial complements of each other – one supplying what the other lacks in the great commercial round" (p. 198). Kinder relates the statement to the mid-century American policy of Manifest Destiny. A stronger point would be that the political terms for regarding South America as part of the United States were in place from the very outset of American travel there. The medium was commerce. Americans had it. South Americans did not. Hence, for example, H.M. Brackenridge, in one of the earliest travel accounts, *A Voyage to South America* (1820), cannot understand why, in such contrast to the United States, the government of Brazil is so oppressive or the lower classes lack such industry. No wonder at the conclusion of his own book on Cuba, *Due South*, Maturin Ballou approvingly cites Jefferson to President Monroe: "That this land naturally belongs to this country is a fact so plain as to have been conceded by all authorities."[8]

Frederick Pike has suggested that American perceptions of Latin America have been conducted by means of the dichotomy Civilization/Nature, the same one employed domestically to conduct the American myth of the frontier.[9] So understood, American travel writing in/on South America from the very beginning repeatedly stages a narrative whereby a civilized traveler regards nature and considers how it might be exploited, developed, or otherwise politically, culturally, and especially economically redeemed, ultimately by being comprehended as part of the United States. Precisely this logic is at work in perhaps the most celebrated narrative, John L. Stephens' two-volume *Incidents of Travel in Central America, Chiapas and Yucatan*. Charged, like Herndon, with an official governmental mission, Stephens travels across a landscape filled with violence and civil war. The Indians are exotic. His own identity is fluid. At one point he is placed under arrest. And yet through it all Stephens moves with assurance and superiority. Even the ruined Mayan cities he comes upon (superbly drawn by his companion, Frederick Catherwood) do not shake him. Indeed, he offers to buy one city, Chopan, for fifty dollars. Why not? Both the surrounding Indians and the owners of the estate appear to be profoundly incurious. Stephens relishes the thought of removing the ruins in their entirety, in order to "set them up in the 'great commercial emporium,' and found an institution to be the nucleus of a great national museum of American antiquities."[10] Compare this to the moment at the outset of the second volume, where Stephens, midway up the volcano of Masaya, contemplates how the thing would be worth a fortune at home, with a hotel on top and a glass of iced lemonade at the bottom (vol. II, p. 13). At such moments acquisition of knowledge about the land and acquisition of the land itself become inseparable.

Neo-imperial engagement

"The American experience at large," Larzer Ziff concludes in his study of American travel writing, *Return Passages*, "was the experience of a movement away from the Old World and into a series of frontiers that shaped the composite nationality of the American people."[11] But of course this movement was not only confined to the interior of the United States, where the direction was westward. It also had to do with the exterior of the United States, where the direction was, in part, southward. One especially striking thing about this particular movement insofar as travel writing is concerned is that it proceeded under the sign of knowledge, pure and simple. Over and over again, from its very inception to the outset of World War II (when numerous travel books appeared, especially in the mid-to-late 1930s, driven by European political unrest), American travel books about South America stage their own motivations in terms of the ignorance of their readers. "South America," writes Hudson Strode in the preface of his *South by Thunderbird*, "is virgin territory. Its greatest expansion is still to come."[12] Thus, the development of the United States is equated with the development of South America, and knowledge of South America becomes a function of America's own knowledge of itself. Strode explicitly declines a political agenda of his own. (He refers his readers to the Marxism of Waldo Frank in *America Hispana* [1943].) Instead, he writes "to present a clearer comprehension of our Southern neighbors by revealing intimate contacts with the people themselves" (*South by Thunderbird*, p. xxi). If he were asked why, in turn, such comprehension is important, he would undoubtedly invoke the traditional protocol of the travel book: it deals in a different sort of knowledge – direct, experiential, sensory – than that of history or political science.

But in the American travel text of South America this knowledge functions as a way of leaving in place – if not reinforcing – larger political and cultural predispositions about a continent easily relegated either to an "exotic" or "romantic" status, or else one simply "poor" and "degraded." Furthermore, the travel writing about South America that developed after the first phase of American engagement took place against a blank slate, strikingly in contrast to comparable texts produced about Europe generally and England in particular; Americans did not regard South Americans in the same way they regarded Europeans. Indeed, with no small irony, Americans regarded South Americans in broadly similar ways to those in which Americans were, in turn, regarded by Europeans, especially the English. What Christopher Mulvey states about the English response to America can be transposed into the American response to Latin America: "With no perceptual scheme ready to receive and to organize impressions, [the English] suffered from a kind of perceptual impoverishment that was quite the reverse of the enriched, imaginatively organized vision that the American brought to his looking at England."[13]

Or, we might add, to the rest of Europe, at least in contrast to the entirety of South America. "South America is still awaiting discovery," writes Carol Crow at the outset of *Meet the South Americans*. "It is one of the few sections of the world which we do not know."[14] It seems a bland enough lament, even if a rather incredible one by 1941, when Americans had been engaged in "knowing" South America for the past hundred years. Other texts, however, make it clear that much of the reason "we" do not "know" South America is because the continent is simply not Europe, either in history or in population.

Hence, James Bryce registers a regret that "a West European race" has not, "to use the familiar phrase, 'got the thing in hand.'" "How men from the Mississippi," he continues, "would make things hum along the Amazon and the Paraná."[15] If only *we* had settled the land: the possibility is woven in various ways into many American neo-imperial accounts of South American travel, such as in Harry Franck's joke concluding *Roaming through the West Indies*: "We could afford to buy all of the West Indies on the basis of the price paid in Denmark, if the sellers would agree to remove all of the population."[16]

Perhaps the best – that is, most unashamed – example of these fantasies of substitution or exchange is a turn-of-the-century romp, *Three Gringos in Central America*, wherein Richard Harding Davis exclaims at one point as follows: "The Central-American citizen is no more fit for a republican form of government than he is for an arctic expedition, and what he needs is to have a protectorate established over him, either by the United States or by another power; it does not matter which, so long as it leaves the Nicaragua Canal in our hands."[17]

In the neo-imperial text, a familiar dualism is repeatedly installed, whereby the poverty of the human presence contrasts with the richness of nature. Thus, for instance, even Davis remarks: "Nature has done so much that there is little left for man to do, but it will have to be some other man than a native-born-Central American who is to do it" (*Three Gringos*, p. 148). One of the most important things distinguishing perhaps the best American travel book of this period, Waldo Frank's *South American Journey* (1943), is simply that this inert dualism is not to be found there. Instead, Frank, who writes in his introductory pages both of his own plans and of the pleas of his friends to revisit South America to give a series of lectures while traveling in Uruguay, Chile, Peru, Paraguay, and Bolivia as well as Brazil and Argentina, demonstrates enormous respect for the culture and politics he encounters.

One instance from Frank's text is illustrative: the subject of Brazilian folk music. Its "organic" complexity makes our own popular music "repulsive with its skin-nervous intricacies bristling about emptiness and inorganic softness."[18] With such observations, it seems, indeed, as if Frank is deliberately overturning the political coding of culture versus nature as employed by the American travel text, and awarding to South American culture the energies of nature that are normally denied to it. Like any traveler, Frank is full of "impressions." Unlike most, he typically expresses them with conceptual flair and sophistication.

Similarly, with the question of prostitutes. Frank finds the "Ibero-American" type "less degraded" than in the United States; his brief pages on their social function as well as their cultural place is typical of how he *thinks* about what he perceives (*South American Journey*, pp. 194–99). *South American Journey* is one of the few American travel books about South America during the neo-imperial period written primarily in an essayistic vein. One reason is simply because lectures – about the importance of a united North and South hemispheric response to social and political problems – structure the author's travel.

Yet there are other reasons for this structure, and all have to do with Frank's awareness of the discursive background that any American faces when writing about travel in South America. He appears resolved to participate differently. Consider his visit to Uruguay. The result is not only a rich meditation on the figure of the gaucho but a stimulating apologia for South America itself, in terms of its numerous republics, each with its own peculiar history, all quite different from the more independent (and more numerous) states of Europe. Notwithstanding the fact that "there must be greater union," Frank concludes, "as I look over the little countries of South America, I find none whose tough personal life does not justify its independence" (p. 156).

Precisely who is Frank to assert such a conviction, the more remarkable against the century-old, sustained American discourse about a thoroughly subordinated South America, with so little integrity as an autonomous political realm? One thing especially should be emphasized: Frank does not purport to be an explorer. He has no scientific project. Roberto González Echevarría has noted how travel literature concerning the New World has been driven by science and how "[t]he rhetoric of the scientific travel narrative is permeated by the figure of [a] narrator-hero who undergoes trials for the sake of knowledge."[19] In the American text, no author better illustrates this figure than Theodore Roosevelt. His account of "zoogeographic reconnoissance" (as Roosevelt puts it), *Through the Brazilian Wilderness* (1914), is as popular a travel book as an American has ever produced about

South America. Hence, today it is particularly interesting to note how insistent Roosevelt is to distinguish between "the ordinary traveler" – who takes no risks and never strays from the beaten path – and "the true wilderness wanderer," who must be "a man of action as well as observation."[20] If we inquire why Roosevelt bothers to make this distinction in the first place, we realize that his own travel is already shadowed by that of another figure.

This figure will soon be as just as decisive for the travel writing that will be produced during the remainder of the century as the figure of the heroic scientific adventure had been for the century already past. Roosevelt's "ordinary traveler" is of course a tourist. Today we can see how an "action" such as Roosevelt's stretches back as far as Herndon. But it does not comprehend Frank, who is no more a tourist than he is a heroic scientist. *South American Journey* in fact inaugurates a species of intellectual commentary by Americans about South America that includes texts as varied as John Dos Passos' *Brazil on the Move* (1963), Joan Didion's *Salvador* (1983), or Oliver Sachs' *Oaxaca Journal* (2001). Apart from being authenticated by actual personal travel, what unites these books is a direct engagement with the politics of their own various discursive circumstances. It will be the pleasure of tourism to avoid these circumstances, just as it will now become the burden of the travel book to try to avoid tourism.

Tourism

At one point in her second travel book on Mexico, *Mexico Revisited*, Erna Fergusson is in the region of the Huasteca Indians, which is, she remarks, "not yet accessible to tourists, nor would tourists be interested in its archaeological finds."[21] Why mention tourists in the first place? Because by 1956 it is simply inconceivable to write about Mexico without mentioning them. Mexico is "tourist conscious" (p. 27). Airlines are making a difference to the Yucatán by opening it up to tourists. A new road has made it possible to speed across the state of San Luis Potisí. The people of Guadalajara "feel injured because their city is so often discovered by tourists only at the end of their stay in Mexico" (p. 207). And so on.

Fergusson herself is a traveler – and so she is interested in archeology (proceeding to give an account which takes the rest of her chapter). Yet tourists are mentioned so often that her travel book keeps assuming the form of a guidebook designed to be read by tourists, full of practical tips, potted history, and a general point of view of "the visitor." This visitor possesses no nationality, or at least none comparable to an interesting moment in Fergusson's first book, *Fiesta in Mexico* (in which she travels like an anthropologist in search of festivals by Mexican Indians). At one point, a Mexican guide tells her that Indians have objected to her presence "because these gringas only take pictures to make fun of us in the United States."[22]

To the Indians, presumably any visitor is an American. For the most part, however, in her first book on Mexico Fergusson does not allow the politics of her national identity to register any emphatic narrative presence, whereas in her second book, tourists now simply comprise part of the narrative (and their national identity has been effaced). Indeed, it is possible to see in travel books themselves the transformation by tourism not only of a country but of a visitor. In Selden Rodman's witty, sophisticated *Mexican Journal* (1958), the author, accompanied by an American friend, is accosted at one point by a Mexican official, who demands to see papers. Rodman has his. The friend does not. Eventually the matter is temporarily negotiated; the official will pass it along in the bureaucracy in the form of a "report" but not before the Mexican friend of the men is outraged on their behalf, protesting thus: "My country *lives* on American tourism. Where would we be without it? And this is the way we treat you."[23]

The contrast between books published before World War II and ones published afterward can be seen over and over again. At the outset of *Now in Mexico* (1947), Hudson Strode notes that his book is not a narrative of a continuous journal, like his earlier *South by Thunderbird* (1937). But this is not the only difference. The writing in the earlier book is lively, sharp, witty. It is as if the pressure to write about so many South American countries visited briefly by plane gives Strode the character of an explorer or adventurer; his narrative is as much about his adventure as about the lands he visits. In the later book he is inescapably among tourists, feels impelled to produce many pages of historical background (despite an announced intention to write something more personal than his history, *Timeless Mexico* [1944]), and concludes with a flurry of clichés that might well be from a tourist guidebook: "Travelers from the States, nurtured on city concrete and gaudy neon lights, might still enjoy the fascination of the primitive in another man's land and delight in antique beauty."[24]

Tourism affects everything about American travel writing, including how examples might be classified. A good indication of the range of American travel writing about Latin America after World War II may be seen by comparing two volumes about French Guiana, one of the smallest and most obscure countries of the continent: Hassoldt Davis' *The Jungle and the Damned* (1952) and Richard and Sally Price's *Equatoria* (1992). Although Davis proposes to travel inland from the capital, Cayanne, up the Maroni River and into unexplored mountains, he arrives ultimately for no better reason than adventure; his is easily the more classic travel narrative.

The Prices, on the other hand, are professional anthropologists, who arrive in Cayanne in order to begin collecting materials for a proposed, government-sponsored museum; the travel detail is more incidental to a larger scientific or political narrative, in which their "ambivalence" about "this strangely anachronistic enterprise" is elaborately theorized and self-consciously articulated at every turn.[25] It is tempting therefore to emphasize the obvious difference between Davis and the Prices as a difference between two grand narratives: Travel and Science.

However, such conclusions ignore how much the two books have in common, a fact that the Prices explicitly acknowledge by quoting Davis five times (in the succession of discursively weighed quotations given on left-handed pages throughout the volume) during the course of their own narrative. Moreover, at the outset, trying to decide whether or not to undertake the museum project, the Prices record the following version of the sheer lure of travel: "In the bland suburban space of our rented Stanford faculty apartment, the idea of embarking on an Ethnographic Mission to the interior of the Guianas exerts that old romantic pull" (*Equatoria*, p. 25).

Similarities do not end here. While not co-authored, the Davis book also includes a wife, Ruth, newly married to the author and herself a professional photographer – whose pictures were subsequently edited, sold, and released as a film by Warner Brothers. Experience in the travel book, in other words, is no more free from commercial taint than it is in the ethnographic text. Furthermore, Davis, rare among travel writers, mentions at the beginning four specific organizations that helped fund his "jaunt," as well as various unspecified companies who contributed funding so that he could check on the tropical fate of their various products.[26]

Thus, it seems that in South America science, now most particularly anthropology, continues to be difficult to extricate from travel. Furthermore, even though neither Davis nor the Prices seem overtly troubled by how tourism might be influencing the sort of text each can produce, we can see how the same sort of energies – representational, commercial, "romantic" – that sponsor tourism in fact now underlie travel itself, of whatever kind. There is a telling moment in his beautifully written wilderness narrative, *The Cloud Forest* (1961), when Peter Matthiessen begins a four-page "note" on cities with a comment that they probably comprise the continent's least compelling destinations, "despite the homage paid to them by travel companies."[27]

So Matthiessen becomes yet another American traveler resolute for the hinterlands. However, by this time, the travel has acquired an additional, inescapable motive: to avoid tourists. By the time Matthiessen writes, to travel is somehow to have to consider them, and to write about traveling is to register in some way how tourism has changed the very project.[28] Insofar as the South American text is concerned, we might say that in recent decades the staging of an author's experience through the ignorance of his readers has been replaced by a direct confrontation of this ignorance embodied in the figure of the tourist.

Consider the role of Thornberry, midway through one of the finest late twentieth-century American travel books, *The Old Patagonian Express* (1979). Like the author, Paul Theroux, Thornberry is a New Englander. Unlike Theroux, he is a tourist. The book is full of tourists. Theroux sneers at them all. However, Thornberry is viewed more indulgently – perhaps because he has lost his tour, perhaps because his sheer hapless ignorance of all he sees in Costa Rica moves Theroux. If so, this ignorance moves him, not simply because he can be superior to it, but because, as a fellow American, Theroux is a hopelessly kindred figure to Thornberry. So they are regarded in South America. So they cannot help but regard themselves.

In fundamental ways, *The Old Patagonian Express* is a travel book that enacts yet another imperial appropriation, not to say incorporation, of the entire South American continent. What makes it distinctive in this regard are two things: first, the project is not scientific, and, second, the motives are so personal. Much of what makes them personal is in fact political: simply through its characterization of tourists, Theroux is trying to work out something of the fateful relation of an American to South America – his inevitable distance from its circumstances and its hopeless folly. The book is not a political critique. Yet within it there exists, if not a political critique, at least political materials so different from the celebration of American power in Herndon's *Exploration* as to constitute a rebuke to it, and the whole tradition of heroic science.

In one emphatic sense, Theroux goes in search of ignorance rather than knowledge, and he finds it, in the form of the vast absence of the Patagonian plains. The result is a failure, however, willed into the character of success. Failure of an at once even more personal and more politically charged sort haunts Moritz Thomsen's *The Saddest Pleasure* (1992), an account of a trip from Ecuador to Brazil that becomes quite possibly the finest American travel book of all – the most politically sophisticated, most emotionally rich – about South America. And, just as Theroux, Thomsen earns his experience in part through the representation both of himself and his country as tourists.

Indeed, even more than Theroux, he acknowledges kinship with them, especially during a moment in response to a tour group in Forteleza. Not so much finally on the basis of their utter isolation from "whatever is real in South America," but because, like him, the four are far from home: "They are almost fatally disoriented. Yes indeed, here, if I am not, is the living proof: travel is the saddest of the pleasures."[29] It may be the case that travel is sad because it is homeless. But emphasizing it here is equivalent in a larger sense to suggesting what Thomsen later quotes his former Ecuadoran partner and friend as saying to him: he does not belong. Reading this stricture in terms of its entire textual tradition, we can rephrase as follows: if the price of "ignorance" about South America is some species of "knowledge" – once scientific, now touristic – it would be better for an American to have remained home.

In an earlier discussion, I have argued "how *The Saddest Pleasure* strives to deconstruct its own 'sovereignty,' both in terms of its specific national tradition and in terms of nationality itself" (*Forgiving the Boundaries*, p. 157). Here, I have tried to discuss how the economic and political dynamics of the tradition have proved enabling as well as disabling for various of its travel writers, even in an age of tourism (which seeks to transcend national boundaries). How sovereign must a national tradition be insofar as travel writing is concerned? On the example of its finest authors: powerful enough to be governed by the coordinates of national identity and yet not so powerful that these same coordinates cannot eventually be searched out, mocked, and even dismissed.

Notes

1. See Desmond Gregory, *Brute New World. The Rediscovery of Latin America in the Early Nineteenth Century* (London: British Academic Press, 1992). Although at the outset Gregory includes the United States within a larger European merchant, banking, immigration, religious, and military as well as travel interest in Latin America, virtually every one of the travel accounts he goes on to discuss is British. Anyone interested in specifically American responses to South America during this period has two scholarly options. Some mention of the texts can be extracted either from the critical biographies included in David Ross and James Schrammer, eds., *American Travel Writers: 1850–1915, Dictionary of Literary Biography*, vol. CLXXXIX (Detroit: Gale Research, 1998) or from a larger discussion of discursive dynamics in Ricardo D. Salvatore, "North American Travel Narratives and the Ordering/Othering of South America *c*.1810–1860," *Journal of Historical Sociology* 9:1 (March 1996), pp. 85–110.
2. Erna Fergusson, *Venezuela* (New York: Knopf, 1939), p. 13.
3. There is no better reason not to offer a country-by-country assessment of American travel writing. Much of it to this day has not been produced in this way because it is a region rather than a country (as earlier it was often the entire continent rather than a region) that provides the experiential ground for the text. Hence, the Amazon rather than the eight countries that contain it rightly forms the object of study in Neil Whitehead, "South America/Amazonia: The Forest of Marvels," in *The Cambridge Companion to Travel Writing*, ed. Peter Hulme and Tim Youngs (Cambridge: Cambridge University Press, 2002), pp. 122–38. Hence also, there will be no attempt in the following discussion to isolate

Mexico or Cuba, despite the fact that each could merit a separate discussion, based simply on the volume of writing respectively elicited, each being more proximately south of the United States than any other country. Hence finally, the reasons for the paucity of attention to Bolivia or Paraguay will be assumed to be part and parcel of the same political and cultural reasons designating Brazil or Argentina as worthy of far more attention.

4. Mary Louise Pratt, *Imperial Eyes: Travel Writing and Transculturation* (New York: Routledge, 1992), pp. 146–55.

5. Ricardo Salvatore, "The Enterprise of Knowledge: Representational Machines of Informal Empire," in *Close Encounters of Empire. Writing the Cultural History of US–Latin American Relations*, ed. Gilbert Joseph, Catherine Legrand, and Ricardo Salvatore (Durham, NC: Duke University Press, 1998), p. 76.

6. Angela Pérez-Mejía, *A Geography of Hard Times: Narratives about Travel to South America, 1780–1849* (Albany: State University of New York Press, 2004), pp. 12–13.

7. William Lewis Herndon, *Exploration of the Valley of the Amazon, 1851–52*, ed. Gary Kinder (New York: Grove Press, 2000), p. 190.

8. Maturin Ballou, *Due South; or, Cuba Past and Present* (Boston: Houghton Mifflin & Company, 1885), p. 300. See Salvatore, "North American Travel Narratives," for a bibliography of selected titles during this period. Among early travel books devoted to Cuba, Richard Henry Dana, *To Cuba and Back* (1859) and Julia Ward Howe, *A Trip to Cuba* (1860) are particularly noteworthy. For a general background – not limited to Americans – see Alan Ryan, *The Reader's Companion to Cuba* (San Diego, CA: Harcourt Brace & Co., 1997).

9. See Frederick Pike, *The United States and Latin America* (Austin: University of Texas Press, 1992).

10. John L. Stephens, *Incidents of Travel in Central America, Chiapas and Yucatan*, 2 vols. (New York: Dover Publications, 1841; 1969), vol. I, p. 115. Such a reflection is of course scarcely conceivable in an American text about Europe, whose very difference as well as distance from the United States abides to be valued, and, if possible, emulated.

11. A. Larzer Ziff, *Return Passages: Great American Travel Writing, 1780–1910* (New Haven: Yale University Press, 2000), pp. 185–86.

12. Hudson Strode, *South by Thunderbird* (New York: Random House, 1937), p. xx.

13. Christopher Mulvey, *Anglo-American Landscapes. A Study of Nineteenth-Century Anglo-American Travel Literature* (Cambridge: Cambridge University Press, 1983), p. 11.

14. Carol Crow, *Meet the South Americans* (New York: Harper & Brothers, 1941), p. 34.

15. James Bryce, *South America. Observations and Impressions* (New York: Macmillan, 1916), p. 420. To be fair, Bryce – whose book is saluted as "admirable" in Strode's Preface – concludes as follows: "[T]he Latin-American peoples may within [another century] grow into something different from what they now appear to the critical eyes of Europe and North America" (p. 421).

16. Harry Franck, *Roaming through the West Indies* (New York: The Century Company, 1920), p. 486. Franck, it might be mentioned, went on to produce two remarkable accounts of four years' travel on the continent, the companion

volumes, *Vagabonding Down the Andes* (New York: The Century Company, 1917) and *Working North from Patagonia* (New York: Grosset and Dunlap, 1921). Barren of stylistic distinction and yet full of interesting incidents as well as consistently thoughtful observations, these enormous volumes (each over 600 pages) comprise some of the most empirical – if not authentic – record of South American travel experience in the whole of the American text.

17. Richard Harding Davis, *Three Gringos in Central America* (New York: Harper, 1896), p. 145. The three friends terminate their journey in Caracas, unsurprisingly hailed as "the Paris of South America." Left-handed compliments fill the pages of American travel books in the neo-imperial period, as, for example, Frederick Hassaurek: "Notwithstanding their ignorance and filthiness, the manners of the rabble of Quito, if not instigated to some quarrel by rum or chicha, are characterized by the utmost politeness." *Four Years Among South Americans* (New York: Hurd and Houghton, 1868), p. 135.

18. Waldo Frank, *South American Journey* (New York: Duell, Sloan and Pearce, 1943), pp. 42–43. For sketches of his governing ideas about the relationship between the United States and South America, see the concluding chapter, "Our Island Hemisphere," concerning, first, "The Three Americas" and then "The One America." In many respects, Frank's convictions seem astonishingly prescient in light of disciplinary developments in Latin American studies today; see Sebastian Faber, "Learning from the Latins: Waldo Frank's Progressive Pan-Americanism," *The New Centennial Review* 3:1 (2003), pp. 257–95.

19. Roberto González Echevarría, *Myth and Archive: A Theory of Latin American Narrative* (Durham, NC: Duke University Press, 1998), p. 107.

20. Theodore Roosevelt, *Through the Brazilian Wilderness* (Mechanicsburg, PA: Stackpole Books, 1994), p. 178. In Appendix A, the starkness of the contrast is somewhat relieved by the introduction of another figure between them, whose travel is subject to more arduousness than the first but who still lacks the auspices of a scientific purpose that so distinguishes the third.

21. Erna Fergusson, *Mexico Revisited* (New York: Knopf, 1956), p. 104. Such knowledge, on the other hand, has been the basis for Fergusson to differentiate herself from tourists in her distinguished series of travel books on South America, as we can see, for example, in the chapter, "Tourist View," from her book on Guatemala (*Guatemala* [New York: Knopf, 1944]). After sarcastically characterizing the timidity of the American tourist, Fergusson joins a tour group of the Alfred Clark organization, and notes that nothing calls forth touristic enthusiasm more than hot cakes for breakfast. "Yes," she concludes, "Mr. Clark knows his tourists well" (p. 36). That is, he knows the tourist, whereas she knows the country.

22. Erna Fergusson, *Fiesta in Mexico* (New York: Knopf, 1934), p. 64. The guide attempts to explain that he is a Mexican, which seems to satisfy the Indians, if only because the man, like the "gringa," thereby joins the category of "conqueror."

23. Selden Rodman, *Mexican Journal: The Conquerors Conquered* (Carbondale: Southern Illinois University Press, 1964), p. 123. Rodman himself cannot help but exclaim just before this about "how much we have to be thankful for at home, living under a system of checks and balances with at least a degree of freedom to damn the powers-that-be." Later in Acapulco he is appalled at the

hordes of American tourists and confesses himself "ashamed at being American" (p. 182). Predating such memoirs as Tony Cohen's *On Mexican Time: A New Life in San Miguel* (New York: Random House, 2000), Rodman finds San Miguel de Allende "more Americanized than ever," even the Indians looking "a trifle self-consciously posed" in their crumbling doorways (p. 279).

24. Hudson Strode, *Now in Mexico* (New York: Harcourt, Brace and Company, 1947), p. 365.

25. Richard Price and Sally Price, *Equatoria* (New York: Routledge, 1992), p. 2. For a discussion of the ethnographic text in travel writing, see Terry Caesar, *Forgiving the Boundaries. Home as Abroad in American Travel Writing* (Athens: University of Georgia Press, 1995), ch. 6. In addition, a number of ostensibly true, anthropological accounts of South America have become subject to the charge of fiction, most notably Florinda Donner, *Shabono: A True Adventure in the Remote and Magical Heart of the South American Jungle* (1982). Tobias Schneebaum's *Keep the River on Your Right* (1969) also deserves mention in this regard.

26. Hassoldt Davis, *The Jungle and the Damned*, Introduction by Lawrence Millman (Lincoln: University of Nebraska Press, 2000), p. 5.

27. Peter Matthiessen, *The Cloud Forest: A Chronicle of the South American Wilderness* (New York: Viking Press, 1961), p. 114. Matthiessen concludes his book with some final questions about a "forbidden" Amazon river and the jaw of an unknown fossil. The thematic of naming continues to the present day in the scientific or quasi-scientific accounts of Amazon travel, as in David Campbell, *A Land of Ghosts* (2005).

28. The most dramatic example is Cuba. To write about Cuba before and then after the Castro government permitted tourism is to write about virtually different countries. Compare Tom Miller, *Trading with the Enemy: A Yankee Travels through Castro's Cuba* (1992) to Christopher Baker, *Mi Moto Fidel: Motorcycling through Castro's Cuba* (2001). Baker's Cuba is wholly mediated through tourism.

29. Moritz Thomsen, *The Saddest Pleasure* (London: The Sumach Press, 1992), pp. 144, 145.

III

SOCIAL SCENES AND AMERICAN SITES

11

VIRGINIA WHATLEY SMITH

African American travel literature

Defining the genre of African American travel writing is more complex than it may seem. Europeans became colonizers, enslavers, and oppressors of mainland African peoples. Contact space on indigenous lands between Africans and Europeans became conflict space, as were the sites of resistance in the New World where slaves were transported. Enslaved peoples' tales of captivity and dehumanization arose immediately in African and New World cultural discourses but, being orally based people without power to counter Europe's control over their bodies, their voices, and their stories, these African slaves resorted to mainland practices by passing on their stories from one generation to the next in oral form. Those displaced African captives who managed to learn the master's tongue, and to garner support from third parties, not only gave their stories to the world in published form, but also ushered in a particular form of writing known as the slave narrative. Moreover, this form, with its specific rhetorical devices, birthed specialized subject matter and a discourse emphasizing the embodied experience of dehumanizing captivity. The captives endured physical shocks to the body and psychological fractures to the mind from being kidnapped and transported away from their homelands across the Atlantic Ocean to New World destinations at which they became sentenced to lifelong servitude as chattel property. The slave narrative thus generated its own sub-genre of travel writing. Specifically, early African American travelers often embarked upon unauthorized liberatory initiatives for the purposes of emancipation, re-identification, regeneration, or self-reliance that frequently conflicted with the principles of Euro-American colonization, slavery, and imperialism. Moreover, these African American travelers inaugurated an eclectic genre of domestic and transnational travel writing which was often sociopolitically motivated on behalf of the collective for racial uplift rather than for mere individualized, European-type, leisure class entertainment – a premise which still holds true in modern times.

The Interesting Narrative of Olaudah Equiano, a Slave, Written by Himself, published in 1789, is invaluable in defining African American travel writing in two ways. First, Equiano's first-person testimony is considered to be the seminal model for the slave narrative, as he reports eyewitness accounts of Europe's institutionalizing the brutal system of slavery by establishing contractual relations with African chieftains or common natives who became complicit in the sales of their own brethren. Kidnapped from his own Ibo tribe in Benin by African kinsmen at age eleven in 1756, Equiano describes the responses of shocked bodies and fractured psyches that captives felt once being stolen from home. He is frequently sold while being transported overland for three months until he reaches the oddity of the sea and the strangeness of white men who house him like cargo in the belly of a slave ship that eventually lands in the Caribbean. At Barbados, Equiano finds himself fated, like other multi-ethnic African captives, to be sold at auction as the property of white men, and then transported to other parts of the New World. One of Equiano's early masters takes him briefly to the American colonies, and specifically to Virginia. There the youth Equiano witnesses the most heinous sight – the dehumanization of a black female slave who is forced to wear a muzzle over her mouth to keep her from tasting the food she is preparing for the master's family. Equiano continually reports such brutalities to the conscripted black body during his ten years of slavery, years that take him throughout the Caribbean, South America, Europe, and North America aboard slave ships, and also to the North Pole, Nova Scotia, Turkey, and the Mediterranean on British warships. Equiano represents his personal narrative of slavery and then freedom as the collective experience of the millions of slaves victimized like or worse than himself. His travels throughout the African diaspora enable Equiano to function as their spokesperson. His is a credible eyewitness account from the perspectives of a slave and then freedman who later becomes a freedom activist in London on behalf of black Britons desiring to emigrate back to Africa in 1784, specifically to the country of Sierra Leone.

All of the rhetorical devices defining embodied discourse in Equiano's seminal slave narrative reappear continually in travel accounts emerging throughout the African diaspora. For example, the "slave ship" and/or black "hole" symbols linked to the conscripted black body also appear in American slave narratives. Solomon Northrup, a freedman of New York, finds himself in a symbolic "hole" after he travels by ship to Washington, DC for a fiddling engagement and is then captured and sold into slavery for twelve years. So hopeless and unending is slave life that Frederick Douglass reports in his 1845 *Narrative* that he, as a youth, had envied the free movement of inanimate ships crossing Chesapeake Bay in Maryland while he,

the human chattel, was doomed to lifelong, static servitude. William Wells
Brown reports visiting slave "holes" in ships traveling between Louisville,
Kentucky, and Natchez, Mississippi, in his 1853 *Narrative*, owing to his
job of fabricating the ages and fitness of unhealthy slaves for his employer,
a slave speculator. The "hole" image also changes into a "womb/tomb"
symbol on land in the 1851 *Narrative* by Henry Box Brown and in the 1861
Incidents in the Life of a Slave Girl by Harriet Jacobs. Brown escapes slavery
by performing a trick of shipping himself in a box to the North. On the other
hand, Harriet Jacobs reports her trick of living for seven years in a "hole"
or small garret in her grandmother's roof in order to escape detection by her
slave owner. The image of the trickster figure determined to escape slavery
often recurs in slave narratives. The small space eventually becomes so detri-
mental to Jacobs that her health suffers and she is finally forced to flee North
to avoid permanent disability. After orchestrating a slave rebellion in Virginia in 1831, Nat Turner, in his third-person *Confession*, reports digging
himself a "hole" underground and remaining undetected for several days.
Modes of escape such as coaches, wagons, boats, or trains also function as
symbolical "holes" of concealment for runaway slaves.

The ship, which served as the prison for the black body during the slave
trade, assumes a different meaning in the emancipatory travel literature
of escaped slaves and freedmen. A few eventually migrated to the British
colonies to retain their earned liberties. In the early stages of the American Revolution, African Americans John Marrant, David George, and
Boston King all report their tales of emigrating to Halifax, Nova Scotia,
which became a new "home" for loyalist African Americans in service to
the British. In their travelogues, all three recall harrowing experiences in
becoming British loyalists because of their specific residences in the Georgia
and/or South Carolina regions. Marrant was born a freedman in New York
in 1755, but his parents relocated to the slave states of Georgia and South
Carolina. Unlike Marrant, both George and King were born into slavery;
George was born, date unknown, in Essex County, Virginia, and King was
born, date unknown, in Charleston, South Carolina. A common thread
of religion connects all three; all report conversions to Christianity during their youth at various times in the 1770s. Marrant succumbs to the
preaching of Reverend George Whitefield, who also influenced Equiano's
conversion. George and King follow their religious callings at local black
churches or through a vision. And like Equiano, they each recount struggling
with worldly temptations. In their escape narratives, Marrant and George
describe their captivities by Native Americans in the Georgia–South Carolina
regions. Marrant had gone into the wilderness to purify his flesh and practice
abstinence, but ended up being held captive by the Creeks for six months.

George had fled to the American Indians to escape a cruel slave master but spent five years performing rigorous labor for the Creek or Natchez Indians.

Various contacts with the British Navy result in their relocations to Birch Town, Nova Scotia, a resettlement area for blacks. After release from British service, Marrant migrates to Nova Scotia voluntarily in 1785 to minister to the black community at the behest of his brother, already located there. At the conclusion of the American Revolution, both George and King face remandment to their slave masters. They accept British offers to relocate them and their families to Halifax around 1785. However, the cold climate drives George and King to look for another safe haven. At different times in 1789, George and King join the Sierra Leone back to Africa movement taking place in England. Each returns with his family to Liverpool, England, where they board another ship bound for Africa. The trip by sea takes seven long, arduous weeks. Many of the immigrants die from the journey or the new tropical climate, including King's wife. George decides to return with his family to England; King remains. He even goes back to England for more training in 1794, and then returns to Sierra Leone in 1796 to teach permanently at Kingwood School.

The British back-to-Africa movement to Sierra Leone also sparks the desire to resettle for other African Americans still located in the United States. Paul Cuffe's interest in emigration is such an instance. Cuffe was born free in Massachusetts in 1795 to an ex-slave father and Native American mother. In his *Brief Account* published in 1812, Cuffe recounts his dream of staging a journey back to Africa that would be redemptive for African Americans enslaved or freed. He even researches the success rates of colonists in 1812, consisting of Europeans, Nova Scotians, Maroons, and African migrants, with whites outnumbering by three-fourths the number of blacks. Cuffe sees an absence of African Americans in the records of new migrants to Sierra Leone and then earnestly adopts the notion that relocation to Africa would be a salvation for them. Cuffe's efforts are well meant; however, the War of 1812 aborts his project, although the British elite admire him for arriving in England with a ship manned by both Native American and African American seamen. All of Cuffe's efforts are of his own volition and sometimes at his own expense. In 1815, Cuffe reignites his Sierra Leone resettlement project and voluntarily pays the passage for many of his new Afrocentric patriots. Before Cuffe's death in 1817, he also succeeds in setting up a trading cooperative affiliated with the Methodist Church and run exclusively by blacks.

Another expression of black body discourse and its forms of mobility appears in the small segment of frontier literature written before and after the Civil War about the exploits of two "black cowboys," James P. Beckwourth and Nat Love. Beckwourth was born in 1789 to a slave mother and white military officer. In his 1856 oral narrative *The Life and Adventures of James P. Beckwourth, A Mountaineer, Scout and Pioneer and Chief of the Crow Nations in Indiana*, Beckwourth, a fair-skinned mulatto, recounts his transient life as a scout for United States troops in the Indian Territory around Des Moines, Iowa. He recalls one occasion of assisting the Army in negotiating a treaty with the Native Americans. His skill earns Beckwourth 700 dollars for this seven-month venture. In another episode, Beckwourth reports guiding General Ashley's Rocky Mountain Fur Company. Though he advises the twenty-member group to carry twenty-five pound backpacks as well as rifles, ammunitions, and blankets in order to survive the frigid cold, they still run out of food. While out foraging for food, Beckwourth wanders straight into the arms of territorial American Indians. Luckily, he has become renowned among the Crow Indians as a negotiator advocating for the rights of Native Americans. Thus, the Crows greet Beckwourth as a hero, and he becomes a "found" son of the tribe – inheriting a wife and Native American family as an inducement to prevent him from returning to the tribe's white enemies. He ultimately becomes a proud son and guardian of the Crow people.

The life of another transient black cowboy is the subject of the 1907 *Life and Adventures of Nat Love*. Born a slave in Tennessee in 1854, Nat Love is emancipated at age fifteen and decides to head West to Kansas. He depicts the cattle center of Dodge City as an unbridled frontier town filled with dance halls, saloons, gambling houses, and wild cowboys. Among them are black cowboys, who assist Love in joining the trade. After passing a test involving breaking in a wild horse, Love earns the short-lived nickname of Red River Dick for his skillful performance and also lands a premium job paying thirty dollars a month. His three-year stint with the Duval group as a cattle driver is never dull and often hazardous. Love escapes threats to his life from sudden hailstorms, charges by cattle, attacks by Native Americans, and sieges by white outlaws. In 1872 when Love joins the Gallinger outfit, that job takes him all over Texas, Arizona, and other Southwestern states. During this transient time, Love reports meeting Buffalo Bill and Yellowstone Kelly. He also acquires the famous moniker of Deadwood Dick after winning roping, riding, and shooting contests in the city of Deadwood, South Dakota, on July 4, 1876. Love leaves a dying profession with regret in 1890. With the rapid rise of the railway industry linking one coast to another, Love joins a growing body of African American males becoming employed as porters by George Pullman, the founding father of the sleeping car industry.

Another form of African American travel writing is the adventure story. The narrative of Thomas Detter is such an adventurous account. Born a free black in Maryland in 1826, Detter relocated to California in 1856; over the years he became masterful at writing owing to his professions as a journalist and congressman. In *Nellie Brown, or the Jealous Wife with Other Sketches* published in 1871, Detter describes his duties as a congressman from Sacramento that require him to travel around the Idaho and Washington Territories. In one of his sketches, Detter reports his encountering of racial discrimination during a stopover in Boise City, the capital of Idaho Territories. The town is rustic, with only a few permanent buildings. When Detter goes to the local saloon to order a drink, the bartender refuses to serve him because of his skin color. Such abrasive insults are the norm in Boise, the author concludes. However, he refuses to allow the white man's bigotry to lower his own self-assessment of being a gentleman. His other travels take Detter to Nevada in the Southwest, the antebellum South, and overseas to Cuba.

Africa never leaves the consciousness of former slaves and their descendants. The loss of Africa as "home" and the "returned body" become rhetorical signatures in other travel accounts by African Americans during antebellum and postbellum times. Africa comes to symbolize re-affirmation for the hybridized, American-born African searching for re-identification and definitions of self-reliance. The three West African countries of Nigeria, Liberia, and Ghana recur as focused sites of study. African Americans Martin Delany and Robert Campbell decided to travel together to Nigeria in 1852, but published separate reports afterwards. Martin Delany was born in 1812 in Charles Town, Virginia, to a freeborn mother and slave father. He eventually became a doctor, political activist, and newspaper owner. In the *Official Report of the Niger Valley Exploring Party* published in 1861, Delany assumes the posture of the field observer who provides minute descriptions of the country's topographical worth and geographical demarcations. He reprises the "ship" symbol since he notes departing on the ship *Mende*, owned by three African American businessmen now living in Liberia. It is Delany's first stop. His comments focus on the country's economy; he makes detailed notes about the coffee, sugar, rice, ginger, and pepper industries thriving there. Delany also observes a need for Liberians to improve methods of drying their products; however, he commends the natives for being willing to improve their quality of production. The schools he thinks are good, and the culture seems heavily Christianized but absent of Roman Catholics. While commending Liberians for trade, he also encourages them to create better means of remaining self-governed. The European presence is obvious also because of ongoing practices of slavery. Delany finds this practice to be totally deplorable and concedes that slavery is not just a system invented or practiced by American whites. In black Liberia, criminals and prisoners of war are routinely sold into slavery. At Lagos and near the Bight of Benin, Delany visits a slave port where he sees captives depart by ship to the New World, which agitates him. His voice immediately assumes a tone of militancy as he vows that slavery will end. He keeps his promise by joining the Union Army at the outset of the Civil War.

Robert Campbell's earlier report on *A Pilgrimage to my Motherland* (1859) conveys an opposite perspective as he consistently focuses on the sociological and humanistic cultural contours. Born in Jamaica in 1829, he forged ties with America when he became employed at the Institute for Colored Youth in Philadelphia. In *A Pilgrimage*, about his trip to Nigeria, Campbell starts his account on the occasion of his introduction to the Alake of the Abeoka tribe. He specifically notes that his negotiator is a white missionary. Campbell is extremely conscious of native dress and the King's semi-nude attire and adornments of gold-trimmed hats and robes. Additionally, he is conscious of polygamy and that the King has three hundred wives. At least ten children are seated at the Alake's feet during Campbell's audience with him. Campbell is also conscious of ceremony – he brings gifts to the chiefs and they provide him with cola nuts, which he learns is a ceremonial food. The Africans at first mistake the light-skinned author for a white man, since the natives are pure black. Campbell, however, dispels the myth that Africans admire only Europeans and light skin. He points to chiefs who consistently accord their highest respects to Reverend Samuel Crowther and his namesake son, both dark-skinned African Americans. Campbell concludes that the governmental operations in Nigeria are efficient, that the architecture is beautiful, and that the security is good. Like Delany, Campbell, too, considers slavery an evil system, but notes significant differences between practices in Africa and the United States. Many of the slaves in Africa hold high government posts as chief officers to the various tribal kings.

In the next cluster of Pan-African antebellum and/or postbellum travel writings, the transnational reporters focus on the state of affairs in Liberia. Alexander Crummell was born in New York City in 1819 to Charity and Boston Crummell, the latter forever instilling the fact that he was a proud member of the Timmanee tribe in West Africa. In 1842, Crummell became an ordained Episcopalian minister, and then later removed to study at Cambridge University in England. Crummell's speech, "The Relations and Duties of Free Colored Men in America to Africa," was given in New York in 1860. In the talk, Crummell takes a pro-Africa, pro-emigration stance but cleverly asks for commitments from his African American audience by using an oratorical method of indirection. He claims not to desire to irritate his brethren by reminding them that America is not their home. Instead, he wishes to remind the sons of Africa of their kinship to their fatherland of Liberia. Crummell is diplomatic in his approach, for he ends his speech by soliciting members of his African American audience to commit to emigration to Africa, and to their evangelism, to service to God.

W. E. B. Du Bois, a global traveler in his time, was also pro-Africa and pro-Liberia. As a returning son of Africa, he renewed bonds and spoke of Liberia in a discourse of romantic wonderment and love. Born in 1869 in Great Barrington, Massachusetts, he became the first African American to graduate with a PhD from Harvard in 1895. His masterpiece, *The Souls of Black Folk* (1903), focused new attention on the importance of the color line in America. His travels abroad led him to appreciate and praise Africa. His 1924 article for *The Crisis* magazine entitled "Little Portraits of Africa" relates his optimistic assessments of the Liberian people, Monrovia the capital, and Africa as a whole. Du Bois provides the romanticized voice and perspective of an African American totally enthralled with "Africa." His love is expressed as he praises the vegetation, the trees, the stars, the animal life, and the people from this distant place where a black person is a free agent. He exalts at the notion of walking unencumbered down a path in the woods. He also expresses wonderment at the bush, the density of trees, and minute ant colonies. Du Bois' moods swing from a thrill at hearing a monkey whine to a feeling of awe at lurking, poisonous snakes. Even the coffee and cocoa plantations appear beautiful to Du Bois. He in essence writes a praise song to Africa. He finds the colors beautiful, the women "comely," and the silence of the bush profound; he concludes that there is no continent on earth more perfect than Africa.

A third group of Pan-African travelers cast their eyes on Ghana, once known during colonization as the Gold Coast. This grouping of travelers includes Richard Wright, Leslie Alexander Lacy, and Sylvia Boone. Their travel accounts capture the urgency and activism swelling in the United States during the 1950s as well as the ensuing 1960s Civil Rights Movement. Ghana is envisioned as part of the solution to American racism, but the three travelers have different responses to the country. Richard Wright was born in Natchez, Mississippi, in 1908 to an illiterate sharecropper and a school teacher. After fleeing to Chicago in 1927, and then removing to Paris, France, in 1946 to gain greater personal and intellectual freedoms, Wright became heavily involved with French intellectuals, their theories of existentialism, and especially their humanist drives to decolonize Africa. In his first travelogue entitled *Black Power: A Record of Reactions in a Land of Pathos* (1954), Wright deliberately creates a political travel narrative not seeking to offer a praise song to Africa like Du Bois' in order to indict

European slavery. Instead of focusing on the people of Ghana, their customs, and President Kwame Nkrumah's strategies for independence from European control, for example, Wright turns his observing eye inward upon his reactions to Africa. He becomes the travel text's subject, not the Africans. His is the exemplum of African American existentialist travel writing where the responses of the outsider travel hero are foremost. All along Wright represents himself not as a native son returning home but as an outsider, an African American disconnected from his roots. To illustrate his distance from originary culture and genealogical roots, Wright playacts the confused subject. He frequently expresses his frustrations with the Ghanaians' different concepts of time, their humid climate, and their incomprehensible tribal languages. Wright lets his reader know that he feels immobilized and alienated because he cannot take a train or bus without the government's permission and must be accompanied by a translator. At all stages in *Black Power*, and also the other two travel books that follow, Wright presents a unique, egocentric form of African American travel writing to illustrate how Western imperialism has ruptured native cultures and/or consciousnesses.

Contrary to Wright's self-focusing about his encounters in Ghana, two African Americans write typical, object-focused narratives and positive accounts about the culture. Born in 1937 to a privileged Louisiana family, Leslie Alexander Lacy in his 1970 travel narrative *The Rise and Fall of a Proper Negro*, writes about black American expatriates in Ghana who cling together almost in a separatist world. Their returned journeys as diasporic Africans recover a motif from the times of slavery. Like him, these exiles have all come to Ghana to search for their identities and to reconnect to Africa. Lacy also recognizes that these expatriates are heirs to the Pan-Africanist teachings of Cuffe, Garvey, and Delany. He also captures the air of excitement: while Nkrumah is making history by creating an independent nation, Du Bois is establishing an intellectual center inspired by his newly sanctioned Ghanaian citizenship. The multiple, indigenous languages of Twi, Hausa, Akan, etc., are not insurmountable because of translators and talented African Americans devoted to modernizing Ghana. Lacy also reports that well-known political activists such as Shirley Du Bois, Julian Mayfield, Julia Wright (daughter of Richard), and a host of painters, sculptors, historians, and translators, are all busily helping Ghana to emerge into the modern world as a technologically competitive nation.

Sylvia Ardyn Boone actually studied in Ghana and also became familiar with the colonies of African American expatriate writers and artists noted by Lacy. Born in New York City in 1941, she became the first African American to graduate with a PhD in Art History from Yale University in 1941. In her 1974 travel book *West African Travels*, Boone reports that she has traveled extensively throughout all five regions of Africa, not just the western parts near Ghana. She indicates that her travel guide to Africa has been written to dismantle Western myths about Africa's backward ways, such as its being labeled as "Third World." Boone praises the way that Africa restores humanity to alienated African Americans, for there is an absence of terror, of surveillance systems, and of incidents of racial slurs that are common in America. She also includes a glossary of terms in her travel book to enable new travelers to avoid pejorative words and phrases. For example, Boone suggests replacing dated words such as "tribe" with the new term "ethnic group," and that "witchcraft" should be rejected in favor of "medicine," etc.

Another site of interest for African American travel writers is France between the periods of 1855 and 1961. *The American Fugitive in Europe; Sketches of Places and People Abroad* (1855) by William Wells Brown recounts the author's escape from American slavery and flight abroad. Brown was born a slave in 1814 in Lexington, Kentucky, and escaped to freedom in 1834 with the aid of a Quaker benefactor. As a fugitive abroad, he reports traveling to France in 1849 as a delegate to the International Peace Congress. He has a sightseer's eye and follows a crowd into the Church of the Madeleine because it was the site of the Revolution of 1848 that dethroned King Louis Phillipe. At the Peace Conference meeting in the Salle St. Cecile, he describes feeling impressed by all the various delegates from Germany, Italy, Greece, Switzerland, Spain, and the United States. He recalls one incident of encountering racism abroad from an American. While traveling to Europe aboard ship, this particular person had been appalled at traveling with a Negro passenger. However, Brown reports that this very same man, who would not have spoken to him in the United States, speaks to him respectfully in Paris. On other excursions, Brown visits the Place de Vendôme and pronounces it to be the Bunker Hill of Paris. He also delights in observing the strollers on the boulevards of Paris.

Gwendolyn Bennett, Jessie Redmon Fauset, and Countee Cullen of Harlem Renaissance fame also traveled to Paris during the 1920s. Gwendolyn Bennett was born in 1902 in Giddings, Texas, but spent her youth in Washington, DC, Pennsylvania, and New York. In her "Diary" entries between June 25, 1925, and August 8, 1925, published in *The Crisis*, she describes her frustrations over finding lodging as a new art student in Paris. In an entry of June 25, Bennett reports becoming upset over being sent back and forth to different places until she settles in at the Hotel Orfila. Being a prudent American does not prepare Bennett for the casual attitudes of Parisians towards sex. She is shocked when the concierge allows her male sponsor to come directly to her room. She worries about her reputation as a lady and quickly suggests that the two go sightseeing. In another entry of June 30, Bennett reports going to a museum to study the paintings of Delacroix, and then stopping on the Boulevard St. Michel for tea after becoming weary of walking. The opera becomes Bennett's favorite form of entertainment.

Jessie Fauset is a much more sophisticated traveler on her second visit to Paris. Born in 1882 in New Jersey, Fauset obtained a master's degree in French from the University of Pennsylvania. In "Yarrow Revisited," published in *The Crisis* in 1925, she contrasts her present status as a mature traveler with her student days abroad. She recalls her reactions years ago to seeing the vibrant and brilliant streets of Paris. Now in October, they seem drab, and she seems annoyed at the constant rainfalls. She notes that she no longer resides in the wild Latin Quarter of her youth but in a quiet hotel. The pension also has no allure; it is damp and cold since the sun rarely penetrates the inside. The dining room also seems shabby. However, Fauset's spirits seem to lift when she begins to observe the ordinary people at work on the streets.

Countee Cullen makes cryptic observations about French etiquette. Born in 1903, he became a popular poet and writer during the Harlem Renaissance. In "Countee Cullen on French Courtesy" in the June 1929 issue of *The Crisis*, Cullen admits that adjusting to the ways of Parisians has taken longer than he had anticipated. After six months, he considers himself an authority on French manners – their politeness and their tolerance levels. For instance, unlike America where one section of the country bears enmity for another, such behavior does not exist in French society. They also do not hurry like Americans, and, therefore, exude a genteel quality in their manners. Even in the most routine of events, such as in purchasing foods, the French, says Cullen, turn the occasion of buying a bottle of wine or purchasing a loaf of bread into a social call and exchange of cordialities. Cullen concludes that Paris is a humanizing experience for African Americans accustomed to America's brusque social rebuffs to them.

A distance from the Harlem Renaissance but still reflecting the black body seeking solace outside of America are the travel writings of James Baldwin and Hazel Scott. Baldwin's most important travel essays are included in his book, *Notes of a Native Son* (1955). Born in Harlem, New York, in 1924, Baldwin became a prolific writer. In later years, he split his time between France and the United States, but never declared himself an expatriate like Wright. In *Notes*, Baldwin describes the difficulties African Americans encounter abroad because they remain unable to immerse themselves in French society. In particular, he notes that African American entertainers now have more monetary problems because the free spending of the 1920s is over and black entertainers are not as much in demand. He estimates that nearly 500 African Americans reside in Paris during the 1950s; the majority of them are veterans of US military service who survive on their government allotments. African Americans seem to cluster together, observes Baldwin. Yet he notes that the expatriates feel freer in Paris, as signified by the glaring absence of the stock responses of "Sir" and "Madam" in their speech patterns that would be demanded by whites in American culture. In France, they simply reply "Yes" or "No" without embellishment or fear of racial reprisal. Baldwin also cites French social customs on the transit system as another example of its free society. In Paris, there is no rude jostling or irritating behavior that is likely to arouse someone's temper. To Baldwin, the French people's forms of politeness and civility are factors that propel African Americans to emigrate, for the daily irritations of racial insults in America are absent.

Hazel Scott's travel account of her life as an expatriate is tinged with comic and tragic memories of her residence in Paris as a performing artist. At the same time, she acknowledges that money enables one to rise above the annoyances of racism. Born in Port of Spain, Trinidad, she grew up in the United States and won a scholarship to the Juilliard School of Music to study the piano at age eight. However, she was only able to accept it at age sixteen. After being blacklisted by the House Un-American Activities Committee in its 1950s hearings and also simultaneously divorcing Congressman Adam Clayton Powell, Scott moved to Paris in 1956. Her article "What Paris Means to Me" was published in the *Negro Digest* in 1961. Scott portrays the city of lights as rehabilitating her emotionally after such devastating crises. She recounts it becoming a second home, complemented by her friendships with expatriate artists, including Billie Holiday and Lester Young. They buoy her spirits during Scott's spates of depression and illness. She suffers greatly when both Holiday and Young die during her three-year residence. However, Scott also brings America to Paris by regularly celebrating traditional holidays and cooking Southern foods for appreciative African students. She paints Paris as a city of magic, culture, the blues, and pain. If there is any evidence of racism, she ignores it; she concludes that financial solvency generally transcends any racial or social barrier in Paris.

A third cluster of travel writers escaping American racism consists of four African Americans who sought freedom or opportunity in Russia between 1823 and 1981. Nancy Prince was born in 1799 in Gloucester, Massachusetts. After growing up in poverty and learning the dressmaking trade, she happened to meet an expatriate African American in 1823 who had become a member of the Russian guard. Following a brief courtship and then marriage, Prince returned to Russia with him in 1824. In one part of her *Narrative* published in 1853, Prince describes the excitement of being thrown into the opulence of the Russian court ruled by Emperor Alexander in St. Petersburg. French and English fashion governs dress, and Prince is conscious of the stately dignity of Emperor Alexander and Empress Elizabeth when they receive her as the wife of a "colored" guard. During her three-year stay, Prince becomes very knowledgeable about court ceremony for festivities, as well as burial rites for court members and the monarchy. In addition, she experiences life-threatening situations: she escapes drowning during a flood in St. Petersburg; she witnesses mob rule during the Decembrist Rebellion of 1825 aimed at overthrowing the monarchy; she witnesses the court's political activities during the War of 1827–29 between Russia and Turkey; and she sees the consequences of the cholera epidemic of 1831. In 1833, she returns to the United States and her spouse dies shortly afterwards in Russia. After providing for her impoverished family, Prince sets off for new adventures in the Caribbean and West Indies.

Travel writers Claude McKay, Langston Hughes, and Audre Lorde go to Russia to see if Communist practices and Marxist theory are truly liberating. Born in Jamaica in 1889, McKay is claimed by African Americans because his novels and poetry connected him to the Harlem Renaissance. In 1921, he visited the Soviet Union. While there, he met Leon Trotsky and other Communist officials. McKay's 1923 article "Soviet Russia and the Negro" was published in *The Crisis*. In it, McKay boldly praises the Soviet Union as the answer to the "Negro problem" as well as the problem of capitalist oppression for any oppressed people. He notes that the American Negro is the prime topic of discussions at the meetings held by the Communist International and attended by Lenin and John Reed, the American journalist. McKay captures the festive air inspired by surging crowds, and stores, schools, factories, and churches draped by red Communist flags. He also consistently praises the Russians for valuing him as a poet while racist Americans denounce both him and his poetry as inferior and uncultured. In Petrograd or Moscow, McKay detects no racial snobbery for the Russians treat all people as equal. He even receives a commission from the state to complete a book. Everywhere he turns, McKay reports, Russian intellectuals as well as ordinary citizens of all ages and classes greet him with warm smiles, contrary to his reception at home in America.

Langston Hughes' trip to Russia also offers a comparative study of racial conditions in the United States. Born in Joplin, Missouri, he became a key creative writer in the Harlem Renaissance, especially because of his poetry. In his article entitled "Going South in Russia" published by *The Crisis* in 1934, Hughes compares the Soviet Union with the American South that still imposes racist social codes upon black people. He recalls how his present trip triggered memories of a visit to the Soviet Union two summers earlier. At that time, the rights accorded to the Russian proletariat had inspired Hughes to comparisons with the rights denied African Americans in the United States and other oppressed peoples in capitalist nations. He visits the "red" South by traveling from Moscow to Central Asia. Riding the train through Central Asia had earlier reminded him of blacks being forced to ride in dirty Jim Crow cars in the American South or African Americans being denied the right to ride in the front of the bus in the North. In this 1933 sequence, Hughes reminds himself that he does not have to ride Jim Crow while he is in Russia.

The travel narrative of Audre Lorde is also politically motivated and critical of American laws that disefranchise its non-Anglo citizens along race, class, and gender lines. Born in 1934 in New York City, Lorde became a leading African American poet and activist for gay/lesbian rights. In "Notes from a Trip to Russia" from *Sister Outsider* (1984), the author discusses her two-week trip to Russia in 1976. Lorde positions herself as an observer/tourist even though her purpose is to attend an African-Asian Writers' Conference. Her trip starts with a nine-hour flight to Moscow. She assists an elderly Russian woman on the flight by removing the woman's coat roll from the overhead storage rack. There is no racial tension, Lorde reflects, which normally would occur in America. In an unescorted walking tour to study the ornate architecture and rich cityscape, she stops at a metro station to observe passengers. The system seems very much like New York; the orderliness and sparse population do not. Even more odd, Lorde sees no black people. Another difference she observes is between American capitalistic greed for individual profit versus Russian Communist communal distribution of wealth. The Soviet government automatically allocated pocket money of twenty-five rubles to all conference participants, which would never occur in America's capitalistic system of hoarding profits. At her destination of Uzbekistan, she concludes that Russians are pleasant people, and feels elated to see a variety of people of color living in Tashkent, whose inhabitants include Asians, Africans, and Iranians.

An educational motive shapes the travel writing of Andrea Lee, who resided one year in Russia as the wife of an exchange student at Moscow State University, 1978–79. Born in 1953 and a Harvard/Radcliffe graduate herself, Lee approached her foreign travel from the perspective of a well-educated woman. In *Russian Journal* (1981), she proves how the reality of a culture undermines assumptions learned in books. Lee provides glimpses into Russian culture while at the same time revealing how her romantic expectations conflict with the reality of Russian life. Her first impressions focus on the lush forests, dark greeneries, and small lakes that she sees while flying into Moscow. These images fulfill her childhood fantasies about Russia, but reality soon sets in. Upon landing, Lee discovers that clearing customs is chaotic and time consuming. Her theoretical textbook language skills as well as knowledge of Russian life soon fail her, too, for they collide with the harsh reality of the Marxist–Leninist world that she has entered. The exterior architecture of Moscow State University with its Slavic, Babylonian, and Corinthian design conflicts with the inside buildings clustered like a fortress. In actuality, the groupings function efficiently like an autonomous city. Lee also discovers that the housing assigned to her spouse in a tower is the best accommodation and is usually reserved for tourists. Thus, the Lees have received special privileges. They have two rooms; normally six students would occupy one of the rooms. Lee soon forgives the drab colors of the beige walls. Elderly women in *babushkas* maintain the housekeeping and guard the keys. Lee never adjusts to the constant surveillance of the Russians, although she does admit that her Western dress still draws attention.

Do African Americans ever travel as leisure-class tourists? The answer is "yes," but the occasions of non-political travel are reported less frequently in the narratives of the black body in motion. One early account is that of Edward Wilmot Blyden. Born in St. Thomas in the US Virgin Islands in 1832, he also emigrated to Liberia. In his travel narrative entitled *West Africa to Palestine* published in 1873, Blyden speaks about an excursion for pleasure from Liberia to Egypt and then Jerusalem. Once arriving in Cairo by steamship, Wilmot incurs problems like other tourists. He feels proud in processing through customs and purchasing rail tickets to the Valley of the Nile, which seem to have gone smoothly. At the Pyramids, he ponders their magnanimity and then ventures inside the dark caverns, which feel like a sepulcher. He wonders what role Negroes played in building the Sphinx. At Jerusalem, he also feels awed at confronting the Temple of Solomon and visiting the Garden of Gethsemane, the Spanish and Polish synagogues, and standing at the site of Jesus' crucifixion. The cross-section of visitors is overwhelming. Blyden concludes that no one can visit Jerusalem without experiencing profound emotional changes.

Another cluster of African American travel writings concern persons self-designated as tourists. David F. Dorr's travels are extraordinary for the times of slavery. Born a slave in New Orleans, Louisiana, c. 1827, Dorr was the son of a white man and a black slave. He was fair enough to pass for white. His master Cornelius Fellowes took Dorr abroad with him to Europe and the Near East from 1851 to 1854. After his return, Dorr eventually published *A Colored Man Round the World* in 1858. His book-length travel narrative starts off in London, and then proceeds to Paris, the Netherlands, Waterloo,

Ghent, Brussels, Rome, Naples, Athens, Egypt, Jerusalem, Damascus, and Jericho. In his entry for Ghent, Dorr speaks about boredom because he had become a seasoned traveler. However, he knows history and especially the city's fame for being the site of the Treaty of Ghent signed there by John Adams and Henry Clay, which officially concluded the War of 1812 between the United States and Great Britain. Dorr also speaks about the Flemish population, the manufacturing of carpets and silks, and the famous Opera house and theatre. One Sunday, he visits a public demonstration of a horse and three people being elevated in a balloon. Dorr indicates that it was not novel to him since he had seen the same act in Paris. In removing to nearby Bruges (with his master), Dorr complains about the bad hotel. He also avoids the traps set by skillful beggars preying on tourists. In the Paris sequence, he returns to his old Hotel des Princes, where the staff extend a welcoming greeting to their guest. In the next chapter, Dorr describes Napoleon's takeover of Paris by military force and appraises the event to be as historically significant as the beheading of Louis XVI in 1793.

In the Depression era, the travel narrative of Sue Bailey Thurman about her trip to Mexico proves interesting as African American tourist literature. Known by her marriage to theologian Howard Thurman, she became a respected reformer, educator, and lecturer in her own right. Her 1930 article on "How Far from Here to Mexico?" appeared in *The Crisis*. On this occasion, she observes that "Negroes" are rare entities in Mexico City. A group would periodically visit there for conferences or jazz performances. Also, Langston Hughes would often visit since his father had become a permanent resident. Still, Thurman ponders why Mexicans lack such curiosity about African Americans. She points out the screening of the film *Imitation of Life* starring Louise Beavers. The Latin Americans are not surprised by the tragic ending because of color line problems for the dark-skinned mother and light-skinned daughter Pecola, who had chosen to pass for white. It seems, so Thurman discerns, that Mexico's close proximity to the Texas border accounts for their reception of American stereotypes of African Americans and their infusing into Mexican culture. The Mexicans expect to see blacks in service positions. Thurman also learns that Mexicans do not realize that African Americans are even citizens of the United States. On another note, she encourages African Americans to travel to Mexico but cautions them to learn the language beforehand.

Finally, Ntozake Shange provides the reader with a rare tourist narrative about Nicaragua during the Sandinista regime. Born in 1948 in Trenton, New Jersey, Shange made her literary mark as a poet and playwright in 1976 when she published her controversial choreopoem *For Colored Girls Who Have Considered Suicide When the Rainbow is Enuf*. Her essay, "All it Took was a Road/Surprises of Urban Renewal" (1998), begins by observing that no roads had existed between Managua and Bluefield, Nicaragua, until the Sandinistas assumed power in 1981. But Shange also realizes her own naïveté, for only gradually in driving across country does she recognize that she is a lone, black North American. While she had conceived of poets forming a bond without color line barriers, it becomes obvious to her that a color line exists in Nicaragua when she finds herself to be an oddity. However, her discomfiture is short-lived after Shange hears familiar rhythm and blues songs by Michael Jackson and Stevie Wonder on the radio. Moreover, she becomes more relaxed when she reaches the home of saxophonist Carlos Johnson in Managua and finds Ruben Daren, the Nicaraguan poet, in attendance. It seems that Johnson has mastered the racial barriers by playing the role of innocent musician; he would go everywhere with his saxophone and be well received. She begins to relax; the small assemblage of poets and musicians forge a special bond that reminds her of a James Brown song: you connect to the culture you live in. Right now, Shange concludes, she is connected in Managua, Nicaragua.

To conclude, African American travel writing draws its expression from the slave experience and the genre known as the slave narrative. From its rhetorical devices of "ship" and "black hole" symbols remarking the kidnapping, transporting, and removing of the black body to distant foreign places in the New World, a particular signature of black body discourse arose intrinsically within the narrative mode. Moreover, in the American colonies and then United States, the escape-to-freedom stories by African American slaves came to be just one aspect of the holistic nature of the slave narrative in its recurrent use throughout the African diaspora. For bondsman and freedman, the quest for liberation and equal rights remained foremost. In searching for equality and answers to cultural gaps in knowledge, the travel writers show a consistent tendency to return to states in Africa for inspiration and renewal, or to look outwards towards Europe, South and Central America, or the Caribbean as alternative sites for cultural regeneration. However, the genre is still in a fluid process of redefinition from emancipatory to tourist literature.

12

SUSAN L. ROBERSON

American women and travel writing

Americans have the reputation of always being on the move. Early in our nation's history, French visitor Michel Chevalier commented that "[The American] has no root in the soil, he has no feeling of reverence, and love for the natal spot and the paternal roof; he is always disposed to emigrate, always ready to start in the first steamer that comes along, from the place where he had but just now landed."[1] Our national identity and literature are marked by the lore of the open road, of "landscapes of continents and the public road," as Walt Whitman celebrated.[2] And our heroes are the explorers and restless souls whose tales of new lands, adventure, freedom, and opportunity form a part of the national myth: Columbus, the 49ers, Huck Finn, Jack Kerouac.

But women too traveled, migrated, moved, often for the same reasons as their husbands, brothers, and fathers. As Annette Kolodny observes of pioneer women who moved West, "Like their husbands and fathers, women too shared in the economic motives behind emigration, and like the men, women also dreamed of transforming the wilderness. But the emphases were different."[3] The reasons women travel may be similar to the motivations that drove men to journey, but the degree to which their choice of travel is free, the kinds of experiences they relate, and the metaphysical roads they travel can be quite different. "The road of the [female] nomad," Deborah Paes de Barros claims, "is not simply traveled in a different manner . . . It is a new space, a space between borders . . ."[4]

Even though women have shared in experiences of travel with men, much of the critical attention to travel has focused on the male traveler or a male paradigm of travel. Eric Leed's monumental *The Mind of the Traveler: From Gilgamesh to Global Tourism* traces the history of travel, but with primarily male examples from Gilgamesh to Claude Levi-Strauss; Larzer Ziff's important *Return Passages: Great American Travel Writing 1780–1910* considers only male travelers; and William Stowe's *Going Abroad: European Travel in Nineteenth-Century American Culture* nods to women travelers like

Margaret Fuller and Lydia Sigourney but focuses on the male experience abroad. Studies like these skew our ideas of American travel writing when they ignore or give only passing comment on women's travel experiences and travel writing, though more recent work by women is bringing attention to American women travelers. Annette Kolodny did much for the critical appraisal of women travelers when she complemented her *Lay of the Land: Metaphor as Experience and History in American Life and Letters* with *The Land Before Her: Fantasy and Experience of the American Frontiers, 1630–1860*; Cheryl Fish's new book, *Black and White Women's Travel Narratives: Antebellum Explorations*, and Sidonie Smith's *Moving Lives: 20th-Century Women's Travel Writing* are among scholarly studies correcting a slanted, even biased, view of American women's travel experiences and travel writing. Indeed, Lewis Perry, in his *Boats Against the Current: American Culture Between Revolution and Modernity, 1820–1860*, observed that "The identification of intellectual opportunity with life on the road [during the antebellum period] imposed severe limitation on women . . . Women could travel across the continent with their families, but when it came to setting forth on new careers, the road was a world where they did not belong." Expecting to find "female modes of protest" in nineteenth-century women's travel writing, Terry Caesar in *Forgiving the Boundaries: Home as Abroad in American Travel Writing* makes the comment that "Women's travel writing enters into no direct dialectical dispute with men's, or no more direct than the humorous mode . . . That is why it is so difficult to locate the exact degree of some specifically female authority." Certainly there have been fewer women travelers than men and fewer published travel narratives by women than by men, as a quick perusal of the extensive bibliography in Michael Kowalewski's *Temperamental Journeys: Essays on the Modern Literature of Travel* attests.[5] But to say that women were circumscribed by gender from taking to the road, or that their narratives must have some degree of protest, is to miss the rich variety of American women's travel experiences and narratives.

Women's travel writing crosses boundaries of genre and purpose, including in its scope not only travel narratives by professional writers but more personal documents by ordinary women who organize their texts and map the self according to the journey, geographic movement providing the root metaphor by which they make sense of their lives.[6] To the extent that "Every story is a travel story," as Michel de Certeau has taught us,[7] women's autobiographies and fictions (though I will not here examine fiction) are also travel stories for they relate spatial practices of mapping the self and making sense of experience, and they provide a way for us to examine how women thought of their mobility and position in the world. These kinds of narratives extend travel writing beyond the more traditional narrative of journeys to foreign lands – to Europe, Africa, Asia – or immigration to a new home at the same time that they broaden our view of women travelers and their mobilities. As well, the peculiarities of the American experience ask us to consider other examples of travel writing: the letters, diaries, and memoirs women wrote about emigrating to and settling in the American West; captivity narratives; and slave narratives. Indeed, Marilyn Wesley counts Mary Rowlandson's 1682 captivity narrative as the "first travel book by a woman published in North America," since it is organized around the "removes" she was forced to make.[8] Slave narratives work as travel narratives for they focus not only on the conditions of the peculiar institution but also on the trafficking of human subjects and on escape from slavery, even if one traveled, as did Harriet Jacobs, to her grandmother's attic. Even Elizabeth Bishop's book of poetry, *Questions of Travel* (1952), is cited as a travel book by Kowalewski for it tells of her sojourn to Brazil and reflects on life in Nova Scotia.

Within this range of genres there is also a range of approaches to writing up the trip. Many narratives imitate, or try to imitate, male traditions of travel writing and do not evidence gender concerns, as when the author objectively describes historic, artistic, or cultural sites. Mary McCarthy's *Stones of Florence* (1959) becomes more historical than personal after the first chapter on tourism as it recounts the political and cultural history of Renaissance Florence, and Ann Zwinger (*Run, River, Run*, 1975), who daringly ran the Green River, works exclusively within the male paradigm of travel writing, citing only texts written by men. As well, the personal journals of women going West follow the format established by guidebooks that map out the route across the terrain. Some women writers, like Sophia Hawthorne, struggle between the objective mode of travel writing and personal reflection, while Willa Cather gives only a passing nod to the influence of guidebooks, and Cathy Davidson more subjectively focuses on the effect of place (Japan) on the self, in *Thirty-Six Views of Mount Fuji* (1993) from "a personal point of view."[9] In addition to the tension between traditional modes of travel writing and the personal, American women's travel writing divides along class lines, with more educated women like Harriet Beecher Stowe, Edith Wharton, and Margaret Fuller writing professionally for publication, while other women write primarily for themselves or family, publication being only an incidental concern. Some women, like escaped slave Louisa Picquet, are not even literate and must relate their tale to an amanuensis and face the "literary appropriation" of her story by male designs (Paes de Barros, *Fast Cars*, p. 48). Because of the variety of travel experiences and travel writings by American women, generalizations about "protest" or "secret journeys" or "nomadic subjects"[10] belie the many concerns and voices evidenced in the rich history of American women's travel writing. Even so, there are some common issues that appear in a number of the narratives and provide a way of characterizing the female traveler and of making some distinctions between men's and women's travel experiences and writing, with the caveats that these issues will not all appear in a woman's text or that men may also address them in their narratives.

Mobility

Historically women have been more associated with sessility than with mobility, with fixity than with motility or physical movement, with home rather than the road. Women have been the ones to whom the traveling or "spermatic" males returned (Leed, *Mind of the Traveler*, p. 224), the faithful Penelope to the wandering Odysseus. Even though women have always traveled, journeying has long been described as a male activity, the public road as a male domain. As Shirley Ardener argues, patriarchy created a "social map" that "constructed some spaces as 'feminine' and others as 'masculine,' using gender difference to inscribe 'spatial difference.'"[11] Those spaces ascribed to women were the private and domestic spaces of the home and family. Because "spatial segregation is one of the mechanisms by which a group with greater power can maintain its advantage over a group with less power,"[12] when women cross spatial, geographic boundaries their movement is seen as a threat to patriarchy and to the social order. That may be why traveling women before the twentieth century were often relegated to the ladies' cabin or why black women, until the Civil Rights Act of 1964, were racially segregated from white travelers; they were still socially and spatially kept "in place."

Doreen Massey points out that "Social change and spatial change are integral to each other,"[13] and so when a woman like Margaret Fuller crosses the threshold of the Harvard College library, when Maria Stewart ascends to the podium of Boston's Franklin Hall in 1832, when the nineteenth-century black itinerant preacher Jarena Lee preaches from the pulpit, or when young Mary Alice Shutes going West gleefully reports that she will ride her pony "straddle like Cow Girls are supposed too [*sic*],"[14] she signals a change in the social order. The freedoms of travel intimate other freedoms and identity transformations that become harbingers of social change. Managing the exigencies of the road – of securing transport, food, and lodging – women like Lee, who made her own itinerant arrangements, and Shutes, who learned to saddle her horse, also gained an independence and self-reliance learned from travel. By challenging immobility and spatial segregation, many traveling women also challenged economic, legal, and ideological restrictions that sought to keep them "in place." For instance, a handful of daring African American women of the nineteenth century like Sojourner Truth, who also challenged racist strictures against mobility, used travel to raise money, to pursue careers, to assert their political rights, thus extending mobility beyond the road and challenging the status quo. Twentieth-century women's travel writing more often evinces the kinds of legal, social, and physical freedoms that earlier women worked to attain. Edith Wharton used her trips to the front lines in France during World War I to expose the devastation caused by the war and to call for America's entry into the war. Charlotte Ebener traveled the globe as a foreign correspondent after World War II, reporting on the growing conflicts in Korea, China, Indochina, and the Middle East. Ann Zwinger traveled the Green River as a naturalist, exercising a great deal of physical motility and strength in her journey. And Frances Mayes, chair of her university's English Department, writes of summers in Tuscany.

Domesticity and the road

Even as women used travel to challenge immobility, they also sought to strike some kind of balance with the domestic and the feminine. Rather than seeing women's travel writing as protest against male paradigms or ideologies of domesticity, I see much of it as a negotiation between mobility and stasis,[15] between new freedoms and traditional ideas and practices of feminine comportment, between the road and home. Annette Kolodny observes that westering women "claimed the frontiers as a potential sanctuary for an idealized domesticity" (*Land Before Her*, p. xiii), and Terry Caesar claims that even as nineteenth-century women traveled abroad "the domesticized space . . . remained the proper province of women" (*Forgiving the Boundaries*, p. 58). Both Kolodny and Caesar's assertions are borne out in the narratives of traveling women, whether they went west or east. Used to conceiving of themselves as domestic women whose "sphere" consisted of home and garden, some women of the Overland Journey transformed the campsite or wagon into a "gypsy" kind of home. "Here I am," writes Harriet Ward in 1853, "sitting on the front seat of the wagon, writing, Willie asleep beside me, Frank seated upon the bed playing her guitar and singing . . . and just a few rods from us, seated around a blazing fire, are the gentlemen of our company, conversing as pleasantly as if they were in the parlour at home."[16] Women who moved to the West often recount how they attempted to create the "ideal home," to become a woman homesteader,[17] and how they managed their domestic duties as wives and mothers. Making a home out of the wild or the foreign seems to be an occupation with women, even into the twentieth century as Maya Angelou relates her living arrangements in Ghana and Frances Mayes describes in great and delicious detail how she converted an abandoned Tuscan villa into a home and mastered the intricacies of Tuscan cooking.

Likewise, antebellum women visitors to Europe sought out the domestic or attempted to associate themselves with the domestic scene even as they journeyed on railway cars, rode horses through the Holy Land, or visited the tourist sites associated with the male-dominated tradition of travel. Thus, Sophia Hawthorne makes sure to describe the domestic scene her traveling family created of the railway car in England, Sarah Haight describes the cozy camps her servants arranged for her in the desert, and Harriet Beecher Stowe lingered over the "bed room, dining room, sitting room" and the "small loophole windows" of Robert the Bruce's caves.[18] At the same time that nineteenth-century women were stretching their legs, their narratives sought to accommodate the ideology of domesticity, gushing over the cozy comfort of their rooms and leaving unquestioned the segregated spaces that consigned the famous author of *Uncle Tom's Cabin* to the ladies' gallery and prevented her from making public speeches. Indeed, antebellum women travelers to Europe worked to shape feminized personae characterized by conventionality, conservatism, and domesticity even as they imitated a male-dominated tradition of travel and travel writing and visited sites associated with male historic and artistic achievement. Even the most nomadic of women travelers, like Jarena Lee, the itinerant woman preacher, made negotiations with the domestic, redefining motherhood and home as she left her child in the care of others to preach the word and reconstructed family out of the communities of African Americans she met on the road.

Home

Even if some women, like Gloria Anzaldúa, had to leave the home, "the source, the mother . . . my family, *mi tierra, mi gente*" to find herself,[19] the home and all it represents resonates in American women's travel writing. Since women are so much identified with home and in fact provide the first "home" for their children, leaving the homesite is often charged with emotions ranging from relief at escape to homesickness. Many pioneer women expressed grief for the lost homes and families left behind in "the States": "I am leaving my home, my early friends and associates, perhaps never to see them again," wrote one woman in 1853 as she set out for the West. The number of letters pioneer women wrote to families attests to the desire to retain contact with home as well as to the effort to define both the old and new homes. Another woman writes to her mother, "There are no turkeys here, and as chickens are three dollars apiece, we are not likely to have any of them ... I will keep your Thanksgiving, and I think it will be on the same day."[20] Carroll Smith-Rosenberg contends that in the "female world of love and ritual" of the eighteenth and nineteenth centuries, letters "provided an important sense of continuity in a rapidly changing society" marked by geographic displacement,[21] as we can see in the stream of letters pioneer women wrote to family and friends back home. Other women, like Stowe and Haight (*Letters from the Old World by a Lady of New York* [1840]), used the letter or "dispatches" to newspapers as a device for writing the travel narrative, providing them with a way to maintain contact with home and of imagining an audience of receptive readers.

At the same time that Stowe maintains epistolary contact with family and friends back home, she is visiting what she takes to be her ancestral home, England. She writes, "Its history for two centuries was our history. Its literature, laws, and language are our literature, laws, and language" (*Sunny Memories*, p. 18). Lydia Sigourney in fact calls England "the Mother Land."[22] Visiting the sites they have read about, Stowe and Sigourney find their cultural, intellectual home, thus signaling their identity both as Americans and as Englishwomen at a time when the nation was still establishing its own identity.

The search for the ancestral home is more complicated for African Americans who journey to Africa to find the home from which their ancestors were forcibly snatched. Disillusioned by the poverty and living conditions in Ghana, Maya Angelou shares her mixed feelings: "We had come home [to Africa], and if home was not what we had expected, never mind, our need for belonging allowed us to ignore the obvious and to create real places or even illusory places, befitting our imagination." Even though she comes "home" to Africa, she finds that, despite the racism of the United States, she still has feelings of homesickness for it. When the expatriate community in Ghana receives a gift of pork sausage, she relates, "We chewed the well spiced pork of America, but in fact, we were ravenously devouring Houston and Macon, Little Rock and St. Louis. Our faces eased with sweet delight as we swallowed Harlem and Chicago's south side."[23] In the end, Angelou returns to her home in the United States having found a lost home in the Old World. This relationship between home and elsewhere, even when home is an uneasy place, resonates through women's travel writing as they use travel and travel writing to define themselves, to find their true "home" or symbol of the self.

New knowledges/new identities

As Eric Leed points out, travel or "the flows of passage not only provide information about the world; they provide information about the self of the passenger" (*Mind of the Traveler*, p. 72). With this new knowledge, the traveler gains new powers, new insights, skills, and identities. One of the truisms of travel is that it transforms the journeying self, unsettling a static self-identity with movement through space and contact with different peoples and places. In fact, one of the purposes of travel has been to broaden one's education, to take the Grand Tour. While the Grand Tour was historically reserved for elite young men, since the modernization of transportation beginning in the middle of the nineteenth century, American women have participated in their own versions of the Tour. When Stowe, Sigourney, and Hawthorne journey to Europe, they are engaging in their own educational tour, visiting those places important to the well-rounded education – the castles, churches, museums that have historical and literary meaning. Especially for these women to whom a university education was denied because of their gender, the journey to Europe provided a way of gaining intellectual capital. Later women like Willa Cather, Edith Wharton, and Mary McCarthy have continued to use the trip to Europe to broaden and deepen their knowledge of European history and art, turning their knowledge into real capital as they published their narratives.

But even when women have not set out to enrich their educations, their travels have provided them with new knowledge about people and places, recording what they encounter in almost ethnographic fashion. Mary Rowlandson's captivity narrative provides readers with valuable information about the Wampanoag Indians at the same time that we see her discovering things about herself: that she can indeed eat horse liver, and use her skill at knitting and her emerging understanding of Indian life to survive the cruelties of her captivity. Nancy Prince, an African American woman who went to imperial Russia with her husband in 1824, relates the customs, holidays, fashions, and politics of Russian life, as well as her ability to learn Russian and French, and sets up a successful business making children's clothes. Like Rowlandson, Prince is able to use her new knowledge to her advantage, creating an "alternate system of exchange" (Paes de Barros, *Fast Cars*, p. 32) in an alien land.

One of the delights in reading travel writing is gaining an armchair acquaintance with other peoples: Madam Knight comments on the behavior of New Haven bridegrooms (*The Journal of Madam Knight*, 1825); with Margaret Fuller we see Native American women of the American Midwest in *Summer on the Lakes*; Edith Wharton provides us an inside glimpse into the harems of Morocco;[24] and we learn a great deal about modern Japanese culture in Cathy Davidson's *Thirty-Six Views of Mount Fuji*, including the interesting note that Japanese girls are better at math than Japanese boys. Many women travelers work to provide readers with the kinds of information about other peoples and places that they might expect, often in a gender-neutral way, but they also pay attention to the kinds of cultural details women readers would be interested in, about homes, child-rearing, sexual arrangements, foods. Like Fuller, their attention is caught by the lives of other women, the pioneer women whose pinched lives belie the freedom of the West, or like Willa Cather, they pause to comment on the English canalman's wife who manages the tiller of the canal boat "with half a dozen children clinging to her skirts."[25] At the same time that many women travel writers attempt to give a kind of descriptive, informative view of foreign lands and people, recounting the histories and accomplishments primarily of men, their eyes are also drawn to domestic scenes and concerns.

While some of the accounts of women are glossed over quickly to return to a phallocentric agenda that recounts the accomplishments of a male-dominated society, in some narratives the female author takes what she learns about women and other people to interrogate patriarchal or oppressive practices. Fuller uses what she has learned about pioneer women in *Summer on the Lakes* to call for a more enlightened education for Western girls and to sharpen her critique of patriarchy in her *Woman in the Nineteenth Century*. A contemporary of Fuller, Jane Storm Cazneau, turned her experience on the US–Mexico border town of Eagle Pass to criticize the peonage system in Mexico that allowed Mexican landowners to make raids into American territory for escaped workers, at the same time that she called for, perhaps coined the phrase, "manifest destiny."[26] Generally content in most of her travel writing to just describe what she sees, Wharton speaks out against the practices of the harem, the "Ignorance, unhealthiness and a precocious sexual initiation" that pervade the lives of Arab women ("In Morocco," p. 204). Gaining political knowledge of El Salvador, Joan Didion gives an astute picture of the civil war and how the United States was manipulated by its "own rhetorical weaknesses" into interfering in a "political tropic alien to us."[27] Most of these women travel writers were content to let their narratives do their political work for them, but Fuller actively engaged in the 1848–49 revolution in Rome, reporting her activities in the series of articles she sent back to the *New York Daily-Tribune*, and Nancy Prince worked to better the lives of the recently emancipated Jamaicans. Turning their new knowledge of political systems into action, both verbal and physical, these women demonstrate a new sense of a political self that has come from their travels.

Whether women have traveled as tourists, simply desiring to gaze upon the sites they have read or heard about, or whether they have immigrated to new homes or escaped from confining locations, their travels have impacted self-identity as these women redefine the self to fit the new environment. They have seen or experienced things new to them and have adjusted, even if unconsciously, to these experiences.

Sexuality

Perhaps what marks the greatest difference between men's and women's travel experiences and writing is sexuality. While men may have engaged in the Grand Tour in part to sow some wild oats, bragging of their sexual exploits, women, who are usually the objects of male sexual conquest, have an uneasy relation to sexual adventure. As one of the editors of *An Inn Near Kyoto*, a collection of twentieth-century American women's travel writing, remarks, "A man alone is a man alone; a woman alone is odd at best, easy prey at worst."[28] In addition to other risks and dangers of the road, women were subject to sexual risk, to themselves being the territory that is explored and conquered by others. For many slave women, travel and sexual risk are clearly interrelated, whether like Louisa Picquet they were circulated as sexual property or, like Harriet Jacobs, they fled to escape the exchange of sexual favors. Focusing on the situation of white, middle-class women, Patricia Cline Cohen points out that as more women began traveling in antebellum America, new standards of comportment for men and women were negotiated and sexually segregated spaces, such as the ladies' cabin on steamboats, developed to protect women from the overtures of male travelers or other discomforts of travel.[29] Not only was the traveling woman at sexual risk, but in the nineteenth century she posed a threat to patriarchy and social order. As Lewis Perry put it in his study of antebellum culture: "The man who traveled was an entrepreneur, perhaps a culture bearer, at worst a scamp, but a woman who traveled was obliged to give reassurance that she was not a threat to morality" (*Boats Against the Current*, p. 185). June Jordan puts the issue more forcibly: "They don't ask you what you are doing in the street, they rape you and mutilate you bodily to let you remember your place. You have no rightful place in public."[30]

Perhaps that is why so many American traveling women either make it clear that they were not at sexual risk or they assured that they would not be subject to strangers' overtures by traveling in the company of others, preferably their husbands. Mary Rowlandson assures her readers that whatever hardships she experienced at the hands of her Indian captors, "yet not one of them offered me the least abuse of unchastity."[31] And when she

was a lone female among the French Legionnaires in Indochina, Charlotte
Ebener relates her own sexual safety amidst the dangers of war: " 'You think
the Legionnaires are criminals and cutthroats who kill just for excitement.
Perhaps we are. But we do not rape sleeping women who are under our protection.' "[32] Although Box-car Bertha, a female hobo of the 1930s, relates
that sometimes women exchanged sexual "expression" for food and quickly
sketches the brutal rape of one of the traveling women, her accounts of sexual abuse and prostitution are rare and may reflect her lower-class status.[33]
The briefly related sexual activity by twentieth-century travelers appears to
be consensual and generally the result of an established relationship, as in
Kelly Cherry's notes on an "underground hotel in Leningrad."[34]

The majority of women who wrote up their travel accounts journeyed
in the company of others, most often their husbands. Stowe takes her husband and several of her children with her when she tours Europe; Sarah
Haight travels the Holy Land with her husband; Sophia Hawthorne travels
with Nathaniel and her children. Pioneer women typically emigrated with
extended families. Edith Wharton's *Motor-Flight Through France* is made
in the company of her husband, Teddy, and friend, Henry James. And Willa
Cather travels to Europe with her friend, Isabelle McClung. Even Joan Didion takes her husband with her to El Salvador, and Cathy Davidson and Ann
Zwinger make it clear that, while their husbands are not always with them
on their travels, they do from time to time join them. By making it clear that
they are not women alone, these authors assure readers that whatever else
they may have transgressed, they were not crossing boundaries of sexual
comportment or threatening established standards of sexual morality. They
probably knew that they had much to risk if they were perceived to be sexually available or active. Indeed, Margaret Fuller, who traveled to Europe,
upset more than conventional ideas of female immobility when she took
Count Ossoli as her lover and bore their child out of wedlock. So shocked
were her friends and acquaintances back in the United States that they were
actually relieved when she and her little family drowned off Fire Island.

Even when sexual adventure is part of the journey, the details are left to
the reader's imagination as they draw the veil on that part of their story.
Even though Picquet's editor, Hiram Mattison, tries to lead her confession to
explicit sexual matters in *Louisa Picquet, The Octoroon: A Tale of Southern
Slave Life* (1861), she resists his attempts to eroticize her and her story.
Wined, dined, and danced by her Mali man, Maya Angelou finds him to
be "exotic, generous and physically satisfying" (*All God's Children*, p. 69).
But she does not reveal the details of her satisfaction and eventually turns
down the honor of becoming one of his wives. Charlotte Ebener falls for
a fellow correspondent but only shares the content of a message she typed

to herself and then threw away. Though they did marry, the relationship that is developed in the narrative remains more professional than intimate. And though the movie version of Frances Mayes' book gets steamy with love scenes as the newly divorced protagonist looks for sexual satisfaction, the book *Under the Tuscan Sun* (1996) is rather tame. She does travel to Tuscany with her partner and they do set up housekeeping together, but the narrative recounts his skills at home remodeling, gardening, and finding good wines, never taking the reader behind closed doors.

It may be that even as the woman traveler dares much in taking to the road, the woman travel *writer* conservatively draws the veil on this most risqué and economically risky of topics – sexual engagements away from home. Indeed, there is a conservative quality in much of women's non-fiction travel writing despite whatever other freedoms or adventures their tales may relate, demonstrating their negotiations between the conservatism of writing for an audience and the radicalism of travel. As well, the study of women's travel writing must negotiate between the ideals of freedom and mobility and the material evidence of so many disparate texts, not all of which celebrate ideological mobility as they narrate geographic movement.

Notes

1. Michel Chevalier, *Society, Manners, and Politics in the United States: Letters on North America*, trans. T. G. Bradford from the 3rd Paris edn, Boston 1839, reprint Research and Social Works Series no. 352 (New York: Burt Franklin, 1969), p. 286.
2. Walt Whitman, *Leaves of Grass*, ed. Harold W. Blodgett and Sculley Bradley (New York: Penguin Books, 1955), p. 133.
3. Annette Kolodny, *The Land Before Her: Fantasy and Experience of the American Frontiers, 1630–1860* (Chapel Hill: University of North Carolina Press, 1984), p. xii.
4. Deborah Paes de Barros, *Fast Cars and Bad Girls: Nomadic Subjects and Women's Road Stories* (New York: Peter Lang, 2004), p. 14.
5. Eric J. Leed, *The Mind of the Traveler: From Gilgamesh to Global Tourism* (New York: Basic Books, 1991); Larzer Ziff, *Return Passages: Great American Travel Writing 1780–1910* (New Haven: Yale University Press, 2000); William H. Stowe, *Going Abroad: European Travel in Nineteenth-Century American Culture* (Princeton: Princeton University Press, 1994); Annette Kolodny, *The Lay of the Land: Metaphor as Experience and History in American Life and Letters* (Chapel Hill: University of North Carolina Press, 1975); Cheryl Fish, *Black and White Women's Travel Narratives: Antebellum Explorations* (Gainesville: University of Florida Press, 2004); Sidonie Smith, *Moving Lives: 20th-Century Women's Travel Writing* (Minneapolis: University of Minnesota Press, 2001); Lewis Perry, *Boats Against the Current: American Culture Between Revolution and Modernity, 1820–1860* (New York: Oxford University Press, 1993),

pp. 184–85; Terry Caesar, *Forgiving the Boundaries: Home as Abroad in American Travel Writing* (Athens: University of Georgia Press, 1995), p. 58; Michael Kowalewski, ed., *Temperamental Journeys: Essays on the Modern Literature of Travel* (Athens: University of Georgia Press, 1992).

6. Theodore Sarbin, "The Narrative as a Root Metaphor for Psychology," in *Narrative Psychology: The Storied Nature of Human Conduct*, ed. Theodore R. Sarbin (New York: Praeger, 1986), pp. 3–21.

7. Michel de Certeau, *The Practice of Everyday Life*, trans. Steven F. Rendall (Berkeley: University of California Press, 1984), p. 115.

8. Marilyn C. Wesley, *Secret Journeys: The Trope of Women's Travel in American Literature* (Albany: State University of New York Press, 1999), p. 21.

9. Cathy N. Davidson, *Thirty-Six Views of Mount Fuji: On Finding Myself in Japan* (New York: Penguin, 1993), p. 287.

10. These are terms used by Caesar, Wesley, and Paes de Barros to characterize American women's travel.

11. Quoted in Alison Blunt and Gillian Rose, eds., *Writing Women and Space: Colonial and Postcolonial Geographies* (New York and London: The Guilford Press, 1994), p. 1.

12. Daphne Spain, *Gendered Spaces* (Chapel Hill: University of North Carolina Press, 1992), p. 15.

13. Doreen Massey, *Space, Place, and Gender* (Minneapolis: University of Minnesota Press, 1994), p. 23.

14. Mary Alice Shutes, *Diary – Eight Hundred Miles Thirty Six Days Covered Wagon – 1862*, ed. LeRoy L. Shutes (Bloomington, IL: L. L. Shutes, 1967), p. 4.

15. See also Wesley, *Secret Journeys*, p. 63, who states that "stasis and movement" are "the basic operations of the female journey."

16. Harriet Ward, *Prairie Schooner Lady: The Journal of Harriet Sherril Ward, 1853* (Los Angeles: Westernlore Press, 1959), p. 27.

17. See Phoebe Judson, *A Pioneer's Search for an Ideal Home* (Bellingham, WA: Union Printing, Binding, and Stationery Co., 1925) and Elinore Pruitt Stewart, *Letters of a Woman Homesteader* (1914; reprint, Boston: Houghton Mifflin, 1988).

18. Harriet Beecher Stowe, *Sunny Memories of Foreign Lands*, vol. 1 (Boston: Phillips, Sampson, and Company; New York: J. C. Derby, 1854), p. 177.

19. Gloria Anzaldúa, *Borderlands/La Frontera: The New Mestiza* (San Francisco: Spinsters/Aunt Lute, 1987), p. 16.

20. Quoted in Susan Roberson, " 'With the Wind Rocking the Wagon': Women's Narratives of the Way West," in *Women, America, and Movement: Narratives of Relocation* (Columbia: University of Missouri Press, 1998), p. 226.

21. Carroll Smith-Rosenberg, "The Female World of Love and Ritual: Relations between Women in Nineteenth-Century America," in *The American Family in Social-Historical Perspective*, 2nd edn, ed. Michael Gordon (New York: St. Martin's Press, 1978), p. 340.

22. L. H. Sigourney, *Pleasant Memories of Pleasant Lands* (Boston: James Munroe and Company, 1842), p. 363.

23. Maya Angelou, *All God's Children Need Traveling Shoes* (New York: Random House, 1986), pp. 19, 120.

24. Edith Wharton, "In Morocco," in *Edith Wharton Abroad: Selected Travel Writings, 1888–1920*, ed. Sarah Bird Wright (New York: St. Martin's Press, 1995), p. 193.
25. George N. Kates, ed., *Willa Cather in Europe: Her Own Story of the First Journey* (New York: Alfred A. Knopf, 1956), p. 42.
26. See Linda S. Hudson, *Mistress of Manifest Destiny: A Biography of Jane McManus Storm Cazneau, 1807–1878* (Austin: Texas State Historical Association, 2001).
27. Joan Didion, *Salvador* (New York: Simon and Schuster, 1983), p. 96.
28. Kathleen Coskran and C. W. Truesdale, eds., *An Inn Near Kyoto: Writing by American Women Abroad* (Minneapolis: New Rivers Press, 1998), p. xii.
29. See Patricia Cline Cohen, "Women at Large: Travel in Antebellum America," *History Today* 44 (December 1994), pp. 44–50.
30. Quoted in Gillian Rose, *Feminism and Geography: The Limits of Geographical Knowledge* (Minneapolis: University of Minnesota Press, 1993), pp. 34–35.
31. Mary Rowlandson, *A Narrative of the Captivity, Sufferings and Removes of Mrs. Mary Rowlandson*, in *Puritans Among the Indians: Accounts of Captivity and Redemption 1676–1724*, ed. Alden T. Vaughan and Edward W. Clark (Cambridge, MA: Belknap Press of Harvard University Press, 1981), p. 70.
32. Charlotte Ebener, *No Facilities for Women* (New York: Alfred A. Knopf, 1955), p. 83.
33. Quoted in Mary Morris, ed., *Maiden Voyages: Writings of Women Travelers* (New York: Vintage, 1993), p. 159.
34. Kelly Cherry, "An Underground Hotel in Leningrad," in *An Inn Near Kyoto*, ed. Kathleen Coskran and C. W. Truesdale (Minneapolis: New Rivers Press, 1998), pp. 305–21.

13

DEBORAH PAES DE BARROS

Driving that highway to consciousness: late twentieth-century American travel literature

The American road narrative moved into new territory in the second half of the twentieth century. These recent literary expeditions reflect a variety of cultural and historic forces: changes in technology, economics, gender roles, migratory patterns, politics, and philosophies as well as the emergence of suburban culture all impact the American literary experience of travel. Two particular elements increasingly construct the American travel narrative: the emergent culture of the car and its resultant highways, and the Modernist (and Postmodernist) concern with the replication of consciousness. As concepts of identity changed, literary genres, including travel writing, had to change in response.

The automobile, available early in the century and an omnipresent necessity after World War II, fostered an American love affair with speed, distance, and the solitary euphoria of piloting one's own vehicle across the miles. Freed from dependence upon the slower, communally directed engines of transportation – the trains, buses, boats, horses, carriages, and ox-pulled wagons – the road now offered a speedy, and indeed a glamorous escape from social conformity. As automobiles became increasingly common they engendered new social institutions. Motels, highways, freeways and interstates, diners and truck stops paved the way for the car trip. The auto became fetishized and romanticized; horsepower, size, and interior accoutrements emerged as subjects of poetry. Rather than a mere vehicle to move the passengers from one point to another, the car itself constituted experience and narrative possibility.

This potential for movement, for literal transport, merged with the century's aesthetic desire for self-representation. In the same manner that the Modernist fictions of James Joyce, Virginia Woolf, Thomas Wolfe, and William Faulkner struggled to reproduce the processes of consciousness and the multifaceted, fluid quality of identity, twentieth-century travel writers endeavored to make the traveling self as much a narrative subject as the

American landscape passing outside the car's window. At times, the literal topography and its populace form merely a background for the author's real topic: the exploration of consciousness. The culture of the highway coupled with a desire to verbally capture the psychological impact of travel – to map the shifts in geography with a correspondent cartography of the psyche – reinterpret and re-cast the genre of American travel writing.

The Beats

The end of World War II brought unparalleled prosperity to the United States, a prosperity marked by a retreat from urban woes into bucolic, middle-class suburbs, a dramatic increase in home ownership, a flood of new college students financed by the recent G.I. Bill, a sky-rocketing birth rate that would later be called "the Baby Boom," the availability of fast and convenience foods, abundant time-saving domestic appliances, and above all, the emergence of a car culture. Henry Ford had dreamed that the revolutionized factory would make it possible for his own workers to buy cars, and by 1950 that dream found realization. The average American family owned a car, and often their newly constructed garage and barely cooled asphalt driveway held two automobiles. Cars defined teenage masculinity, provided status to the workingman, and offered wives freedom from their suburban isolation.

Americans were busy with the processes of becoming – becoming better educated, becoming more familiar with technology, and, above all, becoming more wealthy. They borrowed from European philosophy the notion that humanity must continually seek transcendence, but Americans defined this transcendence in uniquely material ways. Of course, the new prosperity possessed a dark side: the Cold War and anxiety about the bomb and worldwide annihilation, racial tensions and intolerance, an implacable fear of Communism that translated itself into a simple fear of difference, the Red Scare, the emergence of the vastly powerful military industrial complex, the compulsion to conform, nightmares, and bomb shelters were all part of the postwar psyche. If contemporary popular culture re-creates the 1950s as a time of innocent pleasures, it does so only by means of erasure.

And not everyone desired to become rich, to compete, or to celebrate the virtues of the washing machine and the vacuum cleaner. Alienated from a culture of materialism and boosterism, some intellectuals rebelled, leaving a counter-culture legacy that would be called "The Beat Generation." They drove their cars, not to impress or acquire or to arrive somewhere better, but to escape normative culture and to exist in the moment. They drove their cars, not simply to get some place, but for the beauty of driving. Jack

Kerouac's faintly fictive *On the Road* (1955) remains a veritable Bible for this new kind of travel narrative. Influenced by Buddhism, and the desire to be "in the moment" rather than seeking some eventual success, repelled by materialism and eager to escape smothering familial domesticity, Kerouac created a road narrative that countered more traditional tales. His narrator Sal – Kerouac's thinly disguised self playing against the counterpoint of his real-life friends, including Neal Cassady, William S. Burroughs, Allen Ginsberg, Gary Snyder, to name but a few – writes about the road as a place of self-discovery. The different stops along Kerouac's roads, while filled with romance and adventure, are in the end like the American landscape itself: a backdrop for the narrator Sal's emergent self. If Sal – Kerouac's *Doppelgänger* – goes on the road initially to avoid his aunt's domesticity and to find romance, it is ultimately some notion of self that propels his quest.

Inspired in part by jazz structure, Kerouac's prose phrases an idea – the search for "IT" – and then, like jazz, moves into verbal tributaries and impromptu riffs. His narrative leaves the verbal highway and erratically wanders local roads. Kinetic, its rhythms capturing both the jumpiness and the timelessness of the road, the structure of *On the Road* replicates the interior monologue of a traveler. Written as a kind of stream-of-consciousness – "spontaneous" writing Kerouac termed it – the text describes the mental processes of the emergent self resonating against the passing scenery. Although Kerouac's book contains ample and dazzlingly beautiful physical descriptions, these details serve to heighten the self-awareness of the narrator. The landscape performs as psychological metaphor; crossing the Mississippi River becomes a marker of passage into adult experience while the Midwestern landscape signifies Kerouac/Sal's bigger soul. The road map corresponds to a map of the psyche.

Not only did Kerouac make travel literature the literature of self-discovery in new ways; his text also suggested the importance of a teacher, an intellectual model, a sort of Americanized guru. This guru would be cast in the mold of the Western hero, a newly verbal cowboy or a bohemian and intellectual mountain man. Dean Moriarty, a character derived with utter transparency from Kerouac's real friend, Neal Cassady, shapes Kerouac/Sal's experiences. "A western kinsman of the sun, Dean," writes Kerouac about his hero, who is bigger than life, charismatic, and in possession of an irresistible voice.[1] Poet Gary Snyder describes the portrait: "Neal's a beautiful memory because it's so archetypal. My vision of Cassady is of the 1880s cowboys, the type of person who worked the Plains of the 1880s and 1890s . . . Cassady's type is that frontier type . . . he could have been another Jedediah Smith . . ."[2] While the notion of going on the road with a charismatic mentor figure was certainly not unique to Kerouac (and indeed dates back to the most ancient road literature), Kerouac's Cassady combined these more traditional attributes with American "rugged masculinity," a new penchant to explore interior psychological spaces, and a nearly antisocial wildness. The Cassady/Dean portrait empowered several generations of subsequent seekers.[3] Kerouac continues his interior saga in subsequent books, including *The Dharma Bums* (1958), *Mexico City Blues* (1959), *Big Sur* (1959), and *Desolation Angels* (1965), which follow the psychic travel experiences of Kerouac, Cassady, and Allen Ginsberg, and often refer to William S. Burroughs, Gary Snyder, Lawrence Ferlinghetti, Herbert Huncke, and a host of other Beat writers and personalities.

Movement – by car, train, boat, and foot – became essential to the Beat aesthetic. Poets Snyder, Ginsberg, and Ferlinghetti all used this trope. Other writers, like Burroughs, wrote copious journal notes or letters that detailed their cosmic travels. Cassady's posthumously published *The First Third and Other Writings* (1971) as well his *Collected Letters of Neal Cassady* (2004), Gary Snyder's essays in *The Practice of the Wild* (1990), Joyce Johnson's *Door Wide Open* (2000), and Allen Ginsberg's volumes of correspondence bear witness to their travels. For the Beats, the road was the place to celebrate, a space that radically juxtaposed the fixed domesticity that had become modern America. Bucolic suburban life required only material ambition and a competitive desire for bigger, better, and more expensive things. Ironically, it was only in travel, in motion, that the writer could be "in the moment."

It seems important to note that the trope of the charismatic teacher, most particularly in the guise of rugged Western guide, is necessarily, irretrievably masculine and even patriarchal. This image repeatedly marks the travel narratives of authors like Kerouac. The Beats themselves found definition in largely masculine terms, although certainly women like Diane DiPrima, Joyce Johnson, and Carolyn Cassady allied themselves with the movement. Indeed, much of the criticism of the Beats focuses on its sexist elements and its willingness to relegate women to minor and sexualized roles. The result is that the road literature of the period often replicates the traditional notion that the road is a masculine site, a belief that feminists would seek to undermine.

The 1960s: motorcycles, Gonzo Journalism, and the art of self

In 1964 author Ken Kesey took to the road in a gaudily painted 1939 Harvester bus that its riders, the Merry Pranksters, named *Further*. The bus traveled through cities and suburbs as its Pranksters attempted to "turn on" a stale world. Typically driven by Neal Cassady, and frequently ferrying such famed personalities and writers as Tom Wolfe, Kerouac, Snyder, Ginsberg, and musician Jerry Garcia, the bus offered a literal and cosmic journey. Kesey, who had recently published his lauded first novel, *One Flew Over the Cuckoo's Nest* (1962), insisted, "Rather than write, I will ride buses, study the insides of jails and see what goes on."[4] This external exploration would correlate with an investigation of consciousness as the Merry Pranksters experimented with drugs and conducted the Acid Tests, extravagant adventures with sound, light, and psychedelic drugs. "We talked about being the astronauts of inner space," wrote Kesey's friend and fellow Prankster Ken Babbs (Brightman, *Sweet Chaos*, p. 17). By 1969 both Kerouac and Cassady would be dead, while Ginsberg and Snyder retreated into serious study of Buddhism, but their collective travel experiences would inspire another generation fueled by the desire to experience the road in a psychodynamic manner.

Simultaneously, the so-called New Journalism emerged as an alternative narrative strategy. Non-fiction writers claimed the techniques historically associated with fiction – dialogue, inner monologue, detailed, first person sensory description. Dynamic narratives resulted and travel narratives in particular changed from being sometimes staid or formal essays into highly personal, idiosyncratic texts. Inspired by Kerouac's kinetic language, the Beats' endeavor to share Modernism's exploration of consciousness, and the social concerns of the 1960s, writers like Tom Wolfe, Hunter S. Thompson, Joan Didion, and Robert Pirsig created resonant new kinds of travel narratives.

Tom Wolfe's *The Electric Kool-Aid Acid Test* (1968) chronicles his friendship with Kesey and Cassady and their now historic journeys on the "Hieronymus Bosch bus," the aforementioned *Further*. According to Wolfe, a man in Menlo Park, California sold Kesey the 1939 International Harvester school bus for the sum of $1,500.00. Kesey registered the bus in the name of Intrepid Trips, Inc., placed a placard reading "Caution: Weird Load" and invited the Merry Pranksters aboard. The travels begin with "test runs" into northern California and then turn east towards New York and, ostensibly, the World's Fair. The text details the Pranksters' progress forth and back across the continent, their subsequent trips into Berkeley, and later Kesey's Prankster-aided escape into Mexico, where he lived as a fugitive eluding American drug charges. The text concludes with Kesey – tried twice for drug peddling resulting in hung juries and, finally, a *nolo contendere* plea to a much lesser charge – taking the bus and his family north to Springfield, Oregon before returning to the Bay Area to serve six months on a county work farm. Wolfe notes that two months after this departure, Cassady was found dead in Mexico, but against this bleak epilogue Wolfe reminds his reader that "the bus was there," an abiding reminder of the Pranksters' exploration of perception, consciousness, and American culture.

As in Kerouac's earlier work, geographic destination is less important for Wolfe than the process of travel itself. For the Pranksters and Wolfe as their historian, travel was simply an even wilder improvisation, an attempt to take consciousness and perception to a more intense level. The Pranksters had experienced the improvisational musical works of John Cage and Eric Satie. They wanted to create their own riffs, to create improvisational tapestries that both exploited and shocked the world. Drug-laced travel on the bus challenged their own perceptions and exploded what the Pranksters and Wolfe regarded as the mindless tranquility of the hopelessly domesticated bourgeoisie. In this sense, of course, Wolfe's account of the inhabitants of *Further* is really an account of the 1960s. Drugs, rock music, the Grateful Dead, the Rolling Stones, the Hell's Angels, Timothy Leary, Richard Alpert (soon to be Ram Dass), Day-Glo paint, and the anti-war movement pump their kinetic messages through Wolfe's text. *The Electric Kool-Aid Acid Test* tells first-hand the story of cultural rupture, focusing on the shifting, electric dynamism of hip youth culture and it literally roars through the staid fixed suburbias of an earlier world.

To make his account vivid, to make it a real work-in-progress message and not simply a traditional historic account, Wolfe writes with immediacy, uses dialogue, character development, and an eclectic style – fusing prose, poetry, songs, and lists into an enthusiastic rhapsody. Like the Pranksters themselves, Wolfe too wants to improvise and create a new style of language, to write a report where the very language and style is the message itself. In the final note at the end of his book, he writes, "I have tried not only to tell what the Pranksters did but to re-create the mental atmosphere or the subjective reality of it."[5] Inspired by the earlier work of Kerouac and Ginsberg, Wolfe forces narrative and language to do more than describe the travel experience itself, to actually become a part of that experience.

Like Tom Wolfe, Hunter S. Thompson wanted his narratives to fuse with experience and to allow the reader no sense of safe space between the text and the actual event. Like Wolfe, Thompson used detail, conversation, and character, and made himself a part of the story. He too refused to edit experience or to sacrifice narrative form to expository convention. Rather than being sanitized or simply edited out, expletives and seemingly sordid events frequently shape description, once again creating a feeling of immediacy. Sensation, atmosphere, emotion, and consciousness define experience, and the mundane gesture becomes as essential to history as culturally celebrated moments. Thompson recognizes no journalistic boundaries. From his stories, paranoia, pharmaceutically induced visions, and sexually explicit vocabulary comes Thompson's version of the "New Journalism," an energetic, uncensored, seemingly unstructured style that Thompson himself named "Gonzo Journalism." A self-professed "professional journalist," Thompson traveled ostensibly to explore themes and trends in American culture in the 1960s and 1970s. From these travels come his best-known books: *Hell's Angels* (1966), *Fear and Loathing on the Campaign Trail '72* (1973), *The Great Shark Hunt* (1979), and, most famously, *Fear and Loathing in Las Vegas: A Savage Journey to the Heart of the American Dream* (1971), which was dedicated to Bob Dylan.

The adventures of the counter-culture also form the basis for Robert Pirsig's travel narrative in *Zen and the Art of Motorcycle Maintenance: An Inquiry Into Values* (1974). Pirsig's account is largely autobiographical, although he clearly acknowledges making certain alterations for "rhetorical purposes." Following its initial publication, the book gained nearly immediate popular and critical attention. Becoming, in Pirsig's words, a "*kulturbarer* – a culture-bearer" – the text gave expression to certain counter-culture ideas that lay seemingly dormant within the mainstream social experience. He argues that his text reflects the cultural upheaval of the 1960s and 1970s, offering "a serious alternative to material success."[6] Whether or not Pirsig truly offers such an alternative lies in the opinion of the reader; nonetheless there is no doubt that his lyrical "Chautauqua" of the mind and road represents a further conflation of the road, self-discovery, and consciousness. The "red-winged birds," "coastal manzanita and waxen-leafed shrubs" of the American countryside recede in the face of Pirsig's evocation of Buddhism, Kant, and Hume as he attempts to confront and resolve the dualistic quality of modern life, to bridge the perceived chasm between technology and philosophy. Using the Zen notion of Oneness, Pirsig contends that the way people care for vehicles – in particular for their motorcycles – is predictive of both their concern for all things and their own psychic integration. To understand the smallest technical detail of travel, Pirsig tells his readers, is to comprehend the place of the self in the universe.

Like Kerouac's, Pirsig's road trip is fueled by the desire to escape American bourgeois culture and the settled routines of domesticity. For him, as for the Beats before him, outward travel corresponds to inner psychic travel. Like Thompson, Pirsig too becomes the subject of his text; as readers we watch his skill with machinery, the disintegration of his relationship with his son, his refinement of personal philosophy, and his haunted relationship with his past. The text emerges as a sort of super-ego. Moving with ease from one discursive topic to another, from Aristotle to the rainy scenery of Crescent City, *Zen and the Art of Motorcycle Maintenance* offers a fusion of the material and spiritual. It blends philosophy and travelogue, resolves the conflict between Platonic and Aristotelian points of view, merges matter with energy and physics with art, and marries finally its subject and narrator in true postmodern fashion. But the text demonstrates the cost of such cosmic travel; Pirsig's travel book represents the loss-littered, dark side of the road.

Steeped, like Pirsig, in the counter-culture and reared, like Wolfe and Thompson, in the ethos of the New Journalism, essayist and novelist Joan Didion also employs the road as a trope of social and self-discovery. In her 1970 novel, *Play It as It Lays*, her charismatic character Maria uses the road as a space of liberation. Her car becomes analogous to Huck Finn's raft: a clean space where the inevitable corruption of her Hollywood world is temporarily erased. For Maria, the navigation of the freeway system is musical, conducted in concert with the songs on the radio. In the car she consumes eggs, cleans her face, and finds a temporary rebirth of her lost self; as a result, much of the novel's narrative action takes place as she drives. But Maria's freedom is short-lived; she encounters the barbed wire and concrete barriers where the freeway runs out. The road's freedom proves illusory; in truth the highway skirts scrap yards and gas stations in baking-hot empty towns, inevitably always leading back home. The road offers no real redemption.

Didion's essays concerning travel and the road are no less dark. Her words repeatedly trace patterns of movement over highways and mountains, continuously suggesting routes fraught with danger. In the essay "L.A. Notebook" Didion writes about the way the very wind blows, red and hot along the San Gorgonio Pass and Route 66. In another essay, "Some Dreamers of the Golden Dream," Didion remarks about the drive into Fontana and San Bernardino, a ride dotted by dilapidated motels built in the shapes of tee-pees, arriving "only an hour east of Los Angeles . . . but . . . in certain ways an alien place."[7] Lands are settled and abandoned as people attempt the migration towards paradise.

For Didion the road leads once again into the twisted labyrinth of the self, and this fractured self represents the era. In an essay entitled "On the Road," in obvious homage to Kerouac, whose discourse helped shape contemporary travel narrative, Didion meditates on the nature and momentum of travel. Everywhere she goes, Didion maintains, she is asked anew, "Where are we heading?" This query is at once literal, commenting upon what new airport or city or place Didion will visit, but simultaneously a much larger question: where is the culture heading? Indeed, Didion suggests that the answer for both questions is the same: our future destiny is defined by the scope and frenetic quality of our travel. From Los Angeles, to Boston, to Chicago or Dallas/Fort Worth, Didion travels in a "hormonal" momentum, understanding, finally, that the illusion offered by mobility is the illusion

offered by all aspects of American life. She contends that we feel ownership
and control as we move in random patterns from place to place. "I began
to see America as my own, a child's map," she writes; room service reduced
the world to a comfortable (if false) microcosm. "We wanted to stay on
the road forever."[8] American imperialism, the kinetic egotism of the youth
movement, and Didion's own idiosyncratic experience and style find shared
representation in the metaphor of travel. In true New Journalistic fashion, Didion's road links the conscious self with the very essence of culture
itself.

The road and nostalgia

It may be that all fashions reference their antitheses and, if so, this is most
certainly true of later twentieth-century travel writing. Even as Kerouac
and Cassady created a road that focused upon the self, other writers took
a different path and engaged the conventions of travel writing in other
ways. Although certainly influenced by the romantic assertion of individual
perception and identity, these writers also fostered nostalgia for an earlier
era of travel narrative when the subject was, at least in some large part,
the topography of travel. While they were unable or unwilling to avoid the
impact of the road experience, their narratives emerge as both more reflective
and more focused upon landscape and character. Particularly illustrative of
this trend are the works of John Steinbeck, Larry McMurtry, and William
Least Heat-Moon.

John Steinbeck, born to an older generation of Modernists in 1902, was
perhaps most influential in establishing the travel narrative as a genre sympathetic to the American experience. His still famous 1939 novel, *The
Grapes of Wrath*, made the Joads and their over-packed and ill-running
automobile symptomatic not only of the tragic, depression-era Oakies but
also of the American travel experience as a whole. Steinbeck's subject was
neither consciousness nor the meaning of his own life; the novel depicted
exploitive labor practices and indicted a society rooted in inequality. Steinbeck's writerly glance faced outward; his subject found definition in the
larger society. A prolific writer, Steinbeck produced numerous volumes of
fiction and non-fiction; many of these non-fiction texts illustrate Steinbeck's
approach to travel writing. *The Sea of Cortez: A Leisurely Journal of Travel
and Research* (1941), written in collaboration with Edward F. Ricketts,
details Steinbeck's experiences and notes as a marine biologist. By the early
1960s, Steinbeck – then in his sixties himself – expressed an urge to see and
understand America. "For many years," he writes in *Travels with Charley:
In Search of America* (1961), "I have traveled in many parts of the world."[9]

But this travel fails to provide Steinbeck with a real, sensory knowledge of what is truly "American."

The language that shapes the inception of Steinbeck's autobiographical chronicle bears careful note: his vision focuses outward, away from himself. What follows is a travel narrative that collides sharply with the narratives of the Beats and the New Journalists. Just a few years before Wolfe would venture out on the road in the company of Kerouac, Cassady, and Kesey in a bus called *Further*, Steinbeck took to the road in a more solitary fashion, driving a small pick-up truck he named *Rocinante*, in memory of Don Quixote's horse. The very vehicles provide a contrast. Day-glo paint and graffiti covered *Further*; the bus represented the Pranksters' efforts to go further into consciousness and further elude the boundaries of mainstream culture. *Rocinante* marks Steinbeck's reverence for the literature and romance of the past, and his albeit ironic identification with the heroic travel narratives of the past. Steinbeck's journey is nostalgic, as is his very view of the America he will navigate.

Traveling with his French poodle Charley – Charles le Chien – Steinbeck drives across the nation, leaving his home in Sag Harbor, Maine and heading west. As he travels, Steinbeck comments upon New England's seasons and the burgeoning autumn. His drives are frequently punctuated by his notations on the shifting climactic conditions. Against a background of American scenery, Steinbeck encounters a variety of characters, largely working-class individuals in keeping with much of his earlier work. Steinbeck crosses the Midwest and the Mississippi, driving some of the same highways that will shortly be navigated by Kesey's Magic Bus. He eventually reaches the West coast, describing the redwoods with a Woody Guthrie-esque enthusiasm. For Steinbeck, fascination lies in the exterior world, in its picturesque tableau, color, and in the strange vitality of his characters. Steinbeck remarks little upon his own consciousness; indeed his self-confessed purpose speaks of a need to reimmerse himself in the materiality of the American experience. He permits the physical details of his journey – the weather, the textures of word and earth, dialect and differences in voiced language – to play upon his senses and find expression in his text. Ultimately, Steinbeck realizes that it is time to go home, and he resolutely turns his truck back towards Sag Harbor.

Of course, even as Steinbeck explores the literal motifs of travel, he does so with a twentieth-century sense of irony. His companion and interlocutor, after all, is a dog named Charley. He remarks upon his own nostalgia and reveals, not the Americana of the traditionalist, but rather the idiosyncratic, sometimes sweaty experience of the unrelenting and amused observer. Indeed, while on the surface Steinbeck's work differs dramatically from the work of the Beats and the later Gonzo journalists, such distinctions may not be as great as they first appear. Kerouac drove the road to consciousness, yet his book still leaves the reader with an acute memory of the kinetic, visceral details of actual travel. Steinbeck goes out in search of the literal, but his descriptions of the physical leave the reader with the sense that we have shared in the reflections of a mature man re-experiencing and contemplating the roads he had driven some twenty-five years before. The narrator's conversations with his dog suggest at least as much about Steinbeck as they do about the landscape.

Writing from a similar impulse, novelist Larry McMurtry also speaks of a desire to re-experience and "to drive the American roads at the century's end."[10] McMurtry wants to ferry the major highways that quickly link region with region. Deeply immersed in the tradition of travel writing and acutely aware of the literary nostalgia inherent in the travelogue, McMurtry filters his perceptions through words of earlier writers. "I should say that I own three thousand travel books," McMurtry immediately informs his readers (*Roads*, p. 13). He considers how he learned to write by reading countless travel texts. As much about travel writing and tradition as they are about the actual encountered scenes, McMurtry's language and commentary offer a dialogue with these earlier texts and conventions. A vastly literate man, McMurtry meets nearly every sight with a memory of some earlier travel writer. In the end, *Roads* possesses two purposes: to provide a conventional account of travel – complete with roads, directions, and discussions of accommodations – as well as a larger discussion of the genre of travel itself. McMurtry's text serves to establish the significance of travel writing; it places the American tourist squarely in the midst of an historical and significant tradition. *Roads* offers homage to the highway and its scribbling travelers. In the end, McMurtry acknowledges that travel can never be complete, that time necessarily constrains us, limiting the roads we can travel. Opting not to visit the childhood home of Laura Ingalls Wilder in De Smet, South Dakota, McMurtry argues, in a troublingly gendered analogy, that roads are like women because there are: "Just too many nice ones. One simply can't fall in love with, sleep with or marry all the nice women ... As it is with women, so it is with roads. There are just too many nice ones" (p. 294).[11] McMurtry "hurries" home with an "empty feeling." He cannot drive all the world's roads, or even most of them, and he cannot form relationships with all of its women. Reflective and sad, McMurtry concludes only with questions. "Where does the road go? And how is one to marry?" (p. 206). Strangely, McMurtry's literal itinerary and bookish mediation on the art of travel writing ultimately give way to introspection. The rhythms of the road carry the writer literally outward and then, inevitably, turn thoughts inward.

Unlike McMurtry, William Least Heat-Moon drives the "blue highways," the small roads that criss-cross the country. Published in 1982 and, like so many of the books discussed here claiming a nearly cult-like following, William Least Heat-Moon's narrative, *Blue Highways: A Journey Into America* describes an arduous, rural, and thoughtful trip. The author tells us that he thought he coined the term "blue highways," referencing the small blue lines that run between the large red interstates marked on the map. Later though, he notes that as he reads *Black Elk Speaks* (1932) in Oregon's cascades, he sees that Black Elk used the same words. Black Elk writes, "the blue road is the route of one who is distracted, who is ruled by his senses, and who lives for himself rather than his people." Least Heat-Moon notes the clear applicability of Black Elk's words to his own narrative, for he too is "distracted," capricious, and a maverick within the larger materialistic culture of the 1980s.[12]

Least Heat-Moon begins his travels on the vernal equinox, driving his truck named *Ghost Dancing*, heading east on Interstate 70. Thirty-eight, "contaminated" by mixed blood, with a "growing suspicion that I lived in an alien land" (*Blue Highways*, p. 219), he sees his own plight as analogous to that of the doomed Plains Native American tribes – like them he wears a ghost shirt and dances for protection and deliverance in an increasingly hostile world. The name of his truck is interesting, for it both encapsulates his own attitude toward society – as a dangerous entity from which one requires protection – and further establishes the postwar American trope of naming one's vehicle. The car, or truck or bus, emerges as a traveler's *avatar*, a material extension of the narrator's identity.

Ultimately, Least Heat-Moon reads the detailed ground that he drives through the lens of the past; he seeks understanding of the present through history and comprehension of his own alienation from the flotsam of time. His text reads initially as classic travelogue – a cogent inclusion of places, roads, meals, details, and characters. But each detail is understood only through narrative; it is the discussion of past and present accounts that makes each specific meaningful. And similarly, William Least Heat-Moon finds personal meaning, finally, through providing himself with a literal topographical context and a deeper connection with his past. As the journey nears its end, he offers that he has learned a great deal, although not necessarily what he wanted to know because "I hadn't known what I wanted to know" (p. 211). The book concludes with a merging of the literal geography, the personal and previous travel narrative. He absorbs the details of his final drive back into Missouri, noting that he has completed a circle commensurate with the circles celebrated in Native American religion. Reading the slogan on the back of his license plate, a gas station attendant asks him, "Where you coming from, Show Me?" Least Heat-Moon exclaims, "Where I've been." But the final lines of the text are from a Navajo wind chant that counsels the listener that "everything forgotten returns" (p. 412). For William Least Heat-Moon, the physical realities of the road give way to a larger journey and return; his travel narrative is about the return to and the reclamation of self.

A number of contemporary travel narratives reflect the influence of Steinbeck, McMurtry, and Least Heat-Moon's narratives. Of these similarly couched travel accounts, Bill Bryson's *A Walk in the Woods: Rediscovering America on the Appalachian Trail* (1998) may be the best known. Steeped in the realities of the trail, Bryson's best-selling account becomes an effort towards re-engaging the autonomous self. Other writers, like Patrick Symmes in his *Chasing Che* (2000), continue McMurtry's practice of reading place through earlier travel literature. These writers continue to assert the notion that the sights viewed while traveling are metaphorical, corresponding to both psyche and literary history.

Girls on the road

While social condition has often militated against women's travel, women have, of course, always traveled and written. In the later twentieth century the road has emerged as a common theme in women's literary work. These narratives are frequently characterized by several salient features: often the travel narrative acts as a kind of memoir piece; typically the exterior landscape gives way to an inner psychic geography, and quite commonly the female narrator searches for some larger familial connection. The works of Chelsea Cain and Beverly Donofrio exemplify these trends.

Chelsea Cain describes herself as a "psychonaut." With its deliberate homage to Kerouac, Cain's memoir/novel, *Dharma Girl* (1996) once again examines the way the road offers access to a necessary and corresponding inner trail, along which the past and the present, the self and the world can be re-united. But like many female road warriors, Cain finds that self-discovery requires renewed negotiation of maternal relationships. Her rapprochement with the self requires a restructured connection as well with a mother figure. The search for the self on the road also becomes the search for the maternal.

In Cain's case, learning that her mother suffers from cancer, the author decides to travel with her, returning to the Midwest where Cain was once raised on a commune. Riding in the car, Cain realizes that her now middle-aged mother was the fairy tale queen and goddess figure of her youth. Cain recalls games her mother played that provided the young Cain with insight into seasons, love, and death. Cain has long since left the commune, but the two women return so that Cain can regain her Edenic childhood and become newly content in the present. The return to the past requires the presence of the maternal; Cain can only process her identity by accepting her mother. The road – outside of distractions, away from other people, disconnected from social structures, isolated from patriarchy – provides a space for their relationship.

Similarly, Beverly Donofrio's autobiographical text, *Looking for Mary: The Blessed Mother and Me* (2000), details her own travels as she tries to come to terms with motherhood. Donofrio's tensions with her own family are spelled out in an earlier book, the memoir/novel *Riding in Cars with Boys: Confession of a Bad Girl* (1990). Donofrio dislikes her mother for supporting and abetting the patriarchal structure of the Donofrio household. Donofrio's mother – orphaned by her own mother – possesses no comprehension of her daughter's larger aspirations. While loving her own son, Donofrio still feels hostility because of her own lost youth; she is a teenager when she becomes a mother. And Donofrio resents the Virgin Mary as the symbol of a repressive church hierarchy. As *Looking for Mary* opens, Donofrio mourns her empty life and takes a job with National Public Radio, visiting the sites connected with apparitions of Mary. But, noting that the Virgin Mary is as manipulative as Donofrio's own mother, the author becomes preoccupied with her subject.

Donofrio travels to Bosnia, accompanying pilgrims who search for an apparition of the Virgin. Disbelieving and disconnected from both her own mother and her child, and lacking any direction in her life, Donofrio meditates on the symbol of the maternal, on her mother, and her own maternal experience. Through distance, thought, and conversations Donofrio begins to accept herself and to "open her heart" to her relationships. In the process she forges new bonds with her mother and her son. Once again, free from social imperatives, the road allows the fragile bond between women – the bond that Freudians claim as necessarily vexed and the feminists regard as imperiled by patriarchy – to be re-established. By reclaiming her mother, the woman traveler reclaims herself. This same paradigm finds reenactment in a host of contemporary texts; the fiction of such well-known writers as

Mona Simpson, Dorothy Allison, and Barbara Kingsolver attests to this convention.

Still traveling

In exploring women's travel narrative, critic Sidonie Smith claims in *Moving Lives: 20th-Century Women's Travel Writing* (2001), that the automobile becomes a vehicle of transcendence. Similarly, considering recent travel writing in general, Ronald Primeau argues in *The Romance of the Road: The Literature of the American Highway* (1996) that the automobile trip represents a new heroic journey, a quest wherein the driver pursues some objective and finally undergoes psychic transformation. In the twentieth century the car becomes the vehicle for change; the highway is the unencumbered space – perhaps the only unencumbered space – that allows for transformation. While frequently significant in regard to identity formation, the modern road is nearly always, in some way, about the self, and about the way that the self shifts, changes, and finds autonomy. If such autonomy proves difficult in the contemporary world, the road accommodates the need for self. The road – as defined in travel narratives – continuously allows for the re-emergence of the transcendent self. In that sense, it is indeed the site of miracles.

Notes

1. Jack Kerouac, *On the Road* (New York: Penguin, 1976), p. 8.
2. Quoted in Ann Charters, *Kerouac: A Biography* (San Francisco: Straight Arrow Books, 1973), pp. 286–87.
3. Perhaps the most famous psycho-hallucinogenic yet spiritual travel accounts appear in Ram Dass' *Be Here Now* (San Cristobal, NM: Lama Foundation, 1971) and in Carlos Castaneda's *The Teachings of Don Juan: A Yacqui Way of Knowledge* (Berkeley: University of California Press, 1968). Both Dass and Castaneda offer 1960s versions of the teacher/wild man trope.
4. Carol Brightman, *Sweet Chaos: The Grateful Dead's American Adventure* (New York: Clarkson Potter Publishing, 1998), p. 17.
5. Tom Wolfe, *The Electric Kool-Aid Acid Test* (New York: Bantam, 1968), p. 415.
6. Robert M. Pirsig, *Zen and the Art of Motorcycle Maintenance: An Inquiry Into Values* (New York: HarperCollins, 1974), p. 426.
7. Joan Didion, *Slouching Toward Bethlehem* (New York: Farrar, Straus, and Giroux, 1968), p. 3.
8. Joan Didion, *The White Album* (New York: Simon & Schuster, 1979), pp. 176–77.
9. John Steinbeck, *Travels with Charley: In Search of America* (New York: Viking Penguin, 1961), p. 51.
10. Larry McMurtry, *Roads: Driving America's Great Highways* (New York: Simon & Schuster, 2000), p. 11.

11. The attitude towards women expressed in this passage echoes that of Kerouac and the Beats, suggesting that at least for some the road is still largely a masculine space.

12. William Least Heat-Moon, *Blue Highways: A Journey Into America* (New York: Ballantine Books, 1982), p. 219.

CHRONOLOGY

The right-hand column of this chronology lists important works of travel that are written by Americans or describe travel in what is now the United States with a focus on works written in English. A few works of fiction that contain significant travel material are also included. Our selections recognize that these political and geographical categories are inherently fluid and in flux. The list does not claim to be comprehensive, but indicates those works that contributors to this volume see as especially significant and influential. The left-hand column lists selected key historical events that provide an important context for works of travel.

1519–1521	Hernando Cortez's conquest of the Aztecs
1540–1542	Francisco Vasquez de Coronado leads a search for "Cibola," the lost city of gold, across southwestern North America
1562	Jean Ribault tries to establish a Huguenot colony in what is now South Carolina
1587	Founding of Roanoke "lost colony"
1588	Thomas Harriott, *A Brief and True Report of the New Found Land of Virginia*

1598	Don Juan Oñate establishes "New Mexico," destroying Acoma Pueblo in response to an attack on the settlement	
1600–1607	Jamestown colony established	
1608		John Smith, *True Relation*
1609	Henry Hudson explores Hudson River; Champlain discovers Lake Champlain	
1610	Santa Fe established as capital of "New Mexico"	
1612		John Smith, *A Map of Virginia*
1616		John Smith, *A Description of New England*
1620	Pilgrims establish Plymouth colony	
1624		John Smith, *General History of Virginia*; Edward Winslow, *Good News Out of New England*
1626	The Dutch establish the colony of New Amsterdam	
1630	Massachusetts Bay Company establishes its colony	
1630–1647		William Bradford, *History of the Plymouth Plantation* (written)
1630–1649		John Winthrop, *History of New England* (written)
1634	French explorer Jean Nicolet visits Lake Michigan and	

	what is now Wisconsin; English settle Maryland	
1637	Pequot War	
1654		Capt. Edward Johnson, *Wonder-Working Providence*
1664	British seize New Netherland colony from Dutch	
1673–1674	Jacques Marquette and Louis Joliet travel from Lake Michigan down the Mississippi River	
1675–1676	King Philip's War	
1679–1682	La Salle explores the Great Lakes and the Mississippi River and claims the Mississippi Valley for France	
1681		William Penn, *Some Account of the Province of Pennsylvania in America*
1682		Mary Rowlandson, *The Sovereignty and Goodness of God*
1685		Cotton Mather, *Memorable Providences Relating to Witchcraft and Possessions*
1689–1763	French and Indian Wars	
1692	Salem witchcraft trials	
1704		Sarah Kemble Knight, *Journal*; published 1825

1708		Ebenezer Cooke's "The Sot-Weed Factor; or, a Voyage to Maryland"
1729		William Byrd II, *History of the Dividing Line* (written)
1731		Mark Catesby, *Natural History of Carolina, Florida, and the Bahama Islands*
1732		Richard Lewis, "A Journey from Patapsco to Annapolis, April 4, 1730"
1733		William Byrd II, *Journal of a Journey to the Land of Eden* (written)
1740	Popular itinerant minister George Whitefield journeys from Britain to Georgia, initiating the "Great Awakening"	
1744		Dr. Alexander Hamilton, *Itinerarium*
1749		Jonathan Edwards, editor and publisher: *An Account of the Life of the Late Reverend David Brainerd*
1751		John Bartram, *Observations* (published in London)
1754		George Washington, *The Journal of Major George Washington*
1760		Briton Hammon, *The Narrative of the Uncommon Sufferings and Surprising Deliverance of Briton Hammon*

1765	English Stamp Act enacted and met with colonial resistance	William Smith, *An Account of Bouquet's Expedition Against the Ohio Indians*; Major Robert Rogers, *Journals* and *Concise Account of North America*
1766		William Stork, *An Account of East Florida*
1766–1767	Daniel Boone travels through the Kentucky territory	
1773	Boston Tea Party	
1774	First Continental Congress	John Woolman, *The Journal of John Woolman*; Elizabeth Ashbridge, *Some Account of the Fore Part of the Life of Elizabeth Ashbridge*
1775–1783	American Revolutionary War	
1775		James Adair, *History of the American Indians*
1776	Second Continental Congress adopts the Declaration of Independence	
1778		Jonathan Carver, *Travels through the Interior Parts of North America*
1779		Ethan Allen, *Narrative of the Captivity*
1781	Articles of Confederation ratified	
1782		J. Hector St. John De Crevecoeur, *Letters from an American Farmer*

1784		Benjamin Franklin, *Information for Those Who Would Remove to America*
1785	Regular stagecoach routes are established connecting New York, Philadelphia, and Boston	
1789	George Washington elected first President under new US Constitution; publication of first American road map by Christopher Colles	Olaudah Equiano, *The Interesting Life of Olaudah Equiano*
1791		William Bartram, *Travels*
1803	Louisiana Purchase	
1803–1806	Meriwether Lewis and William Clark travel across North America through the uncharted Northwest	
1804		William Austin, *Letters from London*
1805	Zebulon Pike explores the Louisiana Territory	
1807	Robert Fulton's roundtrip voyage between Albany and New York City proves the commercial viability of steamboats	
1809		Royall Tyler, *The Yankey in London*
1811	Steamboat travel begins on the Mississippi	
1812–1814	USA and Great Britain fight War of 1812	

1817	Construction of Erie Canal begins	
1818	First regularly scheduled clippership service between New York and Liverpool; average voyage takes thirty days	
1819		Estwick Evans, *A Pedestrious Tour, of four thousand miles, through the western states and territories, during the winter and spring of 1818*
1820		Washington Irving, *The Sketch Book*; H.M. Brackenridge, *A Voyage to South America*
1821	Opening of Santa Fe Trail	
1822		Gideon Miner Davison, *The Fashionable Tour; or, A Trip to the Springs, Niagara, Quebeck, and Boston, in the Summer of 1821*; Captain David Porter, *Journal of a Cruise Made to the Pacific Ocean*; James Kirke Paulding, *A Sketch of Old England, by a New England Man*; Washington Irving, *Bracebridge Hall*
1825	Completion of Erie Canal; beginning of the Hudson River School of landscape painting	
1826	First American railroad completed (Massachusetts)	

1828		John James Audubon, *Birds of America*; James A. Hall, *Letters from the West*; Giacomo Beltrami, *A Pilgrimage in Europe and America*
1830	First passenger railroad line in USA opens with thirteen miles of track	Basil Hall, *Travels in North America, in the Years 1827 and 1828*
1831	Nat Turner leads slave revolt	James Pattie, *The Personal Narrative of James O. Pattie*; Nat Turner, *The Confession of Nat Turner*
1831–1865	Abolitionist paper *The Liberator*	
1832		Washington Irving, *The Alhambra*; Frances Trollope, *Domestic Manners of the Americans*
1833	Britain prohibits slavery in British colonies	Thomas Hamilton, *Men and Manners in the United States*; Emma Willard, *Journal and Letters*
1834		Henry Rowe Schoolcraft, *Narrative of an Expedition Through the Upper Mississippi*; Gideon Miner Davison, *Traveller's Guide through the Middle and Northern States, and the Provinces of Canada*
1835		Alexis de Tocqueville, *Democracy in America*; Washington Irving, *Tour on the Prairies*; Henry Wadsworth Longfellow, *Outre-Mer: A Pilgrimage*

		Beyond the Sea; Henry T. Tuckerman, *The Italian Sketch Book*; Nathaniel Parker Willis, *Pencillings by the Way* (first edition)
1835–1836	Texas War of Independence	
1836–1838		James Fenimore Cooper, *Gleanings in Europe*, 5 volumes
1836		Washington Irving, *Astoria*
1837		Harriet Martineau, *Society in America*; John Lloyd Stephens, *Incidents of Travel in Egypt, Arabia Petraea, and the Holy Land*
1838	"Trail of Tears," removal of Cherokee Indians from Georgia, resulting in thousands of deaths	Harriet Martineau, *Retrospect of Western Travel*; Fanny W. Hall, *Rambles in Europe*
1839	Slave rebellion on Spanish slave ship *Amistad*	
		Frederick Marryat, *Diary in America*
1840		Richard Henry Dana, Jr., *Two Years Before the Mast*; Sarah Haight, *Letters from the Old World by a Lady of New York*
1841		Caroline Kirkland, *A New Home – Who'll Follow? or, Glimpses of Western Life*; John L. Stephens, *Incidents of Travel in Central America, Chiapas,*

		and Yucatan; Catherine Sedgwick, *Letters from Abroad*
1842		Charles Dickens, *American Notes for General Circulation*; Elder Orson Hyde, *A Voice from Jerusalem*; L.H. Sigourney, *Pleasant Memories of Pleasant Lands*
1843	A thousand settlers move to the Oregon Territory	William H. Prescott, *History of the Conquest of Mexico*
1844		Margaret Fuller, *Summer on the Lakes in 1843*; Josiah Gregg, *Commerce of the Prairies*
1845		Frederick Douglass, *Narrative of the Life of Frederick Douglass, an American Slave*; L.H. Sigourney, *Scenes in My Native Land*; John C. Fremont, *Report of the Exploring Expedition to the Rocky Mountains in the Year 1842, and to Oregon and North California in the Years 1843–44*; Joel Tyler Headley, *Letters from Italy*; Horatio Bridge, *Journal of an African Cruiser*
1846–1848	US–Mexican War	
1846		Herman Melville, *Typee*; Bayard Taylor,

		Views-a-Foot; George Henry Calvert, *Scenes and Thoughts in Europe*
1847		Donald G. Mitchell, *Fresh Gleanings*; Joel Tyler Headley, *The Alps and the Rhine*; William H. Prescott, *History of the Conquest of Peru*; Jane Eames, *A Budget of Letters. Or Things which I Saw Abroad*
1848	First US women's rights convention	Henry T. Tuckerman, *The Italian Sketch Book* (third edition); George Catlin, *Catlin's Notes of Eight Years' Travel and Residence in Europe with his North American Indian Collection*
1848–1855	California gold rush	
1849		William F. Lynch, *Narrative of the United States' Expedition to the River Jordan and the Dead Sea*; Henry Thoreau, *A Week on the Concord and Merrimack Rivers*; Caroline Kirkland, *Holidays Abroad*
1850	Fugitive slave act mandates return of slaves who had escaped to free states	Lewis Garrard, *Wah-to-Yah and the Taos Trail*; Joel Tyler Headley, *Sketches and Rambles*; Bayard Taylor, *El Dorado*; William Cullen Bryant, *Letters of a Traveller*;

William Furniss, *Waraga,*
or the Charms of the Nile

1851   Herman Melville,
Moby-Dick; Clorinda
Minor, *Meshullam! Or,*
Tidings from Jerusalem;
Emmeline Stuart Wortley,
Travels in the United
States, etc. During 1849
and 1850; George
Copway, *Running*
Sketches of Men and
Places; Horace Greeley,
Glances at Europe;
William Ware, *Sketches of*
European Capitals

1852   Harriet Beecher Stowe,
Uncle Tom's Cabin;
Warder Cresson, *The Key*
of David; George William
Curtis, *The Howadji in*
Syria; Daniel Clarke Eddy,
Europa: Scenes and
Society in England,
France, Italy, and
Switzerland; James
Jackson Jarves, *Parisian*
Sights and French
Principles, Seen Through
American Spectacles;
James Freeman Clarke,
Eleven Weeks in Europe;
Samuel Sullivan Cox, *A*
Buckeye Abroad;
Frederick Law Olmstead,
Walks and Talks of an
American Farmer in
England

1853	William Lewis Herndon, *Exploration of the Valley of the Amazon, 1851–1852*; Nancy Prince, *A Narrative of the Life and Travels of Mrs. Nancy Prince*; Henry T. Tuckerman, *A Month in England*; Charles Loring Brace, *Home-life in Germany*; J. Ross Browne, *Yusef; or, The Journey of the Frangi*; Benjamin Silliman, *A Visit to Europe in 1851*
1854	Henry David Thoreau, *Walden*; Harriet Beecher Stowe, *Sunny Memories of Foreign Lands*; William Herndon, *Exploration of the Valley of the Amazon. 1851–52*; Sara Jane Lippincott (Grace Greenwood, pseudonym), *Haps and Mishaps of a Tour in Europe*
1855	Frederick Douglass, *My Bondage and My Freedom*; Ida Pfeiffer, *A Lady's Second Journey Around the World*; Bayard Taylor, *The Lands of the Saracen*; William Wells Brown, *The American Fugitive in Europe*; Cyrus Augustus Bartol, *Pictures of Europe Framed in Ideas*; Henry Ward Beecher, *Star Papers*

1856		Ralph Waldo Emerson, *English Traits*; James Jackson Jarves, *Italian Sights and Papal Principles, Seen Through American Spectacles*; Walter Channing, *A Physician's Vacation; or a Summer in Europe*; Margaret Fuller, *At Home and Abroad*
1857	Dred Scott decision, ruling that slaves and descendants of slaves were not US citizens and, as such, had no rights	William C. Prime, *Tent Life in the Holy Land*
1858		David F. Dorr, *A Colored Man Round the World*; John William DeForest, *European Acquaintance*; Samuel Wheelock, *Mr Dunn Browne's Experiences in Foreign Parts*
1859	Abolitionist John Brown and followers seize US Arsenal at Harper's Ferry, Virginia	Richard Henry Dana, *To Cuba and Back: A Vacation Voyage*; Martin Delany, *Blake or The Huts of America: A Tale of the Mississippi Valley, the Southern United States*; William M. Thomson, *The Land and the Book; or, Biblical Illustrations Drawn from the Manners and Customs, the Scenes and Scenery of the Holy Land*; Charles Eliot

		Norton, *Notes of Travel and Study in Italy*
1860	South Carolina secedes from the Union; Pony Express begins overland mail service	Julia Ward Howe, *A Trip to Cuba*; Nathaniel Hawthorne, *The Marble Faun*
1861–1865	American Civil War	
1861	There are 31,000 miles of railroad track in the USA	Harriet Jacobs, *Incidents in the Life of a Slave Girl*; Charles Dickens, *The Uncommercial Traveller*; Henry Watkins Allen, *The Travels of a Sugar Planter, or Six Months in Europe*; Robert Campbell, *A Pilgrimage to My Motherland*; Paul Cuffe, *A Brief Account of the Settlement and Present Situation of the Colony of Sierra Leone*; Martin Delany, *Official Report of the Niger Valley Exploring Party*
1863	Signing of the Emancipation Proclamation freeing slaves	Nathaniel Hawthorne, *Our Old Home*
1864		Henry T. Tuckerman, *America and Her Commentators: With a Critical Sketch of Travel in the United States*; Elihu Burritt, *A Walk from London*; James Russell Lowell, *Fireside Travels*

1866	Transatlantic cable is completed, linking North America and Europe	Mark Twain, *Letters from Hawaii*; William Dean Howells, *Venetian Life*; J. Ross Browne, *An American Family in Germany*
1867	USA purchases Alaska from Russia	Henry T. Tuckerman, *Maga Papers About Paris*; Charles Farrar Browne, *Artemus Ward in London*; John Wien Forney, *Letters from Europe*
1868		Louis Agassiz, *A Journey in Brazil*; Julia Ward Howe, *From the Oak to the Olive*
1869	Completion of the US transcontinental railroad; Major John Wesley Powell explores the Green, Grand, and Colorado rivers	Mark Twain, *Innocents Abroad*; Francis Parkman, *The Discovery of the Great West*; James Jackson Jarves, *Art Thoughts, the Experiences and Observations of an American Amateur in Europe*; Bayard Taylor, *By-Ways of Europe*
1870	Franco-Prussian War	Sophia Hawthorne, *Notes on England and Italy*
1871		John Hay, *Castilian Days*
1872		William Cullen Bryant, *Picturesque America*; Clarence King, *Mountaineering in the Sierra Nevada*; Helen

		Hunt Jackson, *Bits of Travel*
1873		Charles Warren Stoddard, *South-Sea Idylls*; Edward Wilmot Blyden, *From West Africa to Freetown*; William Root Bliss, *Paradise in the Pacific*; Kate Field, *Hap-hazard*
1874		Margaret Fuller, *At Home and Abroad*; Bishop Henry White Warren, *Sights and Insights; or, Knowledge by Travel*; John Wesley Powell, *Exploration of the Colorado River and its Canyons*
1875		Henry James, *Transatlantic Sketches*
1876	Invention of telephone	Herman Melville, *Clarel: A Poem and Pilgrimage in the Holy Land*; Thomas Gold Appleton, *A Nile Journey*; Henry Martyn Field, *From the Lakes of Killarney to the Golden Isles*
1878	Thomas Edison establishes Edison Electric Light Company in New York City	Henry Morton Stanley, *Through the Dark Continent*; Jessie Benton Fremont, *A Year of American Travel*
1879	Ethnologist Frank Hamilton Cushing travels to Zuni Pueblo	Nathaniel H. Bishop, *Four Months in a Sneak-Box*; Joel Cook, *A Holiday*

		Tour in Europe; Henry James, *Daisy Miller*
1880	Chinese Exclusion Act restricts Chinese laborers in the USA	Mark Twain, *A Tramp Abroad*
1881		Thomas Wallace Knox, *How to Travel*
1882		Clarence Dutton, *Tertiary History of the Grand Cañon District*; David R. Locke, *Nasby in Exile; or Six Months of Travel*; Henry Bacon, *A Parisian Year*
1883	Opening of the Brooklyn Bridge	Mark Twain, *Life on the Mississippi*; James Jackson Jarves, *Italian Rambles*; Henry James, *Portraits of Places*; Andrew Carnegie, *An American Four-in-hand in Britain*
1884		John Gregory Bourke, *The Snake-Dance of the Moquis of Arizona*; Mark Twain, *Adventures of Huckleberry Finn*; Henry James, *A Little Tour in France*; Maturin Murray Ballou, *Due West; or Round the World in Ten Months*; Andrew Carnegie, *Round the World*; William C. Falkner, *Rapid Ramblings in Europe*
1885		Maturin Murray Ballou, *Due South; or, Cuba Past and Present*; Elizabeth

		Custer, *Boots and Saddles*; Samuel Benjamin, *The Cruise of the Alice May, in the Gulf of St. Lawrence*
1887		Marietta Holley, *Samantha at Saratoga*; Maturin Murray Ballou, *Due North; or Glimpses of Scandinavia and Russia*; Jesse Benton Fremont, *Souvenirs of My Time*; William Wetmore Story, *Roba di Roma*
1888	First Kodak box cameras sold	Susan Wallace, *The Land of the Pueblos*
1889		Herbert L. Aldrich, *Arctic Alaska and Siberia, or eight months with the Arctic whalemen*; Frank Stockton, *Personally Conducted*
1890	Yosemite Park created; 200 Sioux killed by soldiers at Wounded Knee, South Dakota	Thomas De Witt Talmage, *Talmage on Palestine: A Series of Sermons*; Lafcadio Hearn, *Two Years in the French West Indies*; Elizabeth Custer, *Following the Guidon*; Maturin Murray Ballou, *Aztec Land*
1891	Thomas Edison patents motion picture camera	
1892		Charles Lummis, *Some Strange Corners of Our Country*; Poultney Bigelow, *Paddles and Politics down the Danube*

1893	Monarchy in Hawaii overthrown and the islands become a US protectorate	Charles Lummis, *The Land of Poco Tiempo*; William Dean Howells, *The Niagara Book*; Elizabeth Custer, *Tenting on the Plains*; Alice Mabel Bacon, *A Japanese Interior*; William Henry Bishop, *A House-hunter in Europe*
1894		John Muir, *The Mountains of California*; Lafcadio Hearn, *Glimpses of Unfamiliar Japan*; William Dean Howells, *A Traveler from Altruria*; Thomas Gaskell Allen, *Across Asia on a Bicycle*; Elizabeth L. Banks, *Campaigns of Curiosity: Journalistic Adventures of an American Girl in London*; Richard Harding Davis, *Our English Cousins*; Charles Warren Stoddard, *Hawaiian Life*
1895		Marietta Holley, *Samantha in Europe*; Frank Collins Baker, *A Naturalist in Mexico*; Richard Harding Davis, *About Paris*
1896		Richard Harding Davis, *Three Gringos in Central America*
1898	Spanish–American War	Poultney Bigelow, *White Man's Africa*; Elizabeth Pennell, *Over the Alps on a Bicycle*; Mabel Todd, *Corona and Coronet*

1900		Walter Hough, *The Moki Snake Dance*; Joshua Slocum, *Sailing Alone Around the World*
1901		John C. Van Dyke, *The Desert*; John Hay, *Castilian Days*
1902		Washington Matthews, *The Night Chant: A Navaho Ceremony*
1903	Orville Wright successfully tests a flying machine	Mary Austin, *The Land of Little Rain*; W.E.B. Du Bois, *The Souls of Black Folk*; Jack London, *People of the Abyss*
1904		Henry Adams, *Mont Saint Michel and Chartres*; Lafcadio Hearn, *Japan: An Attempt at Interpretation*
1904–1905	Russo-Japanese War	
1905		Henry James, *English Hours*; Edith Wharton, *Italian Backgrounds*
1906	San Francisco earthquake destroys much of the city; construction of Panama Canal begins	George Wharton James, *The Wonders of the Colorado Desert*
1907		Nat Love, *The Life and Adventures of Nat Love*; Henry James, *The American Scene*; Henry Adams, *The Education of Henry Adams*
1908	Henry Ford introduces the Model T	Edith Wharton, *A Motor Flight Through France*;

		William Dean Howells, *Roman Holidays*; Albert Bigelow Paine, *The Tent Dwellers*
1909		Henry James, *Italian Hours*; William Dean Howells, *Seven English Cities*; George Wharton James, *Through Ramona's Country*
1910	Mexican Revolution	Harry Franck, *A Vagabond Journey Around the World*
1911		Jack London, *The Cruise of the Snark*; John Muir, *My First Summer in the Sierra*
1912	The Titanic sinks	Jack London, *The House of Pride*; Matthew Henson, *A Negro Explorer at the North Pole*; George Wharton James, *In and Out of the Old Missions of California*
1913		Theodore Dreiser, *A Traveler at Forty*; Harry Franck, *Zone Policeman 88*
1914	World War I begins in Europe; Panama Canal opens for shipping	Theodore Roosevelt, *Through the Brazilian Wilderness*; John Reed, *Insurgent Mexico*
1915		Edith Wharton, *Fighting France*; John Muir, *Travels in Alaska*; George Wharton James, *The Lake of the Sky*

1916		James Bryce, *South America: Observations and Impressions*; John Reed, *The War in Eastern Europe*; John Muir, *A Thousand Mile Walk to the Gulf*; Theodore Dreiser, *A Hoosier Holiday*; Harry Franck, *Tramping Through Mexico, Guatemala, and Honduras*
1917	USA enters World War I; Russian Revolution; Pulitzer Prize established	George Wharton James, *Arizona the Wonderland*; Harry Franck, *Vagabonding Down the Andes*; Edith O'Shaughnessy, *Diplomatic Days*; George Wharton Edwards, *Vanished Halls and Cathedrals of France*; Hildegarde Hawthorne, *Rambles in Old College Towns*
1918	Influenza epidemic kills millions worldwide	Henry Adams, *The Education of Henry Adams*; Louise Bryant, *Six Red Months in Russia*; George Wharton Edwards, *Alsace-Lorraine*
1919		Edith Wharton, *French Ways and Their Meaning*; John Reed, *Ten Days That Shook the World*
1920		John C. Van Dyke, *The Grand Canyon of the Colorado*; Henry Franck, *Roaming through the*

West Indies; Edith
Wharton, *In Morocco*;
Edith O'Shaughnessy,
Alsace in Rust and Gold;
Harry Franck,
*Vagabonding Through
Changing Germany*

1920–1940   Harlem Renaissance

1921   Harry Franck, *Working
North from Patagonia*

1922   Gertrude Stein, *Geography
and Plays*

1924   Mary Austin, *Land of
Journey's Ending*; Clara E.
Laughlin, *So You're Going
to Paris*

1925   Phoebe Judson, *A Pioneer's
Search for an Ideal Home*;
Harry Franck, *Roving
Through Southern China*;
Frank C. Rimington,
*Motor Rambles Through
France*; Clara E. Laughlin,
So You're Going to Italy;
Anita Loos, *Gentlemen
Prefer Blondes*

1926   Ernest Hemingway, *The Sun
Also Rises*; Hildegarde
Hawthorne, *Corsica, The
Surprising Island*

1927   Charles Lindberg flies solo   D.H. Lawrence, *Mornings in
from New York to Paris   Mexico*; Frank C.
Rimington, *Motor
Rambles in Central
Europe*; Amy Oakley,
Cloud-Lands of France

1928		William Carlos Williams, *A Voyage to Pagany*; Dorothy Thompson, *The New Russia*; Theodore Dreiser, *Dreiser Looks at Russia*
1929	US stock market crash marks beginning of the Great Depression	Horace Kallen, *Frontiers of Hope*; Henry Albert Phillips, *Meet the Germans*
1930	Sinclair Lewis wins Nobel Prize	Louis Untermeyer, *Blue Rhine, Black Forest*; Clara E. Laughlin, *So You're Going to Germany and Austria*; Amy Oakley, *Enchanted Britanny*
1930–1940	Severe drought in Great Plains regions leads to "The Dust Bowl" mass migration	
1931		Robert Gordon Anderson, *An American Family Abroad*
1932	Election of Franklin Roosevelt and beginning of "New Deal"	Ernest Hemingway, *Death in the Afternoon*; Harry Franck, *Footloose in the British Isles*; Ernest Peixotto, *A Bachic Pilgrimage*
1933		Gertrude Stein, *The Autobiography of Alice B. Toklas*
1934		Erna Fergusson, *Fiesta in Mexico*; Henry Miller, *Tropic of Cancer*; John

		Dos Passos, *In All Countries*
1936–1939	Spanish Civil War	
1936	Eugene O'Neill wins Nobel Prize	John Gunther, *Inside Europe*
1937	Amelia Earhart and her navigator lost in Pacific	Hudson Strode, *South by Thunderbird*; Henry Albert Phillips, *White Elephants in the Caribbean*
1938	Pearl Buck wins Nobel Prize	John Dos Passos, *Journeys between Wars*; Amy Oakley, *Scandanavia Beckons*
1939	World War II begins in Europe	John Steinbeck, *The Grapes of Wrath*; Adam Clayton Powell, *Palestine and Saints in Caesar's Household*; Erna Fergusson, *Venezuela*
1940		Langston Hughes, *The Big Sea*; Gertrude Stein, *Paris France*; Janet Flanner, *An American in Paris: Profile of an Interlude between Two Wars*
1941	Japanese attack Pearl Harbor; USA enters World War II	Carol Crow, *Meet the South Americans*; John Steinbeck and Edward F. Ricketts, *The Sea of Cortez*; John Gunther, *Inside Latin America*; Henry Miller, *The Colossus of Maroussi*
1943		Waldo Frank, *South American Journey*

1945	USA drops atomic bombs on Hiroshima and Nagasaki; end of World War II	
1946	First assembly of the United Nations	I.F. Stone, *Underground to Palestine*
1947		Edmund Wilson, *Europe Without Baedeker*; Hudson Strode, *Now in Mexico*; John Gunther, *Inside USA*
1948	Creation of state of Israel; T.S. Eliot wins Nobel Prize	F.O. Matthiessen, *From the Heart of Europe*; John Steinbeck, *Russian Journal*; Horace Sutton, *Footloose in France*
1949	People's Republic of China proclaimed; William Faulkner wins Nobel Prize	
1950–1953	Korean War	
1951	Amy Oakley, *Behold the West Indies*	
1952		Hassoldt Davis, *The Jungle and the Damned*; Elizabeth Bishop, *Questions of Travel*
1953		Harlan Hubbard, *Shantyboat: A River Way of Life*
1954	Ernest Hemingway wins Nobel Prize	Richard Wright, *Black Power*
1955	Montgomery bus boycott to protest arrest of Rosa Parks	James Baldwin, *Notes of a Native Son*

1956		Edmund Wilson, *Red, Black, Blond and Olive*; Erna Fergusson, *Mexico Revisited*; Mary McCarthy, *Venice Observed*
1957	Russians launch first artificial satellite, Sputnik I	Jack Kerouac, *On the Road*; Richard Wright, *Pagan Spain*
1958		Ernest Hemingway, *A Moveable Feast*; Jack Kerouac, *Dharma Bums*; Sheldon Rodman, *Mexican Journal*
1959	Cuban Revolution	Mary McCarthy, *Stones of Florence*
1961	Berlin Wall built	Peter Matthiessen, *The Cloud Forest*
1962	Cuban missile crisis; John Steinbeck wins Nobel Prize	John Steinbeck, *Travels with Charley in Search of America*; Eleanor Clark, *Rome and a Villa*
1963	Martin Luther King gives "I Have a Dream" speech; President John F. Kennedy assassinated	Hannah Arendt, *Eichman in Jerusalem*; John Dos Passos, *Brazil on the Move*
1964–1973	US–Vietnam War; anti-war protests	
1964		Clarence Jonk, *River Journey*
1965	Martin Luther King leads civil rights march from Selma to Montgomery, Alabama	Ken Kesey, *Drive Five: Intrepid Trips*
1967	Summer of Love in San Francisco	Martha Gellhorn, *The Lowest Trees Have Tops*;

		John Gunther, *Inside South America*
1968	Assassination of Dr. Martin Luther King	Edward Abbey, *Desert Solitaire*; Tom Wolfe, *The Electric Kool-Aid Acid Test*; Joan Didion, *Slouching Toward Bethlehem*; W.E.B. Du Bois, *The Autobiography of W. E. B. Du Bois*
1969	First landing on the moon	Arthur Miller, *In Russia*
1970	Shooting of anti-war protesters at Kent State University	Leslie Alexander Lacy, *The Rise and Fall of a Proper Negro*
1971		John McPhee, *Encounters with the Archdruid*; Hunter S. Thompson, *Fear and Loathing in Las Vegas*; Joan Didion, *The White Album*
1972		Paul Bowles, *Without Stopping*
1972–1974	Watergate Scandal	
1973	American Indian activists take over Wounded Knee, South Dakota	Ben Lucien Burman, *Look Down that Winding River*
1974	Richard Nixon resigns the presidency	Annie Dillard, *Pilgrim at Tinker Creek*; Robert Pirsig, *Zen and the Art of Motorcycle Maintenance*
1975		Paul Theroux, *The Great Railway Bazaar*; Ann Zwinger, *Run, River, Run*
1976	Saul Bellow wins Nobel Prize	Saul Bellow, *To Jerusalem and Back*

1977	Space Shuttle *Enterprise* completes first test flight	John McPhee, *Coming into the Country*
1978		Peter Matthiessen, *The Snow Leopard*; Martha Gellhorn, *Travels with Myself and Another*
1979	Iranian Revolution; Nicaraguan Revolution	Edward Said, *The Question of Palestine*; Paul Theroux, *The Old Patagonian Express*; Jonathan Raban, *Arabia Through the Looking Glass*; Arthur Miller and Inge Morath, *Chinese Encounters*; Peter Jenkins, *A Walk Across America*
1979–1981	Iran hostage crisis	
1980		Edmund White, *States of Desire: Travels in Gay America*
1981	Identification of AIDS	Andrea Lee, *Russian Journal*; Jonathan Raban, *Old Glory*; Tom Miller, *On the Border*
1982		William Least Heat-Moon, *Blue Highways*
1983		Joan Didion, *Salvador*; Paul Theroux, *The Kingdom by the Sea*
1984		Terry Tempest Williams, *Pieces of White Shell: A Journey to Navajoland*; Audre Lorde, *Sister Outsider*; Peter Matthiessen, *Indian Country*

1986		Barry Lopez, *Arctic Dreams*; Maya Angelou, *All God's Children Need Traveling Shoes*; Mark Salzman, *Iron and Silk: A Young American Encounters Swordsmen, Bureaucrats and Other Citizens of Contemporary China*
1987		Gloria Anzaldúa, *Borderlands/La Frontera*
1988		Paul Theroux, *Riding the Iron Rooster*; Eddy Harris, *Mississippi Solo*; Pico Iyer, *Video Night in Kathmandu*; Tony Horwitz, *One for the Road: An Outback Adventure*; Eric Hansen, *Stranger in the Forest: On Foot in Borneo*
1989	Fall of Berlin Wall	Thomas Friedman, *From Beirut to Jerusalem*; Bill Bryson, *Lost Continent: Travels in Small-Town America*
1990	Iraq invades Kuwait; Gulf War	Eva Hoffman, *Lost in Translation*
1991–1999	War in Balkans	
1991		William Least Heat-Moon, *PrairyErth*; Helen Winternitz, *Seasons of Stones*; Gloria Emerson, *Gaza*; Bill Bryson, *Neither Here Nor There*; Charles Bowden, *Desierto:*

Memories of the Future;
Eddy Harris, *Native
Stranger: A Black
American's Journey into
the Heart of Africa*; Tim
Cahill, *Road Fever: A
High Speed Travelogue*;
Pico Iyer, *The Lady and
the Monk: Four Seasons in
Kyoto*; Tony Horwitz,
*Baghdad Without a Map
and Other Misadventures
in Arabia*; Eric Hansen,
*Motoring with
Mohammed: Journeys to
Yemen and the Red Sea*

1992		Tom Miller, *Trading with the Enemy: A Yankee Travels Through Castro's Cuba*; Thomas Kenneally, *The Place Where Souls Are Born*; Paul Theroux, *The Happy Isles of Oceania*; Richard and Sally Price, *Equatoria*; Moritz Thomsen, *The Saddest Pleasure*
1993	Toni Morrison wins Nobel Prize for Literature	Saul Slapikoff, *Consider and Hear Me*; Eva Hoffman, *Escape into the World*; Robert D. Kaplan, *Balkan Ghosts*; Pico Iyer, *Falling Off the Map: Some Lonely Places of the World*; Cathy Davidson, *Thirty-Six Views of Mount Fuji*
1994		Sheena Berger Gluck, *An American Feminist in*

Palestine; R.W.B. Lewis, *The City of Florence*

1995   Paul Theroux, *The Pillars of Hercules*; Melanie McGrath, *Motel Nirvana*; Bill Bryson, *Notes from a Small Island*

1996   Diana Hume George, *The Lonely Other: A Woman Watching America*; Paul Theroux, *The Pillars of Hercules*; Frances Mayes, *Under the Tuscan Sun*

1997   Jonathan Kaufman, *A Hole in the Heart of the World*; Jon Krakauer, *Into the Wild*; Tim Cahill, *Pass the Butterworms: Remote Journeys Oddly Rendered*

1998   Ntzoke Shange, *If I Can Cook/You Know God Can*; P.J. O'Rourke, *Holidays in Hell*; Stephen J. Dubner, *Turbulent Souls*; Bill Bryson, *A Walk in the Woods: Rediscovering America on the Appalachian Trail*; Karin Muller, *Hitchhiking Viet Nam: A Woman's Solo Journey in an Elusive Land*

1999   Susan Sontag, "Why are We in Kosovo?"; Edward Said, *Out of Place: A Memoir*; Frances Mayes, *Bella Tuscany*; Bill Bryson, *I'm a Stranger Here Myself*

2000		Edward Said, *Reflections on Exile*; Patrick Symmes, *Chasing Che*; Larry McMurtry, *Roads*; Beverly Donofrio, *Riding in Cars with Boys*; Bill Bryson, *In a Sunburned Country*; Frances Mayes, *In Tuscany*; Roff Smith, *Cold Beer and Crocodiles: A Bicycle Journey into Australia*
2001	Terrorists attack New York City and Washington, DC; USA and Great Britain invade Afghanistan	Bruce Feiler, *Walking the Bible*; Christopher Baker, *Mi Moto Fidel: Motorcycling through Castro's Cuba*; Arthur Phillips, *Prague*; Oliver Sachs, *Oaxaca Journal*
2002		Paul Theroux, *Dark Star Safari*; C.M. Mayo, *Miraculous Air: Journey of a Thousand Miles through Baja California, the Other Mexico*; Tim Cahill, *Hold the Enlightenment: More Travel, Less Bliss*; Tony Horwitz, *Blue Latitudes: Boldly Going Where Captain Cook has Gone Before*
2003	USA, Great Britain, and a coalition of other nationals invade Iraq	Jonathan Tilove, *Along Martin Luther King: Travels on Black America's Main Street*; Tom Bissell, *Chasing the Sea: Lost Among the Ghost of Empire in Central Asia*; Ayun

Halliday, *No Touch Monkey!: And Other Travel Lessons Learned Too Late*; William Gibson, *Pattern Recognition*

2004   J. Maarteen Troost, *The Sex Lives of Cannibals: Adrift in the Equatorial Pacific*; Eric Hansen, *The Bird Man and the Lap Dancer: Close Encounters with Strangers*

2005   Franz Wisner, *Honeymoon with my Brother*; Roff Smith, *Life on the Ice: No One Goes to Antarctica Alone*

2006   Jeff Biggers, *In the Sierra Madre*

FURTHER READING

The following list of suggestions for further reading is highly selective and represents only a fraction of the good scholarship available on travel and travel writing. In addition to those works listed below, interested readers may also wish to consult such journals as *Studies in Travel Writing*; *Journeys: The International Journal of Travel and Travel Writing*; *The Journal of Travel Research*; and the *Annals of Tourism Research*.

Anthologies of American travel writing

Brooks, Stephen. *America Through Foreign Eyes: Classic Interpretations of American Political Life*. Oxford: Oxford University Press, 2002.

Cahill, Susan. *Desiring Italy: Women Writers Celebrate the Passions of a Country and Culture*. New York: Ballantine, 1997.

Coskran, Kathleen and C. W. Truesdale, eds. *An Inn Near Kyoto: Writing by American Women Abroad*. Minneapolis: New Rivers Press, 1998.

Gopnik, Adam, ed. *Americans in Paris: A Literary Anthology*. New York: The Library of America, 2004.

Griffin, Farah J. and Cheryl J. Fish, eds. *A Stranger in the Village: Two Centuries of African-American Travel Writing*. Boston: Beacon Press, 1998.

Handlin, Oscar and Lilian, eds. *From the Outer World: Perspectives on People and Places, Manners and Customs in the United States, as Reported by Travelers from Asia, Africa, Australia, and Latin America*. Cambridge: Harvard University Press, 1997.

Kadushin, Raphael, ed. *Wonderlands: Good Gay Travel Writing*. Madison: University of Wisconsin Press, 2004.

Morris, Mary, ed. *Maiden Voyages: Writings of Women Travelers*. New York: Vintage, 1993.

Neill, Peter, ed. *American Sea Writing: A Literary Anthology*. New York: Library of America, 2000.

Nevins, Allan, ed. *American Social History as Recorded by British Travellers*. New York: Holt, 1923.

Powers, Alice Leccese. *Italy in Mind: An Anthology*. New York: Vintage, 1997.

Tinling, Marion, ed. *With Women's Eyes: Visitors to the New World, 1775–1918*. Norman: University of Oklahoma Press, 1999.

Watts, Edward and David Rachels, eds. *The First West: Writing from the American Frontier, 1776–1860*. New York: Oxford University Press, 2002.

Critical studies of travel writing and travel

Baranowski, Shelley and Ellen Furlough, eds. *Being Elsewhere: Tourism, Consumer Culture, and Identity in Modern Europe and North America*. Ann Arbor: University of Michigan Press, 2001.

Bartkowski, Frances. *Travelers, Immigrants, Inmates: Essays in Estrangement*. Minneapolis: University of Minnesota Press, 1995.

Blanton, Casey. *Travel Writing: The Self and the World*. New York: Routledge, 2002.

Caesar, Terry. *Forgiving the Boundaries: Home as Abroad in American Travel Writing*. Athens: University of Georgia Press, 1995.

Chambers, Erve. *Native Tours: The Anthropology of Travel and Tourism*. Prospects Heights, IL: Waveland Press, 2000.

Clark, Gregory. *Rhetorical Landscapes in America: Variations on a Theme from Kenneth Burke*. Columbia: University of South Carolina Press, 2004.

Clifford, James. *Routes: Travel and Translation in the Late Twentieth Century*. Cambridge, MA: Harvard University Press, 1997.

Desmond, Jane C. *Staging Tourism: Bodies on Display from Waikiki to Sea World*. Chicago: University of Chicago Press, 1999.

Edwards, Justin D. *Exotic Journeys: Exploring the Erotics of US Travel Literature, 1840–1930*. Hanover, NH: University Press of New England, 2001.

Evans, Brad. *Before Cultures: The Ethnographic Imagination in American Literature, 1865–1920*. Chicago: University of Chicago Press, 2005.

Groom, Eileen, ed. *Methods for Teaching Travel Literature and Writing*. New York: Peter Lang, 2005.

Holland, Patrick and Graham Huggan. *Tourists with Typewriters: Critical Reflections on Contemporary Travelwriters*. Ann Arbor: University of Michigan Press, 1998.

Hooper, Glenn and Tim Youngs, eds. *Perspectives on Travel Writing*. Aldershot: Ashgate, 2004.

Hulme, Peter and Tim Youngs, eds. *The Cambridge Companion to Travel Writing*. Cambridge: Cambridge University Press, 2002.

Kowalewski, Michael, ed. *Temperamental Journeys: Essays on the Modern Literature of Travel*. Athens: University of Georgia Press, 1992.

Leask, Nigel. *Curiosity and the Aesthetics of Travel Writing, 1770–1840: From an Antique Land*. Oxford: Oxford University Press, 2002.

Leed, Eric J. *The Mind of the Traveller: From "Gilgamesh" to Global Tourism*. New York: Basic Books, 1991.

Löfgren, Orvar. *On Holiday: A History of Vacationing*. Berkeley: University of California Press, 1999.

MacCannell, Dean. *The Tourist: A New Theory of the Leisure Class*. New York: Schocken, 1976.

Mulvey, Christopher. *Transatlantic Manners: Social Patterns in Nineteenth-Century Anglo-American Travel Literature*. Cambridge: Cambridge University Press, 1990.

Roberson, Susan, ed. *Defining Travel: Diverse Visions*. Jackson: University of Mississippi Press, 2002.

Robertson, George, *et al.*, eds. *Travellers' Tales: Narratives of Home and Displacement*. London: Routledge, 1994.

Roject, Chris and John Urry, eds. *Touring Cultures: Transformations of Travel and Theory*. London: Routledge, 1997.

Siegel, Kristi, ed. *Issues in Travel Writing: Empire, Spectacle, and Displacement*. New York: Peter Lang, 2002.

Ziff, Larzer. *Return Passages: Great American Travel Writing, 1780–1920*. New Haven: Yale University Press, 2001.

1 Beginnings: the origins of American travel writing in the pre-revolutionary period

Ausband, Stephen Conrad. *Byrd's Line*. Charlottesville: University of Virginia Press, 2002.

Bauer, Ralph. *The Cultural Geography of Colonial American Literatures: Empire, Travel, Modernity*. Cambridge: Cambridge University Press, 2003.

Brown, Sharon Rogers. *American Travel Narratives as Literary Genre from 1542 to 1832*. Lewiston, NY: Edwin Mellon, 1993.

Franklin, Wayne. *Discoverers, Explorers, Settlers: The Diligent Writers of Early America*. Chicago: University of Chicago Press, 1979.

Imbarrato, Susan Clair. *Traveling Women: Narrative Visions of Early America*. Athens: Ohio University Press, 2006.

Mackenthun, Gesa. *Metaphors of Dispossession: American Beginnings and the Translation of Empire, 1492–1637*. Norman, OK: University of Oklahoma Press, 1997.

Seelye, John. *Memory's Nation: The Place of Plymouth Rock*. Chapel Hill, NC: University of North Carolina Press, 1998.

Zug, James. *American Traveler: The Life and Adventures of John Ledyard, the Man Who Dreamed of Walking the World*. New York: Basic Books, 2005.

2 "Property in the horizon": landscape and American travel writing

Buell, Lawrence. *The Environmental Imagination: Thoreau, Nature Writing, and the Formation of American Culture*. Cambridge, MA: Harvard University Press, 1995.

Kolodny, Annette. *The Lay of the Land: Metaphor as Experience and History in American Life and Letters*. Chapel Hill: University of North Carolina Press, 1975.

The Land Before Her: Fantasy and Experience of the American Frontiers, 1630–1860. Chapel Hill: University of North Carolina Press, 1984.

Lueck, Beth Lynne. *American Writers and the Picturesque Tour: The Search for National Identity, 1790–1860*. New York: Garland, 1997.

Mulvey, Christopher. *Anglo-American Landscapes: A Study of Nineteenth-Century Anglo-American Travel Literature*. New York: Cambridge University Press, 1983.

Reid, John Phillip and Martin Ridge. *Contested Empires: Peter Skene Ogden and the Snake River Expeditions*. Norman: Oklahoma University Press, 2002.

Slaughter, Thomas P. *Exploring Lewis and Clark: Reflections on Men and Wilderness*. New York: Knopf, 2003.

3 New York to Niagara by way of the Hudson and the Erie

Adamson, Jeremy. *Niagara: Two Centuries of Changing Attitudes, 1697–1901*. Washington, DC: Corcoran Gallery of Art, 1985.

Berger, Max. *The British Traveller in America, 1836–1860*. New York: Columbia University Press, 1943.

Bernstein, Peter L. *Wedding of the Waters: The Erie Canal and the Making of a Great Nation*. New York: Norton, 2005.

Conrad, Peter. *Imagining America*. London: Routledge, 1980.

Dubinsky, Karen. *The Second Greatest Disappointment: Honeymooners, Heterosexuality, and the Tourist Industry at Niagara Falls*. New Brunswick, NJ: Rutgers University Press, 1999.

McGreevey, Patrick V. *Imagining Niagara: The Meaning and Making of Niagara Falls*. Amherst: University of Massachusetts Press, 1994.

Sears, John F. *Sacred Places: American Tourist Attractions in the Nineteenth Century*. New York: Oxford University Press, 1989.

Simmons, James C. *Star-Spangled Eden: Nineteenth-Century America Through the Eyes of Dickins, Wilde, Frances Trollope, Frank Harris and Other British Travelers*. New York: Carrol & Graf, 2000.

Simpson, Mark. *Trafficking Subjects: The Politics of Mobility in Nineteenth-Century America*. Minneapolis: University of Minnesota Press, 2005.

Sterngass, Jon. *First Resorts: Pursuing Pleasure at Saratoga Springs, Newport, and Coney Island*. Baltimore: Johns Hopkins University Press, 2001.

4 The Mississippi River as site and symbol

Allen, Michael. *Western Rivermen, 1763–1861*. Baton Rouge: Louisiana State University Press, 1990.

Ambrose, Stephen E. and Douglas G. Brinkley. *The Mississippi and the Making of a Nation*. Washington: National Geographic Society, 2002.

Buchanan, Thomas. *Black Life on the Mississippi*. Chapel Hill: University of North Carolina Press, 2004.

Cox, John D. *Traveling South: Travel Narratives and the Construction of American Identity*. Athens: University of Georgia, 2005.

Foster, William C., ed. *The La Salle Expedition on the Mississippi River: A Lost Manuscript of Nicolas de La Salle*. College Station: Texas A & M University Press, 2004.

Hearn, Lafcadio. *Inventing New Orleans*, ed. S. Frederick Starr. Jackson: University Press of Mississippi, 2001.

Hunter, Louis C. *Steamboats on the Western Rivers: An Economic and Technological History*. Cambridge, MA: Harvard University Press, 1949.

Huser, Verne. *On the River with Lewis and Clark*. College Station: Texas A & M University Press, 2004.

Kruse, Horst. *Mark Twain and "Life on the Mississippi."* Amherst: University of Massachusetts Press, 1981.

McDermott, John Francis. *The Lost Panoramas of the Mississippi.* Chicago: University of Chicago Press, 1958.

Reps, John W. *Cities of the Mississippi.* Columbia: University of Missouri Press, 1994.

Severin, Timothy. *Explorers of the Mississippi.* New York: Knopf, 1968.

Smith, Thomas Ruys. *River of Dreams: Imagining the Mississippi Before Mark Twain.* Baton Rouge: Louisiana State University Press, 2007.

5 The Southwest and travel writing

Handley, William R. and Nathaniel Lewis, eds. *True West: Authenticity and the American West.* Lincoln: University of Nebraska Press, 2004.

Neumann, Mark. *On the Rim: Looking for the Grand Canyon.* Minneapolis: University of Minnesota Press, 1999.

Padgett, Martin. *Indian Country: Travels in the American Southwest, 1840–1935.* Albuquerque: University of New Mexico Press, 2004.

Powell, Lawrence Clark. *Southwest Classics: The Creative Literature of the Arid Lands.* Tucson: University of Arizona Press, 1987.

Schaefer, Heike. *Mary Austin's Regionalism: Reflections on Gender, Genre, and Geography.* Charlottesville: University of Virginia Press, 2004.

Thompson, Mark. *American Character: The Curious History of Charles Fletcher Lummis and the Rediscovery of the Southwest.* New York: Arcade, 2001.

Watts, Edward and David Rachels, eds. *The First West: Writing from the American Frontier, 1776–1860.* Oxford: Oxford University Press, 2002.

6 American travel books about Europe before the Civil War

Baker, Paul R. *The Fortunate Pilgrims: Americans in Italy, 1800–1860.* Cambridge, MA: Harvard University Press, 1964.

Brooks, Van Wyck. *The Dream of Arcadia: American Writers and Artists in Italy, 1760–1915.* New York: Dutton, 1958.

Budd, Louis. *Our Mark Twain: The Making of His Public Personality.* Philadelphia: University of Pennsylvania Press, 1983.

Cady, Edwin Harrison. *The Gentleman in America.* Syracuse, NY: Syracuse University Press, 1949.

Chard, Chloe. *Pleasure and Guilt on the Grand Tour: Travel Writing and Imaginative Geography, 1600–1830.* Manchester: Manchester University Press, 1999.

Dulles, Foster Rhea. *Americans Abroad: Two Centuries of European Travel.* Ann Arbor: University of Michigan Press, 1964.

Earnest, Ernest. *Expatriates and Patriots: American Artists, Scholars, and Writers in Europe.* Durham, NC: Duke University Press, 1968.

Gifra-Adroher, Pere. *Between History and Romance: Travel Writing on Spain in the Early Nineteenth-Century United States.* Madison, NJ: Fairleigh Dickinson University Press, 2000.

Hedges, William. *Washington Irving: An American Study 1802–1831.* Baltimore: Johns Hopkins University Press, 1965.

Levenstein, Harvey. *Seductive Journey: American Tourists in France from Jefferson to the Jazz Age*. Chicago: University of Chicago Press, 1998.

Melton, Jeffrey Alan. *Mark Twain, Travel Books, and Tourism: The Tide of a Great Popular Movement*. Tuscaloosa: University of Alabama Press, 2002.

Nicoloff, Philip L. *Emerson on Race and History: An Examination of "English Traits."* New York: Columbia University Press, 1961.

Smith, Harold F. *American Travellers Abroad: A Bibliography of Accounts Published Before 1900*. Bibliographic Contributions No. 4. Carbondale–Edwardsville: The Library, Southern Illinois University, 1969.

Spiller, Robert E. *The American in England During the First Half Century of Independence*. New York: Holt, 1926.

Stowe, William W. *Going Abroad: European Travel in Nineteenth-Century American Culture*. Princeton: Princeton University Press, 1994.

Tuckerman, Henry T. *America and Her Commentators*. New York: Charles Scribner, 1864.

Wright, Nathalia. *American Novelists in Italy: The Discoverers: Allston to James*. Philadelphia: University of Pennsylvania Press, 1965.

7 Americans in Europe from Henry James to the present

Benstock, Shari. *Women of the Left Bank*. Austin: University of Texas Press, 1976.

Bowen, Frank C. *A Century of Atlantic Travel: 1830–1930*. London: Sampson Lowe Marston, n.d.

Bridgman, Richard. *Traveling in Mark Twain*. Berkeley: University of California Press, 1987.

Gray, Jeffrey, *Mastery's End: Travel and Postwar American Poetry*. Athens: University of Georgia Press, 2005.

Jones, Howard Mumford. *The Age of Energy: Varieties of American Experience (1865–1964)*. New York: Viking, 1971.

Kennedy, J. Gerald. *Imagining Paris: Exile, Writing, and American Identity*. New Haven: Yale University Press, 1993.

Le Clair, Robert C. *Three American Travellers in England: James Russell Lowell, Henry Adams, Henry James*. Philadelphia: University of Pennsylvania Press, 1945.

Longstreet, Stephen. *We All Went to Paris: Americans in the City of Light*. New York: Macmillan, 1972.

Strout, Cushing. *The American Image of the Old World*. New York: Harper & Row, 1963.

Wegelin, Christof. *The Image of Europe in Henry James*. Dallas: Southern Methodist University Press, 1958.

Weintraub, Stanley. *The London Yankee: Portraits of American Writers and Artists in England, 1894–1914*. London: Allen, 1979.

8 Americans in the Holy Land, Israel, and Palestine

Caesar, Judith. *Writing Off the Beaten Track: Reflections on the Meaning of Travel and Culture in the Middle East*. Syracuse, NY: Syracuse University Press, 2002.

Davis, John. *Landscape of Belief: Encountering the Holy Land in Nineteenth-Century American Art and Culture*. Princeton: Princeton University Press, 1996.

Harvey, Bruce A. *American Geographics: US National Narratives and the Representation of the Non-European World*. Stanford: Stanford University Press, 2001.

Obenzinger, Hilton. *American Palestine: Melville, Twain, and the Holy Land Mania*. Princeton: Princeton University Press, 1999.

Seawright, Sarah and Malcolm Wagstaff, eds. *Travellers in the Levant: Voyagers and Visionaries*. Cambridge, UK: Association for the Study of Travel in Egypt and the Near East, 2002.

Starkey, Paul and Janet Starkey. *Travellers in Egypt*. London and New York: I.B. Tauris, 2001.

Vogel, Lester. *To See a Promised Land: Americans and the Holy Land in the Nineteenth Century*. University Park: Pennsylvania State University Press, 1993.

9 Americans in the larger world: beyond the Pacific coast

Cheyfitz, Eric. *The Poetics of Imperialism: Translation and Colonization from The Tempest to Tarzan*. Oxford: Oxford University Press, 1991.

Day, A. Grove. *Jack London in the South Seas*. New York: Four Winds Press, 1971.

Geiger, Jeffrey. *Facing the Pacific: Polynesia and the US Imperial Imagination*. Honolulu: University of Hawai'i Press, 2007.

Green, Martin. *Dreams of Adventure, Deeds of Empire*. New York: Basic Books, 1979.

Herbert, T. Walter. *Marquesan Encounters: Melville and the Meaning of Civilization*. Cambridge, MA and London: Harvard University Press, 1980.

Hietala, Thomas R. *Manifest Design: Anxious Aggrandizement in Late Jacksonian America*. Ithaca, NY and London: Cornell University Press, 1985.

LaFeber, Walter. *The American Age: United States Foreign Policy at Home and Abroad Since 1750*. New York: Norton, 1979.

Lamb, Jonathan. *Preserving the Self in the South Seas, 1680–1840*. Chicago: University of Chicago Press, 2001.

McClintock, Anne. *Imperial Leather: Race, Gender, and Sexuality in the Colonial Context*. New York: Routledge, 1985.

Pease, Donald, ed. *National Identities and Post-Americanist Narratives*. Durham, NC and London: Duke University Press, 1994.

Rennie, Neil. *Far-Fetched Facts: The Literature of Travel and the Idea of the South Seas*. Oxford: Oxford University Press, 1995.

Sanborn, Geoffrey. *The Sign of the Cannibal: Melville and the Making of a Post-Colonial Reader*. Durham, NC: Duke University Press, 1998.

Smith, Vanessa. *Literary Culture and the Pacific: Nineteenth-Century Textual Encounters*. Cambridge: Cambridge University Press, 1998.

Springer, Haskell, ed. *America and the Sea: A Literary History*. Athens and London: University of Georgia Press, 1995.

Spurr, David. *The Rhetoric of Empire: Colonial Discourse in Journalism, Travel Writing, and Imperial Administration*. Durham, NC: Duke University Press, 1993.

Thomas, Nicholas. *In Oceania: Visions, Artifacts, Histories*. Durham, NC: Duke University Press, 1997.

Wrobel, David M. *The End of American Exceptionalism: Frontier Anxiety from the Old West to the New Deal*. Lawrence: University Press of Kansas, 1993.

10 South of the border: American travel writing in Latin America

Elsner, Jas and Joan-Pau Rubiés, eds. *Voyages and Visions: Toward a Cultural History of Travel*. London: Reaktion, 1999.

Glassman, Steve. *On the Trail of the Maya Explorer: Tracing the Epic Journey of John Lloyd Stephens*. Tuscaloosa: University of Alabama Press, 2003.

Hahner, June E., ed. *Women Through Women's Eyes: Latin American Women in Nineteenth-Century Travel Accounts*. Wilmington, DE: Scholarly Resources, 1998.

Hulme, Peter. *Remnants of Conquest: The Island Caribs and their Visitors, 1877–1998*. Oxford: Oxford University Press, 2000.

Madsen, Deborah L., ed. *Beyond the Borders: American Literature and Post-Colonial Theory*. London and New York: Pluto, 2003.

Rodríguez, Ileana. *Transatlantic Topographies: Islands, Highlands, Jungles*. Minneapolis: University of Minnesota Press, 2004.

Szurmuk, Mónica. *Women in Argentina: Early Travel Narratives*. Gainesville: University Press of Florida, 2000.

11 African American travel literature

Andrews, William L. *To Tell a Free Story: The First Century of Afro-American Autobiography, 1760–1865*. Urbana: University of Illinois Press, 1988.

Baker, Houston. *The Journey Back: Issues in Black Literature and Criticism*. Chicago: University of Chicago Press, 1980.

Blassingame, John. *Black New Orleans, 1860–1880*. Chicago: University of Chicago Press, 1973.

Bolster, W. Jeffrey. *Black Jacks: African American Seamen in the Age of Sail*. Cambridge, MA: Harvard University Press, 1997.

Diedrich, Maria, Henry Louis Gates, and Carl Pedersen, eds. *Black Imagination and the Middle Passage*. Oxford: Oxford University Press, 1999.

Gruesser, John Cullen. *Black on Black: Twentieth-Century African American Writing about Africa*. Lexington: University Press of Kentucky, 2000.

Mackenthun, Gesa. *Fictions of the Black Atlantic in American Foundational Literature*. London: Routledge, 2004.

Peterson, Carla. *"Doers of the Word": African-American Women Speakers and Writers in the North (1830–1880)*. New York: Oxford University Press, 1995.

Pettinger, Alasdair, ed. *Always Elsewhere: Travels of the Black Atlantic*. London and New York: Continuum, 1998.

Schmeller, Erik S. *Perceptions of Race and Nation in English and American Travel Writers, 1833–1914*. New York: Peter Lang, 2004.

Smith, Virginia Whatley, ed. *Richard Wright's Travel Writings: New Reflections*. Jackson: University of Mississippi Press, 2001.

12 American women and travel writing

Blunt, Alison and Gillian Rose, eds. *Writing Women and Space: Colonial and Postcolonial Geographies.* New York and London: The Guilford Press, 1994.

Fish, Cheryl. *Black and White Women's Travel Narratives: Antebellum Explorations.* Gainesville: University of Florida Press, 2004.

Foster, Shirley. *Across New Worlds: Nineteenth-Century Women Travellers and Their Writings.* New York: Harvester Wheatsheaf, 1990.

Grewal, Inderpal. *Home and Harem: Nation, Gender, Empire, and the Cultures of Travel.* Durham, NC: Duke University Press, 1996.

Mills, Sara. *Discourses of Difference: An Analysis of Women's Travel Writing and Colonialism.* London: Routledge, 1991.

Paravisini-Gebert, Lizabeth and Ivette Romero-Cesareo, eds. *Women at Sea: Travel Writing and the Margins of Caribbean Discourse.* New York: St. Martin's Press, 2000.

Poling-Kempes, Lesley. *The Harvey Girls: Women Who Opened the West.* New York: Paragon, 1989.

Roberson, Susan L. *Women, America, and Movement: Narratives of Relocation.* Columbia: University of Missouri Press, 1998.

Schriber, Mary Suzanne. *Writing Home: American Women Abroad, 1830–1920.* Charlottesville: University Press of Virginia, 1997.

Siegel, Kristi. *Gender, Genre, and Identity in Women's Travel Writing.* New York: Peter Lang, 2004.

Smith, Sidonie. *Moving Lives: 20th-Century Women's Travel Writing.* Minneapolis: University of Minnesota Press, 2001.

Steadman, Jennifer Bernhardt. *Traveling Economies: American Women's Travel Writing.* Columbus: Ohio State University Press, 2007.

Tinling, Marion, ed. *With Women's Eyes: Visitors to the New World, 1775–1918.* Norman: University of Oklahoma Press, 1999.

Wesley, Marilyn C. *Secret Journeys: The Trope of Women's Travel in American Literature.* Albany: State University of New York Press, 1999.

13 Driving that highway to consciousness: late twentieth-century American travel literature

Clarke, Deborah. *Driving Women: Fiction and Automobile Culture in Twentieth-Century America.* Baltimore: Johns Hopkins University Press, 2007.

Genovese, Peter. *The Great American Road Trip: US 1, Maine to Florida.* New Brunswick: Rutgers University Press, 1999.

Lackey, Kris. *RoadFrames: The American Highway.* Lincoln: University of Nebraska Press, 1997.

McPherson, James Allen. *Railroad: Trains and Train People in American Culture.* New York: Random House, 1976.

Paes de Barros, Deborah. *Fast Cars and Bad Girls: Nomadic Subjects and Women's Road Stories.* New York: Peter Lang, 2004.

Primeau, Ronald. *Romance of the Road: The Literature of the American Highway.* Ohio: Bowling Green State University Popular Press, 1996.

Sachs, Wolfgang. *For Love of the Automobile: Looking Back into the History of Our Desires*. Trans. Don Reneau. Berkeley: University of California Press, 1992.

Shaffer, Marguerite S. *See America First: Tourism and National Identity: 1880–1940*. Washington, DC: Smithsonian Institution, 2001.

INDEX

Abbey, Edward, 41: *Desert Solitaire*, 95
Account (Stork), 19
*An Account of the Life of the Late Reverend
    David Brainerd* (Edwards), 24
Adams, Henry, 130–31: *The Education of
    Henry Adams*, 131; and the
    European past, 130; *The Letters of
    Henry Adams*, 130; *Mont Saint
    Michel and Chartres*, 130; and the
    USSR, 135
Adler, Judith, 26
adventure narratives, 202
The Adventures of Huckleberry Finn
    (Twain), 72, 171
Africa, 118, 132, 135, 202, 204–05, 220
    back-to-Africa movement, 200
African Americans
    as entertainers, 138, 207
    in Europe, 120–21, 136, 137–40
    in Jerusalem, 211
    in Mexico, 212
    in Middle East, 157–58
    in Nicaragua, 212–13
    in Palestine, 157
    in Russia, 208–11
    as tourists, 211–13
    travel writing by, 7–8, 24, 34, 197, 213
    travel writing by women, 205–06, 218,
        221
All God's Children Need Traveling Shoes
    (Angelou), 140
"All it Took was a Road/Surprises of Urban
    Renewal" (Shange), 212–13
Along Martin Luther King (Tilove), 34–35
Amazon, 182–83
    development of, 182
*An American Feminist in Palestine: The
    Intifada Years* (Gluck), 160

*The American Fugitive in Europe; Sketches
    of Places and Peoples Abroad*
    (Brown), 120, 206
*American Indians: First Families of the
    Southwest* (Huckel), 80
The American Rhythm (Austin), 92
American Scenery (Willis), 51
American travelers, 5–7, 140–42
    disappointed with Palestine,
        151
    ignorance of, 180–81, 184, 190
    and New York, 48
    preconceptions of Palestine, 151
    privileged, 127
    see also tourism
"Americanness," 6, 7
    and the "expat," 6
    and genre conventions, 3
    and landscape, 5
Ancient and Honorable Tuesday Club,
    15–16
Angelou, Maya, 220, 224: *All God's
    Children Need Traveling Shoes*,
    140
anti-Semitism, 157
Anzaldúa, Gloria, 219
Ardener, Shirley, 217
Arendt, Hannah: *Eichman in Jerusalem: A
    Report on the Banality of Evil*,
    158–61
art and artists, 108–09, 114
    in the Southwest, 89, 91–94
Ashbridge, Elizabeth: *Some Account of the
    Fore Part of the Life of Elizabeth
    Ashbridge*, 22
Austin, Mary: *The American Rhythm*, 92;
    Land of Journey's Ending, 92; *The
    Land of Little Rain*, 92

Cambridge Companions to ...

AUTHORS

TOPICS